NCAA:
The Voice of College Sports

NCAA: The Voice of College Sports

A DIAMOND ANNIVERSARY HISTORY
1906-1981

by Jack Falla

Published by the
National Collegiate Athletic Association
Mission, Kansas

Library of Congress Cataloging in Publication Data
Falla, Jack, 1944-
NCAA, the voice of college sports.
Bibliography: p.
Includes index.
1. National Collegiate Athletic Association — History — 20th century.
2. College sports — United States — History — 20th century.
I. Title.
GV347.F34   796'.06'073   81-14120
ISBN 0-913504-70-X   AACR2

FIRST EDITION

To the former Barbara Spelman Baldwin of Northampton, Massachusetts, and to the people at 22 Bacon Street and 306 Washington Street, for the badminton, basketball, football, hockey, volleyball, soccer, swimming, stickball and all-around good times we have there. You are good sports, all.

CONTENTS

FOREWORD

The first president of the National Collegiate Athletic Association, Capt. Palmer Pierce of the U.S. Military Academy, once referred to the fledgling Association he headed as "the voice of college sports." We do not know if he realized at that time in the early 1900s that this voice still would be heard today, 75 years after the gavel brought order to the first NCAA Convention in 1906.

It was at the first Convention that the foundation of the NCAA's structure was cast — no one individual or no group of individuals were to determine the policies of the Association. Rather, these decisions were to be made as a result of the collective will of the member colleges and universities, and it is this will of the members that has become "the voice of college sports."

A call for football reform came in 1905. In the eyes of many, football, with its mass-momentum formations and "anything goes" philosophy, had reached an unacceptable level of violent play. Society clamored for the college game to adopt stricter rules. Significantly, the response to this public outcry led to the initial meeting that was to be the forerunner of the NCAA.

Following World War I, sports and entertainment enjoyed a nationwide boom. Athletic competition became more important to the people of the day, to the extent that fans and athletes alike desired competition beyond regional lines. As a result, it was not long before the NCAA membership established the first national collegiate championships — the National Collegiate Track and Field Championships in 1921.

Events during the 1940s and '50s made the public aware of the need for regulation of the college athletic scene to avoid exploitation and excesses. The Association responded with the Sanity Code, the beginnings of the regulation and enforcement machinery of today. The 1950s and '60s brought the influence of television to the campuses; and the NCAA membership, anticipating the inevitable impact it would have on college attendance, quickly moved to establish policies regarding the effect of this new electronic device.

During the 1970s came the call for expanded opportunities for women athletes. And, at one of the most significant Conventions since that of 1906, the membership in 1981 answered this call by expanding both the governance and competitive structures of the NCAA to provide representation and participation for women.

History is a record of the responses of people and groups of people to changing times and the alternating moods of society. The NCAA has responded well to the changing needs of its members. So, it is appropriate as we celebrate the NCAA's 75th anniversary to look back with pride at the accomplishments of the nation's colleges and universities and express a deep sense of gratitude to the countless individuals who have played a part in the Association's history. At the same time, it is in the character of the NCAA also to take a forward look at those issues that lie ahead. I am confident the Association will continue to be successful as it responds to the needs of its members.

WALTER BYERS
Executive Director
NCAA

ACKNOWLEDGMENTS

Anyone undertaking to write a history will necessarily incur a large debt to those who assist with the great amount of research essential to such a project. The author's specific obligations are too numerous to list in full detail, but I feel compelled to acknowledge some individuals without whose help there would be no book.

At every stage in the preparation of this book, I received generous help from NCAA Publications Editor Timothy D. Schmad; I should like to record here my warm gratitude for his hard work and reliability.

NCAA Assistant Executive Director Ted C. Tow read and edited each chapter, supplying many suggestions and much sound judgment. Other NCAA executives who read and made suggestions on portions of the manuscript or who assisted with the research were Executive Director Walter Byers, Controller Louis J. Spry and Assistant Executive Directors Thomas C. Hansen, William B. Hunt and Thomas W. Jernstedt.

I am particularly grateful to NCAA Director of Publishing Wallace I. Renfro, who first offered me the opportunity of writing this book and who offered much advice and encouragement, particularly in the difficult early going.

Though he is allegedly "retired," former NCAA Controller Arthur J. Bergstrom was an invaluable source of guidance and information. His monographs on various facets of the Association's history were among my most valuable resources.

On a more personal level, I must acknowledge the perphaps unwitting contribution of my children and their school friends, who so graciously acquiesced when they suddenly learned so many of their backyard "home games" would be rescheduled as "away games" during the 15 months this work was in progress.

JACK FALLA
Natick, Massachusetts

CHAPTER ONE

" . . . and many a grevous fall."

We will begin with the sticking of the pig.

We will begin here because, to understand the forces bonding sport to education and later giving rise to a coalition such as the National Collegiate Athletic Association and its predecessors, it is necessary to have a grasp of the curious evolution of the game of American football. And American football begins not in America but in the British Isles in medieval days. More particularly, it begins with the November ritual of the sticking and butchering of the family pig.

We will not stick the pig, however, without noting, in the interest of historical accuracy, that the football we are about to see played in medieval England can trace its origins all the way back to 1697 B.C. and a soccer-like game, *tsu-chu,* played by the Chinese.

Games similar to *tsu-chu* are played later by the Japanese *(kemari),* Berbers *(koura),* Greeks *(episkiros)* and Romans *(harpastum).* In fact, the British farmer probably learned his crude form of football from the Romans during the occupation from 43 to 407 A.D.

None of which saves our pig.

This business of sticking a pig is as precise as it is grisly. The farmer must slip his blade in at a certain mark just about the breastbone, then draw it quickly upward, severing an artery and killing the pig. The blood will go to the making of black pudding. Indeed, the best thing about the pig is its total utility. The heart and liver will be eaten the night of the sticking. The intestines are scraped to become chitterlings. Pork chops and bacon are put up for the winter. And the bladder — well, now, the bladder will provide our

1

farmer with a little fun. And sometimes a little trouble, as well.

After a day or two of this bloody business of sticking and butchering pigs, a farmer hardly can be blamed for wanting to disport himself in the great outdoors in the last crisp days of autumn. For this, he will blow up or stuff the pig's bladder to use as a ball in a pasture game that might charitably be called football — it calls for use of feet and a ball — but, more accurately, is a form of rural mass mayhem.

We still have the delightful Middle English verse of Alex Barclay's "Eche Time and Season" as testimony that a good many pig bladders became footballs:

> "When men be busy in killing of fat swine,
> They get the bladder and blow it great and thin.
> . . . Eche one contendeth and hath a great delight
> With foote or hand the bladder for to smite."

Later in the same poem, we have the poet's view of this impromptu football as a vigorous affair:

> "If it fall to grounde they lift it up agayne,
> This wise to labor they count it for no pain,
> Renning and leaping they drive away the colde.
> The sturdie plowman, lustie, strong and bolde
> Overcommeth the winter with driving the football,
> Forgetting labor and many a grevous fall."

Eventually, these games attract more than just the "sturdie plowman." From a kick-about in the fields, this primitive football game proliferates to the point where games will match the greater part of the male population of neighboring towns in a furious contest, the only object of which is to kick the inflated bladder into the center of the opponent's town. This done, there follows a great outpouring of joy, fueled by a greater outpouring of ale.

The game is a violent affair in which hedges, animals, fences and crops (and, in one case, a house) are routinely trampled as the tide of battle swirls destructively over the countryside. Rules are simple — there aren't any.

Despite the game's inherent violence — "a bloody muthering practice," one English preacher calls it — football proves widely seductive. It spreads from pastures to city streets, where its violence now poses a threat not only to property, but to law and order and the lives and limbs of bystanders. It is in London in 1314 that football players first feel the effects of the public disapproval that, in differing forms, will threaten the existence of the game into our own century. King Edward II bans the sport, addressing thus the citizens: " . . . there is a great noise in the city caused by hustling over large balls . . . from which many evils might arise, which God forbid, we command . . . on pain of imprisonment, such game (not) to be used in the city."

The ban is not enforced in rural areas until 1349, when relations between footballers and the monarchy grow markedly more strained. King Henry III sees football not only as a threat to law and order, but to national security, as well, in that it engages the energies of young men who should be better occupied with their obligatory archery practice. Henry III bans the game everywhere in a proclamation that refers to football as a "foolish game."

The ban continues through successive monarchies and football is forced underground, being played only in rural areas where the police can be bribed to look the other way.

It isn't until the 16th century that James I bows to the pressure of sportsmen (who have been playing the game anyway) and revokes the ban on football. The game emerges from its dark ages as a more controlled, though no less brutal, affair. The chaotic, town-to-town demolition derbies of Henry III's day now give way to a game confined to one field where a team receives points for kicking a ball across a predetermined goal line. The rules — perhaps better described as "customs" — prohibit running with the ball and forward passing. Other than this, football remains a violent game in which players are routinely maimed and sporadically killed. There is no reason to think Puritan pamphleteer Phillip Stubbs exaggerates when he writes in 1583:

> *"They have the sleights to meet one betwixt two, to dash him against the hart with their elbowes, to hit him under the short ribbes with their griped fists, and with their knees to catch him upon the hip and pick him on his neck, with a hundred such muthering devices: and hereof groweth envie, malice, rancour, cholar, hatred, displeasure, enmitie, and what not els, and sometimes murther, fighting, brawling, contortion, quarrel, kicking, homicide, and great effusion of blood."*

That about covers it.

Football's further evolution limits the number of players on a team and produces goal posts so that points might be scored via a skillful kick. But the malignancy of violence essentially is unchecked. Rule changes do not clot the "great effusion of blood."

By the late 16th century, however, there arises a new point of view regarding football. The opinion that eventually will see football wedded to education and that, four centuries later, will see the game raised to its present stature in America is first expressed around 1570 by one Richard Mulcaster, headmaster of the Merchant Taylors School in England. "Football," observes Mulcaster, "strengtheneth and brawneth the whole body, and by providing superfluities downward, it dischargeth the head and upper parties, it is good for the bowels, and to drive downe the stone from both the bladder and the kidnies ... "

Football can be good for you, Mulcaster thinks. It is a radical thought at the time.

Mulcaster's enlightened sentiments are, and for 300 years remain, the minority view. In general, schoolboys and university students play football on their own time and under the scowls of their schoolmasters, men who obviously find the game more suited to farmers than to would-be gentlemen.

The breakthrough — more important than it seems at the time — does not occur until 1828, when another educator, Dr. Thomas Arnold, a man in the Mulcaster mold, becomes headmaster of England's Rugby School and immediately incorporates sports into the school's curriculum.

Dr. Arnold's decision is most significant. From this time on, football (and, later, many other sports) will have its fortunes tied directly not to clubs or towns or government or the military or any of the myriad social institutions that might have supported it, but instead to schools. When headmaster Arnold formally bonded sports to education, it is doubtful that he or anyone of his day could foresee how insoluble that bond would be.

It is around Arnold's time that two types of football become clearly discernible. One permits a player to run with the ball; the other requires that the ball be advanced only with the feet. Football's evolutionary path comes to a fork. While it may seem inconsequential whether a school plays the "handling" game or the "dribbling" game, the choice of one or the other will set off reverberations that will be felt in America a century later and that will produce a greater conflict than one might imagine among American colleges.

Plainly, the two games evolving here are rugby and soccer. Rugby is reported (though the report is hard to verify) to have enjoyed a rather dramatic beginning in 1823 in an intramural game at Rugby School when a student, William Webb Ellis, did a very natural, if then illegal, thing. He picked up a ball and ran with it. His team-mates viewed this as a breach of sportsmanship and, so the tale goes, practically ostracized the poor lad in what must rank as one of history's more severe illegal-procedure penalties. Ellis, however, later is vindicated and, in fact, honored by a bronze plaque com-memorating his act. It reads:

> *"This stone commemorates the exploit of William Webb Ellis who with a fine disregard for the rules of Football as played in his time first took the ball in his arms and ran with it thus originat-ing the distinctive feature of the Rugby game. A.D. 1823."*

The divergence is formalized in 1863 when Cambridge University publishes a set of rules prohibiting running with the ball. Later in the same year, representatives of various British football clubs (these being made up of alumni who want to keep playing after they have graduated) meet in a tavern and establish the London Football As-sociation. The association publishes 14 rules. Rule Nine reads, "No player shall run with the ball."

"Football," as our medieval farmer knew it, has now disappeared. It is replaced by rugby on the one side, soccer on the other.

Given football's popular and violent origins, its adoption by the educational establishment and its evolutionary branching into two sports, it is now necessary that we leave England for America. It is in the United States in the late 19th and early 20th centuries that we first see the unparalleled influence of sport, initially on a few college campuses and later throughout the American educational system.

Football, of course, does not make a dramatic arrival in America. The original, barnyard, "anything goes" version of the game is played in New England as early as 1609. Here it meets the same fate it earlier met in England: Boys and young men embrace it, only to have politicians ban it. The town fathers in Boston in 1657 go so far as to impose a fine of 20 shillings on anyone caught playing football. This, they say, is the result of injuries to citizens caused "by boyes and young men playing at football in the streets . . . "

The game nonetheless survives. By the 1820s, we find reports of football games at the Ivy League schools — Harvard, Yale and Princeton. These games are not faculty-sanctioned affairs but in-tramural games organized by and for the students. Most notorious of these matches is an annual clash between freshmen and sophomores at Harvard on the first Monday of the fall term. The day is called "Bloody Monday," suggesting the fundamental nature of football has changed very little since medieval days. The Harvard faculty, pressured by the Cambridge townsfolk, bans the Bloody Monday games in 1860.

It is important to note that the game played at Harvard and other colleges is more akin to rugby than to soccer; that is, it permits use of the hands and, in general, is considered a rougher version of the game. The choice of which sort of football to play — handling or dribbling — seems of little moment to us now. But, for the players of these early days, this choice will become the first major divisive issue in American college sports, and its resolution will have a profound effect on the conduct of all future college athletics.

Despite the popularity of rugby football, soccer football is able to find a home at two prestigious American colleges, Princeton and Rutgers. It is rather common knowledge today that when these two schools play each other in the now celebrated "first football game" on November 6, 1869, they play a game more akin to soccer than to rugby, a game, in fact, that is governed by a modified version of the rules of the London Football Association.

Soon after the Princeton-Rutgers game, two other major Eastern colleges, Columbia and Yale, adopt the soccer-style game. Predictably, with four schools playing the same game, it is only a matter of time before representatives of these schools do what groups with common interests always do — hold a meeting.

The meeting in 1873 of representatives of the teams from Princeton, Rutgers, Yale and Columbia accomplishes much more than its stated purpose of drawing up a set of rules. It illustrates both the coalescent and divisive effects of sport upon colleges.

Agreement on the rules is easy. The four schools agree to play a game that for all practical purposes is soccer. But persuading other schools to follow their lead and adopt soccer as the universal form of football proves to be more difficult.

There is a fifth prominent football-playing school that does not attend this 1873 rules-making meeting and that has no intention of agreeing with anyone to play anything other than the game it always has played. That school is Harvard, and the game is rugby, or the "hands-on" game.

Harvard, even in these days, is more than two centuries old and is an institution of incomparable prestige. It already has produced two presidents, a Supreme Court justice and writers such as Emerson and Thoreau. It is, more than any other American institution, the leader of the young country's political and intellectual development. Its status as a minority of one is of no account to Harvard. It clings stubbornly to its handling game which, by now, bears the parochial title "the Boston game."

Harvard stands so isolated on this issue that it literally cannot schedule a game with any other American college and instead is forced to turn to Canada where, in 1874, the Harvard Football Club persuades the team from McGill University of Montreal to journey to Cambridge for a pair of games. The first game will be played under "Boston" rules, the second under all-Canada rules. The Canadian rules provide for free kicks, drop kicks, use of an oval ball and a rectangular field (the Boston game is played on a square field) and, in general, mark another evolutionary step toward the more open game of football we know today. Also foreshadowing things to come is the series' paid gate — 200 spectators at 50 cents each, the proceeds used to defray McGill's travel expenses.

Harvard wins the first game and ties the second, but that is not of much consequence. The important and unexpected result of this series is that the Harvard players and fans take more enthusiastically to the Canadian game than to the Boston game. "Football," reports the Harvard Advocate after the series and with reference to the Canadian version, "will be a popular game here in the future." That has to be one of sports' great understatements.

The next year finds Harvard holding out an olive branch of sorts to the soccer-playing schools by asking Yale to meet in a football game to be played under "concessionary rules." It is Yale, however, that ends up doing most of the conceding; and the Harvard-Yale game in New Haven on November 13, 1875, is, in essence, a rugby game which Harvard wins, 4-0. Again, the score is not important. What is important is the opinion of two chilled spectators huddled among the 1,200 at the game. Jonathan Potter and W. Earle Dodge, two Princeton students, become so impressed with the rugby-style game — that is, a game permitting use of the hands — that they soon prevail upon Princeton to give up soccer and adopt rugby as its form of football. And so, at last, Harvard is to have its way and U.S. college football will come to mean rugby football rather than the somewhat less violent soccer football. This is the critical turn down a road that in 30 years will bring football to the brink of self-destruction.

Intercollegiate squabbling (in these days the prevailing method of getting things done) by no means ends with the agreement to play a particular type of football. In fact, the arguing has hardly begun.

On November 23, 1876, it is Yale that picks up its ball and goes home. Yale, Harvard, Princeton and Columbia are meeting at the Massasoit Hotel in Springfield, Massachusetts, for the purpose of forming an organization to be called the Intercollegiate Football Association, a praiseworthy attempt to bring some order to the prevailing chaos of collegiate sport, particularly football. The association is in its fourth hour of organizational life when it slams head-on into the political reality of intercollegiate sport — namely, that no one can make people do something they don't want to do. There comes to the floor of the meeting a seemingly innocent proposal calling for several football rules changes, among them a provision that will reduce the size of a squad from 15 to 11. Yale opposes the change. Harvard, Columbia and Princeton approve it. The motion passes, 3 to 1. This time the score is important. Yale immediately pulls out of the association. Three years will pass before Yale is brought back into the fold by the persuasions of its football captain, Walter Camp.

Yet, this sort of squabbling is a benign annoyance compared to the deadly malignancy of violence.

Scattered newspaper reports of the late 1870s note that football is becoming a rougher game, relying more on the use of heavy, strong men. The Lehigh Burr goes so far as to claim, "to make a good football player, one must forget his position as a gentleman."

The open-field tackling of unpadded ball carriers is vicious enough, but what truly puts the emphasis on size and strength is a dull convention of the game called the "scrummage," a system of putting the ball in play. In the scrummage or "scrum," as it is popularly known, eight men assemble in what is called "the pack." The ball is placed between the packs of the two teams, whereupon follows mayhem. The ball may not be touched by any player until it is kicked clear of the scrum, at which point it may be picked up and advanced by one of the backs. Players in the pack link arms for greater solidarity, while players at the back of the pack literally push against the buttocks of their teammates, driving them forward. Kicking, punching and butting are common.

The scrum is not only dangerous, it is also bad box office. The New York Times reports of an 1879 Yale-Princeton game, "For nearly 10 minutes, the men struggled without gaining 10 feet either way, the backs of each side being nothing but interested onlookers."

The scrum is the obvious manifestation of the tactic of mass play. It is to make the game even more dangerous when to mass is added momentum.

In the 1879 Harvard-Princeton game, we see Princeton unveil a new tactic called "guarding the runner." Here a player runs on either side of the ball carrier to prevent his being tackled from the side. They thus insure either a violent head-on tackle or a jolting hit from behind.

Besides the legitimate violence, games of these days are marred by an inexplicable leniency in the rules — punching an opponent is punishable by no more than a warning.

By 1883, we see football degenerate to a point where the Harvard Committee on Athletics says it is a game "no longer governed by a manly spirit of fair play" but instead pervaded by "a spirit of sharpers and roughs." The committee orders the Harvard Football Club to disband.

Incredibly, the team does not disband — at least, not for another two years — and the reason it does not disband presages, more plainly than any incident thus far, the growing power and problems of college athletics. The reason is money.

By the time the Harvard committee makes it pronouncement, Harvard and Yale already have agreed to play their now-traditional annual game at the Polo Grounds in New York City. Harvard is in the process of spending $13,000 to redesign its field, and Yale is seeking to acquire property near the college to build a new field of its own. Both schools are relying on the anticipated gate receipts of their forthcoming game to help meet costs of the new fields. The Harvard Football Club is able to prevail over the Harvard faculty. The Harvard-Yale game is played before a record gate of 10,000. Sport has dictated college policy. And in this we can see the tail's first ominous wagging of the dog.

While football attendance swells, violence on the field continues unabated until, at the end of the 1884 season, we see Harvard and Columbia dropping football and withdrawing from the ineffective Intercollegiate Football Association. Harvard's parting shot is to call football "brutal, demoralizing to teams and players and extremely dangerous."

The Intercollegiate Football Association reacts to its critics by making token improvements in the game. It advocates use of paid referees and makes some of the more blatant fouls, such as slugging, punishable by game ejection. The association, by now also awakened to the problems caused by the scrum and acting on a suggestion put forth by Yale's Walter Camp, has eliminated this boring and brutal battle for ball control by simply awarding a team undisputed possession. The changes seem to work, producing, for a few seasons, a less violent game. Criticism lessens, even to the extent that Harvard returns to the association in 1886. But worse trouble lies ahead. It already has arrived in 1884 in the form of a human wedge.

The straight wedge or "V-trick" is invented at Princeton and used for the first time on an unsuspecting Pennsylvania team at Philadelphia on October 25, 1884. The Tigers gain 45 yards on its first use.

The V-trick is the tactical innovation of Princeton quarterback Richard Hodge, whose idea is to have his players form, literally, a human wedge, with the Princeton ball carrier safely in the middle and the apex of the wedge aimed directly at the opposing line.

The wedge is an effective, if violent, tactic — "mass play" is the popular term — and it catches on quickly, as do various means of defending against it. One of the more popular defensive tactics is to hit the apex man in the jaw. Another calls for the defensive players to dive under the legs of the men in the wedge, knocking them down and stripping away the ball carrier's protection. But to get the full picture of the spiral of violence in the 1880s, we have to look at famous Yale lineman Pudge Heffelfinger, a man with his own system for stopping the wedge. Pudge takes a running leap, draws up his knees and smashes into the apex man. This works nicely. We might note, too, that it is Heffelfinger who first invents the practice of a lineman pulling out of the line to lead the interference. Heffelfinger mows down would-be tacklers with his crunching shoulder blocks.

By the 1890s, college football is in the curious predicament of proving increasingly popular on campuses, where 120 schools now field teams, and less popular in the press, where criticism accelerates.

"There is no sport outside of a bullfight," claims the New York Herald, "that provides the same degree of ferocity, danger and excitement as that shown in an ordinary intercollegiate game of football."

But the Herald reporter who wrote that has not seen the ultimate in mass-momentum plays, a tactic to be known as "the flying wedge." It will be a giant step toward the near self-destruction of football.

The flying wedge is conceived in Boston by a construction engineer, chess expert and student of military tactics, Lorin F. Deland. Deland is a Harvard fan (the fact that he is not also a Harvard alumnus is testimony to the growing attraction of football to the public) who comes up with a play he says embodies the Napoleonic concept of "multiplying mass by rapidity." Deland gives his secret play to Harvard captain Bernard Trafford.

Harvard first uses the flying wedge against Yale — who else? — at the start of the second half of their game in 1892.

Yale has nine men strung along its 45-yard line in preparation for Harvard taking the ball on the kickoff (in these days, a team kicks off to itself, much as is still done in soccer). The last two men on the right side of the Yale line are in for a bad time of it. Harvard's Trafford puts the ball in play by tapping it back to halfback Charlie Brewer. The flying wedge is already in motion. From Brewer's right, four of Harvard's biggest men come charging, single file, across the field intent on blasting a hole between Yale's two outside linemen. From Brewer's left comes a diamond-shaped, five-man wedge — a modification of the old V-trick — ready to escort the ball carrier through the gap. The play gains 30 yards before the Yale pursuit stacks it up by grabbing legs.

The combination of mass and momentum embodied in the flying wedge produces more shattering full-speed collisions and, understandably, more injuries than any previous formation.

Now football's critics are not to be found only in a newspaper's sports department. After a particularly violent game in 1894, Army and Navy decide to discontinue their series. Across the nation, disenchanted school officials and the general public are calling for the banning of mass-momentum plays. "To make matters worse," writes football historian Col. A. M. Weyand, "there was no authoritative body that could take the necessary action."

The loosely organized and never-too-effective Intercollegiate Football Association is now virtually dead, Harvard and Columbia having withdrawn to leave only Yale and Princeton. The day temporarily is saved when the University Athletic Club of New York seizes the initiative and invites representatives of Harvard, Pennsylvania, Princeton and Yale to form a football rules committee. Delegates from these schools, along with football official Paul J. Dashiel of Johns Hopkins, meet at the club on February 23, 1894.

The newly formed rules committee, like the association before it, makes a few — too few, it will turn out — rules changes, aimed as much at stopping public criticism as at improving the game on the field of play. They add a linesman to the crew of game officials, reduce playing time from 90 to 70 minutes and outlaw use of the flying wedge on kickoffs. However, they stop short of outlawing all mass-momentum plays, an apparent concession to coaches and players who tend to like the game pretty much the way it is.

By now, coaches have invented derivatives of the flying wedge. The "guards back" and "tackles back" plays all move linemen into the backfield for the purpose of forming a phalanx of blockers.

Less than a year after formation of the football rules committee, Harvard and Yale play a game in which six players, three from each side, have to be helped off the field. The Boston Post calls the match "a most atrociously brutal game throughout."

The new rules committee also proves helpless in eliminating interschool squabbling, even among its own select members. Harvard temporarily discontinues athletic relations with Yale after the aforementioned "brutal" game of 1894.

It is at about this time that another sports-related problem begins to show itself, a problem that, in the long run, will prove even more troublesome than football violence. Hired athletes or "tramp" football players begin showing up on college rosters. The specter of the twin issues, recruitment and eligibility, begins to cast what will be an ever-darkening shadow.

But the game thrives, increasing in popularity and violence. Another new tactic, the "hurdle play," is introduced. While it doesn't prove as popular as the flying wedge, it will serve to show what we might consider the high-water mark of dangerous play.

In the hurdle play, a small back is given the ball. The back takes a running leap onto the arms of two of his teammates (and up the back of the center) and literally is flung, feet first, over the defensive line, hurtling through the air at a height of five or six feet.

The ultimate defense of the hurdle play is invented by Princeton in 1902 and is worth our attention if we are to appreciate fully the state of the game in this era. When Columbia throws little halfback Harold Weekes across the line in a hurdle play, the Princeton defense counters by hurling one of its own players, Dana Kafer, into the air to intercept Weekes. The ensuing midair collision puts Weekes and Kafer out of the game, probably to their mutual relief and undoubtedly to their mortal well-being.

By 1903, we hear not only journalistic complaints against the violence of football, but legislative protests, as well. Several state legislatures vote on bills that will outlaw college football. While none of the bills passes, the votes are close enough that the football rules committee feels compelled to declare itself publicly in favor of a less violent game it terms "open" football.

The committee backs its public posture, albeit weakly, with a few rules changes. One change requires that there be seven men on the line, thus effectively preventing guards and tackles from dropping back and leading mass-momentum plays. It seems like a good rule until we realize it applies only between the 25-yard lines. From the 25-yard line to the end zone it's still "anything goes." In this light, the change appears to be little more than a pacifying token cynically tossed to the game's critics.

The simple fact is that coaches and players tend to be, insofar as tactics are concerned, a conservative lot who like football the way it is. Let the newspapers and legislatures wail. Football still has many friends. There are 45,000 in the stands at the 1905 Harvard-Yale game. One of them is Theodore Roosevelt, a Harvard alumnus, former varsity boxer and, at this time, the President of the United States.

President Roosevelt is an unabashed football fan. He is the first of our presidents to use football analogies in his public speeches. "Don't flinch, don't foul and hit the line hard" is one of his favorites.

Like any elected officeholder, Mr. Roosevelt is careful to keep his political fingers closely pressed to the public pulse. And what he is feeling in 1905 is a growing and profound sense of outrage by the American people against the game of college football.

The evidence is not only in the newspapers. One of the great theatrical successes of this season is a play called "The College Widow," a farce about the foibles of college athletics and, in particular, the violence of football.

On the more serious side, the 1905 season will produce a total of 18 deaths and 149 serious injuries attributable (or at least attributed) to football. Public opinion, in the case of college football, apparently is justifiable. The general attitude is best expressed by Chancellor James Roscoe Day of Syracuse University: "One human life is too big a price for all the games of the season."

The season is not yet half over before President Roosevelt decides to bring the power and prestige of his office to bear on the problem. On October 9, 1905, with due publicity and ballyhoo, Roosevelt summons to the White House several football leaders, among them representatives of Harvard, Princeton and Yale, for a discussion of what the President sees as the two choices facing the college game — reform or abolition. Roosevelt, ever one to extol the virtues of sport and the robust life, makes it plain that he favors rules changes that will make the game less dangerous and thereby restore it to public favor. The delegates agree — they are hardly in a position to do anything else — and the President receives their assurances that the matter will be a priority at the December meeting of the rules committee.

What happens after the White House conference is an affront to the presidency and a disservice to football. The football rules committee meets in Philadelphia and, Roosevelt's wishes notwithstanding, takes no action to make the game better or safer.

Meanwhile, the crisis is growing.

Columbia and Northwestern suspend football. California and Stanford substitute rugby (by now a separate game) for football, and Harvard President Charles Eliot is threatening to abolish the game on his campus.

The rules committee is beginning to get its share of blame for the state of the game. The prevailing attitude toward the committee in these days might have been best expressed a few years later by Capt. Palmer Pierce of the U.S. Military Academy, who claimed that the rules committee was widely viewed as "a self-constituted, self-perpetuating and irresponsible body, which, in order to make the rules more favorable to the playing talent available at particular institutions, had degraded a once noble sport to the plane of a brutal gladiatorial contest."

Had the 1906 season followed the same violent course as its predecessors, college football today might be nothing more than a curiosity of our athletic past. Pressured by public opinion and urged by common sense, more schools would have turned to soccer or rugby as alternatives. But what happens next is one of those rare and singular acts of personal initiative upon which history so often turns.

Henry M. MacCracken, chancellor of New York University, seeing clearly the steady descent and grim future of football, takes it upon himself to call a special meeting of the football-playing colleges of the nation, a meeting not sanctioned by the rules committee.

Thirteen Eastern colleges agree to attend MacCracken's conference, a rather appreciable number considering that the invitation does not come from any formal or recognized organization. The delegates meet in New York City on December 9, 1905, and decide to take it upon themselves to reform the game. They vote to reconvene in New York on December 28 and again to send out invitations to any football-playing college. This time, 62 schools send delegates.

The conference immediately becomes more than a mere meeting of the minds (as the White House Conference had been) due to the actions of one of the delegates, Capt. Palmer E. Pierce of West Point.

Pierce persuades the assembly to create a formal organization to be called the National Intercollegiate Football Conference. The delegates agree but, significantly, leave the restricting word "Football" out of the name and call the new organization the Intercollegiate

Athletic Association of the United States (IAAUS). Within seven years, this association will be renamed the National Collegiate Athletic Association — in Pierce's words, "the voice of college sports."

But this is late December 1905, and the fledgling organization is nothing more than a roomful of men with the common problem of finding a way to save football from falling off the precipice of violence toward which it has been careening for a thousand years. It is here that Pierce again steps in, initiating a series of three shrewd organizational moves, not the less astute for their tactical simplicity. In less than a half day, Pierce and the IAAUS create the machinery that will save college football.

First comes the vote to create a formal association, thus forming an instrument for taking collective action. This done, there is a motion that the new association create its own football rules committee. This is agreed, though clearly the new committee poses a challenge to the authority, not to mention the egos, of the established American Football Rules Committee. Again, Pierce maneuvers cleverly. Rather than directly challenging the established but ineffective old rules committee, Pierce and the IAAUS issue an invitation to the old committee to join forces with the new group in changing the rules of the game.

The choice for the old committee is simple and, we may imagine, uncomfortable — either join with the new rules committee of the IAAUS in a cooperative effort to save football, or refuse to join forces and stand revealed, or at least labeled, as a minority of stubborn obstructionists.

The old committee agrees to merge ("amalgamate" is the word they use) on a temporary basis, the latter stipulation seemingly a face-saving measure.

Representatives of the two committees meet in New York on January 12, 1906. In what appears to be an insignificant preliminary decision, the newly-amalgamated committee elects William T. Reid of Harvard as secretary. Harvard is not a member of the IAAUS, and Reid's election makes it obvious that the old committee is to have some real power in this new alliance. But more important is that the secretary's post to which Reid is elected has been, since 1894, the exclusive domain of the legendary Walter Camp. As secretary, Camp was responsibile for putting the old committee's rules changes in writing. In effect, Walter Camp wrote the rules of football. But among the criticisms leveled at football in the early 1900s is that many of the rules are vague and difficult for officials to interpret. When Reid takes over as secretary, he immediately sets about recodifying and clarifying the rules of the game.

Whatever resentment members of the old rules committee might feel toward the upstart IAAUS, it is to their everlasting credit that the amalgamated committee works smoothly and well.

While the old rules committee required a unanimous vote to bring about a rules change, the new committee — officially called the American Intercollegiate Football Rules Committee — requires only a majority vote. Changes come quickly. The forward pass is approved. Loose balls no longer can be kicked. Hurdling is prohibited. A one-yard neutral zone between the offensive and defensive lines is established. Playing time is reduced from 70 to 60 minutes. And first-down yardage is increased to 10 yards, thus requiring the gaining of 10 yards in three downs for a first down rather than the mere five yards in three downs that encouraged the relentless use of line-smashing plays. Most important, the committee effectively eliminates mass-momentum plays (such as guards back and tackles back) by requiring that there be at least six men on the offensive line at all times. This time, the rule does not include the "between the 25-yard lines only" proviso of the old football rules committee.

The changes work.

At the end of the 1906 season, even Harvard's President Eliot, never a great proponent of football, intones, "I must say that football has been greatly improved this year. It has less injuries and is much more openly played."

Another educator is reported as saying of the IAAUS, "The remarkable amalgamation with the old football rules committee marked a distinct triumph for the association, resulting not so much in changing the rules . . . but even more in a better public sentiment."

And Walter Camp makes it official, saying flatly that football now is reinstated "in public favor."

This amalgamated rules committee, in reality an arm of Pierce and MacCracken's new IAAUS, has reached out and plucked the game from the edge of the precipice. It performs this rescue mission in 16 days, from December 28, 1905, to January 12, 1906.

But the establishment still has face to save. For the absurd period of 10 years, the IAAUS (which becomes the NCAA during that decade) passes a standard motion instructing its football rules committee "to communicate with the representatives of Yale, Princeton, Harvard, Pennsylvania, Cornell, Annapolis and Chicago University, who constituted the committee that formed the football rules committee during 1905, and propose that the committee be amalgamated into one which shall formulate rules under which football shall be played in (the coming year)."

And each year, the IAAUS or NCAA rules committee chair tactfully reports to the Convention, as does Henry L. Williams of Minnesota in 1910, that the amalgamated committee "worked together throughout the year in perfect harmony and accord."

Establishment sensibilities aside, the speedy and dramatic work of MacCracken, Pierce and the IAAUS rules committee does not go unnoticed in college circles. Membership in the IAAUS increases from 28 to 39 by the end of 1906 and to 49 by 1907. Palmer Pierce, the president of the new association, sounds more like a prophet when he says in 1907, "I firmly believe the IAAUS will finally dominate the college athletic world. It stands for purity, for rational control, for fair play.... As its aims and methods become better understood, its strength will grow until its influence will become truly national."

There is still something overlooked here. Beyond the salvation of a venerable old game, and transcending the politics of the new athletic alliance, lies the universal of sport, the spontaneity of the player and his game. Our old pig-butchering medieval farmer would not recognize the football of 1906 as the same game he played with a pig bladder in the pastures a thousand years before. Yet, despite its twisting course through history, football remains a fine way to disport oneself in the last crisp days before winter. And as that, it should be preserved.

CHAPTER TWO

" . . . in keeping with the dignity and high purpose of education."

Headmaster Arnold did a shocking thing in the 1820s by making athletics a part of the curriculum at The Rugby School in England. In one stroke, he brought together two rather diverse groups — students and teachers — on grounds other than the traditional one of scholarship.

School-sanctioned sports bring together the youthful, active, physical and oftentimes boisterous student-athlete and the older, more sedentary, cerebral and generally quieter academician. These are generalizations, to be sure; there are always bookish students and vigorous teachers. But as coaches are wont to say, "I get older every season but my seniors are always 21." This fact alone assures a constant discrepancy between those who play a sport and those who administer it.

It will not surprise us, then, when we see that the 28 delegates coming into the meeting room at New York City's Murray Hill Hotel on December 29, 1906, for the first annual IAAUS Convention are not rabid college sports boosters or outspoken athletic reformists. They are, almost to a man (there is, as yet, no woman delegate), college professors. Twenty-one of the 28 accredited delegates carry the title "professor." Four others are listed as "doctor."

Despite their association's dramatic success in saving football, these men are not (it seems almost unfair to say it) dashing or swaggering or colorful men; not men of, say, the Teddy Roosevelt mold. We see very quickly that this is not to be a meeting powered by the force of anyone's rhetoric or personality. Rather, it will plod along in time-honored organizational paths. What these men do may strike us as dull history, but it is actually shrewd politics. The delegates, a handful of men representing fewer than one-quarter of the nation's sports-playing colleges, are about to lay the foundations of the country's first truly successful intercollegiate athletic alliance, an organization that will neither tear apart along the strained seams of regionalism nor self-destruct from internal squabblings.

To appreciate the early maneuverings of the IAAUS, we should look for a moment at what actually happened back in 1905; that is, let us put football aside and examine what other issues were discussed in those formative days.

Acting on the fact that it is a formal alliance rather than an ad hoc group, the IAAUS elects officers and appoints an executive committee charged with drawing up a constitution and bylaws.

The man elected president is Capt. Palmer Pierce of West Point, one of the driving forces behind the move toward formal organization. Vice-president is H. D. Wild of Williams College, and the secretary-treasurer is Louis Bevier Jr. of Rutgers University. The names are not as important as the sudden fact that the big four Northeast powers of the first Intercollegiate Football Conference — Columbia, Harvard, Princeton and Yale — are not members of the new Association; for the first time in the history of American college athletics, the big four are on the outside looking in.

That original 1905 meeting (it was not yet properly a convention) also passes a motion that, for ease of administration and fair representation, the country be divided into seven geographical districts, each district to be represented on the executive committee. Again, the following names may mean little to us today. But consider the schools, states and sections of the country that for the first time are in position to make their influence felt in intercollegiate athletics. Joining the representatives of West Point, Williams and Rutgers on the executive committee are William L. Dudley of Vanderbilt, Chancellor Frank Strong of the University of Kansas and President Herbert Welch of Ohio Wesleyan. The South and the Midwest are to be heard.

This executive committee meets three times between the first general meeting of 1905 and the Convention of 1906. During this time, the committee draws up a constitution and bylaws, going about the job with a little eloquence, a lot of workmanship and, as we are about to see, a good deal of vision.

There is, on this morning in 1906, no great Jeffersonian oratory ringing down the corridors of the Murray Hill Hotel. Rather, this whole Convention seems to be shaping up as a great bore.

The meeting begins with the drone of the call to order, followed by a call of the roll. Capt. Pierce then appoints a committee on credentials and promptly adjourns the Convention, thus allowing the new committee to do its work.

It is already late morning when the delegates reconvene to hear Pierce read the minutes of the 1905 meeting. This chore done, Pierce appoints a nominating committee, not a particularly startling move on the face of it but an interesting one, nonetheless. Pierce, of course, is required by the new constitution and bylaws to appoint a nominating committee. The interesting thing is that by making such a provision, the executive committee gives clear evidence of its intent that the IAAUS is not to be an organization controlled by any one man, group of men or bloc of schools. Rather, it is to be an organization controlled by the collective will of its members, made manifest through the instrument of committees.

The nominating committee is particularly powerful because it proposes the names of members who will be elected to the first official Executive Committee, and it is the Executive Committee that will conduct the day-to-day business of the Association throughout these early years.

Members of the nominating committee come from Dartmouth, Colorado, Missouri, Ohio Wesleyan, Syracuse and West Point. Only the South is without representation. While this committee may have a slight Northeastern bias, again there is the conspicuous absence of the old "big four" schools.

We might imagine more than a little impatient shuffling in the meeting room as the delegates listen to Capt. Pierce report that the constitution and bylaws drawn up the preceding winter by the original executive committee are now ratified by 35 colleges and universities; Pierce, ever a meticulous man, proceeds to read the list of ratifiers.

The First Constitution

The content and language of the original constitution are worth our inspection.

What the presidents and chancellors of the ratifying schools approve is an instrument obviously designed for the systematic development and long organizational life of the new Association. We can judge, simply by the language and directness of the constitution, that the fledgling IAAUS is an organization of institutional representatives with a clear idea of where they want to go and an equally clear disinclination to restrict their activities to the narrow area of college football. In the writing, as in the oratory, there are few eloquent flourishes, just a here-to-there simplicity:

"Article 1: The name of this Association shall be the Intercollegiate Athletic Association of the United States.

"Article 2: Its object shall be the regulation and supervision of college athletics throughout the United States, in order that the athletic activities . . . may be maintained on an ethical plane in keeping with the dignity and high purpose of education."

And so it goes, through the division of the country into seven districts, the setting of dues at $25 per school, the stipulation of the titles and duties of officers and so on. Some of it appears to be rather mundane, until we come to Article 8. Here, in one sentence — practically in one word — the new Association matter-of-factly, almost offhandedly, lays the cornerstone for its administrative success and political survival:

"Article 8. The Colleges and Universities in this Association *severally* (italics added) agree to take control of student athletic sports, as far as may be necessary to maintain in them a high standard of personal honor, eligibility and fair play, and to remedy whatever abuses may exist."

They "severally" agree. That is not precisely the same as saying they "collectively" agree.

It is not hairsplitting fancy but a fundamental philosophical premise that underlies the use of the word. What is implied here, and later spelled out clearly in the bylaws, is one of the Association's governing principles — home rule.

We shall see, in the bylaws and elsewhere, that no group of states' rights proponents ever embraced more tightly the home-rule philosophy than do this country's colleges in 1906, particularly when the subject is athletics, an area in which most schools are very much on their own.

What these institutions "severally" agree to in 1906 is that they may act "separately" thereafter.

If this seems a weighty argument for one word to sustain, we can see the matter set forth with unmistakable clarity in Article 7 of the bylaws. This article, and the one preceding it, are addressed to the related issues of eligibility and amateurism. Article 7 of the bylaws says, in part:

> "The acceptance of a definite statement of eligibility rules shall *not* (italics added) be a requirement of membership in this Association. *The constituted authorities of each institution* (italics added) shall decide on methods of preventing the violation of the principles laid down . . . ."

At the Convention, Capt. Pierce will admit that, when the bylaws were drawn up the preceding March, "definite rules of eligibility made mandatory upon all members of the Association were judged impractical . . . ."

A sound judgment. If previous experience showed, as it did, that other associations could not even reach agreement among their members on the urgent matter of debrutalizing football, unanimity on issues as sensitive as amateurism and eligibility seems a faint hope indeed.

The "Principles of Amateur Sport," as they appear in these first bylaws, are clear and laudable. They prohibit proselyting, athletic scholarships, athletic recruiting of prep school students, use of professional players, use of players who are not bona fide full-time students and unsportsmanlike conduct by players, coaches or fans. But to attempt to take from each college — in fact, from each faculty — the prerogative of running its own athletic program might undo the new Association or, at the very least, retard its growth by raising internal arguments and animosities.

New members of the IAAUS may be attracted by the very real prospects of their having something to gain, not by the implied threat of their having something that must be surrendered. If the IAAUS wavers (and it does) on the matter of enforcing its eligibility code, it does so to preserve the principle of home rule and to keep the Association together. (The day is soon coming, however, when the collective membership will get off the fence, coming down with both feet firmly planted on the side of amateurism and enforcement.)

The founders of the IAAUS, in drawing up the first constitution, go well beyond the concerns with one sport, namely football, to get to the heart of the larger issue, namely the need for a coalition of all colleges concerned with the wider area of intercollegiate athletics in general. Well and good. We should note, however, that the 28 schools sending delegates to this Convention are less than half the number that sent delegates to the 1905 meeting at which the main topic was football. Obviously, the salvation of college football is of much more immediate concern to college administrators in 1906 than is the need to join with each other in any more encompassing sort of association.

Problems in Growth and Membership

The colleges remaining outside the IAAUS in 1906 vastly surpass, in numbers and prestige, the 35 schools that are members. For example, Harvard, Yale, Stanford and the U.S. Naval Academy are among those remaining outside the fold. Save for Harvard, Yale and Navy being represented on the amalgamated football rules committee, these schools show little interest in the new Association. As an example of their resolve, when the IAAUS early in 1907 sends Harvard, Yale and Navy special invitations to join the Association, Harvard issues a flat refusal, Navy takes the matter "under advisement" and Yale does not reply. At this stage, the IAAUS is hardly a bandwagon.

With the constitution and bylaws ratified — that is, with the foundation firmly in place — Capt. Pierce sees what the new Association has to do; and early in the afternoon of this first Convention, he sets about to do it.

Pierce addresses the Convention. He speaks in the passive rather than in the active voice. Perhaps this should not surprise us, the passive voice being the voice of a group, not of an individual.

"It is intended to exert every effort," he says, "to increase the membership until all colleges and universities of any athletic importance subscribe to our constitution and bylaws and thereby agree to do their share properly to control and purify college athletics."

Pierce gets immediate support from an unexpected but prestigious source, Amos Alonzo Stagg. Even at this early stage of his career, Stagg is a legend as the successful football coach at the University of Chicago (a school that has not joined the Association). He rises and addresses the Convention, "speaking earnestly in advocacy of a national organization to regulate athletic sports," according to Secretary Bevier's minutes.

"Such an organization," Stagg tells the Convention, "could do much . . . in exerting a salutary ethical influence, raising the standard of student athletic sports for honesty, fair play and manliness."

There is no record of it, but it is not hard to imagine the applause when Stagg announces that he firmly expects the University of Chicago to join the Association.

Speaking to the same topic, E. J. Bartlett of Dartmouth talks after Stagg and expresses his hope "that the success of the past year will result in a great increase in the membership of the Association so that it may enroll also the large universities of New England and the Middle States."

Emboldened by the powers within, and apparently not intimidated by the powers without, the IAAUS makes a risky — we might almost say foolish — move.

The boldest of the young group's steps begins with a routine motion — virtually the same one that carried in 1905 — to direct the Association's Football Rules Committee for 1907 "to communicate with the representatives of Yale, Princeton, Harvard, Pennsylvania, Cornell, Annapolis and Chicago universities, who constituted the committee that formed the football rules committee during 1905, and propose that the committees be amalgamated into one which shall formulate rules under which football shall be played in 1907."

All familiar ground so far. But there is a second part to the motion, an instruction that carries with it the suggestion of organizational muscle flexing.

"Second. If this amalgamation be not accomplished, then the above named committee of seven shall proceed to formulate rules under which football shall be played by institutions enrolled in this Association."

With this rather thinly disguised ultimatum to the old football rules committee, the IAAUS determinedly crosses the Rubicon.

The old football rules committee, hardly in a position to rebuff the organization that in the public mind (and in reality) saved college football, again agrees to the amalgamation.

The combined committees work together, in what Chair Henry L. Williams of Minnesota later will call "the most cordial relationship and harmony," as one body known as the American Intercollegiate Football Rules Committee.

One wonders at the size and consequences of the schism that may have resulted if the old football rules committee had refused to join with the IAAUS committee.

Eligibility and Amateurism

Beyond its primary work of salvaging football and structuring itself as a formal organization, the IAAUS is quick to move ahead into another issue and another sport. The issue is eligibility and, while problems of eligiblity exist in all sports, the sport with the biggest problem in 1906 is baseball.

As we have seen, the Association's leaders are realistic about their organization's practical ability to enforce either the Principles of Amateur Sport as set forth in Article 6 of the bylaws or the eligibility rules as defined in Article 7. Nevertheless, these rules are set down in great detail, eligibility rules alone making up almost one-third of the total bylaws. There appears to be, even at this early date, a consensus among member schools as to what conditions *should* exist, even though it admittedly is impossible for the Association to bring about these conditions.

The eligibility rules are clear and stringent:

> "No student shall represent a college or university in any intercollegiate game or contest who is not taking a full schedule of work . . . . who has at any time received, either directly or indirectly, money, or any other consideration. . . . who has competed for any prize against a professional . . . . who has participated in intercollegiate games or contests during four previous years."

The rules also stipulate that "No student who has been registered as a member of any other college or university shall participate in any intercollegiate game or contest until he shall have been a student of the institution which he represents at least one college year."

Finally — and most surprisingly in view of the Association's admitted lack of enforcement powers — Bylaw 7 requires all candidates for any varsity position on teams of IAAUS members to fill out a 15-question eligibility card. The card, however, is not to be filed with the IAAUS but with the player's college.

The questions on the card are specific and are designed to find out if an athlete has ever competed professionally, has used up his eligibility at another school or is competing for his school for money or other considerations. The tone and intent of the eligibility card are best exemplified by its final question:

> "Are you under any contract or understanding expressed or implied to engage in athletics at (name of college) for money or other consideration or emolument to be received from any source whatever, either directly or indirectly?"

To which question is appended:

> "On my honor I state that the above answers contain the whole truth, without any mental reservation."

The athlete is required to sign and date the card.

The intent is obvious. The Association is serving notice that, although it lacks enforcement powers, it considers it important, in Capt. Pierce's words, "to annunciate clearly ... the principles of amateur athletic sports ... and, further, to set up a code of eligibility rules *which might stand as a norm for enactment as fast as circumstances shall warrant.*" (Italics added.)

This, as we shall see, is not to be especially fast. Still, it is surprising that a new organization made up of a minority of the nation's colleges is willing to plunge so quickly into the murky questions of amateurism and eligibility. After all, it is not these issues, but, as we have seen, the more urgent matter of football rules reform, that gave rise to the Association in the first place.

However, as football draws crowds, grabs headlines and generally retains its position as the flagship of every college's athletic program, the issues of amateurism and eligibility are beginning to crystallize around the less visible sport of baseball, and, more specifically, around a particularly troublesome activity called "summer baseball."

Amateurism and "Summer Baseball"

College baseball gets its start in 1859 when Williams and Amherst play a game at Pittsfield, Massachusetts. The game soon thereafter is taken up by Harvard (which finds it necessary to supplement its roster with Cambridge "townies"), Tufts, Yale, Dartmouth and most of the country's major colleges. Baseball quickly becomes a major college sport, at least as measured by participation.

College baseball, however, never generates the spectator appeal of college football, one reason being that another brand of baseball is running slightly ahead of the development of college baseball — a brand first called "professional," then "major league" and, finally, "Organized Baseball."

By the early 1900s, baseball, unlike football, is an established professional sport drawing millions of paying customers a year. If football offers a boy a chance to get an alumni-subsidized college education and perhaps a few dollars under the not-too-well-policed table, baseball offers the chance for outright, legal, salaried employment. This employment is not restricted to the major leagues but is more apt to be found in the burgeoning minor or semipro leagues. Furthermore, since baseball is a summer sport, college ballplayers can make a few extra dollars during a season when they are not attending classes.

There is no shortage of playing opportunity. The Northwestern League, the country's first minor league, is founded in Rockford, Illinois, in 1879; within eight years, there are nine minor leagues — from the California League to the New England League — all eager for the services of good players.

When college athletes increasingly begin to turn to baseball as a means of summer employment, the issue naturally arises: Does a college student who accepts pay for playing baseball during a time of year when it does not interfere with his studies thereby become a professional and suffer the loss of his intercollegiate eligibility?

No issue, not even the need for curbing violence in football (on which, of course, there is a consensus) engenders as much debate among IAAUS members and so taxes the solidarity of the Association as does the issue of summer baseball.

The feeling at a majority of IAAUS schools is that these original "boys of summer" do indeed, by associating with professionals, and regardless of whether or not the student in question takes money, place themselves in the class of professionals and thereby forfeit their college eligibility.

Amos Alonzo Stagg perhaps best expresses this position when he says he "stands for the highest standard . . . and would not allow professionalism to creep into college sports through this channel."

But a significant number of schools adopts the opposing viewpoint. They argue that even though a college player plays with a professional team in the summer and makes money doing so, he should not be subject to loss of eligibility any more than an actor who plays summer stock would lose his or her eligibility for college theatricals.

In the first year of his tenure, Capt. Pierce observes that the issue of summer baseball and amateurism could prove more troublesome in the long run than all the more-publicized problems of football. We see a suggestion of this issue at the first Convention when H. D. Wild of Williams, as spokesman for the Association's First District, begins his report (the first in the Association's history) not with any self-congratulatory recounting of the strides made in football, but with a reference to what he sees as greater awareness among some colleges of strict enforcement of eligibility rules, particularly in regard to baseball. As an example, Wild refers to Dartmouth College, which "reports last spring they had a baseball team made up of ineligibles that beat the regular team once, and that with a little training, would have been much superior. The students there," says Wild, "now take a strict enforcement of the rules as a matter of course."

But what holds at Dartmouth does not hold at all schools; and though there is to be no debate on it at this first Convention, the issue of summer baseball will consume over the next five years more hours of floor debate than will the issue of football rules reform.

Predictably, as the hour grows late, the delegates decide to address the problems of summer baseball the way we expect them to — by turning the matter over to a committee. A motion by E. J. Bartlett of Dartmouth proposes that "the question of preparing rules governing summer baseball in its relation to amateur eligibility be referred to the Executive Committee for consideration and future action."

That action, though no one foresees it, will be much slower in occurring than was the swift action that saved football.

The first Convention touches on one more sport, and one more issue, before adjourning for the year.

Basketball

Of less urgency than the reform of football and of less complexity than the eligibility issues posed by baseball is a kind of administrative problem presented by a relatively new sport, basketball.

Basketball, unlike other sports, is not so much a product of evolution as of invention. It is designed in 1891 with necessity being very much its mother and Dr. James Naismith its father.

Naismith, a physical education instructor at the International Young Men's Christian Association Training School (today Springfield College) in Springfield, Massachusetts, delights in bringing his students outdoors for football in the fall and baseball in the spring. Alas for Naismith, the long, cold New England winter leaves him with a bored and increasingly hostile group of students, clearly unhappy at being forced to take their hour-a-day recreation indoors. Naismith (apparently a man well ahead of his time) tries indoor versions of soccer (it leads to broken windows), rugby (tackling on the wooden floor is vicious) and lacrosse (windows again). In desperation, Naismith one day nails two peach baskets to balconies at either end of the gym, uses a soccer ball for play and thus invents basketball, although for a short time his grateful students try to call the game "Naismith ball." Naismith also publishes 13 rules for his new game, which immediately proves popular and is rather easy on the windows.

The first intercollegiate basketball game takes place February 9, 1895, when the Minnesota State School of Agriculture beats Hamline College of St. Paul, Minnesota, in Minneapolis by a score of 9-3 and then immediately (and opportunistically) lays claim to the "State

Championship of Minnesota."

By 1901, Harvard, Columbia, Princeton, Cornell and Yale organize the Eastern League, while Dartmouth, Holy Cross, Amherst and Williams form the New England League. It is interesting to note that women are in the vanguard of basketball's development. Vassar and Smith, both women's colleges, add basketball to their sports programs in 1892.

Although originally designed by Naismith as a noncontact sport, basketball quickly goes the way of football, with rough-play the norm and games greatly slowed by a succession of players parading to the free-throw line. As was the case with football, basketball players and coaches hear public criticism of the game's violence and outcries for rules reform.

It is difficult, however, to legislate changes in basketball's rules because the game has neither a uniform code of rules nor a central governing body. There are regional differences in rules and rules interpretation, and there are no fewer than three national associations involved in the supervision of the game. These organizations are the YMCA, the Amateur Athletic Union and, in 1906, the IAAUS.

Again, as is the case with baseball, the first IAAUS Convention wastes little time with a floor debate. The issue simply is shipped off to a committee. On the motion of C. W. Hetherington of the University of Missouri, the Executive Committee is charged with examining "the question of proper measures to be taken in view of the present diversity of rules for basketball, to the end that uniformity may be attained under some recognized authority."

From its first days of organization, the IAAUS is much inclined to the committee system of problem-solving. And from the first, the organization's powerful Executive Committee reflects a geographical diversity, the presence of men of academic bent and the conspicuous absence of Ivy League or Eastern bloc influence, at least in any disproportion.

The last thing the delegates do on December 28, 1906, is to pass unanimously a motion instructing Secretary Bevier to elect the following members to the influential Executive Committee: Capt. Pierce is to continue as president, Henry L. Williams of Minnesota is vice-president, Bevier will continue as secretary-treasurer. The district representatives on the committee will be, from the First District, Professor Wild of Williams; the Second District, Capt. Pierce; the

Third District, William L. Dudley of Vanderbilt; the Fourth District, C. E. St. John of Oberlin; the Fifth District, Vice-President Williams, and the Sixth District, C. W. Hetherington of Missouri.

The Convention thereupon adjourns to meet again at the call of the Executive Committee, a call that will come exactly one year later.

The work of this first Convention — the approval of the constitution and bylaws, the commitment to work through a permanent committee structure, the addressing of the twin issues of amateurism and eligibility, the decision to expand the scope of the Association's work from football to baseball and basketball — shows us that what began as a hastily convened ad hoc committee is now, at the end of 1906 and after only one year of existence, an intercollegiate athletic alliance of influence, diversity and as yet untested potential. The tests are soon in coming.

CHAPTER THREE

"... a proper share of the burden ..."

"In unity is strength, and all the ills of college athletics would be near solution if every college became an active partisan of this organization."

Such is the uncharacteristically sweeping observation of IAAUS President Palmer Pierce in 1907. But, like the preacher who might do better delivering his sermons to those not in church, Pierce is speaking to the converted, the delegates of the 49 member institutions at the second Convention in 1907.

It is obvious to Pierce, as it must be to much of the membership, that however carefully it is organized, however spectacular its early success, the IAAUS will not become a long-lasting force for good in college sports until it can claim membership of a majority of the nation's colleges and universities. As long as the likes of Harvard, Yale, Stanford and Princeton remain outside the fold, the IAAUS is a minority voice wanting not only strength, but prestige.

Membership and Growth

While the Association in these early years continues to give its attentions to the specific problems of football, baseball, basketball and track and field, and while it grapples with new definitions of amateurism and seeks to find a workable eligibility code, the chief concern of the Association's leadership is with the politics of growth.

Such is the sense of urgency regarding its development that the Association's three-man Committee on Membership includes the president and the vice-president, Capt. Pierce and Henry L. Williams. The third member is James A. Babbitt of Haverford College. The Convention's mandate to the committee is not simply to launch a membership campaign, but specifically "to secure the membership of the *larger* (italics added) universities." Even more specifically, the committee is charged with trying to bring Harvard, Yale, Princeton, Cornell and Annapolis into the fold. In this, the committee is a total

The Principles of Amateur Sport and the Call to Uphold Them

Palmer Pierce was one of the leading advocates of his day of the need for a national organization to govern intercollegiate athletics. In this speech to the 1907 IAAUS Convention, Pierce not only issues his call for a national organization to govern intercollegiate athletics, but also discusses the importance of the principles of amateur sport.

"The purpose of this Association is, as set forth in its constitution, the regulation and supervision of college athletics throughout the United States, in order that the athletic activities in the colleges and universities may be maintained on an ethical plane in keeping with the dignity and high purpose of education. All institutions enrolled as members agree to take control of student athletic sports, so far as may be necessary, to maintain in them a high standard of personal honor, eligibility and fair play, and to remedy whatever abuses may exist.

"The necessity of a widely organized effort to raise college sports to a higher plane and keep them there must be evident to everyone who gives the subject proper consideration. The spirit that justifies victory by any means fair or foul is still too rampant, and a great educational movement to correct this is of the highest consequence. The effect upon the national character of permitting intercollegiate contests to be conducted under false pretenses; of considering victory alone, and not the means of gaining it; of looking with a favoring eye upon concealed proselyting and professionalism; of thinking continually of winning, instead of the sport itself, and of depreciating legitimate academic work in favor of athletics, must be admitted to be seriously bad. The average American young man is already prone enough to indulge the spirit of rivalry; enamoured enough of the end to be gained irrespective of the means, without having these tendencies increased by unfair play and low standards of sportsmanship on his athletic fields. There can

failure — at least at first.

The approach to be used is a personal letter from Capt. Pierce to the presidents of the five universities. The letter is persuasive, respectful and conciliatory, offering the schools in question favorable changes in the bylaws. The most notable comes in Article 5, providing for the makeup of the all-important Football Rules Committee.

---

be no question but that a boy or young man, who is habituated to the endeavor to win games by means that he knows to be unfair and against the rules, later will play the game of life with the same ethical standards.

"A national organization of universities and colleges is needed, but to be truly effective, it must have a sufficient membership to be truly national. It may justly claim the cooperation of all college and university faculties that have at heart national control of athletics for the elimination of abuses and the better utilization of the innate love of manly sports in the upbuilding of strong and vigorous manhood.

"The Association hopes to accomplish its purpose largely by educational means. It is endeavoring to disseminate throughout the great mass of college students of our land true ideas of what amateur sport really is, to establish well-defined notions of its principles and to obtain strict adhesion to them. 'Sport for Sport's Sake' might well be its motto. This organization wages no war against the professional athlete, but it does object to such a one posing and playing as an amateur. It smiles on the square, manly, skillful contestant, imbued with love of the contest he wages; it frowns on the more skillful professional who, parading under college colors, is receiving pay in some form or other for his athletic prowess.

"This Association does not require acceptance of any particular set of eligibility rules. It does, however, bind its members to line up to the well-known principles of amateur sport. It does not take from any institution its independence, except independence for violation of the ethics of amateur athletics. It does not interfere with the formation of local leagues of two or more allied institutions; rather, it encourages such. In a word, this is a league of educated gentlemen who are trying to exercise a wise control over college athletics, believing that the good effect will react on every playground of every schoolhouse of the United States."

"It was the consensus of opinion of the delegates," writes Pierce to the presidents, "that this article should be so amended that your institution should name one member of the rules committee, provided it join this Association." (This offer was not made to Annapolis, which already enjoyed membership on the amalgamated Football Rules Committee.)

"The idea is to make plain to you," continues Pierce at his diplomatic best, "our desire to secure your membership for no other purpose than the betterment of college athletics throughout the country. There is no selfish motive, such as a desire to get control of the Football Rules Committee. We want representation but not control."

Besides the gambit of the bylaws changes, Pierce also offers his strong moral persuasion.

"It is the earnest desire of our Association that your institution should be enrolled in its membership. This is desired in order that new impetus may be given to the movement for better conditions in college athletics by the prestige and influence that will come from your joining in the work . . . . The Association is one from which any institution can withdraw whenever it sees fit. Therefore, your institution will lose none of its independence if it should join us in the work . . . . Your athletics, no doubt, are properly controlled, but we need your powerful influence to assist in elevating (athletics) throughout the country."

No answer. By October 20, 1907, Pierce has heard nothing from any school. He tries again with a follow-up letter. The response is discouraging. Yale and Princeton still do not respond. Harvard and Cornell refuse to join. Annapolis, as noted earlier, takes the matter "under consideration."

Pierce presses on, recommending to the membership "continuance of these efforts to induce these important institutions to join this Association," believing, he says, that the big schools must soon see " . . . the necessity and practicability of a national reorganization."

There will be several years and another football crisis before Pierce's prediction comes true.

Meanwhile, the IAAUS is not about to concern itself with size at the expense of function. The work goes on.

In an important and prophetic speech to the Convention in 1907, Pierce looks ahead to the work he believes the national organization can accomplish one day. He is remarkably accurate.

"It may become," he says, "a clearinghouse of athletic ideas for the whole country; a central bureau of propaganda concerning college athletics; an agency of practical reform." This reform is to come "by suggesting and urging methods of purifying athletics, by establishing . . . needed rules of play; by becoming a strong central authority on college athletics." To which he adds, most prophetically of all, "It (the IAAUS) has not endeavored to control by force of authority. Its work has been suggestive. I should regret to see any other means become necessary. However, I believe the Association will develop slowly along the best lines suitable for control of athletics." Do we hear in this the first hint that "suggestion" might someday be followed by "enforcement"?

New Members

Regardless of the absence of some of the major institutions in these early years, the IAAUS begins to grow by force of its own momentum. Let football's old "big three" remain aloof. Colleges across the country, particularly from the Midwest, begin to apply for membership in the Association.

In 1908, Northwestern, Iowa State, Penn State and Kansas are counted among the new members. Then, in 1909, comes the first big breakthrough. Harvard joins the IAAUS, as do Brown, Columbia, Bates, Tennessee, Norwich, Arkansas, Mississippi, Delaware, Indiana, the College of the City of New York and others.

IAAUS membership grows from 38 in 1906 to 67 by 1909, with the member schools representing a combined enrollment of more than 100,000.

"The need for this organization is now being widely recognized, and its methods and aims are meeting with approval," says Pierce. "In time, all the institutions of the country, of any athletic importance whatever, will become members and take their proper share of the burden of controlling college athletics."

Pierce is right. By 1912, membership increases to 97 colleges representing an enrollment of more than 120,000. Princeton, Yale and Annapolis still are not in the fold but by now it seems only a matter of time.

"We can never feel satisfied," says Pierce, "until every college . . . in the land joins in this work, which has for its object the proper control and development of collegiate athletics."

The IAAUS is moving toward its goal of becoming truly national in character. This progress is formally recognized by a name change in 1910.

The NCAA

The change occurs with neither fanfare nor debate. It happens routinely, as though the membership spontaneously decides it is time to take the next logical step in the organizational evolution. So casual is this name change that it is noted in the report of the Convention of 1910 in a small section entitled "Miscellaneous Business," almost as though it is an afterthought.

There is an amendment proposed at the 1910 Convention that would change the name of the organization from the Intercollegiate Athletic Association of the United States to something called the "National Intercollegiate Athletic Association." This does not come to a vote before another amendment is offered "to make the name of the Association the National Collegiate Athletic Association." This latter amendment carries and, by unanimous vote, the IAAUS becomes the NCAA.

The reasoning behind the change is simple. The key word is "National."

"On account of its really national character," says Pierce, "and, incidentally, to secure a more distinctive name, it is proposed to call this organization in the future, 'the National Collegiate Athletic Association.'"

Continuing his theme of association, Pierce says, "a national organization is necessary ... to make the best of the educational features of college athletics."

To the end of furthering growth of the NCAA, Pierce foresees a new dimension to the organization's involvement in college sports. What today we call "public relations" (or, more often in the context of college athletics, "sports information") in Pierce's day is called "propaganda." He urges the delegates to bring "our ideals before the student bodies ... by word of mouth and by articles in the college papers and periodicals. I cannot urge you too strongly to continue this advertisement of our aims and ideals. The national association must largely depend on you to act as independent agents to carry on the propaganda for sane and well-controlled college athletics."

Interestingly, the treasurer's report for 1909 suggests that the IAAUS already has placed a high priority on public relations. The greater part of the organization's expenditures in this year are for printing and mailing. Reprints of several Convention addresses are sent to college presidents and released to campus newspapers, "all with the endeavor," says Pierce, "to educate the masses and the students to higher athletic ideals."

If Pierce and the members of the NCAA are concerned with promulgation of the philosophy of amateurism, they are no less concerned with the day-to-day practicalities of regulating the various sports that, in the main, make up "college athletics." At this time, these are baseball, basketball, football and track and field.

Continuing Problems of Baseball and Amateurism

The question of summer baseball continues to be the most vexing problem facing the organization simply because the whole problem is wound up inextricably with the issues of amateurism and eligibility.

If football reform is the NCAA's most notable early success, baseball reform for some time will prove to be the organization's most frustrating failure.

In 1906, the Association's Committee on Summer Baseball takes what we charitably might call a "soft" stance on whether or not a college baseball player may play for a professional team in the summer without suffering loss of his amateur eligibility. On the one hand, the committee takes a firm position on the matter of amateurism — "the playing of baseball in summer for gain is distinctly opposed to the principles of amateurism," reads the report. On the other hand, it has difficulty reconciling this with the principle of home rule. The result is that the Association's first resolution on summer baseball, passed in 1907, says, "While the responsibility for the details of rules rests with the individual institution, the Association expects a bona fide enforcement of the principles of amateur sport and invites a report to its Executive Committee for investigation and appropriate action."

There is, in the absence of any enforcement machinery at this stage, no indication of what "appropriate action" will mean. There also is no record of a complaint.

Yet, the summer baseball question is such a serious one that it affects the growth of the Association. For example, no New England schools join the Association in 1908, most of them giving as their reason, according to Frank W. Nicolson of Wesleyan, "that they do not have rules prohibiting summer baseball and therefore do not feel that they would be welcome in the Association."

What summer baseball is doing in these early years is forcing a crisis between the Association's two fundamental principles — amateurism and home rule. The result is that the Committee on Summer Baseball proposes that the Association rethink its definition of amateurism. On December 28, 1908, the Convention approves a motion "that a committee be appointed to formulate a law of amateurism or a definition of an amateur that will more nearly realize, if possible, the ideal of the amateur concept."

The resolution passes. As if to underscore the divisiveness of the issue, its passage is followed by a lengthy and formal debate. If it does not solve the problem of summer baseball, the debate at least has the distinction of producing some of the most impassioned rhetoric of these early years.

Amos Alonzo Stagg, after acknowledging that "the enforcement of our eligibility rules has failed more in connection with baseball than with any other sport," goes on to take an uncompromising stand against summer baseball, drawing a far-reaching and, it strikes us now, not inaccurate conclusion.

"Just the moment we allow men to play on our baseball teams who are professionals," says Stagg, "just that moment will begin a new evolution of professional football . . . . break down the amateur spirit of college athletics by passing this rule and it is my prophecy that in a few years you will find that many of our large cities will be supporting professional football teams composed of ex-college players . . . . the passing of this rule would be an unceasing catastrophe."

But the other side of the issue proves not to be without its equally articulate and impassioned friends, including one J. P. Welsh of Pennsylvania State University.

"The student in good collegiate standing," argues Welsh, "who earns money during the summer vacation is not sick. He does not need treatment. He needs to be let alone in the full, free, untrammeled exercise of his American citizenship, which entitles him to life, liberty and the pursuit of happiness, which," Welsh adds tersely, "sometimes means money."

Two years pass. In 1910, the Committee on Summer Baseball can only report its rather curious finding that "a large number of colleges report that they enforce the amateur law, (but there is) a decided difference of opinion as to what that law is."

The earlier resolution calling for a new definition of amateurism produces, in the end, only more perplexity, as described in 1911 by Paul C. Phillips of Amherst, who chairs the Committee on Amateur Law.

Phillips says that the committee is inclined to a definition of amateurism that would exclude not only the college player who plays for money, but also the one who competes with or against professionals; but (and it proves a rather large "but") " . . . from information gathered this year through this committee . . . our undergraduates are not yet ready for such an amateur rule as we would like to propose . . . moreover, it is the wrong method of approach. It would seem wiser to start in each college a tasteful but vigorous campaign of education on matters of amateurism, leading up to a wholehearted adoption by our student bodies of some reasonable and untrammeled definition of an amateur and a rule allowing only such to represent our various colleges in intercollegiate athletic relations."

If this thinking appears to be a laying of the corpse at the dormitory doorstep, it also is an accurate assessment of student attitudes at the time. A 1908 survey of undergraduates at three New England colleges — Amherst, Wesleyan and Williams — shows students favor college athletes being allowed to play summer baseball, and they favor it in overwhelming numbers: 272 to 65 at Amherst, 237 to 37 at Williams and 118 to 67 at Wesleyan.

"Like the poor," laments R. G. Clapp of Nebraska in 1911, "the summer baseball question is always with us." Indeed, after five years of debate within the Association, the issue of summer baseball seems no closer to solution but it is bringing the issue of amateurism into sharper focus.

Basketball

Basketball, like football before it, proves an easier matter than baseball. Here the problem is not so much one of controlling the nature of players as of controlling the nature of the game.

The problem with basketball during these formative years is that it is a sport governed by no fewer than three sets of rules — those of the Intercollegiate Basketball Rules Committee (a group not yet affiliated with the IAAUS, a situation reminiscent of that which existed with the "old" Football Rules Committee); the Young Men's Christian Association, and the Amateur Athletic Union.

As was the case with football, the IAAUS in March 1907 tries to amalgamate its own Basketball Rules Committee with the existing Intercollegiate Basketball Rules Committee. As was not the case with football, the "old" basketball rules committee gladly accepts the IAAUS's invitation to, in Pierce's words, "come under the jurisdiction of this Association." In brief, the arrangement is that the IAAUS will bear the expenses of maintaining what will be called the Basketball Rules Committee, but this committee may consist of members whose colleges are not yet affiliated with the IAAUS. For example, in 1908, the first full year of the merger, representatives of Yale and Princeton (non-IAAUS members) sit on the committee.

Progress comes fast, almost as fast as it did in football and, happily, much faster than is the case with baseball. The first step, taken at the 1907 Convention, is for the Association to formally recognize basketball as a college sport, " . . . to be controlled and safeguarded as other intercollegiate games."

The Basketball Rules Committee moves first to suggest that all colleges restrict themselves to games only against other colleges, thereby eliminating the situation wherein a college team would often find itself playing a club team, such as a team sponsored by a YMCA, under the latter's rules. It is not uncommon in these days for a barnstorming college basketball team to play several noncollege or club teams under YMCA or AAU rules. The invariable result is that the college players are called for a great many fouls, most as a result of unfamiliarity with the rules rather than deliberately rough play.

"I have seen many accounts in newspapers," says Pierce, "in which uncomplimentary remarks are made of the college players on account of the numerous fouls awarded against them. Such occurrences are very apt to bring (college basketball) into disrepute."

The policy of colleges playing only other colleges is adopted, whereupon the committee moves on to tackle a problem that almost seems to have been invented with basketball itself — officiating.

In perhaps one of sports' great understatements, Basketball Rules Committee member Ralph Morgan of Pennsylvania says, "It is not easy to officiate a game of basketball."

This point of view being widely accepted, the rules committee in 1908 appoints a Central Board of Officials. This group, in turn, publishes a directory of officials.

"Officials who have been placed in this directory," says Morgan, "are presumably the most competent men from the several parts of the country."

The listed officials are kept up to date on rules changes and interpretations by committee mailings and by a series of four IAAUS-sponsored rules interpretation meetings held in different sections of the country prior to the start of the college basketball season. At one such meeting, in New York on December 4, 1909, Morgan credits the meeting's leader, R. B. Hyatt of Yale, with presenting the rules of basketball "in a manner absolutely impossible on the cold pages of a rules book."

The Basketball Rules Committee also appears to be ahead of its time in its insistence on the ongoing evaluation of its officials. Report blanks are given to the captain or coach of every college team. These are filled out with comments on the work of the officials at each game. The cards are then turned over to the committee to be used in assessing the competence of officials.

Given this exemplary level of cooperation among colleges on matters concerning college basketball, the actual rules changes prove rather easy to agree upon and implement.

The criticism of college basketball in these early days is that it is too rough; not rough to the point that it presents a threat to life and limb, but "rough" in a different, almost ethical sense. This sort of "rough" play, according to some, reflects badly on the character of the college athlete.

In 1908, the Intercollegiate Basketball Rules Committee moves quickly, making two important rules changes designed to reduce rough play. The committee adds an umpire to the list of game officials, specifying his duties as being "to follow the players who have not the ball." The second major change provides for disqualification from the game of any player making five fouls. Ralph Morgan claims that these two innovations not only will reduce fouls "but will have a good moral effect upon the players." By 1910, the committee also has added the rule against charging and feels confident enough to report publicly that basketball is "gaining steadily in popularity and the collegiate rules are gaining throughout the country . . . the crusade of the rules committee is bearing fruit."

Its involvement with basketball leads the Association from rules making and the supervision of officials into another new area — publishing. In 1908, the IAAUS assumes responsibility of publishing the Official Basketball Guide, heretofore published by the AAU and YMCA.

Track and Field

Like basketball, track and field is an area of marked early success for the Association.

It is not surprising that track is one of the earliest sports to emerge on college campuses. In fact, it is unquestionably mankind's oldest, if not "original," sport. In prehistoric times, man undoubtedly enjoyed better chances of survival to the extent that he could run and leap in his escapes from predators. There may be no prize for winning a race against a cave bear, but there is surely a reward for not losing.

The manufactured events of Olympian days — the dashes, running broad jump, javelin throw — surely had their roots in man's earliest physical endeavors and have survived, surprisingly unchanged, into the events of our own day.

The first recorded college track meet takes place in England, where Oxford meets Cambridge in 1864. In the United States, the newly formed Intercollegiate Association of Amateur Athletes of America (the IC4A) holds its first meet in 1876 at Saratoga, New York. Here Horace H. Lee of the University of Pennsylvania becomes the first United States athlete to run 100 yards in 10 seconds. In 1893, Pennsylvania hosts Princeton in a relay race competition that later will become the Pennsylvania Relay Carnival, forerunner of the Penn Relays.

Track is popular with students, relatively inexpensive and certainly free of the roughness that plagues football and basketball and the professionalism that mars baseball. Track quickly establishes itself on the nation's campuses. It is, in terms of participation, a major sport and one in which the IAAUS takes an early interest.

As early as 1908, the Association appoints its first Committee on Track and Field. The committee quickly discovers that, as is the case with basketball, track is handicapped by a mishmash of different sets of rules. Besides the rules of the IC4A, there also are rules books published by the New England Intercollegiate Athletic Association, the Intercollegiate Conference of Athletic Associations, the Southern Intercollegiate Athletic Association, the AAU and the YMCA.

The first move is obvious. The Committee on Track and Field appoints a subcommittee to formulate a set of intercollegiate rules for all track and field events. By 1910, a committee headed by the indefatigable Amos Alonzo Stagg has produced the NCAA's own codification of track and field regulations.

The committee's second step to improve college track takes the NCAA onto more new ground. "This Association," reads the committee report of 1910, "should become responsible for preserving and publishing the intercollegiate records of its members." The motion passes, and the committee appoints another subcommittee, charging it with collecting all records of intercollegiate meets, passing on new records and, at the end of each year, publishing a handbook that will contain all intercollegiate meet results and individual records. Palmer Pierce's "propaganda" machinery increasingly takes the form of the modern-day sports information office.

The Committee on Track and Field also mentions, but stops short of taking, another step onto unfamiliar ground. For the first time, it raises the prospect of an NCAA-sponsored national intercollegiate competition.

"Your committee conceived that it was inadvisable at this time to plan for the machinery which would be necessary to manage an intercollegiate meet of the Association."

The report sounds, and in fact is, negative on the matter. But the issue is raised and discussed and, for the next 10 years, will gain momentum until the machinery is not only constructed, but running smoothly.

The Second Football Crisis

The future looks bright for the Association in 1909. Aside from the problems posed by summer baseball and the general desirability of gaining the support of some of the nation's bigger schools, the Association appears to be growing in stature, responsibility and membership and is becoming increasingly involved in rules making and regulation of a growing number of college sports. We may safely say at this point that the Association has progressed beyond what anyone might have expected four years earlier. Its future looks clear and promising until the past reaches into the present and says "stop."

Death and football come together again.

On October 16, 1909, Navy quarterback Earl D. Wilson receives fatal injuries after being hit by a flying tackle in a game against Villanova. Two Saturdays later, a relentless series of Harvard line smashes, all run over Army tackle Eugene Byrne, leaves the cadet lineman dying on the field. Another two Saturdays later, on November 13, Virginia fullback Archer Christian dies of head injuries received on a line-bucking play in a game against Georgetown.

Thirty-three football players are killed in this bloody season. Apparently, the rules changes made by the IAAUS in 1905 are insufficient. But the type of action taken then is going to have to be taken again, just as fast and, this time, with longer-lasting results.

Syracuse Chancellor James Roscoe Day represents the opinions of a growing number of college administrators when he tells the 1909 Convention, "Any game that kills, in different parts of the country, college men every season and every year maims a number equal to the attendance of the average American college should be changed so as to eliminate its fatal features or be excluded from our colleges entirely. . . . it is the most popular of college games, but the killing of one man a season would be a toll which it could not justify by all that it ever has done for the colleges."

General John Mosby, the "Grey Ghost" of Civil War fame, speaks for an increasingly disenchanted public when he says, "I believe that cockfighting is unlawful in Virginia . . . . why should better care be taken of a chicken than a schoolboy?"

Even the most ardent proponents of college football see the problem. In an exchange between giants, Amos Alonzo Stagg writes to his friend, Yale coach Walter Camp, after the 1909 season, "We have certainly got to do something, Walter, for the season has been a mighty bad one for a number of individuals, as well as for the game."

These men echo the sentiments of a public that is once again crying out for the reform or the abolition of football. In fact, the New York and Washington, D.C., school systems drop the game as an interscholastic sport. This crisis is, if anything, even more serious than the preceding one; out of it comes the last substantial threat to the growth and jurisdiction — in fact, to the existence — of the NCAA.

During the 1905 football crisis and the months in which the IAAUS was being formed, the "big three" of college football — Harvard, Yale and Princeton — while refusing to join the new Association, did in no way hinder its early efforts at football reform. Now, however, the "big three," spurred by public pressure, inexplicably try to take the problem into their own hands, not in opposition to the IAAUS but as separate powers who believe they still have the power and prestige to control the game. They are wrong.

On December 7, 1909, three weeks before the IAAUS Convention, President A. Lawrence Lowell and football coach Percy Houghton of Harvard meet in Boston with President Arthur Hadley and football coach Walter Camp of Yale. Lowell and Hadley agree to the idea of their colleges sponsoring a new intercollegiate committee to address the problem of football rules reform. In short, Yale and Harvard plan to create a second rules committee, independent of the IAAUS. They hope to do this with the support of other New England colleges. Both presidents plan to present their idea at a forthcoming meeting of New England colleges in Cambridge.

Coincidentally, a day before the meeting of New England colleges, Princeton President Woodrow Wilson writes to Hadley saying that he (Wilson) has long been considering joint action by the "big three."

As it turns out, Harvard and Yale do not gain the support of the Conference of New England Colleges for the simple reason that Hadley is not in attendance to plead his case. Instead, he is detained by another meeting at Yale. Even though Harvard and Yale appear to lose the opportunity to build a wider base of support in New England, the sudden interest of Princeton and Woodrow Wilson raises the possibility of the "big three" finally coming together in a formal alliance. These three prestigious Eastern schools would be a formidable force, one that might well eclipse any efforts by the IAAUS.

Hadley and Wilson meet in New York on December 22, 1909, to talk of the problems facing football and of possible action by the "big three." To his surprise, Hadley finds that Wilson holds "a more emotional view of the situation" than either he or Lowell. Instead of a few rules changes that would leave the character of the game essentially unchanged — this being the position of Hadley and Lowell — Wilson wants, in Hadley's words, "sweeping demands concerning safety . . . and a threat (that colleges) abolish the game if they are not complied with." Hadley and Lowell shy away from radical reforms, and they also do not want to present their rules changes in terms of an ultimatum.

After meeting with Hadley, Wilson is noncommittal about joining with Harvard and Yale. Hadley, however, says that they will proceed with or without Princeton. After returning to Princeton and further considering the matter, Wilson agrees to send a representative of Princeton to join with Camp and Houghton in their deliberations regarding football rules changes.

Had these three powerful schools joined forces during the first football crisis four years earlier, it is likely they would have succeeded in reforming college football to their own liking, that other schools would have followed along and the IAAUS never would have been born. Such was the prestige of the "big three" in 1905. However, we have an entirely different atmosphere in 1909. Now a majority of the nation's football-playing institutions are members of the IAAUS; to these member schools, as well as to a growing segment of the sporting public, the "big three" (and especially Walter Camp) still are associated with the "old" football rules committee or, as it is sometimes called, "the committee of misrule."

Yale's Hadley thinks the influence of the "big three" is so great that their joint reform movement will have adequate public undergraduate support, "so that if the big committee (meaning the Intercollegiate Football Rules Committee made up of IAAUS representatives and members of the "old" committee) insists on irrational revision, we can go our own way and carry our own undergraduates with us."

But Hadley has overestimated the national sway of Harvard, Yale and Princeton. The "big three" cartel is a disaster from the start.

First, Hadley is shocked by a letter from Lowell late in December, saying that the Harvard Corporation has decided the school will join the IAAUS and will attend the Association's Convention on December 28, 1909.

Another surprise to Hadley is Woodrow Wilson's insistence that the three schools join in advocating not small rules revisions, which Wilson finds technical and microscopic, but major changes that will end mass play forever and make the game more open and attractive.

Meanwhile, the IAAUS Football Rules Committee once again "amalgamates" with the old rules committee and, on February 5, 1910, holds the first of a series of meetings designed, once more, to save college football. It is not until March 7 that the now-tentative alliance among Harvard, Yale and Princeton holds its first meeting devoted to football rules reform. Lowell's assertion on this occasion that "the other colleges are looking to us for guidance" now sounds hollow and presumptuous.

The decline of the once-awesome power of football's Eastern triumvirate is never seen more dramatically than here in 1910. While the Intercollegiate Football Rules Committee, in a series of meetings through the winter and early spring, once more comes up with the rules changes that will save college football, the Harvard-Yale-Princeton meetings limp along, producing little more than a report that echoes the intercollegiate committee's report, and this long after the former is published. Significantly, Yale's Walter Camp (a member of both committees) refuses to sign the Harvard-Yale-Princeton report, allegedly because it is merely an endorsement of the measures adopted by the larger committee.

Princeton coach William Roper has another thought, however, regarding Camp's actions: "If you pardon me for saying so . . . Mr. Camp is violently opposed to the new rules for one single reason, because Yale's style of play is practically destroyed, there being no further pulling or pushing of the runner allowed. As this practically eliminates the old bucking game, at which Yale has been so proficient, and which to my mind is the dangerous part of football, naturally Camp is opposed to the rules as changed."

Roper, regardless of whether he is right about Camp's motives, is absolutely correct in assessing the net effect of the new rules — they will eliminate mass play and make the game safer.

Among the more important rules changes to take effect in the 1910 season are these: (1) Seven men from the offensive team must be on the line of scrimmage; (2) interlocking interference and the pulling or pushing of the ball carrier is prohibited; (3) the offensive player first receiving the ball is allowed to cross the line of scrimmage at any point; likewise, a forward pass can cross the line of scrimmage at any point (these changes eliminate the necessity for longitudinal lines on the field); (4) an incomplete forward pass results in a down being charged to the offensive team (rather than a down plus a yardage penalty, as formerly was the case); (5) pass interference, the flying tackle and crawling by the ball carrier are made illegal, and (6) the game is restored to 60 minutes duration and divided into four quarters, allowing a player leaving the game for any reason other than disqualification to return in the next quarter.

At the 1910 Convention, Football Rules Committee Chair Henry L. Williams can report to the members (which now include Harvard), "On all sides the consensus . . . seems to agree that the game under the new rules has been made comparatively safe and reasonably free from danger . . . the excessive danger, which previously existed and to which the public and those interested in the welfare of college players and schoolboys rightfully objected, has been overcome."

As for the "big three," the ultimately ineffectual response of Harvard, Yale and Princeton not only shows us the decline in influence of this once-powerful Northeastern bloc, but also points out the corresponding rise in the national stature of the NCAA. If Presidents Hadley, Lowell and Wilson actually had held and been able to exercise the measure of influence they thought they possessed, it seems reasonable to suppose that, by just such measure, the prestige of the new NCAA would have been reduced. Thus, there seems a more profound meaning to one of Palmer Pierce's opening remarks at the 1910 Convention: "The importance of the work done by the Football Rules Committee cannot be overestimated."

The committee definitely saved college football, and it may well have saved the NCAA in the process.

CHAPTER FOUR

"Its object shall be . . ."

The decade from 1910 through 1919 is the last period in which we logically can consider the growth of the NCAA in a chronological sense. So rapid is the progress in these 10 years, so vast the new areas of sport and athletic administration undertaken by the Association, that hereafter we shall have to examine the work of the NCAA on a topical, rather than sequential, basis. But for now, let us look at the growth and changes in the way they occurred. This is the decade of transition for the NCAA.

This is also a decade of transition for the world, a transition that will have its impact on American colleges. Europe and Asia are in a state of unrest. Germany, under Kaiser William II, for several years has been pursuing a course of naval expansion that by 1914 will make her the second strongest naval power on earth. England warily views the German expansion as a challenge to its naval supremacy. To the east, the combined forces of Bulgaria, Serbia and Greece go to war against Turkey and the crumbling Ottoman Empire in 1912. The world outside of America is a place of shifting boundaries, warring armies and the first signs of another reordering of the balance of world power.

Therefore, it should not surprise us — and probably did not surprise him — when, in 1913, Palmer Pierce (it is Major Pierce now) is reassigned by the Army to a military training camp in the Midwest. On the one hand, this might be viewed as standard operating procedure for the Army. On the other hand, and in retrospect, it also may be a hint of the country's quickening military pulse.

Whatever the reason, when Pierce steps down from the NCAA presidency, the election of his successor illustrates dramatically the Association's growth in prestige. The barest lingering notion of doubt as to the NCAA's stature and potential longevity must be discarded at once when LeBaron R. Briggs is named as the Association's second president. It is not that Briggs is a nationally renowned figure; it is that he is a dean at Harvard University.

Sitting in the audience when Briggs takes the chair on Tuesday, December 30, 1913, is Joseph E. Raycroft of Princeton University; thus, two of the former "big three" institutions are now NCAA members. Yale will follow in 1915. From this point on, the history of the NCAA no longer is the chronicle of a struggle for growth, acceptance and survival; instead, it is a record of rapid development on several fronts by a widely supported organization that is increasingly interested in the development of all facets of intercollegiate athletics.

The Committees

This new momentum shows itself in the rapid branching out of the Association's committee structure. Between 1911 and 1918, the NCAA adds four more committees on sports to the existing committees on football, basketball and track and field. There is the Committee on Association Football (Soccer), 1911; the Committee on Swimming and Water Sports, 1913; the Committee on Wrestling, 1917, and the Volleyball Rules Committee, 1918. In the same period, the Association begins a discussion of involvement in tennis, boxing and riflery.

Further evidence of the Association's growing and divergent interests is seen in the appointment in 1913 of a Committee to Study Methods of Athletic Regulation and Control in Other Countries and a Committee to Assist in Adjustment of Athletic Differences Between Colleges and in 1915 a standing Committee on Publication of the Rules, as well as several other committees, the most important of which will be a committee of three to study constitutional changes.

Amateurism

There are also the first hints that the Association now is beginning to accept the idea that the spirit of amateurism may not flourish everywhere without something stronger than ideals to back it up.

It is LeBaron Briggs, in his first speech from the president's chair in 1913, who uses a form of the verb "enforce."

"For however much men ought to be above sordid considerations of reward and punishment, they are not; and without these
sordid considerations, we might subject our students to what
President Eliot (of Harvard) calls 'too great a strain on their
higher motives.' Appeal to chivalry, but strengthen this appeal
to chivalry by *enforcing* decency . . . ." (Italics added.)

Briggs' remark has more to do with the action of players than of
administrators, but the message is clear: If the NCAA truly is going
to reflect the will of its members, it may have to do so with something
more than moral suasion.

At this stage, the Association is well along in the matter of "enforcing decency" via its rules-making actions and its work with game
officials. It still has a way to go, however, in adopting a universally
accepted definition of amateurism. While action on game rules has
been dramatic and swift, action on determining a standard of
amateurism to which all athletes and athletic departments will
adhere is to be slow and frustrating.

Publication of Rules

The Association also is moving into the area of promotion, as was
seen in earlier remarks by Palmer Pierce. The rules committees are
not charged simply with codifying regulations, but also with the
matter of promulgating these changes to the extent that the rules are
available not only to all member colleges, but to secondary schools,
youth athletic associations, the news media and interested fans. This
is one of the reasons that, in 1914, the NCAA makes its Committee on
Publication of the Rules a standing committee. There is also an
important move at this time to take the publishing of rules out of the
hands of a commercial printing firm, The American Sports Publishing Company (a division of A. G. Spalding & Brothers, the sporting
goods manufacturers), and to place it in the hands of the NCAA.

The argument in favor of such a move is put forth as early as 1914
by Joseph E. Raycroft, chair of the Committee on Publication of the
Rules. "The Association has no control over the rules, since the
copyright is in the name of the American Sports Publishing Company, so that the NCAA has not the right to give permission to print
the rules, nor have (we) the right to reprint the rules without permission." Raycroft also raises the objections that the price of the rules
books is too high (45 cents each for the books governing football, track
and field and basketball) and that footnotes to the rules make it

appear as though a certain Spalding ball or piece of equipment has been declared "official" and must be used in all contests.

Within two years, the rules books on volleyball, basketball and swimming are published under joint copyright of the NCAA and the American Sports Publishing Company. The track and field rules books are published solely by the NCAA. Increasingly, the work of the various rules committees is taking the Association further into the field of communications. (In the years to come, the Association will depend heavily on individuals from member institutions in assisting with editing of the rules. Of special importance are those who serve as secretary-rules editor of the various committees. As an example of this dedicated leadership, David M. Nelson, athletic director at the University of Delaware, serves on the Football Rules Committee from 1958 to 1981 and is secretary-rules editor of the committee from 1967 to 1981.)

Constitutional Changes and a New Definition of Amateurism

All things considered, the NCAA during this period appears to be on solid ground and moving ahead on all fronts. But growth is not without its problems; in 1916, there arises a question as to whether the original constitution and bylaws, now more than a decade old, are adequate to define and govern this suddenly powerful Association. Heretofore, Article 2 of the constitution seemed adequate on the most basic question of all, the purpose of the NCAA. "The objective shall be," it says, "the regulation and supervision of college athletics throughout the United States in order that the athletic activities in the colleges and universities of the United States may be maintained on an ethical plane in keeping with the dignity and high purpose of education."

But, as we have seen, the NCAA already has gone beyond that objective to confront myriad problems facing all facets of intercollegiate athletics. Therefore, President Briggs appoints a committee in 1915 to study and, if necessary, revise the constitution and bylaws.

The committee's first recommendation, which passes easily in 1916, is to rephrase what is probably the most fundamental paragraph of the constitution. Article 2 is changed to more accurately reflect the actions and direction of the Association. It now reads: "Its object shall be *to study various important phases of college athletics, to formulate rules governing athletics and to promote the adoption of recommended measures,* in order that the athletic activities in the colleges and universities of the United States may be maintained on an ethical plane in keeping with the dignity and high purpose of education." (Italics added.)

There are also two important bylaw changes made by the 1916 Convention. First comes a change in Article 7 of the bylaws. Article 7 establishes a lengthy list of eligibility rules and is accompanied by a list of the 15 questions that make up each athlete's "eligibility card." The committee, on approval of the membership, omits the elaborate set of eligibility rules and inserts in its place a short statement simply saying that these "suggested rules will be sent on request to any college desiring them."

There now arises a disagreement between the committee and the Convention delegates concerning a change in Article 6 of the bylaws, the one entitled "Principles of Amateur Sport, " that is addressed to problems of proselyting and the playing of those ineligible as amateurs.

The committee wants to take out the specific reference to "the playing of those ineligible as amateurs" and to insert in its place a definition of amateurism written by the non-NCAA-affiliated Athletic Research Society (see Chapter Five). The Convention will not approve deletion of the existing wording but does approve the definition of amateurism which now becomes part of Article 6. The definition reads:

> "An amateur athlete is one who participates in competitive physical sports only for the pleasure and the physical, mental, moral and social benefits directly derived therefrom."

At last, an amateur is to be defined by what he is, rather than by what he is not.

Control of Football Rules

At the same time the Committee on the Revision of the Constitution is studying its changes, there takes place a little-noted dinner in a private room in the Biltmore Hotel in New York. The purpose of this dinner foreshadows by a full year (and there must be men in the room who sense it) one of the most symbolic changes in the Association's history.

On a night in February 1915, the revered Walter Camp, for more than 30 years the Yale representative on both the "old" and "amalgamated" football rules committees, invites to dinner the members of the "old" committee and the seven members of the NCAA Football Rules Committee. After dinner, Camp announces that, following completion of the current meeting of the "amalgamated" rules committee, he will resign his seat on the old committee. NCAA committee Chair Henry L. Williams reacts to this appropriately, it seems: "This was a matter of great regret to both committees .... his name is indelibly graven on the rules of football."

Williams is right. Camp exercised great influence over not only the rules, but also the evolution of football. By 1915, however, this annual "amalgamation" procedure is, in Williams' words, "a process which has come to be a mere formality." The truth is that the "old" football rules committee exists more in form than in substance. Since all of the colleges represented on the "old" committee are now members of the NCAA, it is the NCAA's Football Rules Committee that, in effect, determines the rules of the game. Therefore, it should surprise no one when, in 1916 (a decade since the first merger of the two committees), NCAA Football Rules Committee Chair E. K. Hall is able to report as follows:

"At the last meeting (of the NCAA Football Rules Committee), for the first time, this Association, which has steadily grown in size and strength until it has now received into its membership every institution that was represented on the 'old' football rules committee, took into itself, as it were, and made official for the first time in its history, the so-called 'old' rules committee by specifically inviting its members to membership on the rules committee of this Association. This step was of more than passing significance, as the rules of football for the American schools and colleges were thereby brought entirely under the direction and jurisdiction of this Association."

What might have been a kind of civil war between the two committees 10 years earlier concludes in 1916, not only peacefully but with a 10-year record of productivity.

"Code of Ethics"

One of the first actions of the NCAA Football Rules Committee in 1916 is to take a step away from simply changing and codifying rules and to move toward publishing something called "A Code of Football Ethics." This is in no way a part of the rules but is, instead, a plea for high standards of sportsmanship issued by men who love the game. The preamble to this code reflects the committee's and the Association's broadening philosophy:

"...the first obligation of every football player is to protect the game itself, its reputation and its good name. He owes this to the game, its friends and its traditions. There can be little excuse for any player who allows the game to be smirched with un-sportsmanlike tactics."

The code then goes on to address itself to such practices as holding, "beating the ball" (i.e., going offsides deliberately) and talking to officials and opponents in an abusive or insulting way. The last two sentences of the code explain the way in which it differs from the rules and also give us some insight to the Association's growing concern not only with the spirit or attitude that should characterize intercollegiate competition, but also with the public image of this most visible of all games:

"The football code is different (from the rules). The football player who intentionally violates a rule is guilty of unfair play and unsportsmanlike tactics, and, whether or not he escapes being penalized, he brings discredit to the good name of the game, which it is his duty as a player to uphold."

It will not be too many more years before the realization of the fact that a "code of ethics" needs a code of enforcement to support it.

Another link to the old days of the original IAAUS is broken on the morning of December 27, 1918. The Association's 13th Convention is called to order at 10:30 a.m. in the Hotel Astor in New York City. At the same time, a few miles away at University Heights, funeral services are being held for Henry M. MacCracken, former chancellor of New York University and, for all practical purposes, the founder of the NCAA. This irony is not lost on MacCracken's longtime friend and associate, Dean Louis Bevier Jr. of Rutgers, a delegate to the original IAAUS. Bevier introduces this resolution:

"Resolved, that the National Collegiate Athletic Association, re-membering gratefully that its original organization was due to the action of the late Chancellor MacCracken of New York University, desires to place on record ... its profound regret that his long and distinguished career has come to a close ... we should express our appreciation of him as an educational leader, an able organizer and a man of vision .... "

The resolution passes in what then is termed "a rising vote," later to be called a standing ovation.

Faculty Control

As the Convention gets down to work later in the day, we see another indication of the Association's tendency to broaden its involvement with college athletics. There now passes a resolution that deals not with the regulation of athletics by athletic departments, but with the place of the athletic department within the college or university. The resolution says, in part, that it is the sense of the membership "that in every college and university, the Department of Physical Training and Athletics should be recognized as a department of collegiate instruction, directly responsible to the college or university administration."

In short, the Association is advocating the placing of athletics under faculty control, a corollary to which is the suggestion that coaches be made year-round staff or faculty members.

The timing, in late 1918, could not be better for a move that will, in effect, lift athletics out of the realm of extracurricular activity run by alumni, students or quasi-independent athletic associations and onto the level of a cocurricular activity.

Timing is good for such a philosophic shift because colleges and universities are entering a period of postwar reconstruction in 1918. World War I had ended in November, six weeks before the NCAA Convention. The war was disruptive to American higher education and especially to intercollegiate athletics.

World War I

United States colleges and, of course, college teams, see their ranks rapidly depleted following Congress' declaration of war on Germany on April 6, 1917. This declaration comes at the request of President Woodrow Wilson, the former Princeton president whom we last saw trying to make football safer for its participants and who now is intent on making "the world safe for democracy."

Wilson's call is answered. Enlistments during 1917 and 1918 drain the campuses of students and result in the curtailment or outright suspension of intercollegiate athletics. The state of many college athletic departments is well phrased by LeBaron Briggs, who says in 1917, "Practically all our men from varsity squads are gone or are subject to immediate call. At any time, we may hear that men who were closely associated with them have been killed. Our bigger games, those with Yale and Princeton, have been great public spectacles such as we do not like to be responsible for in times like these."

In the place of organized varsity athletics, many colleges decide to

cooperate with the government by instituting Reserve Officer Training Corps or Naval Training Unit programs. Military training in
some form is practically universal on the campuses. At Yale, there is
foot drill three times a week.

Athletic programs are pared to the bones. While the NCAA, consistent with its home-rule policy, leaves each member institution free to
pursue its own course during the war years, the Association does
adopt several resolutions intended as policy guides. To wit: Athletics
are to be made "subservient to military preparation." Members
should place greater emphasis on intramural, rather than intercollegiate, sport, "with a view to promoting the participation of all
students." Professional coaches are to be used only when absolutely
essential. There is to be no preseason practice, no scouting and no
training table. The number of game officials and the fees paid to them
are to be kept as low as possible.

The war temporarily retards the growth of intercollegiate athletics; but in the longer run, it gives momentum to the NCAA's position
that athletics and physical education should enjoy a higher status on
campus. Fully 35 percent of the men called to arms in the war years
are rejected as unfit for military service. When these figures become
known, it is the NCAA that urges via a resolution in 1918 that
"increased emphasis be placed upon health and physical efficiency for
all college students," and that this take the form of "required courses
of health instruction and physical education." This emphasis indeed
is the case on many campuses as physical education begins to acquire
a higher status. Yet, as the war ends and America's men come pour-
ing out of the service and back to the campus, it is intercollegiate
athletics that dominates the college sports spotlight. This is not an
unmixed blessing, as R. Tait McKenzie of the University of Pennsylvania observes at the start of this athletic revival in 1919: "When the
American people are interested in anything, whether it be Belgium, a
Victory Loan or intercollegiate sport, they indicate it by an outpouring of cash, and it is interesting to see how this has affected the
problems with which our Association is immediately concerned."

Postwar Problems

Some of the things McKenzie alludes to are the reappearance of the
training table in all its prewar luxuriance, preseason practice, summer athletic camps and scouting. And there are occasional instances
where the boy representing his college at a football game on Saturday
can be found playing under a different name for a local professional

football team on Sunday.

It is discouraging. "The abuses with which 13 years of discussion have made us familiar," laments McKenzie, "have grown rank and luxuriant, and it is little wonder that we are confronted this year with predatory bands of heroes, trained on the battlefields for the more serious combats of the gridiron, combining in casual clubs to pick up what loot they may in Sunday games, with lowered standards of sportsmanship, contaminating the atmosphere of the college team near which they are, with offers of easy money under an assumed name."

The postwar athletic revival and the appearance of professional teams once more have underscored the twin issues of amateurism and eligibility as the biggest problems facing the NCAA. Yet the Association, for all of its idealism, is still without any sort of machinery to enforce its policies and regulations. Home rule remains the guiding principle. This fact is emphasized by Palmer Pierce (reelected to the presidency of the NCAA in 1918 while still serving in France), who takes the chair in 1919 and once more affirms the Association's commitment. The NCAA, says Pierce, "does not attempt to govern, but accomplishes its purposes by educational means, leaving to the affiliated local conferences the responsibilities and initiative in matters of direct control."

The Association, however, does adopt a resolution emphasizing its position that its members generally want to associate only with institutions whose eligibility code "is in general conformity with the principles advocated by this Association, such as the freshman rule" (i.e., freshmen not eligible for varsity teams), the one-year migratory rule, the limitation in years of athletic participation and the amateur rule.

The decade that began with the NCAA embroiled in the second football crisis and a test of its prestige has ended with the Association stronger, more widely accepted and respected and clearly the closest thing to an authoritative body on all matters of intercollegiate athletics. By 1919, there are 170 colleges and other institutions holding regular, joint or associate membership in the organization. This membership count represents about 400,000 students. The Association is involved directly in 11 sports: football, basketball, baseball, track and field, swimming, soccer, volleyball, wrestling, boxing, riflery and tennis. Involvement comes through its rules committees, publishing activities or, as in the case of riflery (1917) and tennis (1918), simply by voting to recognize these as intercollegiate sports.

As the Association presses ahead on so many fronts, we will begin to consider its progress in specific areas and important issues — such as the evolution of eligibility regulation and an enforcement procedure — rather than in a chronological sequence of sometimes distantly related events. It is enough to say for now, as Palmer Pierce says in 1919, with the country and the NCAA preparing to enter the 1920s, that "the Association has grown because the seed sown in 1905 fell on fertile soil."

CHAPTER FIVE

" . . . peace . . . even though we have to fight for it."

No problem, except the constant effort to maintain amateurism in college sports, is as severe, complex, threatening and of as long duration as is the NCAA's often stormy relationship with the Amateur Athletic Union. Yet, stripped of the charges, counter-charges and occasional acrimonious rhetoric, the central issue in this now-epic struggle can be reduced to a single word, jurisdiction.

To understand fully the difficulties that will later arise between the United States' two largest amateur sports-sanctioning bodies, it is necessary that we step back from the threshold of the Roaring Twenties into pre-Civil War America, here to review for a moment the growth of amateur sport as it occurs *outside* the colleges.

Amateur Athletic Clubs

Like a giant magnet, the clanking machinery of early industrialized America draws the population from the countryside into the cities in the early days of the 19th century. This industrialization produces, as a social byproduct, jobs, money and a class of city-dwelling factory workers. Because of constraints of space and time, the city worker has fewer opportunities to participate in sport than does his rural counterpart. However, with so large a potential audience gathered in one place, it should not surprise us that commercial amusements, including spectator sports, become popular with the masses and profitable for the promoters.

Boxing, wrestling, rowing and foot racing are all popular spectator sports, each lending itself to betting and the offering of purses. These activities, in time, produce a class of professional athletes. One of the favorite ploys of these days is for a professional runner or rower to go into a town where he is unknown, talk like a boastful yokel about his athletic feats and eventually persuade the townsfolk to put up a purse backing a local runner or oarsman against the braggart. The professional, of course, easily wins the event and pockets the money.

It is not until the time of the Civil War that there arises any great concern over the difference between amateur and professional sport. But by the mid-1860s, there begin to be formed several amateur athletic clubs — themselves a product of urban development — that have as one of their goals the sponsorship of teams and athletic events so that amateurs might compete on a reputable basis under sponsorship of the clubs and only against other amateurs.

Richest and most powerful of these organizations is the New York Athletic Club, founded in 1860. It has a constitution and bylaws and sponsors meets that are open only to other club-affiliated amateurs. In 1876, the New York A.C. publishes its official definition of an amateur: "An amateur is any person who has never competed . . . for public or admission money, or with professionals for a prize . . . nor has at any period in his life taught or assisted in the pursuit of athletic exercise as a means of livelihood."

If this does not define precisely what an amateur is, it is rather precise about what an amateur is not.

The National Association of Amateur Athletics

By the 1870s, there are athletic clubs in most major United States cities; and there is a growing feeling of need for a national or umbrella organization that will exercise control over all of the clubs and, thereby, over amateur athletics in the United States. Preliminary attempts at forming such a controlling body end in failure. But on April 22, 1879, a group representing several athletic clubs, mainly in and around New York City, forms the National Association of Amateur Athletes of America (N4A). The N4A immediately takes over sponsorship of the annual amateur championship games — heretofore conducted by the New York A.C. — and sets about trying to organize other games and championships. The new association also begins to hear, and tries to settle, various cases involving violations of the amateur code. But the N4A begins its descent to inevitable dissolution when a series of decisions goes against its single most powerful member, the New York A.C.

Founding of the AAU

In 1888, the New York A.C. withdraws its support from the N4A and, with 15 other clubs, forms a new association that is to be a challenger to the N4A for control of amateur sport.

This new association calls itself the Amateur Athletic Union. It is formed on January 21, 1888. In one year and seven months, it will deal a death blow to the N4A. On August 25, 1888, at a meeting on Travers Island, New York, the AAU board of governors passes a resolution barring any amateur athlete from competing in AAU games if he has competed in any "open" games not governed by rules of the AAU. The board specifically cites N4A meets, underscoring the point that N4A rules are not approved by the AAU.

The situation now is that an athlete must choose between AAU- and N4A-sanctioned meets with the foreknowledge that competing in N4A events will bar him from competition in all future AAU events.

The AAU deals the N4A another severe blow in 1889, when it declares that AAU athletes will not take part in the games to be sponsored later in the year by the University of Pennsylvania and administered under the rules of the Intercollegiate Association of Amateur Athletes of America (IC4A). This action is taken because the IC4A is a member of the N4A; such a ruling will drive a wedge in the relations between these two allied organizations. (It is the AAU's contention that colleges should control all intercollegiate meets, but open meets involving colleges and noncollege clubs should be under the rules of the AAU as the amateur sanctioning body.)

Indeed, the AAU's "wedge" has the desired effect. The IC4A resigns its membership in the N4A and joins the AAU. The AAU responds by remitting penalties against IC4A athletes who previously had com- peted under N4A rules. By the summer of 1889, theN4A is stripped of its power and support. It disbands and its members are assimilated by the AAU.

The AAU then broadens its considerable powers in 1891, when it reorganizes, changing from a union of individual clubs to a union of district associations. It also claims jurisdiction over 23 sports, includ- ing all college sports. But by 1899, the AAU drops claims for jurisdic- tion over football, soccer, baseball and rowing, while retaining con- trol over basketball, lacrosse and, its flagship sport, track and field. It will be ramifications of this claim of jurisdiction that will bring about conflict between the AAU and the NCAA.

The Olympic Games and the
International Olympic Committee

Despite the efforts of the colleges and athletic clubs to control it, professionalism is rampant in sports by the 1890s. To counteract this growing trend and to promote friendship among nations, a French nobleman, Baron Pierre de Coubertin, calls a meeting in 1894 of representatives of all countries interested in helping to bring about a revival of the Olympic Games. The first games are scheduled for Athens in 1896. It is at de Coubertin's first meeting that the International Olympic Committee (IOC) is formed and charged with organizing the games.

Although the United States forms its own American Olympic Committee (AOC), which is recognized by the IOC, the first U.S. Olympic team is formed less by the efforts of a committee than by the work of William Sloane of Princeton. Working with several volunteers, Sloane puts together an Olympic team made up of both collegians and club athletes. In the next two Olympiads, we see the composition of the United States entries vary from a team made up mainly of collegians competing in Paris in 1900 to a team of mainly club athletes competing at St. Louis in 1904. It is not until the 1906 Olympic Games (the four-year interval has not yet been established) that the United States is represented by a team selected by the American Olympic Committee and financed by a nationwide drive for an Olympic fund. The days of voluntary participation by American athletes are over.

In 1906, the AOC concentrates its 35-member team in the track and field events. It falls to the track-oriented AAU to play the major role in planning and conducting United States participation in the games through its representatives on the AOC. Most of the planning for the 1906 Olympics is done in 1905, prior to the founding of the NCAA. At this point, the AAU is the only organization in the country with the ability to perform such a task.

While the 1906 team dominates the track and field events, the United States entry is not sufficiently diversified to be competitive in other sports. As a result, for the first time since the revival of the Olympics, another country, France, wins the unofficial overall competition.

As we have seen, it is also in 1906 that the IAAUS, forerunner of the NCAA, is formed. Plainly, as evidenced by the very existence of such bodies as the IAAUS and AAU, the idea of control of amateur athletics is beginning to grow. It is not yet evident — what with the

IAAUS being largely preoccupied with its football crisis — but the stage is being set whereon relations between these two giant sports bodies will have a great deal to do with the shaping of amateur athletics in the United States. These relations are not always to be harmonious.

Early Conflicts and Cooperation
Between the Colleges and the AAU

It is interesting to note that at the first IAAUS Convention in 1906, President Palmer Pierce reads a letter from AAU President James E. Sullivan. The letter urges an alliance between the two groups, though with the hint that the AAU is to be the dominant organization.

"It is up to the officers of the Amateur Athletic Union," writes Sullivan, "to advocate and work for an organization among the colleges to be known as the American Intercollegiate Association to control all college sports." Sullivan goes on to say that his proposed collegiate organization "be formed and allied with the Amateur Athletic Union."

The IAAUS takes no action on Sullivan's proposal but proceeds, as we have seen, with formation of the Committee on Summer Baseball and the Basketball Committee to examine problems facing colleges in those two sports. Early conflict with the AAU is practically inevitable since baseball and basketball are sports over which the AAU claims jurisdiction.

The most serious conflict arises in basketball, where, even before formation of the IAAUS, the AAU was insistent on enforcing its rules on college teams that played against AAU-afflilated club teams. Should a college team play a non-AAU affiliated team, the AAU automatically would suspend the college players from further competition with AAU teams.

At first, the colleges react by publishing their own set of rules, independent of the AAU. In 1907, Palmer Pierce is speaking for a subcommittee on basketball of the Executive Committee of the IAAUS when he says, "After talking with the representatives of the AAU, I am convinced that the intercollegiate basketball rules are not suitable for athletic club, YMCA and schoolboy players. It therefore seems well to retain a distinction between the rules for these different classes . . . . I suggest that it be understood that college players shall not arrange games with any of the above-mentioned classes."

In cases where colleges do play club teams, it becomes IAAUS policy that such games be played under AAU rules. Pierce also recommends that the Basketball Rules Committee, organized in 1905 to formulate rules for the college game, be invited to come under the jurisdiction of the IAAUS. This happens peacefully in 1907.

Surprisingly, the major difference between the *playing* rules of the IAAUS and those of the AAU (this as opposed to *policy* rules such as the AAU's insistence on competing clubs being AAU-registered) is that the college player may make a play after dribbling, while a player who dribbles under AAU rules is then required to shoot. Such a relatively minor difference might suggest that the principles of control and jurisdiction are of much more import here than are the finer points of game competition.

Basketball continues to be played under three sets of rules (collegiate, YMCA, AAU) until 1915, when the Basketball Rules Committee of the NCAA meets with a similar committee representing the YMCA. The two committees merge and adopt a single set of rules to govern YMCA and collegiate play. Shortly hereafter, the AAU indicates its willingness to join with the NCAA and YMCA in writing the rules for basketball and publishing the official basketball guide.

In May 1915, representatives of the NCAA, YMCA and AAU meet and draw up one set of basketball rules that later will be published under the auspices of all three organizations. Such is the desire of each group to maintain its individuality and stature, however, that part of the publishing agreement states that, in the first year, each organization will be listed in order of its chronological relationship to basketball (i.e., YMCA, AAU, NCAA), but in each succeeding year, the order will rotate. This cooperative arrangement in basketball will exist until 1936. Unfortunately, the relationship between the NCAA and AAU in other sports and on other issues is not to be as cordial.

Attempts at a Federation for Amateur Athletics

Beginning in 1907, representatives of various sports and youth organizations — principally colleges, public and private schools, Boy Scouts and YMCAs — join in a group called the Athletic Research Society. The group is formed as a forum for discussion of problems in athletic administration. In 1911, the Athletic Research Society appoints the National Federated Committee, charged with implementing decisions of the society. More specifically, it is charged "to unite the national organizations interested in play and recreation in a comprehensive educational campaign, to develop wholesome play sentiments among the youth of the land, to widen the public consciousness of the moral and social values of play and athletics and to determine and seek to put into operation the best forms of administration."

Attempts to form and enlarge such a federation reflect the widespread dissatisfaction with the AAU's control of amateur athletics. An article in the American Physical Education Review, June 1912, decries the fact that "the Amateur Athletic Union insists that it is the only national controlling body for athletics in this country in spite of the fact that it has a membership of only 538 clubs and a registration of only 18,861 ... this unfortunate autocratic position of the (AAU) will never bring the athletic forces together under its banner."

The article goes on to criticize the typical AAU-affiliated club with doing "little or nothing to promote the educational view of athletics. The prime object of these clubs," the article charges, "seems to be to corral the 'star' athletes in order to beat some other club, win a meet and furnish a spectacle.

"This viewpoint of (AAU) ... is wholly at variance with the trend in educational institutions ... which is toward a scheme of athletics which will not only serve expert performers, but also will interest and stimulate every man and boy of athletic age to take part in wholesome competition. For the colleges ... playgrounds, etc., to accept the (AAU) as the national controlling body would mean the adoption of a viewpoint wholly out of sympathy with the general policy and objectives of these organizations."

Besides its criticism, the article also cites the rather practical fact that 85 percent of the country's gymnasiums, athletic fields and swimming pools belong to organizations that are independent of the AAU.

Unlike the AAU, the proposed national federation will have no central registering body but instead will let each athlete register with his own organization, which then will vouch for his eligibility and amateur status.

The AAU withholds its support from the federation movement. This opposition by the AAU to the formation of a federation prompts Athletic Research Society President W. P. Bowen to say in 1914: "Since unity is important in (amateur sport), there is need for a democratic organization in which all the interests will be represented. Cooperation by all is essential; any attempt on the part of one interest to dictate to all the others or to monopolize control is like all the other schemes in the interest of one class, destructive of best results and, in the end, suicidal for the group attempting it."

Despite the federation's broad base of support from so many amateur sports governing bodies — including the NCAA — opposi-·tion from the AAU prevents its formation. Initiative for such a feder-ation fades away as the United States enters World War I and most athletic programs are de-emphasized.

While it is blocked in its attempt to form a federation, the Athletic Research Society achieves notable success in its definition — actually redefinition — of an amateur athlete. In fact, the definition is one point on which the AAU and the Athletic Research Society are in almost verbatim agreement.

In 1914 the society adopts its definition of an amateur, the same definition that will become a part of the NCAA constitution:

> "An amateur athlete is one who participates in competitive physical sports only for the pleasure and the physical, mental, moral and social benefits directly derived therefrom."

In 1916, the AAU accepts a similar version, discarding the earlier definition based on the technical violations that disqualify an athlete as an amateur.

AAU Control of U.S. Olympic Committee

The war results in the cancellation of the 1916 Olympic Games. However, after the signing of the armistice, members of the AAU-dominated American Olympic Committee, wishing to see this body continued, call a meeting to begin plans for the 1920 Olympics at Antwerp. The committee, which meets at the New York A.C. on December 12, 1918, consists mainly of the same members and officers originally appointed at the discretion of former AAU President James E. Sullivan. As Arnold W. Flath of the University of Michigan later will point out in his doctoral dissertation, the committee that meets in 1918 has " ... neither constitution, bylaws nor rules of procedure."[1]

At its meeting, the AOC decides that it now will form a continuous committee that will be representative of the various organizations interested in the Olympics. Invitations to be represented on this committee are sent to 14 arbitrarily selected groups, including the NCAA. Even with a realigned committee, however, the majority of votes still rests in the hands of AAU members. It is this new AOC that

[1]Flath, Arnold W., "A History of Relations Between the National Collegiate Athletic Association and the Amateur Athletic Union of the United States (1905-1963), Stipes Publishing Company, Champaign, Illinois, 1964.

nominates and selects the 1920 U.S. Olympic team. Nowhere is the disproportionate influence of the AAU more evident than on the AOC nominating committee — a group made up of nine AAU members and not more than one representative from any other organization, including the Army, Navy and NCAA.

Logistics for the 1920 Olympics are handled badly. So loud and public are the complaints from athletes concerning the transportation, accommodations and general management of the United States team ("sanitation was conspicuously absent ... drinking water was terrible," says one athlete, describing the teams' lodgings) that, following the Olympics, there arises a general feeling among several sports bodies, including the NCAA, that there is a need for reorganization of the American Olympic Committee. To this end, the NCAA, on December 29, 1920, adopts a resolution "favoring the organization of an Olympic association, to be made up of bodies like this that have to do with participation in the Olympic Games."

The delegates to the NCAA Convention then specifically charge Palmer Pierce with the task of trying to implement this resolution. The job will prove taxing and, at times, annoying.

Reorganization of the American Olympic Committee

So widespread is criticism directed against the AOC for its handling of the 1920 Olympics that even the AOC itself decides to appoint a subcommittee to study the possibility of reorganization. On February 5, 1921, the AOC accepts a report from its subcommittee on reorganization. The report calls for formation of an American Olympic Association to take charge of management and fund-raising for the U.S. Olympic effort. But the reorganization plan still has the preponderance of votes resting with the AAU. Specifically, under the new plan, the AAU will directly control 33 delegate votes, with the possibility of indirectly controlling nine more votes as the result of a provision calling for "regional delegates to be designated by the president of the American Olympic Committee and selected by him." Under the plan, the NCAA is to have 16 votes and all other organizations — such as the Army, Navy, U.S. Golf Association, etc. — three votes each. However, at a later meeting, the reorganizing committee decides to reduce the number of NCAA delegate votes from 16 to three. The number of AAU votes is to stand at 33. Palmer Pierce protests that such a move now is beyond the powers of the committee.

The new plan is adopted, however; and 10 days after the abrupt and arbitrary reduction of its voting strength, the NCAA formally withdraws its support from the movement to organize an American Olympic Association.

In a letter to AOC President Gustavus T. Kirby printed in the New York Times, Pierce says, "If the National Collegiate Athletic Association, the undergraduates of the members of which number 350,000, is prevented from exerting its influence in the selection of the contestants for the Olympic Games, their managers and trainers, and the conduct and control of the contests, an influence commensurate with its position in amateur sport, it is much better that it should remain independent."

Pierce adds that he hopes for one of two solutions: "First, the organization of an American Olympic Association that would be truly representative of all interests concerned, or second, the taking over of the entire responsibility for the proper conducting of the Olympic Games by the (AAU)."

It is obviously the first solution that Pierce and the NCAA favor.

Kirby replies "that the representation of the various bodies on the reorganized American Olympic Committee would be reconsidered and finally determined at the October meeting."

In the May-to-October interval, Palmer Pierce makes several strenuous attempts to arrange a conference with AAU representatives to discuss "the affiliation with the Amateur Athletic Union of amateur athletic organizations like our own, or the formation of a federation."

In response to this request, Pierce receives a reply from AAU President Robert S. Weaver on September 22, 1921. Weaver says, in part:

> "I just received today your wire dated September 17 regarding a meeting in Washington on October 5 between representatives of the AAU, YMCA, the Army and Navy and (NCAA). I certainly feel that the suggestion for this meeting is a very good one indeed, but I regret to state that it will be impossible for me to leave my business at this time to come east for the meeting. I am today writing Mr. Rubien (AAU Secretary Frederick W.), appointing him as our representative and suggesting to Mr. Rubien that he get in touch with you immediately on receipt of my letter .... I assure you of my heartiest cooperation .... "

But Rubien does not contact Pierce; when Pierce takes the initiative in inviting Rubien to the proposed October 5 meeting, the AAU secretary replies, "The Amateur Athletic Union of the United States cannot at this time participate in such a conference, as it is definitely committed to the American Olympic Association by a vote of its board of governors."

The tone of Pierce's reply to Rubien suggests the NCAA president is perplexed but nonetheless eager to reach an accord.

"I had hoped to have the (AAU) represented at this conference," writes Pierce, "which is to be a friendly one, having as its purpose the discussion of some means of nationalizing the activities concerned with the United States' participation in the Olympic Games. It might be that as a result of a friendly discussion of the question at issue, you could convince the gentlemen present of the advisability of joining in the plan formed by the subcommittee appointed by the general Olympic committee.

"I note that it is your opinion that the plan of the American Olympic Association will be a really national organization. I seriously question this unless the cooperation and support of such organizations as the YMCA, the Playgrounds Association, the Boy Scouts and the (NCAA) are secured . . . . I hoped for your presence today in order that we might discuss it pro and con, without heat or bitterness."

Rubien's answer, if not heated and bitter, is at best testy:

"Your letter of even date delivered by messenger is at hand. I must decline the invitation because I am not at all in sympathy with the objects you have in mind in calling a meeting of this kind practically on the eve of the meeting of the American Olympic Committee for October 15, and in view of the great amount of time given to this subject by the reorganization committee of which you are a member, and the definite plans proposed by this committee, approved by all the national governing bodies of amateur sports on the Olympic program . . . . As you well know, the proposed constitution of the American Olympic Association provides for membership of such organizations as the NCAA and YMCA and such other organizations . . . whose activities are wholly in amateur sports, and such organizations as you mention can be elected if they comply with these requirements."

At the October meeting of the AOC, the representation of the colleges is fixed, with the NCAA having three representatives and other intercollegiate athletic organizations and regional conferences given 20 votes; thus, a total of 23 votes are in the hands of those representing the collegiate community. A committee composed of

Pierce, Kirby and a representative of the IC4A is appointed to select the associations and regional conferences to be invited to send delegates to the December formation conference of the American Olympic Association.

In an attempt to further clarify the situation as regards the colleges and to secure a satisfactory solution to what he still sees as the problem of non-AAU groups being underrepresented, Pierce takes it upon himself to name a committee, including the secretary of the AAU and president of the AOC, and calls a meeting for November 4. Once again, it is AAU Secretary Rubien declining to attend, doing so with a trace of impatience:

> "In view of the fact that we have gone a great way out of our way to help form an American Olympic Association, giving many organizations a complimentary representation, many of our (AAU) officials feel that we have gone far enough, and I am inclined to believe that if there is a continuance of this propaganda to form a federation as you suggest, many of the board of governors will be inclined to the view 'that every shoemaker should stick to his last' and insist on Olympic affairs being governed by the national governing bodies of the sports on the Olympic program only, and ignore professional organizations who claim to control amateur sports."

The National Amateur Athletic Federation

Meanwhile, with Pierce and the NCAA seemingly at a standoff with Rubien and the AAU, Secretary of War John W. Weeks, in a letter to AOC President Kirby, also suggests the formation of a national association composed of all existing amateur sports organizations. Weeks goes so far as to submit a proposed constitution for such a federation, which he suggests be called the National Amateur Athletic Federation of the United States. In his letter, Weeks also echoes Pierce's objections to the actions of the AOC reorganizing committee, saying that, should the proposed reorganization be put into effect, the representatives of the War and Navy Departments will not be given permission to commit to them.

Weeks' proposal, though first applauded by Kirby, is later defeated at a meeting of the AOC; the defeat is attributable to the bloc voting of AAU members.

Following defeat of Weeks' proposal, the AOC adopts the plan of its reorganizing committee and forms the American Olympic Association. The AOC appoints Palmer Pierce to its nine-member committee on Olympic Games.

In reporting the results of the AOC meeting to the NCAA Convention in December 1921, Pierce criticizes the newly formed American Olympic Association on grounds that, in restricting itself only to the Olympics, it is too limited in scope and, more to the point, it also is undemocratic in its composition.

"The Amateur Athletic Union has at least 33 votes," explains Pierce, "and its allied members sufficient more to give it a majority. It is provided that, at a quadrennial or special meeting, a member is entitled to a number of votes equal to the number of delegates, and a single delegate present may cast the full number of votes to which the member is entitled. This provision is not democratic and makes the organization not truly representative in character. It is possible that a single delegate at a meeting may . . . have votes sufficient for control."

Acting on Pierce's criticism, the NCAA passes a resolution refusing membership in the American Olympic Association, at the same time endorsing the idea of the National Amateur Athletic Federation.

The Army, Navy and YMCA also decline membership in the American Olympic Association.

If there is a particular point at which relations between the NCAA and AAU worsen from constant disagreement to an almost formalized opposition, it is on April 18, 1922, when AAU Secretary Rubien says, in reference to the widening rift between the two organizations, that the AAU is "prepared to fight to the last ditch."

Secretary of War Weeks' plan for an organization of amateur sports bodies is realized on May 8, 1922, when the NCAA, YMCA, Army, Navy and other non-AAU affiliated organizations draw up a constitution and bylaws for the National Amateur Athletic Federation (NAAF).

Rather than remain apart from the Olympic effort, the NAAF expresses early its willingness to join the American Olympic Association if the NAAF is given equal voting power with the AAU and if the AAU drops its claims to jurisdiction over certain sports.

In reply to the NAAF's overtures, AAU President William C. Prout claims such proposals "would eliminate the AAU as a sports governing body."

With relations apparently getting worse between the American Olympic Association and AAU on the one side and the NAAF and NCAA on the other, Col. Robert N. Thompson, the capable and widely respected president of the American Olympic Association, steps into the breach and, by dint of personal diplomacy, brings about a compromise wherein changes in the AOC's constitution lead to the NCAA, Army, Navy and other NAAF groups joining the American Olympic Association.

Under terms of the compromise, the NCAA and AAU are to have three votes each; however, the AAU is acknowledged in the association's constitution as being the governing body in track and field, swimming, boxing, wrestling and gymnastics.

With Thompson's compromise in effect, the American Olympic Association begins preparations for the 1924 Olympics as the most representative body in the history of this country's Olympic participation.

Thompson has brought about a temporary lull in the conflict between the NCAA and the AAU. The lull does not last long.

The Charles Paddock Case

Problems flare anew in May 1923 when Charles Paddock, a student and world-class sprinter at the University of Southern California, accepts an invitation to compete in an international meet in Paris. Paddock accepts this invitation with the approval of both the university and his local association of the AAU.

However, as Paddock is on board a train for New York, where he is to board a ship to France, the AAU announces that he will be unable to compete in Paris unless it (the AAU) makes an exception to an earlier ruling prohibiting competition abroad by American athletes in 1923 on grounds that such athletes are needed in the United States to help create public interest in preparations for the 1924 Olympic Games at Paris.

The AAU refuses to make an exception for Paddock although precedent for an exception was set when the AAU earlier granted a Yale-Harvard track team permission to compete in England vs. Oxford and Cambridge. Despite the AAU's position, Paddock sails for Paris and participates in the International University Athletic Games, turning in a strong performance that includes equaling a world record in the 150-meter dash. After his record-tying run, Paddock says, "The AAU hasn't any authority over members of the National Collegiate Athletic Association and can't dictate to them."

Upon learning that Paddock has in fact competed in the Paris meet in defiance of the AAU, Secretary Rubien announces that he (Paddock) is automatically disqualified as an amateur within the jurisdiction of the AAU, the obvious implication being that Paddock's action will now leave him ineligible for the U.S. Olympic team.

Upon learning of the AAU decision, NCAA President Pierce issues this statement supporting Paddock: " . . . since there seems to be no question as to the amateur standing of Mr. Paddock, he has a perfect right to take part in (the Paris college meet). It is difficult to conceive that by doing so, his amateur status would be affected. The (AAU) might subsequently prevent his competing in track and field events under their direction but certainly could not debar him from other games."

An editorial in the May 7, 1923, New York Times generally seems to favor Paddock: " . . . far too much importance has been attached to Paddock's participation in the Paris meet . . . . He also knew, as does everybody else, that the AAU controls only its own meets but has a working agreement with the International Federation. It can forbid Paddock to take part in these but cannot bar him from other amateur competition. The AAU is a fine and important organization, but not all amateur athletes belong to it, nor can it compel a man to affiliate with it against his will . . . . Arguments can be advanced for both sides in this controversy, but the wisest policy for both right now would seem to be let the matter rest."

But that editorial plea is in vain. The matter will not rest.

There now breaks out a squabble within the ranks of the AAU. On May 16, the Southern Pacific Association (the regional AAU group that first approved Paddock's participation in the Paris meet) refuses to enforce the decision of the AAU's national body in disqualifying Paddock.

Paddock himself, upon his return to the United States in June, says, "I certainly hope to try for the American Olympic team next year. If I can run well enough to make it and the AAU offers opposition to my selection because of the fact that I competed in the meet at Paris, I can only look for support from the University of Southern California; the NCAA, of which it is a member, (and) the National Amateur Athletic Federation . . . . "

The AAU takes no action on the Paddock case at its fall meeting. It is not until a meeting of the American Olympic Committee on December 22 in New York that AAU President William Prout takes a firm public stand against allowing Paddock to try out for the Olympic team. He goes on to say that this position will not be reconsidered unless Paddock retracts alleged statements in which, Prout charges, he vilified the AAU.

"As long as I am president of the Amateur Athletic Union," says Prout, "and as long as Paddock maintains his present attitude, just so long will I refuse to affix my signature to any certificate of amateurism of his. And I say I am justified."

Once again it is Col. Thompson, in the now-familiar role of peacemaker, who steps into the debate, asking Palmer Pierce to write Paddock and ask him (Paddock) to submit his case to the AAU committee especially appointed to hear it.

Pierce wires Paddock: " . . . I recommend, at the suggestion of the president of the American Olympic Committee, that you apply for reinstatement to the special committee appointed by the Amateur Athletic Union to consider your case."

The Paddock case is the main topic at the NCAA's 1923 Convention, and the delegates pass a resolution providing that the facts of the Paddock case be given to the press. The resolution further asserts that American colleges have "rights to determine the eligibility of their students to compete in intercollegiate athletic meets in this country and elsewhere."

Acting on Pierce's advice, Paddock applies for reinstatement by the AAU in order that he might be declared eligible for the 1924 Olympics. At last, on March 17, 1924, the special committee of the AAU reinstates Paddock on a vote of 4 to 1, after which AAU President Prout comments on the reinstatement: "The Paddock matter has been given a great deal more attention than the ordinary case that comes before the AAU . . . due to the fact that Paddock was used without his knowledge as an instrument to demonstrate what some people hoped was the fact that the position of the AAU has been weakened. The AAU, during the various controversies that have been raging during the past two years, has demonstrated that its position is stronger than ever."

The reinstatement ends this particular case, but it clearly delineates a battle line along which the NCAA and AAU will continue to skirmish, contesting each other's jurisdiction and control, particularly with regard to the American Olympic Committee.

NCAA and NAAF Discontent
With AAU Olympic Role

At a December 31, 1923, meeting of the American Olympic Association, the NCAA and NAAF are unsuccessful in a combined bid to have certification of the amateur and citizenship status of athletes taken from the hands of the individual sports governing bodies and placed in the hands of the Olympic Committee. Opposition to this proposal comes mainly in the form of bloc voting by the AAU delegates, who believe passage of such a regulation will greatly curb the power of the AAU as a governing body.

On January 24, 1924, Pierce renews his charge that the AAU is using the Olympic Games as a means of arbitrarily controlling the sports under its jurisdiction and that the AAU is trying to gain absolute control of all matters connected with American participation in the Olympics. Pierce explains precisely what this will mean to United States colleges:

"The colleges are thoroughly awake to the danger of the attempt that is being made through certain sports governing bodies of this country and abroad to obtain centralized control of athletics. The (AAU) has been actively engaged since the Olympic Games of 1920 in fostering an international sports federation. This body has enunciated a rule that 'No amateur athlete can compete in any foreign country without a certificate from the sports governing body of his own country of that sport in which he wishes to engage.' Since the (AAU) is a member of the international federation and claims jurisdiction over track and field, swimming and other sports in which the colleges are vitally interested, it means that if this regulation is accepted, no college could participate in international intercollegiate athletics except by permission of the (AAU)."

Despite this obviously widening rift between the NCAA and the AAU, the onset of spring and preparation for the Olympic Games once again bring a momentary lull in the feuding.

Under AOC President Thompson, United States' participation in the 1924 games is successful and well managed. United States collegiate athletes once again make up the core of the team. There are 47 undergraduates on a track and field team of 121 members. Of 250 points scored by Americans in track and field events, 195 are scored by college-trained athletes.

NCAA and Others Withdraw From the AOA

The post-Olympic year of 1925 brings no major clash between the NCAA and AAU, but trouble flares anew in 1926. The AAU refuses to stop its member athletic clubs from approaching undergraduates during the college semesters and persuading such athletes to join the club teams. This is a shaking of the NCAA's philosophical foundation, that amateur sport is most properly a part of the educational process.

When athletic directors from the Big Ten Conference publicly request AAU President Murray Hulbert to forbid AAU-affiliated clubs from signing Big Ten athletes as members during the school year, they receive a curt reply stating that the AAU will not comply with this request.

Palmer Pierce later will describe the tone of Hulbert's reply as "offensive" and claim that the AAU's position "shows that the AAU has little, if any, sympathy with the larger purposes of the NCAA, which are to make athletics an integral part of the educational program."

Denying that the AAU has any quarrel with the NCAA or any sports governing body in the United States, Hulbert replies to Pierce's remarks with the curious assertion, "I am for peace and harmony and will get it even though we have to fight for it."

College and AAU relations are strained further when, at the quadrennial meeting of the AOC in 1926, bloc voting by AAU delegates dominates each issue. In the end, the AAU delegates succeed in electing former AAU President William C. Prout as president of the American Olympic Committee, replacing Col. Thompson. The election of Prout leads the New York Times to observe, "The AAU is right back in the saddle where it was years ago when the late James E. Sullivan ruled with a firm hand."

Unable to contest the dominance of the AAU in the American Olympic Association, the NCAA, Navy, YMCA, NAAF and other groups resign from the AOA in 1927. Speaking to the NCAA Convention prior to the vote to withdraw, Pierce says:

> "Now that the AAU has assumed complete responsibility, again the outlook is far from promising. Since the NCAA is in such a helpless minority, it seems to me the part of wisdom to withdraw entirely from administrative participation . . . . It is my belief that the AAU cannot succeed in its efforts to perpetuate its system of control upon amateur sport. It is un-American and out-of-date. It places responsibility for amateurism on the individual instead of on the organization he may represent. The athletics of the United States have become too well and completely organized to make it necessary or desirable that every athlete should be required by the order of a foreign organization (i.e., the AAU-supported International

Amateur Athletic Federation) to sign a registration card and pay a fee to the AAU before he can compete for the Olympic Games."

Pierce concludes by urging the NCAA to inform the AAU "that the colleges of this country once again deny its authority in any way to control the participation of their undergraduates in intercollegiate athletics, here or abroad."

The Big Ten Conference also withdraws from the AOA; in so doing, Maj. John L. Griffith, conference commissioner, sets forth the three main objections of the colleges to AAU control of the association:

"1. The constitution of the Olympic Association was so changed ... last month as to deprive the national organizations that composed the federation of any influence in relation to America's part in the Olympic Games and place the control in the hands of one member of the Olympic Association, the Amateur Athletic Union.
"2. The centralization of control in the hands of the AAU restored an unsatisfactory situation that the American Olympic Association was organized to correct.
"3. The constitutional changes engineered by the AAU representatives changed the basis of participation upon which the colleges, the YMCA and the Army and Navy joined the Olympic Association in 1921."

Gen. Douglas MacArthur's Request for Olympic Reorganization

With the withdrawal of so many organizations from the AOA, it appears in 1927 that the American Olympic team for 1928 is to be basically an AAU team. However, the death of AOC President Prout in August 1927 brings about the election of Brig. Gen. Douglas MacArthur as the new president of the AOC. MacArthur's first priority is an effort to persuade the defected organizations back into the Olympic association; in this, he is successful. In December 1927, the NAAF votes to rejoin the AOA; a few days later, the NCAA adopts a resolution saying:

"Being assured that the tryouts for the Olympic Games of 1928 will be conducted on the 1924 basis, in the interest of amity and international sport, the Association accepts the invitation of the president of the (AOC) to resume membership in the American

Olympic Association.

The breach between the colleges and the AAU is still far from healed. On April 16, 1928, Big Ten Commissioner Griffith shakes the uneasy truce with a much-publicized statement in which he calls for the formation of a new and more representative Olympic association that will "end the domination of the (AAU) over American amateur athletics."

Griffith further exacerbates matters by referring to the leadership of the AAU as "cheap politicians" who gained control "over the best elements of our athletic public by intimidation." The intimidation Griffith refers to is the threat of disbarment of any athlete competing in an amateur event not under AAU sanction.

Gen. MacArthur makes no immediate response to Griffith's remarks; but following the Olympics, he makes his views known in a special report to the President of the United States:

"The complicated chancelleries of American sport . . . are even more intricate perhaps than are political chancelleries. To abstain from the conflicting interests of various sports bodies and yet to demand of all support for the Olympic movement has been a problem which at times appeared insurmountable. It is my most earnest recommendation that, within the next few months, an athletic congress be called under the auspices of the (AOA) of all amateur sports associations in the United States, attended by the leading athletic figures of America, wherein the various athletic problems that have been agitating the nation during the immediate past shall be thoroughly discussed without crimination or recrimination . . . and policies and standards fixed so definitely as to thoroughly chart the course of American athletics for the immediate future."

MacArthur's call to reorganize American amateur sport is echoed by Palmer Pierce, who claims the selection of coaches, managers and athletes for the 1928 Olympics was not conducted in accordance with the AOA constitution. Pierce points out that, instead of the Olympic Track and Field Committee selecting the team members as is specified in the AOA constitution, the Olympic tryouts for the 1928 team had been part of the annual national championships of the AAU, a meet conducted by the AAU and not by any Olympic committee.

A Brief Reconciliation

At its 1928 Convention, the NCAA, on Pierce's initiative, appoints a committee "to discuss with (the AAU) the registration system and the relations between that body and the colleges."

Before any meeting takes place, however, further trouble develops between the colleges and the AAU. It begins when Northwestern University announces it will schedule contests with teams not subject to AAU control, this action being the result of the AAU's refusal to sanction a swim meet between Northwestern and the Chicago Athletic Association. The reason given by the AAU for its refusal to sanction the Chicago meet is that Northwestern athletes had competed during the previous summer in meets not sanctioned by the AAU.

Northwestern Athletic Director Kenneth L. "Tug" Wilson issues a statement saying, in part: "The AAU has not charged that the men violated any amateur laws. Their only offense in the eyes of the AAU is that they competed in meets not controlled by the AAU. Northwestern University does not acknowledge that the AAU has supreme control over swimming and other sports, and in the future, we will schedule our meets with colleges, universities and such clubs as are not subject to AAU control."

The Northwestern incident leads to the Big Ten Conference breaking relations with the AAU on January 18, 1929. "No longer will the Western Conference (now the Big Ten) bend under the yoke of the AAU," says Commissioner Griffith. "We are tired of its continued demands and general attempts to dominate our affairs."

For its part the AAU, through Secretary-Treasurer Daniel Ferris, says that "the AAU never claims to control intercollegiate activity of any sort. It is only when AAU athletes compete that the AAU is forced to watch over them." Ferris calls Griffith's remarks "a smoke screen."

Despite these fundamental and public problems, Avery Brundage, now president of the AAU, appoints a committee to meet with the NCAA in an attempt to settle the differences.

The NCAA and AAU special committees meet on April 15, 1929, in New York. Surprisingly, they come to terms almost immediately with some important concessions being made to the colleges.

The AAU agrees to amend its rules to provide for certification of a college athlete by the college he represents and not by the AAU. The AAU also resolves "that amateur competition within the territorial jurisdiction of the AAU by an undergraduate representing his college ... in other than AAU competition will not subject such competitor to the discipline of the AAU."

With the colleges having hereby taken a large step toward control of their own sports, the NCAA now turns its attention to the Olympic problem, specifically the reorganization of the American Olympic Association.

A special committee of the NCAA meets with representatives of the AOA in New York on December 30, 1929. The NCAA suggests to the Olympic Association that it reorganize to become "a democratic organization truly representative of the athletic bodies interested in the (Olympics)."

Again, the NCAA initiative proves successful and the AOA reorganizes in 1930. The key point in the reorganization is that now there is to be fixed representation on the executive committee of the AOA — the NCAA and AAU are to have three representatives each, the War Department, Navy and IC4A will have one representative each and 10 additional representatives are to be elected by a two-thirds vote of members of the executive committee.

Another AOA constitutional revision provides for the appointment of Olympic Games committees for each of the Olympic sports in which the United States competes. Each committee is to include among its members " . . . four representatives of the (NCAA) if the game or sport is one in which the NCAA holds national championships or . . . fosters competition on a nationwide basis; four representatives of the (AAU) if the game or sport is one over which the AAU has jurisdiction . . . ."

With agreement on registration and the reorganization of the AOA, the long and bitter feud between the NCAA and AAU comes to a halt — albeit a temporary one — eventually culminating in formal Articles of Alliance signed by both organizations.

The decade of the 1930s is characterized by generally peaceful and cooperative relations between the NCAA and AAU, not restricted solely to the Olympic effort but also extending into the area of rules making. NCAA President Charles Kennedy of Princeton, who takes over from the retired Palmer Pierce in 1930, urges that the various NCAA rules committees foster cooperative arrangements with the AAU to develop greater uniformity in national and international rules. This is accomplished by overlapping committee membership, with the most notable success coming in swimming and basketball.

The 1932 Olympics, held successfully in the United States, pass without serious conflict between the NCAA and AAU. In fact, NCAA President Kennedy praises "the spirit of cooperative endeavor" between the organizations, and AAU President J. Lyman Bingham says the year 1932 "finds the AAU again in complete harmony with all sports governing agencies."

This spirit prevails through the 1936 Olympic Games, although there are widespread political protests about the games being held in Nazi Germany.

Following the 1936 games, the NCAA takes a large step toward equally shared control of the Olympic Games. John L. Griffith, Big Ten commissioner and now NCAA president, advocates and then obtains an equal number of games committee members — six each for the NCAA and AAU — in the sports of track, swimming, boxing, wrestling and gymnastics.

World War II and the Start of the Pan-American Games

The outbreak of world war in 1938 leads to cancellation of the 1940 Olympic Games. But there now arises the idea of staging a competition in the Western Hemisphere to be called the Pan-American Games.

In 1940, a committee of the AAU, meeting with representatives of the NCAA, investigates the possibility of staging such games. The AAU makes the decision to go ahead. The NCAA seems inclined to support the games but the issue must go before the Convention.

While the NCAA favors the idea in principle, the colleges are understandably hesitant to support the AAU's suggestion that the United States entry in the Pan-American Games be managed by the AOA. The colleges are not eager to see more power vested in this group and agree to the move only after assurances from AAU President Brundage that the Pan-American and Olympic committees "will be separate and distinct."

On February 24, 1941, the AOA is renamed the United States of America Sports Federation (USASF), the change made in order that it might have jurisdiction over the Pan-American Games.

The effort goes for naught, however, as the bombing of Pearl Harbor on December 7, 1941, and the declaration of war by the United States ultimately leads to the USASF withdrawing from the Pan-American Games.

At the end of World War II, the USASF, at its quadrennial meeting to begin plans for the soon-to-be-restored Olympic Games, once again changes its name and becomes the U.S. Olympic Association (USOA), forerunner of the U.S. Olympic Committee (USOC).

In 1946, at the urging of NCAA President Wilbur C. Smith, Big Ten Commissioner Griffith and Eastern College Athletic Conference (ECAC) Commissioner Asa Bushnell are named vice-president and secretary, respectively, of the USOA. It is also in 1946 that the NCAA and AAU jointly adopt the Articles of Alliance, among the provisions of which is the AAU's recognition of "the right of member colleges of the NCAA to govern themselves and to compete among themselves or with nonmember colleges, under eligibility rules considered satisfactory to the NCAA."

The signing of the articles probably marks the high point of NCAA-AAU relations, as attested by Tug Wilson: "The recognition of the true worth of the NCAA to the U.S. Olympic Association . . . has resulted in the utmost harmony and finest cooperation that has ever existed between your Association and the AAU."

But it is not long before trouble looms again. Following the 1948 Olympics, Avery Brundage, the former AAU president who is now president of the USOA, publicly states his belief that "college athletes who receive scholarships because of their ability in sports become, in fact, professionals."

Surprisingly, it is AAU President James Rhodes who takes a position against Brundage and nearer to the NCAA's stance when he declares himself in favor of both academic and athletic scholarships as long as they are limited to books and tuition. But Brundage's viewpoint moves from opinion to policy in 1951 when the USOA president warns "that subsidized college athletes, rewarded financially for their talent alone, will be ineligible for the 1952 Olympics at Helsinki."

No such ineligibilities occur, however, because on January 17, 1952, the NCAA Council proposes and the Convention passes a new NCAA Principle Governing Financial Aid. The statement says:

> "Any college athlete who receives financial assistance other than that administered by his institution shall not be eligible for intercollegiate competition."

Thus, a standard is set — eligibility still rests in the hands of the colleges.

NCAA Olympic Committee

Financial aid of a different sort becomes an issue as the 1956 Olympics approach. Fund-raising becomes important. In 1954, the

NCAA decides that rather than appointing temporary NCAA Olympic committees, which have as one of their main duties the raising of funds to help support the Olympic effort, the scope of the Olympics and the constant need for fund-raising is such that the NCAA should establish an ongoing Olympic Committee. This committee's initial responsibility is largely in fund-raising, but committee Chair Willis O. Hunter of the University of Southern California proves prophetic when he says, "There will no doubt be other assignments given to the NCAA Olympic Committee . . . in its relationship with the U.S. Olympic Association."

True to Hunter's prediction, the NCAA Olympic Committee in 1957 requests and receives increased NCAA representation on several USOA games committees, giving the colleges a stronger voice in Olympic affairs.

Events Leading to Cancellation of the Articles of Alliance

On the surface, relations between the NCAA and AAU are harmonious during the early and mid-1950s, so much so that representatives of the two groups meet in 1956 to try to draft a common amateur code. However, behind this apparent detente there takes place a number of unpublicized incidents and an accumulation of complaints by the colleges concerning the AAU's administration of amateur sport and its cavalier attitude in dominating Olympic matters.

For example, during what the NCAA International Relations Committee Report later will describe as "frustrating sessions" of the USOC executive board in 1958-59, the NCAA strongly advocates rotation of board members and members of games committees to obtain new ideas and possibly relieve the situation of personal animosities. The only way this rotation can be approved, however, is with a provision that the rule will not be retroactive, so that the incumbent AAU members will not rotate off for another eight years. Seeing that this is the only way to reach the objective, the NCAA members accept this AAU provision and an agreement is reached. But the agreement is to no avail because it later is rescinded by an AAU-led voting bloc before it can affect any incumbent board or committee member.

During this time, the NCAA also proposes an Olympic development and fund-raising program with equal membership of the AAU and NCAA.

Says an NCAA report on the plan, "The program made progress, but was kept under constant harassment, delays and opposition from AAU personnel."[2]

Meanwhile, other grievances are building up against the AAU. A list of complaints compiled by the NCAA include:

1. The AAU has a "dictatorial attitude"[3] (using the NCAA term), with reference to established policy in sports in which it is the international representative. The NCAA charges that AAU decisions are based less on the good of the sport in question and more on the self-interest of the organization or individuals involved.
2. Complaints registered with the AAU are not investigated.
3. The AAU has withheld invitations to athletes to compete in foreign meets when that participation would prevent the athlete from competing in an AAU event.
4. The AAU has neglected the area of research.
5. AAU track meets "are poorly managed, as are United States tours of foreign teams."

A particularly bitter incident occurs in 1959 when the AAU's national basketball committee disapproves a planned United States tour by the Swedish national basketball team during which the Swedes would have played several college teams. The AAU committee then asks the International Basketball Federation to suspend Swedish team members should they play in the United States without AAU approval.

This action and the collective weight of the grievances preceding it prompt the NCAA to cancel the Articles of Alliance in April 1960. At the same time, the NCAA announces it will not honor suspensions imposed on college athletes by the AAU.

More Negotiations

In 1960, the NCAA, still not wishing to discard the idea of some sort of working arrangement with the AAU, appoints a special committee to review NCAA relations with the AAU and USOC. The committee meets in June 1960 with a similar committee representing the AAU and meets again in December of this year with the AAU committee

[2]The National Collegiate Athletic Association's International Relations Committee, "A Historical Overview of the United States Olympic Committee," November 24, 1972, page 11.

[3]Ibid., page 11

and USOC representatives. Neither meeting produces a settlement, largely because of repeated refusals by the AAU to commit any of its proposals to writing.

Meanwhile, unrest is developing among United States track, basketball and gymnastics coaches regarding control of these sports by the AAU. In fact, it is with the urging of the National Association of Basketball Coaches that the National Basketball Committee of the U.S. (primarily the rules-making body) seeks recognition from FIBA (the international governing body) to become the country's national governing body for basketball, in which role it hopes to supplant the AAU. The move ends in failure at a FIBA meeting in Rome when the proposal is dismissed by FIBA President Bill Greim, who is also an AAU representative. Nevertheless, basketball, gymnastics and track coaches continue to agitate for separate federations to control their sports.

After repeated frustrations in trying to reach a new alliance with the AAU, the NCAA special committee announces in May 1961 its conclusion that the AAU " . . . is no longer truly representative of all interests in certain sports and is certainly not the best representative group for NCAA interests in specific sports."

The committee suggests that new organizations be formed in basketball, gymnastics, track and field and swimming and that, hereafter, whatever organizations "contribute most in the development and support of any sport in the United States should be the officially recognized representative to the sport's international federation or should have at least equal representation."

The committee goes on to recommend "that definite steps must be taken to break the stranglehold of the AAU if the NCAA is to acquire its rightful place in international representation" and, in view of this, " . . . the U.S. Olympic Committee organization is completely outmoded and should be reorganized . . . . "

Perhaps the most discouraging finding by the NCAA committee is that "the AAU people were not inclined to agree to anything unless we were willing to 'deal.' They set forth certain possibilities of conceding certain changes in the area of international representation, but only on the basis that the NCAA ... withdraw support of the National Basketball Committee's effort to be recognized (as the national governing body)."

The NCAA makes no such concession; in May 1961, the special committee breaks off negotiations with the AAU, formally dissolves the Articles of Alliance and, most importantly, recommends to the

NCAA Executive Committee "that the NCAA lend all its effort to bring about the formation of new organizations to represent the United States in basketball and gymnastics to the international federations."

The committee goes on to suggest that these new organizations be made truly representative of all amateur sports interests, including, among others, the AAU.

The New Federations

On October 1, 1961, 88 representatives of various sports organizations meet in Chicago to discuss formation of new federations. This and subsequent meetings produce, by the end of 1962, three new national federations — the U.S. Track and Field Federation, the U.S. Basketball Federation and the U.S. Gymnastics Federation.

The new federations give many organizations, among them the nation's high schools, a more proportionate control over a particular sport.

In October 1962, the AAU declares that it will not recognize, much less accept an invitation to join, any of the newly formed sports federations and will "rule ineligible any athlete who competes in a federation event sponsored by a high school or college."

Largely because of this action by the AAU, the NCAA Council recommends that member colleges withdraw from membership in the AAU "until such time as that organization indicates a cooperative attitude toward federation members." It also recommends that "colleges not enter athletes in AAU competitions unless the event also is sanctioned by the appropriate federation."

Federal Intervention

Fearing a disruptive effect on the 1964 Olympics and on all of United States amateur sport, Attorney General Robert F. Kennedy in October 1962 calls a meeting in Washington of representatives of the USOC, NCAA, AAU and other sports bodies. An agreement — a truce called the "Washington Alliance" — at first is agreed to; however, two weeks later, it is renounced by the AAU.

On November 12, Kennedy tries again and brings about another general agreement on a truce, the so-called "House Olympic Coalition," that needs only ratification by the parent bodies to go into effect. However, this agreement also is repudiated by the AAU convention later in the same month.

Following rejection of two Federally negotiated plans, President John F. Kennedy asks the nation's sports leaders to submit their dispute to the arbitration of Gen. Douglas MacArthur.

Although MacArthur is not given full arbitration powers, he succeeds in working out an agreement in January 1964. There are three key points: (1) Immediate amnesty is to be granted to all athletes previously disqualified for Olympic consideration for competing in "unsanctioned" meets; (2) an Olympic Eligibility Board is to be formed, consisting of three members of the AAU and three members of the U.S. Track and Field Federation (as duly constituted agent of the NCAA), and this board is to pass upon the eligibility and qualifications of every candidate for the 1964 U.S. Olympic team; (3) an "athletic congress" is to be called, made up of representatives of all major amateur sports bodies and instructed "to devise a permanent plan under which all organizations dedicated to amateur athletics . . . pool their resources so that by a united effort we may be able successfully to meet the challenge from any nation in the field of athletics and sport."

Under terms of MacArthur's plan, the U.S. Track and Field Federation (USTFF) is given jurisdiction over meets involving high school and college athletes, while any athlete who is not a high school or college student must have an AAU card to compete in USTFF meets.

The MacArthur Compromise produces a moratorium lasting through the 1964 Olympics, but 1965 brings more problems and a serious setback for the nation's colleges.

The Sulger Amendment

In a decision that turns back the clock 35 years, the USOC board of directors, meeting in May and June of 1965, approve an amendment (hereafter called the Sulger Amendment) to the USOC constitution specifying that the majority of votes on each Olympic games committee (there is one such committee for each sport in which the United States participates) must be reserved for the internationally recognized governing body of that sport. For example, the AAU automatically would have 23 votes on the 45-member Track and Field Committee and would have a similar majority in basketball and other sports in which it is the internationally recognized governing body. The Sulger Amendment passes on the strength of bloc voting by AAU members of USOC in conjunction with various independent franchise holders that caucus with the AAU. The amendment passes despite the opposition of the armed services, NCAA, YMCA and the National Federation of State High School Athletic Associations.

This change in the individual games committee structure relegates the colleges and high schools to what one NCAA delegate calls "a completely subservient role." Indeed, the NCAA no longer is merely a minority, but is now just a segment of the minority. The Sulger Amendment effectively restores the imbalance that existed in the 1930s.

After the discouraging outcome of the USOC meetings, a majority of the NCAA membership recommends that the Association (1) withdraw from the USOC, (2) establish more federations in other sports, (3) look into possibilities of Federal supervision of amateur sport, (4) ask Congress to investigate and restructure the USOC and (5) refrain from making appointments to any Olympic games committee.

The country's high schools, equally distressed, request via their national organization that Congress examine the USOC with an eye to seeing "that all areas of the United States and all amateur sports programs ... be justly and equitably represented on the Olympic Committee."

As the NCAA moves toward withdrawal from the USOC, it is dissuaded by the forceful appeal of Association President Everett D. Barnes and Big Ten Commissioner William R. Reed, who are both of the opinion that diplomacy and continued discussion eventually will lead to the USOC accepting the views of the schools and colleges. It is an assumption that once more proves incorrect and which Reed later renounces. A year after an NCAA committee begins negotiations with representatives of the USOC, Reed finds himself telling the 1967 NCAA Convention that, contrary to his earlier beliefs, "there does exist a coalition between the AAU and the independents (individual franchise holders) which constitutes control of the USOC and which appears to serve the interests of the AAU."

Reed's change of opinion comes partially as a result of the "test issues" of applications for USOC membership by the USTFF and the new federations in basketball and gymnastics. Membership of the new federations is vigorously opposed by the AAU and finally is defeated.

Sports Arbitration Board
Meanwhile, the entire issue of the national structure of amateur

sport once again comes to the attention of the Federal government. In January 1967, a Sports Arbitration Board (SAB) is appointed by Vice-President Hubert H. Humphrey, who is acting on a directive from the U.S. Senate. The task of the SAB is to examine problems relating to sanction, jurisdiction and Olympic representation. However, contrary to what its name suggests, the SAB does not enjoy full powers of an arbitrator. In 1968, the NCAA offers to submit to arbitration by the SAB if the AAU will agree. The AAU declines.

"The AAU, as far as we can see," says NCAA President Marcus L. Plant, "holds that no one can put on a track meet without its permission. This is and will continue to be totally unacceptable to us."

Denied power of arbitration, the SAB, like others before it, ends in failure.

Deteriorating NCAA-USOC Relations

Despite its open dissatisfaction with the organization and procedures of the USOC, the NCAA continues its role in strengthening the U.S. Olympic team. In the late 1960s, the NCAA gives new impetus to three sports — water polo, volleyball and soccer — by establishing national championships in them. It adds the decathlon, a prestigious Olympic event, to the NCAA track championships. The Association also continues to support the USTFF and the federations in basketball, gymnastics, wrestling and baseball.

Wrestling is an interesting case in point. It is in events surrounding this sport that we see the AAU's full influence and control over the USOC.

At its quadrennial meeting in 1969, the USOC rejects the membership application of the U.S. Wrestling Federation, at the same time tabling membership applications from the USTFF and the Women's Basketball Association. But a year later, undoubtedly to the surprise of the USOC and others, the international governing body for wrestling (FILA) disaffiliates the AAU as the internationally recognized United States governing body for wrestling. FILA does this on grounds that the AAU is a multisports body and, therefore, does not conform to a FILA rule that all national governing bodies must be single-purpose in nature. Logically, in the aftermath of the AAU's disaffiliation, the U.S. Wrestling Federation applies for USOC membership and recognition as the nation's governing body in wrestling.

Understandably shocked by FILA's decision, the AAU persuades the USOC to intervene in its behalf. Hereupon, the USOC steps into the momentary vacuum, declaring itself the "intervening" governing body. On January 20, 1971, at a USOC board of governors meeting in Denver, the officers of the USOC amend that body's constitution to give themselves authority to approve or deny the application of any organization to become this country's representative to an international sports governing body. At a later meeting at Greenbrier, West Virginia, the USOC board adopts a motion requiring a favorable two-thirds majority vote of USOC directors for any organization seeking international recognition. Thus, without the USOC board's approval, the U.S. Wrestling Federation may not even *apply* for recognition from FILA.

With the U.S. Wrestling Federation effectively in check, the AAU now seeks and obtains the intervention of IOC President Avery Brundage who, along with AAU President Clifford Buck, persuades FILA to reconsider its decision and to return the international wrestling franchise to the AAU, despite the fact that the AAU is not a single-purpose organization.

These maneuverings dismay and disillusion NCAA Olympic Committee Chair Edward S. Steitz, who, following FILA's reversal, analyzes the issue for the NCAA membership:

"At Greenbrier at the USOC biennial meeting, a motion was passed whereby a sports body, such as a federation, in order to be recognized by the USOC, must obtain a favorable vote of two-thirds . . . . This divisive legislation is interpreted by NCAA representatives as a means of doing all that is possible to prevent one of the federations from being designated the governing body for that particular sport. In addition, before a sports body may apply to the international governing body for membership, it must have the approval and recognition of the USOC . . . . *This, in effect, places control of (all) international competition in the hands of the USOC board* (italics added), which, in turn, is governed by the organizations which hold international franchises . . . . Before any change can be made in membership, the change must be approved by two-thirds of the people who hold present membership."

It is apparent to states and others that, under this rule, there is little likelihood of any change in the status quo.

Steitz, a veteran international authority, goes on to suggest that continued NCAA membership in the USOC should be contingent upon three USOC constitutional changes: (1) repeal of the Sulger Amendment giving the national governing body an automatic majority on all games committees, (2) repeal of the amendment saying that the USOC may recognize only one national governing body in a sport and that the organization recognized also must be a member of the international sports federation and (3) repeal of the amendment saying the USOC must give prior approval before any organization can apply for international recognition.

"NCAA members of the Olympic Committee feel," says Steitz, "(that) a radical change must take place within the structure of the USOC itself before the school-college system ever will receive its due identity and respect, (that is) *having a voice and vote commensurate with the contribution it makes in various sports.*" (Italics added.)

Once again, despite the difficulties, the NCAA fulfills its responsibilities for the 1972 Olympics in Munich. But on October 25, 1972, the NCAA Council — the Association's 18-member policy board — votes to withdraw the NCAA from the USOC. NCAA Executive Director Walter Byers comments: "The situation is worse now than in the '60s. The only external force that has the clout to bring about reorganization is the agency that gave the USOC its original charter, Congress."

While all previous government efforts at finding a *modus vivendi* had ended in failure or, at best, in short-term, patchwork solutions, this time, spurred by the NCAA's withdrawal from the USOC, Congress vigorously tackles the problem — but, at first, with no better results.

In 1974, the Amateur Athletic Act — an amalgam of bills introduced by Senators John Tunney, James Pearson, Marlow Cook, Mike Gravel and Warren Magnuson, passes the Senate but is not brought up for a vote in the House. If passed, the bill would have created a national Amateur Sports Board of five members appointed by the president of the United States with the advice and consent of the Senate. This board then would revoke all existing charters (including the USOC's) and issue new ones, with an eye to making certain that a majority of the charters for individual sports did not end up being held by one group. The board also would have created a National Sports Development Foundation to collect and supervise funds for the furtherance of amateur athletics. In short, the Amateur Athletic Act would have brought amateur athletics very much under government control. The thought of such government control obviously displeases IOC President Lord Killanin of Ireland, who reminds President Gerald Ford that the IOC limits government influence in Olympic sports and that, even if the Amateur Athletic Act should pass, government intervention in the affairs of the USOC or any other internationally recognized sports governing body could result in the United States being barred from the games.

The Amateur Sports Act

Undaunted by the failure of the Amateur Athletic Act and apparently not intimidated by Killanin's warning, President Ford in 1975 appoints a 22-member Presidential Commission on Olympic Sports to be chaired by Gerald B. Zornow, chair of the board of Eastman Kodak. The commission includes several athletes, members of Congress and private citizens from within and outside the amateur sports community. The President's overall charge to the commission is to determine what factors tended to impede proper development of the United States' international sports effort and to make recommendations for changes.

After a year of study, the commission releases a two-volume, 613-page report recommending a national reorganization designed to meet three main needs: (1) to provide a means of settling disputes among sports organizations as to which will receive international recognition; (2) to provide a means by which all sports-governing bodies receive equitable representation on the national governing body, and (3) to set up a central policy-making forum to direct fundraising activities for amateur sport, particularly the Olympics.

There is also a mandate in the report that any jurisdictional or franchise disputes be submitted to and settled by the American Arbitration Association.

Charles "Bud" Wilkinson, former football coach at the University of Oklahoma and a member of the commission, says of the report's recommendations that "once such a mechanism is in place, once the people who deserve to govern a sport really govern it, most of these petty squabbles will die away."

With only a few modifications, the report of the President's Commission becomes the landmark Amateur Sports Act.

Rather than creating a new central sports governing body, the act reorganizes the USOC (which already enjoys the advantage of IOC recognition) and places it atop a vertical structure of all national sports-governing bodies. The act requires that at least 20 percent of each governing body be composed of athletes. It also provides that some of the traditionally less influential sports groups, such as the YMCA, be involved in the decisions of each governing body.

In cases where national organizations such as the NCAA and AAU are contesting for control of national governing bodies, the act calls for arbitration in choosing which governing body will best represent the sport and serve the nation's interests.

In April 1978, encouraged by the impending passage of the Amateur Sports Act and by the earlier (1974) repeal by the USOC of the Sulger Amendment (the amendment that had given the national governing body of any sport an automatic majority on the individual Olympic games committees), the NCAA rejoins the about-to-be-reorganized USOC.

The bill passes the Senate, literally at the last minute, by voice vote at 4 a.m. on the final day of the 95th Congress — October 15, 1978 — after the Senate and House have been in continuous session more than 60 hours. It is signed into law by President Jimmy Carter November 8, 1978. The major provisions of the Amateur Sports Act are:

1. That the USOC be reorganized into a central policy-making organization for amateur sport, in which all major interests will be directly or indirectly represented.

2. That there be qualifying standards for any organization wishing to gain and maintain USOC recognition as the national governing body for a particular sport. (We will discuss the specific criteria in a moment.)

3. That there be a mechanism for "binding arbitration" by which an organization, believing itself better qualified than the incumbent to act as governing body for a particular sport, could challenge the incumbent for recognition as such.

4. That there be general recognition of the right of athletes to compete in international events, free of unwarranted interference.

The act unquestionably increases the USOC's powers, making it the "coordinating body for amateur athletic activity in the United States directly relating to international amateur athletic competition." However, there are two important safeguards. The act makes clear that the USOC's "coordinating" authority is nonmandating; that is, the USOC has no direct power over other organizations. The act also specifies that this limited coordinating power applies only to international competition. Thus, the USOC has no power over what is called "restricted competition" — domestic competition in which the participants are drawn from a limited class, such as college students. For example, the USOC has no power with reference to college or high school basketball competition.

The act also is specific in setting qualifying criteria for any organization seeking the right to act as the national governing body for a particular sport. The five most important criteria are autonomy, open membership, athlete representation, representation of major interested organizations and nondiscriminatory sanctioning.

The most important of these provisions is the one requiring a national governing body to be autonomous and separately incorporated. Says attorney Michael Scott of the NCAA's Washington, D.C., legal firm, himself a specialist in amateur sports law: "This requirement, quite bluntly, spelled the end of the AAU as a multisport national governing body in the Olympic movement . . . . What it has meant as a practical matter is that the AAU has been required to spin off its various Olympic sport divisions into independent national governing bodies. Consequently, a person or organization interested in swimming, for example, no longer has to affiliate with the entire AAU complex, involving a multiplicity of sports, in order to be involved in the administration or development of swimming."

One remarkable impact of this provision is that amateur track and field, historically the most important of all AAU-controlled sports, forms a new governing body, "The Athletics Congress," formally severing all relationships, even clerical ones, with the AAU. More remarkable, in view of the 50-year-old conflict between the AAU and NCAA in track and field matters, is that the NCAA-supported Track and Field Association/USA joins The Athletics Congress, uniting all major track and field interests in a single organizational structure.

The criterion calling for a governing body to have "athletic representation" means that the board of directors of each governing body must consist of at least 20 percent active or recently active athletes. "This new notion of athlete participation in policy making," says Scott, "has been spectacularly successful. Not only have the athlete representatives . . . performed their duties in an intelligent and constructive manner; they also have learned about . . . the complex problems involved in the running of a major sports program."

In requiring representation of major organizations concerned with a particular sport, the act calls for a "reasonable direct representation" for any national sports organization that conducts international-class programs in its sport, thus opening the way for representatives of the NCAA, Association for Intercollegiate Athletics for Women, armed forces or similar sanctioning bodies to have a voice on a national governing body.

If there is a weakness in the act, however, it may well be in the provision calling for "binding arbitration" in a dispute over which organization is to be the national governing body for a particular sport.

The complaint procedure, as stipulated in the act, says that any interested person who thinks a national governing body is not in conformity with the various criteria may file a complaint with the Olympic Committee and be heard formally by a disinterested group of USOC executive board members. The act goes on to provide that if either the complaining party or the national governing body is dissatisfied with the findings of the hearing panel, it may take the matter to binding arbitration under the auspices of the American Arbitration Association. Under the act, the USOC or the arbitrators may place the national governing body on probation or altogether revoke the USOC's recognition of that national governing body.

Actually, the provision for binding arbitration is not unique to the 1978 act. It was first placed in the USOC constitution in 1974. Thus, arbitration is both USOC constitutional policy as well as Federal law. Whether it is workable is another matter.

In 1977, the U.S. Wrestling Federation (USWF) files a demand for arbitration against the incumbent national governing body in wrestling, the wrestling division of the AAU. It is the intent of the USWF to replace the AAU as the USOC-recognized national governing body. In September 1978, after extensive hearings before three independent arbitrators appointed under the procedures of the American Arbitration Association, the arbitrators issue their award, stating that the USWF is in fact entitled to replace the AAU wrestling division as the national governing body member of the U.S. Olympic Committee for the sport of wrestling. The award subsequently is confirmed in Federal courts. However, the decision of the arbitrators and the courts never is carried out.

When the USOC board is called upon to implement the decision, it takes the position that it cannot recognize the USWF as its national governing body for wrestling until the USWF is recognized by the international sports federation for wrestling, FILA. "In effect," says attorney Scott, "the USOC 'punted' on the meaning of its own binding arbitration award and handed the matter to the international federation abroad."

In 1979, FILA declares that it will decide for itself the identity of its member in the United States and that it (FILA) is not bound by decisions of United States courts or the American Arbitration Association.

"Congress has no power . . . to pass a law which regulates either the IOC or any of the international federations," explains Scott, "and we presently are witnessing what may be the beginning of a major confrontation between this country and the international federations on the subject of whether the arbitration procedures under the Amateur Sports Act or the private international federations are to dictate the question of national governing body status. The question is enormously important, since if the international federations are in the last analysis to prevail, then challenge arbitrations under the act are for all practical purposes meaningless."

But, this weakness notwithstanding, the act appears to have the potential for bringing to a close a dispute that was beginning to assume proportions of the Hundred Years' War.

"I frankly believe," says Scott in a September 19, 1980, speech at Syracuse University, "that the act in its infancy is showing strong signs of good health . . . . To date, at least, the organizational conflicts which have plagued amateur sport for so many years appear either to have been solved or to be quiescent . . . . It, of course, remains to be seen whether the end product will be the shared objective of us all — an amateur sports structure which produces the best opportunities for participation and excellence for the most number of Americans — but it seems to me we have cause for optimism at this point."

If Scott is right, and if the act fulfills the intent of Congress, then it well may be said to have been a peace worth fighting for.

CHAPTER SIX

" . . . the electronic free ticket."

Art often foreshadows science, as is the case with two cartoons from the 1870s, each of which precedes major developments in the field of electronic communications. On March 15, 1877 — this being the year after Alexander Graham Bell first demonstrates his telephone — the New York Daily Graphic prints a drawing depicting a perspiring, wild-eyed orator shouting into a primitive microphone, out of which emerges a tangle of wires carrying the speaker's voice to Boston, Peking, San Francisco and other cities. Given the invention of the telephone, it is perhaps not that big a step to discern the coming of radio. But in an even more surprising artistic prediction, this one appearing in an 1879 edition of Punch, artist George Dumaurier shows two people sitting by a fireplace viewing a sporting event on a screen placed over the mantle. An announcer's voice is coming over the telephone.[4]

In the space of two years, these cartoonists have predicted not just radio and television but, in the case of Dumaurier, the linking of these two electronic developments with sport. Only a few more years will go by before the actuality of sports broadcasting will make itself felt throughout America.

A crude sort of sports broadcasting takes place before the turn of the century when, in 1898, the Dublin Daily Express charters a steamer fitted with antenna to follow the racing yachts in the Kingston Regatta. The steamer's radio sends back coded "wireless" mes-

[4]Barnouw, Erik; "A Tower in Babel," Oxford University Press, New York, 1966, page 7.

sages (practically a minute-by-minute account of the race) to a shore station. The messages then are decoded and telephoned to the newspaper, where they are printed.

As telegraphy and telephony begin to establish themselves as viable businesses, there is growing demand for further technical innovation; it is only natural that the American colleges should become involved in this burgeoning field of electronic communication. It is Reginald A. Fessenden, a professor of electrical engineering at Western University (now the University of Pittsburgh), who achieves a major breakthrough in 1901 by superimposing his voice on an electrical wave, thus transmitting the human voice without the use of wires.

This early type of wireless radio sees limited military use during World War I. After the war, radio quickly comes to play an everyday role in the life of the nation. In fact, radio's growth is as much social phenomenon as technical advance.

As an example of radio's proliferation, we find in 1920 only one station, KDKA in Pittsburgh, licensed to broadcast; but by 1922, there are more than 500 radio stations on the air, including 72 operated by colleges and universities.[5]

The early 1920s also mark the beginning of what has since come to be known as "The Golden Age of Sport," and it is not surprising that sports soon become a radio broadcasting staple. The earliest radio broadcasts consist of news, music and religious programming, but it isn't long before RCA general manager David Sarnoff seizes the opportunity to broadcast to the nation's sports-minded public. On July 2, 1921, RCA broadcasts the heavyweight title fight between Jack Dempsey and Georges Carpentier from Jersey City, New Jersey. Thanks to the enthusiastic support of fight promoter Tex Rickard, the bout is broadcast in about 100 theaters, dance halls and fraternal lodges in the Eastern United States, most of which levy a $1 admission charge with the proceeds to go for "aid to devasted France." An estimated 300,000 listen to the fight, and sports broadcasting is on its way to becoming a national phenomenon.

The broadcasting of college sports begins less than a year and a half after the Dempsey fight, when American Telephone and Telegraph's corporately owned station WEAF in New York City broadcasts play-by-play coverage of the October 28, 1922, Princeton vs. University of Chicago football game via long distance lines from Stagg Field, Chicago. Four weeks later, WEAF broadcasts the Harvard vs. Yale

[5]Ibid, page 4.

game from New Haven, Connecticut.

During the 1920s, Americans by the millions raise radio from the status of novelty to that of household necessity. Americans spend $222 million on radio sets in 1923 and then nearly triple that figure over the next five years, reaching $650 million by 1928.

By the early 1930s, the proliferation of radio (it becomes available in cars in 1927) is fast making sports broadcasting — particularly the games of major-college football teams — an entertainment commonplace. All of this is well and good for the radio stations and their listeners. However, the colleges providing the sports events seem to have some confusion as to how to deal with the electronic media.

In the beginning, many colleges simply give away radio rights, rationalizing that the broadcast provides more publicity for the team. Some schools, realizing that the product made available free on the radio might hurt gate attendance, charge rights fees to the broadcasting companies.

The first concerted approach to the question of college sports broadcasting comes from the Southwest Athletic Conference. The seven institutions making up the conference vote to sell all radio rights to conference games to a major oil company sponsor for a fee of $14,000, to be shared equally among conference teams, with an additional $300 per game to be paid to the home team whose game is broadcast.

Elsewhere in the country, the whole issue of broadcast "rights" seems considerably cloudier than it does in the Southwest Conference. On the one hand, the radio stations are arguing that the broadcasting of games is a public service for which the station should not be required to pay; on the other hand, the colleges are countering with the argument that the radio station is in fact capitalizing on this "public service" by selling advertising time and that radio broadcasts may diminish the return from ticket sales.

At the same time (the early 1930s), colleges begin to feel some of the effects of the Great Depression. Paid attendance at college games is down, though it is still a matter of some conjecture and argument as to whether the decrease is due to the economic bad times or to the availability of games on the radio. By 1935, the effects of radio on gate attendance and the entire issue of broadcast rights reaches the floor of the NCAA Convention. C. L. Eddy, delegate from the Case School of Applied Science, presents this assessment of the conflicting viewpoints of the large and small schools:

"There is a difference of opinion with regard to the broadcasting of football games. Most of the larger institutions broadcast their important games, feeling that the number of their friends interested so far exceeds the seating capacity that broadcasting is not likely to reduce their attendance. On the other hand, the smaller institutions feel that broadcasting definitely cuts down their attendance, and hence it is not a wise policy to broadcast."

Be it due to the broadcasting of games or the economic convulsions of the Depression, attendance at college football games is down about 15 percent in 1934. It is no doubt more than coincidental that the 1935 Convention — even though football attendance has staged a slight recovery in 1935 — appoints a three-man special committee charged with studying the effects of radio broadcasting on attendance at intercollegiate athletic contests.

After a survey of faculty representatives and athletic directors, the special committee reports in 1936 that "a satisfactory answer to the important question of whether radio broadcasting adversely affects attendance at athletic events appears difficult, if not impossible, to obtain." The only finding reported with certainty is that there exists a consensus among officials of the lesser athletic powers that the broadcasting of their games or the broadcasting in their area of the games of major national powers *does* reduce gate attendance.

In regard to the issue of broadcast rights, the committee is more definitive, reaching a conclusion that later will become a fact of broadcasting life; namely, that "the broadcasting privilege is a proper subject of sale."

The committee goes on to offer the conclusions that a visiting team has no right to award broadcast privileges except as granted through the courtesy of the home team and that no athletic conference arbitrarily can bind all its members to any sale of broadcasting rights.

The NCAA's longstanding philosophy of home rule clearly is evident where radio is concerned. The Association at this stage merely determines that broadcasting rights do exist and may be sold by a member institution. Hereafter, the matter rests in the hands of the individual colleges.

The nationwide upswing in attendance in the late 1930s seems to indicate that for the average fan, seeing the game is preferable to sitting beside the family radio. Radio, by its very nature and by the nature of sport, does not pose major problems. It will be another story with television.

Early Days of Television

It is with great reluctance that the Westinghouse Corporation in

1919 grants Vladimir K. Zworykin, one of its engineers and a former communications specialist in Russia's czarist army, permission to pursue his experiments with television. At first, Westinghouse officials see little hope of television becoming a reality. They are amazed when in December 1924, five years after giving approval to Zworykin's experiments, the engineer produces and successfully demonstrates to corporate executives the first electronic television system.[6]

By the mid-1920s, other firms have begun experimenting with television. In 1927, AT&T holds a public demonstration of television in New York City. Throughout 1928, General Electric conducts television tests over experimental station W2XAD. On September 11, 1928, the first television drama takes place; it is the play "The Queen's Messenger," with the video portion supplied by W2XAD and the audio coming over radio station WGY.[7]

As was the case with radio, it does not take long before sports and television begin the first flirtations of what will lead to a seemingly indissoluble, if occasionally stormy, marriage.

"Sports events proved an especially powerful attraction. In every television city, groups clustered around tavern TV sets," says historian Erik Barnouw describing the early days of television.[8]

The first intercollegiate sports telecast occurs on May 17, 1939, when NBC experiments with the telecast of a Columbia-Princeton baseball game played at Baker Field. The first football telecast is a 1940 Pennsylvania vs. Maryland game at Franklin Field in Philadelphia.

Television's development and popular acceptance are slowed by World War II; but in the first few years after the end of the war, television quickly asserts itself as one of the country's dominant entertainment mediums. It is proving itself at the expense of movies, radio and, not surprisingly, sports.

In the mid-1950s, cities with television stations begin to note waves of theater closings (64 theaters close in Chicago, 55 in New York); radio listening drops measurably; restaurants and night clubs reportedly feel the impact; book sales are down — and there is a marked decline in attendance at sports events in most TV cities.[9]

[6]Ibid, page 66.

[7]Ibid, page 231.

[8]Barnouw, Erik; "The Golden Web," Oxford University Press, New York, 1968, page 244.

[9]Ibid, page 286.

Concern by the NCAA

By 1948, the NCAA membership is concerned enough about television that it devotes part of its annual Convention to a round-table discussion on the effects of game broadcasts on gate attendance.

The discussion only serves to underscore the widely held belief among the member institutions that television does, in fact, pose a threat to in-stadium attendance and gate receipts. In 1949, though there are still only three million television sets in the country, the NCAA commissions Crossley, Inc., of New York to conduct a study on the impact of television on football game attendance. Researchers gather information in only four East Coast cities, and the results prove inconclusive. The research notwithstanding, many colleges continue to believe they are being hurt by the unrestricted telecasting of major games; the subject is once more a major issue at the January 1950 NCAA Convention. This time, the membership deems the television question pressing enough to warrant appointment of a Television Committee, charged with examining the whole issue of college sports on television. Later in 1950, acting on its own initiative, the Big Ten Conference announces that none of the games played by its member institutions will be televised during the 1950 season.

Meanwhile, the NCAA Television Committee approaches the major networks and forms a joint research committee to unearth further data regarding the effects of television on game attendance. The complexity of the problem and the contradictory nature of much of the existing research prompts this joint committee to seek the help of the National Opinion Research Center (NORC), a nonprofit social research group affiliated with the University of Chicago.

Before the 1950 football season, the NCAA asks the NORC to evaluate and summarize all existing surveys and to recommend a research program that will provide the Association with definitive findings. The first NORC report, based on existing data and given to the NCAA in August 1950, does, in fact, support the position that television has an adverse effect on attendance. Further research carried out by the NORC during the 1950 season and given to the NCAA in 1951 shows unmistakably that, whereas football attendance increases in areas without television, it decreases when facing television competition. The attendance losses, as we might expect, are greatest in areas where there is the largest television set ownership and in those areas where more local games are available on television. The largest losses attributable to television occur among colleges telecasting their own home schedules. Across the nation, the reduction in college football attendance directly attributable to football on television is 11.4 percent from the 1947-48 pretelevision average.

Television Restrictions

In 1950, there are virtually no restrictions on football telecasting. But in 1951, as a result of the NORC's preliminary studies, the NCAA, through its TV committee, launches a program of limited telecasting with designated games of the week and with some "blackout Saturdays" for each area. The blackouts are intended to enable researchers to evaluate more accurately television's effect on attendance.

At the same time the NCAA adopts its program of experimental television controls, it directs the TV committee to develop by 1952 a more comprehensive plan for the controlled televising of college football. The NCAA's approach to television is, at this stage, the most farsighted of any of the nation's major sports bodies.

While the experimental television controls and blackouts of 1951 may help the researchers, they do nothing to reverse the continuing decline in game attendance. This does not surprise TV committee members Thomas J. Hamilton and Ralph Furey, who claim in the 1951 TV committee report that most college administrators "well knew, even before the first scientific studies...that the problem being built up by the new television medium was a real poser and would have to be solved successfully — and speedily — if collapse was to be avoided in the existing structure of intercollegiate football."

The Association's action is speedy and decisive. By an overwhelming vote of 163 to 8, the 1952 NCAA Convention endorses a television policy, the keys to which are found in the words "limited," "live" and "controlled."

The 1952 NCAA Television Policy

The 1952 NCAA television policy is based on the now generally accepted belief that "unrestricted live television would seriously jeopardize the future of college football and the intercollegiate, intramural, athletic and physical training programs dependent upon football." This belief then must be reconciled with another widely held belief among members that, in the words of a TV committee report, "efforts should be continued to find ways to promote the public interest in television without destroying attendance at college football games."

The Association clearly wants to find ways to live with this communications giant. Indeed, preliminary results of the NORC surveys, as well as the TV committee's research, show that the two extreme positions are untenable. A complete ban on televised football likely would encounter great public displeasure, while a return to totally unrestricted television would continue and probably accelerate the decline in attendance. Thus, the membership's directive to the 1952 TV committee is to design a plan establishing a *modus vivendi*. The resolution reads, in part:

> "...that the members of the NCAA agree upon a program of *limited live television for 1952, controlled and directed by the NCAA* (italics added) and having the following objectives:
> 1. To minimize the adverse effects of live television upon attendance at college and high school football games.
> 2. To spread television, within the limits of such controlled plan as may ultimately be adopted, among as many colleges as possible.
> 3. To provide television to the public to the extent consistent with the first two objectives."

The Association further resolves that no member shall make any television commitment for the 1952 season prior to the presentation and adoption by the membership of the TV committee's plan. No one is quite sure what the plan will contain; but whatever it is, the approach to television is to be a united one.

This eight-man 1952 TV committee is chaired by Robert A. Hall of Yale and has a four-man steering committee made up of Hall; the Association's newly appointed executive director, Walter Byers; J. Shober Barr of Franklin and Marshall College, and ECAC Commissioner Asa S. Bushnell. It is Bushnell who ultimately will be responsible for the implementation of the plan. While there is a great deal of discussion about placing on the steering committee a television executive sympathetic with the college viewpoint, it finally is decided that the committee might be better served by Bushnell because of his complete familiarity with college athletic administration. The choice is a sound one. Asa Bushnell will be the NCAA's television director from 1952 to 1970, during which time college football in general and televised football in particular will enjoy unprecedented and almost uninterrupted success.

The committee goes to work in February 1952. After conversations with all interested parties — networks, stations, set manufacturers, advertising agencies, potential sponsors and various consultants — it reports to the membership in May that it has a plan embodying "as completely as possible the three basic principles established by the Association's directive."

The main provisions of the plan submitted to the membership for a referendum vote are:

1. Twelve Saturday afternoon dates shall be made available for "sponsored network telecasts."
2. Sponsor or sponsors must provide national coverage on each of the 12 dates.
3. There will be only one game telecast nationally on each of the 12 dates, except that small-college games of regional interest may be added or substituted by local stations.
4. The 12 games in the series "shall be widely distributed geographically with respect to their points of origin."
5. Games other than those in the series may be telecast only with the specific approval of the NCAA Television Committee.
6. A member college may appear on television only once per season.
7. No member college shall be obligated to televise any of its games, home or away.
8. "Sponsor(s) shall be organizations of high standards which meet traditional college requirements of dignified presentation."

When balloting closes on June 8, the referendum produces an impressive majority of 185 to 15, or 92 percent of the membership voting in favor of the committee's plan. A follow-up study of these results shows that the minority is not made up solely of colleges opposed to television limitations, but also includes some institutions still advocating the elimination of televised college football.

Other Television Dangers

When the TV committee first sets about its complicated business, it is concerned chiefly with the dangers posed by unlimited football telecasting. The committee is not far along in its interviews, however, when it begins to realize that while television's threat to gate revenues may be the most obvious problem, it is by no means the most insidious question posed by television. A potentially more disturbing threat to the future of college football is inherent in the financial and publicity rewards to be reaped by some schools for their participation in nationally or regionally televised games. In a special letter accompanying the 1952 television referendum, the TV committee sounds this warning:

> "(The TV committee) is convinced that any previous rewards for athletic success pale in comparison to the rewards of television, which constantly multiply as more television sets are installed . . . and the networks expand to all corners of the nation . . . . The rights for a few network games, now measured in thousands of dollars, will be measured in millions of dollars . . . . The 1952 Television Committee of the NCAA is of the unanimous conviction that steps must be taken by the colleges of the nation to meet this problem."

The committee's immediate answer to the problem is " . . . to urge most strongly the continuation of the one-appearance rule."

First Network Contract

After adopting the television plan for 1952, the TV committee on June 24 declares itself ready to receive bids from networks, agencies and sponsors interested in acquiring rights to the 1952 NCAA football television series. A bid of $1,144,000 by NBC appeals to the steering committee because at this time, NBC is the nation's leading sports network; in addition, its bid includes the promises that it will promote the series via a vigorous publicity campaign and will create a special NCAA football production unit solely for these telecasts. The network agrees to aid in researching the effects of television on college football. The TV committee awards the contract to NBC; and by late August, the network has signed the country's largest corporation, General Motors, as a sponsor.

It is NBC and General Motors that select the games to be broadcast in this inaugural season of the agreement. The NCAA TV committee participates only to the extent of assuring that the final schedule meets the stipulations of the plan.

The first NCAA football national telecast schedule: September 20, Texas Christian at Kansas; September 27, Princeton at Columbia; October 4, Michigan at Stanford; October 11, Texas A&M at Michigan State; October 18, Cornell at Yale; October 25, Purdue at Illinois; November 1, Ohio State at Northwestern; November 8, Oklahoma at

Notre Dame; November 15, Alabama at Georgia Tech; November 22, Southern California at UCLA; November 29, Army vs. Navy at Philadelphia.

True to its word, NBC launches a publicity program that, combined with the wide appeal of college football, produces one of the highest-rated sports shows in television history.

A special season preview, "Kickoff 1952," airs September 14 and is dedicated to football's "Grand Old Man," Amos Alonzo Stagg, who makes a personal appearance on the show. The network hires Dave Camerer, a former Dartmouth football player, to serve as media information officer and issue weekly news releases on forthcoming games. NBC also provides a theme for half-time shows, wherein announcer Bill Henry interviews various college presidents and high-ranking administrators regarding the value of sport in American education.

The series is a hit from the beginning. The opening game is carried by 63 stations, seen on 18,711,800 television sets and receives a Neilsen rating of 33.1 (i.e., the percentage of all sets tuned to the NCAA game). The share of audience (i.e., percentage of sets in use tuned to the game) is a dominating 61.8. And this is only the beginning. On November 29, the Army vs. Navy game is seen on a record 20 million television sets, draws a 50.0 Neilsen rating and a 75 share of audience. The game is carried on a 65-station hookup, the largest network to carry a college football game up to this point.

In keeping with the NCAA's objective of gaining some television exposure for smaller colleges playing regionally popular games, NBC persuades each of the stations carrying the game-of-the-week telecast to substitute a local game on at least one Saturday during the season. As a result, 51 different college teams appear on television during the 1952 season.

A particularly farsighted provision of this first television plan is the "sold-out, nondamaging clause." This states that games sold out in advance may be made available to television *if* such is the wish of both schools and *if*, in the opinion of the TV committee, this can be done without appreciable damage to other football games being played in the area.

Still, there are problems. In 1952, college football attendance continues its downward trend. There is speculation among NCAA member institutions as to whether there ever can be a productive coexistence between college sports and television. Doubt grows when the research firm of Benson and Benson reports following the 1952 season that "beyond doubt . . . the competition of televised games continues to hurt college football attendance."

At first glance, the figures tell a sad story. For the country as a whole, paid attendance at college football games in 1952 is about what it was in 1951. However, among those colleges facing television competition, there is a 16 percent decrease in attendance from the pretelevision 1947-48 base. Meanwhile, those colleges that are not exposed to any television competition see a 10 percent attendance increase over the base. Closer analysis, however, shows that this first comprehensive plan for televised sport does, in fact, accomplish its primary objective — it reverses not the loss, but the *rate of loss*.

For example, in 1950, when there are no restrictions on telecasting, colleges in heavily saturated television areas (heavily saturated being defined by researchers as areas where 40 percent or more of the families own television sets) experience a 25 percent decrease in attendance, while colleges in nontelevision areas enjoy a 15 percent increase. Thus, under conditions of unrestricted television in heavily saturated areas, television produces a 40 percent decline in expected in-stadium attendance. In 1952, however, with the NCAA television plan in effect, the differential between the loss in attendance in television areas and the gain in attendance in nontelevision areas is not 40 percent but 26.7 percent, which, according to the 1952 NORC report, "reflects the success of the NCAA plan in reducing the attendance losses which would otherwise have occurred in TV areas."

But the NCAA TV committee is under no rosy illusions. "The more television, the greater the loss; the less television, the less the hurt," the committee reports after the 1952 season. It does concede to researchers the point that "without the limited program, it is not hard to estimate what would have happened to attendance." What would have happened is that in-stadium attendance would have been 13 percent worse than it was.

Legal Issues

Continuing decline in football attendance is not the only problem facing the Association's TV committee. There also arises the crucial legal question of whether or not controlled television is in restraint of trade.

From the beginning of discussion about controlled television, a small segment of the Association's membership and others outside the college community (particularly those concerned with a plan of restricted television being launched by the National Football

League) take the position that restrictions on the right to telecast constitute illegal infringements on the autonomy and privilege of individual institutions. The NCAA hesitates to go ahead with its plan when, on October 9, 1951, the U.S. Justice Department brings suit against the National Football League, seeking to enjoin the league from continuing its plans for controlled television. However, there is no direct threat to the NCAA following the Justice Department's announcement that action against the NFL is a test case and that no action will be taken against other sports or leagues until there is a ruling in the NFL case.

The NCAA TV committee attorney, Joseph L. Rauh Jr., together with Dean Charles B. Nutting of the University of Pittsburgh law school and Ralph W. Aigler of the University of Michigan law school, examines the question and urges the NCAA to go ahead with the television plan. Says Aigler in January 1952: " . . . I have talked about it (the TV plan) with a good many men around the United States, men who were distinguished law teachers, men who were distinguished at the bar, with very large practice and experience in antitrust litigation; (and) on the basis of my own study, on the basis of what I have learned from them, I would have no hesitancy in saying to the NCAA as my client, 'you are not running any great risk in going ahead.' "

Aigler is right. On November 12, 1953, a Federal court in Philadelphia rules that controlled television, if reasonable, is a legal restraint of trade. The decision puts the NCAA's television plan on firm legal ground.

A Serious Threat to Attendance

But the idea of "living with" television — indeed, of it being possible to live with television — still is not on firm economic ground. So rapid is the proliferation of television that by 1953, two-thirds of the families in the nation own a set and nine-tenths of all colleges are in statistically defined "heavy-saturation" areas. Furthermore, one-tenth of all colleges remaining outside television areas are small schools in terms of football attendance. Research also shows that one-third of the families that do not own a television set are, for the most part, not college football fans. As far as college football is concerned, television has blanketed the country. And the NCAA is still looking for a *modus vivendi*.

"It is the sense of the member institutions," says 1952 committee Chair Robert A. Hall of Yale University, "to continue to take the middle road between those institutions . . .who would ban live television completely and those institutions . . .who would, by rejection of all action, permit the monopolization of television by the very few . . . ."

In 1953, the second year of a television plan, the TV committee, now chaired by Robert J. Kane of Cornell University, states its not yet wholly supportable belief that "the future of NCAA policy lies neither in a complete ban of live television at the one extreme nor in unrestricted live television at the other extreme, but rather in the middle course of moderation and reasonableness."

The 1953 television plan retains the one-appearance rule and provides for geographic considerations in scheduling so that colleges in all parts of the country have an opportunity for television appearances. The plan is approved by a 95.3 percent majority of the Association's membership. The game of the week once again will be carried by NBC, this year with an increase in the rights fee from $1,144,000 to $1,723,366. Again, the television series is successful, achieving an average 61.4 share of audience; but as the nation's television sets click on, the college's turnstiles click ever more slowly. Attendance drops 3.5 percent from 1952, forcing the TV committee to report following the 1953 season: "The televising of college football games continues to constitute a serious threat to attendance . . . and to the future of both intercollegiate football and the athletic and physical education programs dependent upon it."

The Trend Reverses

The dramatic turnaround comes suddenly in 1954. This year begins an almost unbroken 26-year trend of increased game attendance and strong television ratings. College football at last seems to have learned to live profitably with television, or with what one member calls "the electronic free ticket." The reason for this suddenly compatible relationship lies partly in the Association's restrictions and controls and partly in the curious nature of the individual college football fan.

The most interesting characteristic of the college football ticket buyer, researchers say, is that he is less a fan of college football than he is a fan of some particular college football team. NORC researchers report to the NCAA in the early 1950s that "most fans concentrate their interest — and, to an even greater degree, their attendance — on one, two or three teams." A study of college football fans in Boston and Pittsburgh conducted for the NCAA shows that four-fifths of the college football fans in both cities concentrate more than two-thirds of their attendance on the games of only one college. With a policy of unrestricted television, such as existed in the disastrous season of 1950, many of these fans could stay home, assured of being able to watch their favorite college team on television. However, with the advent of the game of the week and the "one-appearance" rule, the individual fan is likely to see his favorite team on television only once at most and, more likely, not at all. Thus, since 1952, even though the college football fan is assured of seeing a game on television each week of the season, he nonetheless must buy a ticket when he wants to see his favorite team.

Even before the 1954 attendance increase, the NORC says of the NCAA's one-appearance rule, "It was this feature of the NCAA plan which helped most to shave the attendance losses in television areas in spite of television saturation."

In 1955, the Association modifies the one-appearance rule to permit a maximum of two television appearances by a member school, thus maintaining restriction in principle while adding a degree of scheduling flexibility. Fortunately, the ruling does not slow down the now-accelerating trend of in-stadium attendance increases.

From 1955 to 1959, college football attendance increases from 17.3 million to 19.6 million; and, though television ratings drop slightly, advertiser interest remains strong and rights fees paid to the Association climb from $1.25 million in 1955 to $2.2 million in 1959. During this period, the NCAA maintains a consecutive series of one-year contracts with NBC. Beginning in 1955 and continuing to 1959, the network adopts a policy of using the same principal announcers for each national telecast. In this period, Lindsey Nelson and Red Grange become known to millions of viewers as the voices of college football.

The relationship between college football and the television industry is so stable during the 1955-59 period that the TV committee feels compelled to report in 1959 that this "degree of stabilization (is) sufficient to warrant the NCAA's negotiation of longer-term contracts . . . such arrangements would make the football program more attractive to national sponsors seeking continuity in their advertising and would strengthen the NCAA's television position."

Thus, in 1960, the NCAA for the first time adopts a two-year plan, signing a $3,125,000 per year contract with CBS. These will be the only two years that the NCAA is under contract to CBS. The network announces that its choice as announcer for the games is Curt Gowdy, a still relatively obscure former play-by-play man for the Boston Red Sox.

The Successful 1960s

The 1960 season is as symbolic as it is successful. While 1954 is important because it marks the reversal of the downward trend in game attendance, 1960 perhaps is even more significant because it sees college football attendance restored to the levels of the pretelevision era.

Aggregate crowds of 20,403,409 — an all-time record and nearly three-quarters of a million more people than watched games in 1949, the last of the truly pretelevision years — attend 2,711 college football games. The showing is more impressive in light of the fact that in 1960, nearly 75 percent of all college football games are played opposite a regional or network game telecast. But the lure of live action proves irresistible. In the end, the loyalty of the college football fan to his team and his apparent desire to "be there" is what permits college football to live so productively with network television.

In its postseason analysis, the 1960 TV committee regards the record attendance "as proof that the NCAA Football Television Plan, given time to produce the benefits which it seemed to promise from the outset, has accomplished the objective which has always been paramount — to preserve and promote the game of intercollegiate football. The committee believes that continued restrictions will bring continued advantages."

The committee's premise proves true. In-stadium attendance increases steadily from 20.7 million in 1961 to 22.2 million by 1963. Remarkably, television ratings also move sharply upward, from 11.6 to 13.4 in the same three-year period. Television and college football seem locked in a constant upward spiral. Even the now-surging popularity of the National Football League seems to have little or no effect on the college game, as eloquently noted by football historian Allison Danzig in the December 2, 1963, New York Times:

> "The interest in intercollegiate football has been tremendous all season. In the light of the figures, the constant belittling of the college game and the claims that its public is deserting it for the professional brand can hardly be taken seriously . . . . Texas and Oklahoma played to 75,504, their 18th successive sellout. Attendance records for a single game have been set this year at

Penn State, Army, Navy, Notre Dame, Tennessee, Georgia
Tech, Florida, Kansas and Washington, as well as at other
colleges.... Though an image has been created of the professional player as a fire-eating gladiator, impervious to pain and a
Goliath of monstrous strength, the public still turns out 22
million strong to see the poor little puny college upstart die for
dear old Siwash."

A Threat from the Pros

Danzig's reference to the professional game is not without merit.
Professional football experiences its own surge in popularity in the
years following the now-famous Baltimore Colts-New York Giants
overtime championship game of 1958. By 1961, the NFL actively
considers expanding its television coverage to include both Sundays
and Saturdays. NCAA TV committee Chair James J. Corbett of
Louisiana State University sees the possibility of professional football on Saturday as "a threat of dilution of the protection earned by
the colleges by voluntary imposition of restricted television for more
than a decade."

Congress agrees with Corbett. Federal legislation averts the threat
of competition from either live or filmed professional football on any
Saturday during the course of the college season. "It was particularly
gratifying to the Television Committee," says Corbett, "to note this
undeniable evidence of realization by the Congress of the United
States that college football is an asset to the country warranting
preservation."

The Continuing Spiral

The upward spiral of college football's popularity — live and on
television — continues unabated through the 1960s. In 1964, the
Association switches networks, moving from CBS back to NBC and
signing a two-year contract worth $6,522,000 per year. Televised
college football now is available in 99 percent of the country, prompting the 1964 TV committee to observe, "Football goes virtually
everywhere with television." In this year, the weekly telecast is seen
in an average of 12.7 million homes, with a major attraction such as
the Army-Navy game topping 17 million homes. Further measure of
the series' standing in the eyes of its sponsors is seen in the lineup of
major advertisers for 1965 — Chrysler, Gillette, Goodyear, RCA,
Texaco and United Airlines.

In 1966, its 16th year of restricted television, the Association breaks a precedent in its television negotiations. Rather than awarding broadcast rights via open bidding, the TV committee negotiates directly with ABC, the suddenly sports-oriented network that, from this year through 1981, will carry all NCAA weekly games. Backed by a 92.5 percent affirmative vote of the membership, the NCAA signs a two-year contract with ABC for $7.8 million per year.

The TV committee also liberalizes its two-year policy, agreeing to make a decision on future rights *before* the expiration of the contract. In effect, the 1966 contract with ABC is more like two consecutive two-year contracts, the understanding being, according to committee Chair Herbert J. Dorricott, that "if no substantial alterations of the 1966-67 plan are felt necessary by the NCAA membership or the TV committee, ABC retains the package for 1968-69." Under these terms, total rights fees for four years will amount to $32,200,000. The contract also provides for the first major exposure for smaller teams, specifying that four College Division championship games must be televised. Principal announcers for the ABC series are Chris Schenkel, Bill Flemming and former Oklahoma coach Bud Wilkinson, while a relative unknown by the name of Keith Jackson makes occasional appearances.

Again, as if there is no ceiling for it, the concurrent spiral of attendance and television ratings continues. For the four years of the ABC agreement (the two-year contract is renewed for 1968-69 by a near-record 96.1 percent majority vote of the membership), ratings increase from 12.3 to 13.9, while attendance goes from 25.3 million to 27.6 million.

Expanding Coverage

The most important facet of the NCAA's 1968-69 plan is its emphasis on expanding television coverage to other sports. In renewing its contract, ABC agrees to continue carrying the four College Division football championships and to add coverage of five other NCAA championship events — gymnastics, swimming, track, volleyball and wrestling. The network also adds a series of 11 weekly football highlight shows and a postseason highlight show. The contract renewal also introduces the concept of a "wild-card" game — a game the network may select at the last moment to be televised nationally in a double-header presentation. The network plays its wild card wisely, choosing the November 28 Notre Dame vs. Southern California game. The game breaks all existing college football television records, delivering 23.3 million homes and being seen by 37.3 million viewers.

Another new feature in the 1968-69 contract is the addition of two night-game telecasts to be allowed by the NCAA with the understanding that one of the games will be on the first Saturday of the season. This has the dual purpose, as explained by TV committee Chair William J. Flynn of Boston College, of "making the public conscious that college football is back in town . . . and at the same time showing college football to a tremendous audience in prime time."

The plan succeeds as never before in striking a near perfect balance between, as Flynn puts it, "giving the fans enough television but not so much as to hurt the gate." Despite the worst weather since 1962, college football attendance hits a record 27,055,846 in 1968, an increase of more than half a million over the previous year. In the larger perspective, through 15 seasons of uninterrupted increases, college football attendance has climbed 62 percent above the 1953 level.

Under the supervision of ABC Sports Director Roone Arledge, producer Chuck Howard and directors such as Chet Forte and Don Ohlmeyer, the technical quality of NCAA football telecasts rises to unprecedented heights. Video techniques such as dual isolation and slow-motion replay, along with expert analysis and color commentary, prompt the 1969 TV committee to agree with the network's claim that it is indeed "the nationally recognized leader in sports telecasting."

Part of the strength of the television series rests with those making the schedule. In this, network executives demonstrate a shrewdness bordering on clairvoyance. The network reaches a high point in scheduling savvy in 1969 when it schedules the December 6 Texas vs. Arkansas game for national television. An ABC staff memo, written before the college football season begins, says "(the) game could not only be for the Southwest Conference title, but for the national championship as well."

This prediction not only comes true, but, to combine luck with genius, President Richard Nixon attends the game. He takes time for a half-time interview with Chris Schenkel and, after the game, presents a "No. 1" plaque to Texas coach Darrell Royal. The postseason TV committee report notes of this bit of scheduling, "For ABC and college football this was a masterpiece — but no accident."

Two years later, in what committee Chair James H. Decker describes as "the scheduling heights," ABC chooses in *March* a schedule that later leads to television appearances by five unbeaten teams on the final three television dates of the season.

In 1969, the centennial year for college football, it perhaps is symbolic of the age that television and game attendance soar again to new heights. The television series reaches an all-time high of 15.6 million total homes per game, while game attendance is up more than a half-million to 27.6 million. One of the highlights of the season is an ABC one-hour special presentation in prime time — "One Hundred Years of College Football," a documentary capturing the spirit, tradition and color of the college game.

While measurably successful, the centennial season ends with the well-earned but much regretted retirement of Asa Bushnell as director of the TV program. Bushnell, the only program director during the first 18 years of the TV plan, is described by Flynn as "the backbone, the historian, the balance wheel, the guiding light (who) has handled all the big and little problems over the years."

The 1970s

Yet, such is the momentum of the television series and such is the widespread popularity of college football that even without Bushnell at the helm, the spiral continues whirling upward into the 1970s. In 1969, the NCAA signs another two-year agreement with ABC, this covering the 1970 and 1971 seasons at a rights fee of $12 million per year. The first year of the new contract produces more records, with 16.2 million average homes per game and a record single-game viewing audience of 37.3 million for the November 28 Notre Dame vs. Southern California wild-card selection.

Realizing the value of the scheduling flexibility offered by the wild-card provision, the Association liberalizes its next contract — again with ABC and covering the 1972 and 1973 seasons — to permit the network to delay selection of its last eight games of the series. Under this contract, ABC executives do not have to make these late-season selections until the Monday before a Saturday telecast, thus assuring the greatest possibility of presenting the most attractive and significant games on national television.

Once again, attendance continues to climb throughout the 1972 and 1973 seasons, reaching 31.3 million in 1973. And, while television ratings drop slightly, viewing remains strong at slightly better than a 12 Neilsen rating and a one-third share of audience. Rights fees during this period are now up to $13,490,000 per year, with the rate for one nationally televised game at $487,857 and a regional game at $355,000.

As has been the practice since 1952, the greater part of the rights fees goes to the institutions whose game is televised, while a small percentage — ranging from three to eight percent over the years — goes to the NCAA to cover the expenses of the TV committee and the implementation of the plan. Other NCAA services benefiting through the 1970s from this small assessment include the post-graduate scholarship program, football promotion activities, an expanded enforcement program, sports development projects, reimbursement for travel to championships and construction of the national office building.

Just when it appears that the marriage of college football and television is on its highest and firmest ground, there is a small but ominous sign of trouble. The 20-year climb of football attendance ends in 1974, when attendance slips from 31.3 to 31.2 million. It is a drop of only 0.15 percent, but it is enough to raise the question of whether or not the game is being overexposed. And that question might be given more legitimacy by the fact that as attendance drops, television ratings rise. Has the balance at last been upset?

No. Attendance moves upward again in 1975, and it appears that the 1974 dip was just a statistical spasm caused by the nationwide economic recession of that year. The 1975 attendance gains amount to a half-million, while television ratings get back over the 13 mark. This pattern of steadily rising attendance accompanied by strong ratings will carry on into the 1980s.

One of the biggest changes in the NCAA's approach to its television agreements comes in 1977. Following approval by a 304 to 65 vote of the Association's membership, the TV committee, chaired by Seaver Peters of Dartmouth College, awards a four-year contract (as opposed to consecutive renewable two-year contracts) to ABC. The contract runs from 1978 through 1981 at rights fees averaging $30 million a year. By 1981, a national television game is worth $600,000, while regional games carry rights fees of $426,779. Once again, the contract is aimed at gaining exposure for all levels of college football, requiring the network to air the Division I-AA, Division II and Division III Football Championships and the NCAA championships in five other sports. Beyond that, the plan leaves in the hands of network executives the actual selection of games to be broadcast and states specifically that " . . . neither the (TV) committee nor its members shall attempt to influence these selections."

Throughout its dealings with television, the Association maintains its adherence to the principle of home rule — no member institution need appear on television if, for any reason, it does not wish to — and adheres also to its principal of limited appearances. But in this case, there is a modification. There are now some special exceptions to the two-appearance rule, providing the possibility that some institutions may be allowed a third appearance on certain dates, such as Thanksgiving or for the wild-card game. However, no team may appear in a wild-card game more than once during any two-year period of the plan.

The contract benefits all NCAA-sponsored varsity sports since part of the eight percent of the rights fees going to the Association is earmarked to provide a major portion of the funds used to pay travel expenses of all participants in NCAA championship events. Other proceeds from the contract will continue to fund the postgraduate scholarship program and to pay the expenses of administering the television plan.

Historically, the most interesting feature of the 1978-1981 plan lies not in its differences from previous plans but in its fundamental similarity to the original plan designed in 1952. The primary objective is, almost word for word, the same as appeared three decades earlier:

"The purpose of this plan shall be to reduce insofar as possible the adverse effects of live television upon football game attendance and, in turn, upon the athletic and related educational programs dependent upon the proceeds therefrom."

Perhaps the only philosophic departure from previous plans is the intent of the 1978-1981 plan to permit more exposure for more schools, an intent clearly reflecting the will of the members. "When development of the 1978-1981 plan was undertaken," reports 1978 TV committee Chair Capt. John O. Coppedge, "the committee was advised that the NCAA membership favored exposure for a greater number of colleges, despite the long-held theory that games of general national interest would cause less harm to attendance at concurrent games than (would) regionalized television patterns presenting more games of significant local interest."

This objective is met immediately as the total number of teams appearing on football telecasts jumps from 55 teams accounting for 82 television appearances in 1977 to 76 teams accounting for 116 television appearances in 1978, the first year of the new plan.

This provision of the plan in no way damages game attendance, which rises to a record 34.3 million in 1978 and to 35.5 million in 1980 as the now much-traveled *modus vivendi* proves a fast track indeed.

In 1981, more exposure for more teams remains an important aspect of the football television negotiations. This added exposure comes in a different form, however. Once again, a four-year agreement is reached (for the 1982 through 1985 seasons), but this time the agreement is with *two* national networks as both ABC and CBS come to terms with the Association. The combined total for the new package negotiated by the NCAA Football Television Committee and its chair, Wiles Hallock of the Pacific-10 Conference, is $263.5 million, more than double the 1978-1981 figure. Team appearances grow from 116 to 140, a 20.6 percent increase.

Cable Television and ESPN

The NCAA's early grapplings with the issue of television focus mainly on the question of establishing and implementing a program that will allow the colleges to live compatibly and productively with the new medium. This step alone represents a rather sensible and, as we have seen, exceptionally farsighted approach. Television in the early days means conventional, freely available, sponsor-supported, over-the-air broadcasting. In the late 1940s and early 1950s, however, there are rumors of the coming development of subscription, or what is then called "pay-as-you-see," television. These rumors do not escape the attention of the Association's TV committee.

As early as 1952, committee Chair Robert Hall is reporting to the membership, "If television offers irresistible premiums for sports glory today, the TV committee wishes to point up and underline the more serious problem which will be posed when pay-as-you-see television arrives."

During these early years, there also are references to subscription television, the coming of which, in 1952, is seen as being no more than three years away. While the timetable is inaccurate and the technical language (e.g., pay-as-you-see) somewhat imprecise, the main point is that from its first consideration of television, the Association foresees and is concerned with the problems to be posed by the introduction of alternative forms of television delivery.

The originally estimated three years increases to nearly three decades, when in the late 1970s, it is subscription cable television that establishes itself as the dominant alternative form of delivery.

The lessons learned by the TV committee during its early struggles with conventional broadcasting enable the Association to deal effectively with cablecasting. A unique and widely beneficial program is arranged with one of the nation's leading cable networks, the Connecticut-based Entertainment and Sports Programming Network (ESPN).

In March 1979, the TV committee reaches agreement with ESPN for national cablecasts of intercollegiate contests of member institutions and allied conferences. The agreement is for two years — renewable at the NCAA's option after one year — and the regular-season segment carries a modest initial annual rights fee of $720,000, all of which is to go to the competing institutions. More significant is the content of this national series. For the first time, a great number of the nation's lesser-known colleges will gain the benefit of national television exposure, and much of this exposure will come in sports seldom before seen on national television. Specifically, the contract will result in the cablecasting of a minimum of 230 intercollegiate games and events.

The agreement also provides that ESPN will present at least one cablecast of each NCAA championship in all three divisions. Rights for this programming are $420,000 per year, and use of the Association's name and marks adds $150,000 annually. An important exception here is that this provision does not include the NCAA basketball championship, which is committed to conventional network television. But for the first time, the traditionally less-visible sports such as cross country, fencing, skiing and water polo are assured contractually of at least one national telecast.

While the rights fees for the cablecasts are not comparable to those paid by the over-the-air networks, Capt. John O. Coppedge, chair of the TV committee, finds the arrangement with ESPN " . . . attractive, considering the newness of the venture and (of) the industry itself."

More Legal Issues

The proliferation of cable television systems during the 1970s, combined with the viewing public's continually increasing demand for sports programming, soon leads to the widespread practice of retransmission of over-the-air broadcasts by various nonnetwork cable companies. This raises several legal issues, among them the questions of copyright royalty payments and the legality of the NCAA's Football Television Plan.

A 1978 revision in the Federal Copyright Act requires for the first time that cable systems pay for retransmitting over-the-air broadcasts. As it is, a substantial majority of college sports telecasts fall under this requirement.

The revisions in the act set up an unusual system by which the cable television royalties are to be paid and received. Through the Copyright Royalty Tribunal, distribution of fees for 1978 are made. The tribunal rules that the right to recover royalty fees for cable retransmissions of sports event telecasts is held by several interest groups, among them the colleges and universities represented by the NCAA, unless the contract with the broadcaster of the event specifically states otherwise. The tribunal's decision is an important victory for college sports interests. The payment of nearly $200,000 claimed by the NCAA for the colleges it represents is a new and potentially important source of revenue for the college athletic programs.

In the issue regarding the legality of the NCAA's Football Television Plan, a Federal judge in Columbus, Ohio, in 1980 denies a cable television company's motion for a preliminary injunction that effectively would have suspended application of the plan. Warner-Amex Cable Communications, Inc., seeks the order so it can present cablecasts of Ohio State University football games on its QUBE system in Columbus. ABC-TV, the network carrying the NCAA football series, is a codefendant with the NCAA.

The judge holds that Warner failed to demonstrate a strong or substantial likelihood of success on the merits of its claim that it had been injured by the defendants' acts under the antitrust laws. He adds that Warner has failed to show that it would be irreparably injured if the court did not grant the injunction.

The preliminary injunction would have posed a significant threat of substantial harm to the defendants and the member institutions of the NCAA, the court holds. The court also rules that Warner had not demonstrated it would serve the public interest.

Following the ruling, Warner does make arrangements in order to comply with the NCAA Football Television Plan and presents the Ohio State telecasts.

Basketball and Television

On few related issues is the will of the Association's members as markedly diverse as it is on the matters of football and basketball on television. While there is overwhelming majority support for the NCAA's program of limited, live and controlled televised football, the approach to basketball remains more "laissez faire." Of course, college basketball, with its indoor arenas, smaller seating capacities and on-campus following, generally is less apt to suffer attendance damage because of television than is football, a game with far more seats to fill and one which can be affected greatly by the weather. It is perhaps not so surprising, therefore, that basketball television rights remain from the beginning in the hands of the individual colleges and the various conferences, with no NCAA restrictions.

The single and very important exception to this policy is the annual National Collegiate Division I Men's Basketball Championship.

The championship final (the Final Four) proves itself a strong television attraction as early as 1946, when it is broadcast locally for the first time by WCBS-TV in New York City. An estimated 500,000 see Oklahoma A&M (now Oklahoma State) beat North Carolina, 43-40, to become the first team to win consecutive NCAA titles.

The finals are telecast nationally for the first time in 1954; and beginning in 1963, there is a national telecast of the finals each year. But the full impact and benefit of television is not felt until 1969, when the NCAA signs a contract with NBC to televise the championship game. In this case, the game turns out to be an unprecedented third straight national title for UCLA. Return to the NCAA from sale of the broadcast rights amounts to $547,500, almost triple the return from previous national-championship telecasts.

Records come and go quickly in the 1970s, as college basketball enjoys its greatest surge of popularity. In 1971, NBC records the largest audience ever for a network telecast of the semifinals; in 1972, the UCLA vs. Florida State final becomes the highest-rated basketball broadcast of all time. The record is short-lived. A year later, the UCLA vs. Memphis State game, broadcast in prime time, gets a record 20.5 share and is seen in a record 13.5 million homes. By this time, the championship is so popular that NBC agrees to allow the TVS network to carry those early-round championship games not carried by NBC. In 1978, NBC expands its own early-round coverage to include the four regional championship games. Extending coverage still further, NCAA Productions — a production unit directly operated by the NCAA — televises all of the regional semifinals.

Under terms of the 1980-1981 contract between the NCAA and NBC, the network carries a minimum of 11 championship games in addition to those carried by TVS and NCAA Productions. But even this level of television exposure does not raise the specter of attendance damage. Tickets to the NCAA Division I Men's Basketball Championship finals usually are sold out — as many a chagrined fan can attest — nearly one year in advance.

A change occurs in 1981 as CBS Sports is awarded live domestic rights to televise the championships in 1982, 1983 and 1984, thus ending an 11-year span in which NBC aired the event. In addition to the tournament package, CBS also commits to broadcast regular-season college basketball games each year during the agreement. As in the past, NCAA Productions will carry any tournament games not aired by CBS.

Through technical advances that would have amazed observers of that 1939 Princeton vs. Columbia baseball telecast, the various events in the cablecast series are transmitted via satellite (RCA's Satcom I) to the receiving earth stations of those cable systems subscribing to the ESPN service. But outer space, earth stations and satellites not withstanding, the end result, the linking of sports with television, would not have amazed George Dumaurier, that Punch cartoonist whose brush predicted it all more than a century ago. Nor, most likely, will it surprise viewers a generation hence when the once-called "electronic free ticket" will still be bringing the best in intercollegiate athletics to what, collectively, may be the largest sports audience in the world. And if present trends continue, television will be serving its audience without making the originally feared inroads on game attendance. In the end, the success of college sports on television rests perhaps less with the viewer than with that fan who on many occasions shows that he prefers the bleachers to the armchair.

CHAPTER SEVEN

" . . . putting our athletic houses in order."

"Aidos is stolen away by secret gains."
Thus quoting the Greek poet Pindar, R. Tait McKenzie of the University of Pennsylvania on December 29, 1910, delivers to the NCAA Convention one of the most scholarly and eloquent addresses in the history of the Association. His talk — it approaches more nearly a lecture — is called "The Chronicle of the Amateur Spirit." In it, he traces the birth, growth, degeneration and renaissance of this spirit of amateurism or, as he calls it, this "aidos."

Aidos is a Greek word for which there is no exact English equivalent; but as McKenzie defines it, aidos is a quality " . . . opposed to both insolence and servility, that, while it puts into a man's heart the thrill and joy of the fight, restrains him from using his strength like a brute or from cringing to a superior force; that wins for him honor and respect, in victory or defeat, instead of terror from the weak and contempt from the strong. It includes the scrupulous respect for personal honor and fairness that would make a team elect to risk a probable defeat rather than win through the services of those who do not come within the spirit of a gentlemen's agreement. It is that spirit of modesty and dignity that obeys the law, even if the decisions seem unjust, instead of piercing the air with protestations."

It is this aidos, says McKenzie, that must be at the incorruptible core of amateurism. Historically, this has not always been the case; and McKenzie's lecture is well documented with examples, all of them predating intercollegiate sport by several centuries.

There is, in particular, the case of one Astylus of Croton who becomes, depending on one's point of view, either the world's first tramp athlete or the first victim of unprincipled recruiting. Astylus, an Olympic athlete in the first century B.C., establishes a lofty reputation by winning the prestigious stade race and the long race in two successive Olympics. Such victories reflect well on the citizenry of Croton. However, in the Olympics of 75 B.C., Astylus does not enter the competition as a representative of Croton; instead, influenced by the persuasions and inducements of the tyrant Hieron of Syracuse, Astylus enters and competes as a Syracusan. There being in these ancient times no legal sanctions against such perfidy — and most assuredly no sanctions against tyrants — the citizens of Croton feel compelled to show their displeasure by destroying all the statues of Astylus, banishing him from the city and converting the house they had given him into a common prison.

In historical fact, says McKenzie, transgressions against the spirit of aidos are almost as old as sport itself. The bribing of officials and competitors is frequent enough in the ancient Olympiads that, in the third century B.C., the Greeks place this inscription at the entrance to Olympic Stadium: "Not with money but with speed of foot and strength of body must prizes be won at Olympia."

McKenzie goes on to document the gradual decay of the amateur spirit, the concurrent rise of a professional class of athletes and finally the ultimate debasing of sport in the gladiatorial and wild-beast shows of the Romans — "this cesspool of athletic corruption and disgrace."

Fearful even at this early date that intercollegiate sport in the United States might suffer a degeneration of the spirit of amateurism, McKenzie pleads for "pursuit of (a) campaign to restore sport to those for whom it was designed, the regular student body." He decries what he sees as the tendency of increasing gate receipts and fast-growing publicity of college sports to put pressure on rules committees and athletic authorities "to consider the spectator rather than the man for whom the game should be designed ... it is the professional motive, which is gain, replacing the amateur motive, which is the thrill of the contest."

It must be frustrating to McKenzie as well as to the other delegates in the room that at this early juncture in the Association's history (so early that McKenzie's speech follows by just a few hours the resolution to change the name of the IAAUS to the NCAA), the organization is essentially an advisory educational association and not a regulatory body. Therefore, despite all of McKenzie's oratorical skill, the strongest action he realistically can suggest in 1910 is that the NCAA "cultivate by a campaign of education in player and spectator alike that wholesomeness of mind, that aidos... that makes the sting of defeat nothing when weighed with the consciousness of having won dishonorably."

Rhetoric is a long way from regulation. Members in these early days point to Articles 6 and 7 of the bylaws, these spelling out rather specifically the "Principles of Amateur Sport" (Article 6) and the list of "Eligibility Rules" (Article 7). But the practical fact is that the Association lacks the size, strength and inclination to enforce its own rules. Furthermore, such is the Association's uncompromising adherence to its fundamental principle of "home rule" (or "institutional control," as it will come to be known) that any measure of regulatory authority is not something that may be exercised, willy-nilly, by the officers of the Association. Rather, it remains a tightly held prerogative that first must be given by the membership. The general feeling in 1910 is that it is too early to give a four-year-old organization, however commendable its record thus far, this sort of power. Beyond this is the fact that the good intentions of Bylaws 6 and 7 are superseded by the all-important provisions of Article 8 of the constitution. Entitled "Control of Athletics," the article says that "... legislation enacted at a conference of delegates shall not be binding upon any institution if the proper athletic authority of said institution makes formal objection to same." And backing up this bit of constitutional thunder is the bylaw provision specifying that acceptance of any definite set of eligibility rules is not to be a condition of membership in the NCAA.

Up to now, the Association has concerned itself directly with the actual playing of games and only indirectly with the spirit with which these games are played. The Football Rules Committee is a compelling example of the effectiveness of cooperative effort in the regulation of on-field play. But attempted regulation of this spirit of amateurism, this amorphous aidos, will prove a more difficult challenge than legalizing the forward pass or prohibiting the flying tackle. To extend its influence into this sensitive area, the Association will have to reconcile its policies on amateurism and eligibility with its fundamental principle of institutional control. This can be done only by means of a mandate from the members, who, if McKenzie's speech is any indication, seem threatened enough by this corrosion of the spirit of amateurism to at least begin to think about collective action.

One of the first steps toward this broader policy of athletic self-regulation comes in December 1918, when the Convention authorizes appointment of a special committee appropriately called the Special Committee on Extending the Influence of the Association. The committee is to survey the membership to determine its main concerns with the conduct of intercollegiate athletics.

After analyzing questionnaires returned by more than 70 percent of the Association's membership, the committee reports in 1920 that there are three areas that are cause for concern among college presidents, athletic directors and faculty representatives: (1) " ... there is widespread suspicion, distrust, dissatisfaction and criticism relating to intercollegiate athletic practices. There is probably not a single educational institution in America carrying on intercollegiate athletic activities that is not under suspicion from some source or other;" (2) "There is general conviction that athletic standards have been growing steadily worse throughout the country since the war," and (3) "The ideals of the NCAA are endorsed by all the college presidents ... and other college officials with whom your committee has corresponded, and *there is a unanimous demand for a satisfactory remedy for the athletic evils under indictment.*" (Italics added.)

The committee concludes that the problem is so serious that it "justifies the investment of such time and money as may be necessary for its solution."

Arbitration Committee

On the evening of December 29, 1920, shortly after the special committee concludes its report, the Convention, at the request of President Palmer Pierce, gives the Nominating Committee authority to create a nine-member Arbitration Committee (one member from each NCAA district) "to deal with charges of proselyting or eligibility" and a three-member Central Committee (perhaps more accurately called an appeals committee) as "a court of last resort for such cases of proselyting or eligibility as are not cleared up by the local conference authorities or district representatives."

The idea is ahead of its time. The Central Committee hears no cases in its first year; and though Pierce cites "the advisability of making greater use of this agency," the committee goes through its second year with neither accusation nor rumor brought before it. Perhaps the best statement of the prevailing regulatory philosophy of this era, and one of the main reasons members are reluctant to make use of the Arbitration Committee, is put forth in 1920 by Yale President Arthur T. Hadley. In a letter to the NCAA Committee on Extending the Influence of the Association, Hadley writes: "My personal opinion is that the evils you mention cannot be effectively dealt with on the lines hitherto recommended by the NCAA. If A is an honorable businessman and has dealings with B, he assumes B is acting in good faith. If B's agents do not seem to be acting squarely, he keeps quiet until he has laid the facts before B; and B generally straightens the matter out. If B does not do so, A has the choice of two things — either to discontinue his dealings with B, or to keep on dealing and say nothing. It is not proper for A to continue his dealings with B and indemnify himself for his grievances by talking about them in public."

Hadley's remarks carry an image of the old gentlemen's club code and an undertone of laissez faire.

The 10-Point Code

The prevailing viewpoint as expressed by Hadley and the lack of real regulatory powers on the part of the Association do not stop the membership from taking the half step of declaring its principles in a 10-point code, adopted in December 1922. The code urges members to organize in sectional conferences (which presumably will have their own strict regulations regarding amateurism and eligibility). The other key points of the code, which members are "urged," but not directed, to adopt, include: abiding by the Association's definition of amateurism,[10] adopting the freshman rule, adopting rules against participation by members in professional football, limiting varsity eligibility to three years, eliminating participation by graduate students, maintaining absolute faculty control of athletics, suppressing betting and prohibiting participation on noncollege teams.

There is no question as to where the Association stands in principle; the only question is how to persuade all of its membership to stand with it. As late as 1926, in debate on the Convention floor, F. G. Folsom of the University of Colorado and the Rocky Mountain Conference says of so fundamental a tenet as the amateur rule, "This

---

[10] An amateur is defined by Article 7 of the constitution as " . . .one who engages in sport solely for the physical, mental or social benefits he derives therefrom, and to whom the sport is nothing more than an avocation." Any participation in sport for gain in any form is considered a violation.

amateur rule is a trespass upon the authority of a college to lay down its own rules and determine what is best for the students."

The nation's colleges gradually move toward a firmer policy of collective regulation. The reason is not that the ingrained desire for home rule gets weaker, but that the equally ingrained desire for highly principled athletics gets stronger.

The Carnegie Foundation Report

In 1930, the Carnegie Foundation completes and makes public a 14-year study of intercollegiate athletics. The study originally was made on petition of the NCAA. The findings are not entirely pleasant. Foundation investigators — after visiting 112 institutions, interviewing 86 college presidents and vice-presidents and a similar number of athletic directors, head coaches and others charged with the conduct of intercollegiate sports — find many instances of the recruitment and subsidization of athletes and report several cases where intercollegiate sport is not under faculty control but is rather unduly influenced by overzealous alumni and coaches.

Reactions to the report are mixed. Some feel it is unfair to single out specific schools or to generalize from specific violations, but the general attitude toward the report is probably best expressed by Dean C. W. Mendell of Yale, chair of the NCAA's Special Committee to Study Carnegie Foundation Bulletin No. 23. Mendell calls the report "...the first constructive view of the athletic situation....It is a friendly and useful report, and we believe that all the colleges, after reviewing their own code of sportsmanship, can wisely use it as a check on their own situation."

When the furor dies down, it appears that the Carnegie Foundation's report adds momentum to the growing trend toward athletic regulation and enforcement.

Investigations of Recruiting and Subsidizing

As college sport moves into the 1930s, there appears to be a growing doubt as to whether the problems connected with recruiting and subsidizing of athletes can be solved unless the NCAA is given a stronger regulatory role. In 1931, in remarks entitled "A Return to Sanity," E. K. Hall of Dartmouth, chair of the Association's Football Rules Committee, offers his prediction that "the day is steadily and rapidly approaching when the school or college which makes football a business instead of a sport will have great difficulty in finding suitable opponents." Hall goes on to urge the membership toward cooperative action against transgressor institutions; and, though he stops short of suggesting compulsory acceptance of NCAA regulation, he does suggest that members refuse to schedule games with colleges whose policies are suspect and urges "a reasonable amount of discriminating and fearless ostracism."

This idea of collective action against transgressors gains momentum in 1933 when the Association appoints a special committee to study recruiting and subsidizing, with particular attention to the regulatory powers and policies of the nation's various conferences. This is strictly an investigative committee and one that holds no regulatory power. Besides determining that there are abuses in the areas of recruiting and subsidizing, the committee also reports that there are variations and inconsistencies in the different conference codes. There is no uniform code or standard, not even the NCAA's.

The committee findings prompt the 1934 NCAA Convention to adopt its own code on the recruiting and subsidizing of athletes. The code terms "unjustifiable" almost all forms of recruiting and subsidy except legitimate on-campus employment at standard wage rate, and, in the case of recruiting, a coach's reply to an applicant-initiated inquiry. The code is evidence that the membership accepts the committee's conclusion: "Recruiting and subsidizing go hand in hand . . .they are so closely related that it is almost impossible to consider one without considering the other. *They have grown to such a universal extent that they constitute the major problem of American athletics today.*" (Italics added.) Despite this realization, implementation of the NCAA's code still rests with the various conferences and not with the Association itself. The NCAA's role is still advisory, at best.

The same sort of study-report-reaction cycle starts around again in 1935, when the membership adopts a resolution appointing a committee of three to "make a thorough study of all the influences that are in any way inimical to the best interests of intercollegiate sport." This time the report and the reaction to it are stronger than usual.

In adopting the resolution to appoint the committee, the membership agrees that recruiting and subsidizing "represent a real emergency." Adding fuel to this long-smoldering fire are the committee findings that gambling, postseason bowls, amateur vs. professional football games, drinking at college games and a lessening of faculty control at some schools all constitute real threats to college sport. But to this, the committee emphasizes that recruiting and subsidizing are "*of such importance in scope as to bring about the downfall of intercollegiate athletics."* (Italics added.) As to the existing codes and the power of the Association to enforce them, the committee concludes, somewhat frustratingly: "The Association by its very nature has no police power. It is the responsibility of each individual institution to correct its own shortcomings. The Association's code but points the path to follow. This situation presents, in the opinion of your committee, the strongest of challenges to the fundamental common sense and integrity of the administrators of our colleges . . . . "

On the one hand, the Association seems well aware and very much concerned about the growing problems of college sport; but on the other hand, there is still a pronounced reluctance to do much more than "point the path to follow."

It is not until 1940 that the Association takes a major step toward regulation, this coming on December 31, 1940, when the Convention authorizes the Executive Committee to proceed as necessary to investigate alleged violations of the Association's amateur regulations and to issue interpretations of the NCAA constitution. In effect, the membership is adding investigative and, to some extent, judicial powers to the advisory and legislative authority already held by the Association. However, the only constitutional sanction that may be taken against a member institution is termination of membership. This requires a two-thirds vote of the members. There still are no provisions for other sanctions. The beginning of the 1940s seems to have brought about majority acceptance of the concepts of investigation and adjudication, but the concept of enforcement is not yet on the horizon.

What we do see on the horizon are the gathering storm clouds of World War II. With the outbreak of war, the NCAA once again lends its weight to the national defense effort, advocating use of college athletic facilities by the armed services and pledging its support to the government. Though the Association encourages members to continue their intercollegiate athletic programs during the war years, this hardly seems the best time to try to implement a new program of athletic regulation. Thus, the momentum of the 1930s is temporarily slowed. There is little movement toward regulation until after the war.

In the mid-1940s, several conditions combine to impel the NCAA membership to assign to the Association some responsibilities in the area of rules enforcement. For one thing, there is evidence of professional gambling on college basketball and football games; there are accompanying rumors that gamblers are trying to "fix" some contests. There is also, in the years after the war, a marked increase in transcontinental recruiting and intersectional scheduling, all brought about by the advances in air travel. At the same time, there is a proliferation of postseason bowl games, with college teams competing intensely to gain invitations to one of these lucrative events. Finally, Congressional passage of the G.I. Bill of Rights makes available millions of dollars in Federal funds to exservicemen who choose to pursue a college education. The sudden availability of so much "scholarship" money seems to create a more favorable public image of financial aid. It also puts a new emphasis on aid to student-athletes. Should an athlete be an exserviceman, he now can get tuition and living allowance from the government with no obligation to take part in any sport. The temptations to "sweeten the pot" are obvious.

The Sanity Code

The NCAA, reacting to these fast-developing postwar changes, calls a special Conference of Conferences to meet in Chicago July 22-23, 1946. (We should keep in mind that it is the nation's individual athletic conferences that at this time are generally considered to be the prime regulatory bodies.)

Delegates to this midsummer Conference of Conferences draw up the first draft of a statement entitled "Principles for the Conduct of Intercollegiate Athletics," which will prove to be one of the most influential documents ever written by the Association.

These "principles" actually are drawn up more in the form of a questionnaire, which will go to all NCAA member institutions and is designed to determine the extent to which certain principles are accepted by the members. The "principles," at this stage, are a suggested common rallying point and not a firm policy. The principles concern adherence to the definition of amateurism, the holding of student-athletes to the same "sound academic standards" as those of the student body, the awarding of financial aid "on the basis of qualifications of which athletic ability is not one" and a policy of recruiting that basically prohibits a coach or anyone representing a member institution from soliciting attendance "of any prospective student with the offer of financial aid or equivalent inducement."

Not surprisingly, the overwhelming majority of NCAA members endorse the "principles," which now have become known colloquially as the "Sanity Code," this name arising because of a prevailing belief that adherence to such principles is necessary to restore sanity to the conduct of intercollegiate athletics.

So strong is the support for this Sanity Code that, in 1948, the principles that started out as a questionnaire become adopted as Article 3 of the NCAA constitution. By amending its constitution, the Association in effect makes it incumbent upon its members to assume responsibility for the observance of certain standards in their athletic programs. But the Convention does not stop here. For the first time, it takes the next logical — but heretofore so difficult — step toward a realistic program of regulation. The membership passes a resolution giving to the leadership of the Association the authority to establish a rules-enforcement mechanism as a means of implementing and supporting the Sanity Code. It is perhaps as important as the passage of the code itself that there is, at last, an expressed desire by member colleges to surrender a small part of their individual authority for the overall good of intercollegiate athletics.

The Sanity Code is more than regulation; it is regulation with enforcement. An executive regulation, issued as part of the code, sets up a three-member Constitutional Compliance Committee, "authorized to make rulings . . . regarding the interpretation of the constitutional language and . . . to answer inquiries as to whether stated practices, actual or contemplated, are forbidden by or are consistent with the provisions of the constitution. *Such rulings and answers shall be deemed final and authoritative* (italics added), subject only to reversal by vote of the Association in Convention assembled."

The Sanity Code also provides for appointment of fact-finding committees to investigate specific allegations and complaints, as the investigative function is given its place alongside the regulatory and enforcement functions.

In 1948, the first year of the Sanity Code's application, the Constitutional Compliance Committee considers 20 complaints against members alleged to have violated some part of the code. "Some of the complaints have proved groundless," reports the committee; "others have resulted in the situation being corrected; the remaining complaints have not yet been disposed of because professional or further investigation is involved, and it will take some time before all the facts can be collected."

In fact, administrators, coaches and students under suspicion of code violations do not always prove cooperative. Even as the compliance committee goes about its work; and as the press and public praise the Sanity Code as an important step in the preservation of true amateurism, there is mounting opposition to the code, with many schools and colleges specifically voicing opposition to the rules governing financial aid and recruiting. In short, the complaints strike at the heart of the code.

Further complicating the problem is the fact that the only penalty provided under the code is expulsion from the NCAA for those found in violation. It is a severe penalty, and its severity is one of the causes of the constitutional crisis of 1950.

Seven cases of institutions found to be in violation of the code are brought before the Convention in January 1950, and motion for termination of membership on grounds of noncompliance is made against the schools. The motion carries by a 111 to 93 majority but not by the constitutionally required two-thirds majority. The motion therefore is declared defeated and the schools in question retain their membership. Judging from the closeness of the vote, it appears that the Sanity Code can be as practically divisive as it is potentially helpful. While the vote of the membership may represent a triumph for the Association's constitutional democracy, it does little to enhance the status of the Sanity Code.

Criticism of the code increases, and even the plea of NCAA President Hugh C. Willett at the 1951 Convention fails to rally the members behind it. Referring directly to the code, Willett says: "We have entered the field of so-called 'regulation.' It would be dishonest and ungracious of me not to acknowledge the progress we have made in bringing to the consciousness of our members the great need of putting our athletic houses in order."

The Sanity Code does raise the consciousness of everyone connected with intercollegiate sports, but as a practical instrument of regulation, it is a failure. Willett's call is too late. The tide of opinion has turned, not so much against the principles of the Sanity Code as against the severity of the loss-of-membership penalty and perhaps against the entire concept of cooperative — rather than solely institutional—regulation.

The 1951 Convention repeals the Sanity Code and instructs a constitutional committee to develop recommendations and proposals for rules enforcement. These new proposals, which actually have their origins in the Sanity Code, are to be presented to the 1952 Convention.

The downfall of the Sanity Code is not the end of the concept of athletic regulation and enforcement; rather, it marks the faltering and perhaps too-hurried first step at the beginning of what is to become a slower, more methodical and better-supported approach to cooperative preservation of the spirit of amateurism.

The 12-Point Code

In the year between the repeal of the Sanity Code and the enactment of new enforcement legislation, the NCAA Council, in a move to lessen what it terms "the pressures which are intensifying emphasis upon athletics" and to counteract a statement by USOC President Avery Brundage that "subsidized college athletes rewarded financially for their talents alone" will be ineligible for the 1952 Olympics, issues a sort of interim athletic code. This 12-point code is approved by the Council August 29, 1951; and, while it is more or less advisory at this point — there being no enforcement legislation to back it up — it will evolve in the years to come as a fundamental part of the Association's position regarding the conduct of intercollegiate athletics. The 12 points are:

1. Confine practice sessions to the recognized season of the sport or limit and rigidly supervise out-of-season practice.
2. Limit the number of games in each sport, particularly football and basketball.
3. Reexamine postseason games in the light of pressures they create.
4. Urge reconsideration of the free-substitution rule (football).
5. Insist upon normal academic progress toward a degree for purposes of eligibility.
6. Deny eligibility to any athlete not admitted under the institution's published entrance requirements.
7. Limit the number and amount of financial grants to athletes.
8. Top-level institutional administrators should "enlist the support of true lovers of wholesome college athletics, particularly in alumni areas, to reduce undesirable recruiting."
9. Demand strict adherence to the letter and spirit of the rules, once they have been established by regional or national groups.
10. Rule ineligible any athlete who knowingly enters into collusion for the purpose of receiving gifts or subsidy beyond that regularly permitted by the institution or conference.
11. Eliminate excessive entertainment of prospective athletes.
12. Give close attention to the curriculum of the athlete to

assure that he is not diverted from his educational objective.

1952 Legislation

These 12 points are at the heart of new regulatory legislation passed by the Convention in 1952. Included in this legislation is a new "Principle Governing Financial Aid":

"Any college athlete who receives financial assistance other than that administered by his institution, shall not be eligible for intercollegiate competition; provided, however, that this principle shall have no application to assistance received from anyone upon whom the athlete is naturally or legally dependent."

Implicit in the statement is recognition of the fact that athletic ability may be taken into account when making scholarship awards but that the institution is the only proper source and administrator of such aid.

In other major improvements over the Sanity Code, the legislation adopted in 1952 creates a more democratic and flexible enforcement machinery. This time regulation and enforcement are to be the responsibility of four bodies — the Membership Committee, the Subcommittee on Infractions, the NCAA Council and, finally and most appropriately, the membership assembled in Convention.

The key group is the Membership Committee, a nine-member body made up of the NCAA president and the eight district vice-presidents. It is this committee that is charged with considering complaints against member institutions. Such complaints and charges then are investigated by the Subcommittee on Infractions. The findings of the subcommittee then are reported back to the Membership Committee.

The Membership Committee reports its findings to the NCAA Council. It is the Council, not the Membership Committee or Subcommittee on Infractions, that is empowered to take action against a member institution. But this time there are choices. The Council may suspend a member or place a member on probation for a given number of years, with such penalties allowing for eventual reinstatement of the member institution. The Council also may ask the Convention to terminate a specific institution's membership, but no longer is this the only choice as it had been under the Sanity Code.

The 1952 legislation also gives the Council authority to take action between Conventions rather than forcing it to have all of its decisions subject to the vote of the Convention before implementation.

A Committee on Infractions

These new rules and procedures, while spreading out the responsibilities of regulation, obviously place the burden of enforcement directly on the shoulders of the Council. It proves a heavy burden indeed. In 1953, the Council reports that a disproportionate amount of its time is being taken up by matters related to enforcement. By 1954, the Association once again must revise its procedures. The first move is to eliminate some duplication of effort by abolishing the Membership Committee and replacing it with a Committee on Infractions.

The Committee on Infractions is to be made up of members who are also on the Council. Thus, there is a heavy burden on some Council members but not on the Council as a whole. It is the Committee on Infractions that now becomes the Association's investigative body, the primary fact-finding body in all cases. This committee reports its findings to the Council for action. To speed up the investigative and administrative work, the 1954 revisions also authorize the hiring of an assistant to the executive director, with specific responsibilities in the areas of regulation and enforcement. In 1955, E. G. "Ted" Whereatt fills that position. He is followed a year later by Arthur J. Bergstrom.

As another facet of this more comprehensive approach to regulation and enforcement, the delegates to the 1954 Convention approve the launching of a national certification plan. This program requires the chief executive officer of each member institution to certify in writing his school's compliance with all applicable NCAA rules and regulations. The certification plan seems a manifestation of the longstanding principle of faculty control being the first step in any regulatory process.

The national certification plan is a success from the beginning. By 1955, 391 of 398 chief executive officers have signed forms indicating compliance with the Association's rules and regulations.

Adding further moral, if not practical, support to the NCAA's regulation and enforcement program is an unsolicited resolution of support received in 1954 from the American Football Coaches Association.

The sweeping changes made in 1952 and 1954, though they will be modified and strengthened, will remain unchanged in principle for a period of about 20 years. This time, there is no thought of repeal; instead, the now-acknowledged need for regulation and enforcement appears to be the enduring legacy of the short-lived Sanity Code.

The first strengthening of the procedural machinery comes in 1956, when the NCAA Council supports the recommendation of the Committee on Infractions, chaired by A. D. Kirwan of the University of Kentucky, that a member institution must "show cause" why its membership should not be suspended or terminated if it retains a staff member found to have violated NCAA rules. The Council also takes the position that, in some cases, the identity of staff members causing violations may be disclosed.

Further underscoring the relationship between academics and athletics, the membership in 1956 authorizes its officers to forward reports of certain infractions cases to the appropriate regional academic accrediting organization.

The Enforcement Procedure: 1964-1973

General support notwithstanding, regulation and enforcement are at best unpleasant activities. By 1961, the NCAA Convention finds it must strengthen the commitment to its program by means of an amendment to Article 2 of the constitution. The article, as amended, specifies the obligation of member institutions to apply and enforce NCAA legislation. It also directs that the enforcement program be applied to any member institution that fails to fulfill this obligation.

Despite this constitutional change, the work of the Committee on Infractions, now chaired by George H. Young of the University of Wisconsin, Madison, remains difficult. In the words of James K. Sours, a committee member from Wichita State University, "Oftentimes institutions are not as fully cooperative as they might be . . . institutions in some instances have ignored the request of the committee for information or for an appearance by an institutional representative." Sours' remark comes in 1964, following another review by the Council of the procedures of the infractions committee. The result of this review is, once again, strengthening of the Association's regulation and enforcement procedures. The procedure set down in 1964 will govern all NCAA investigative enforcement proceedings until 1973. It calls for all judgments and most fact finding to be done by committees and maintains the basic principle that, in the final analysis, an institution and its representatives are regulated by their peers and not by a centralized, monolithic authority. From 1964 to 1973, the enforcement procedure works like this:

A three-member Committee on Infractions directs the investigation, analyzes information, makes initial finding of facts and, finally, recommends penalties. The NCAA staff assists the committee in conducting the investigation. But all material collected by the staff is given to the committee prior to the filing of an official inquiry and prior to any appearance before the committee of a representative of the institution in question.

After examining the facts and holding a hearing for the involved institution, the committee reports its findings to the Council. Once again, it is the Council that bears the major burden of enforcement. After reviewing the findings of the Committee on Infractions and after considering all other information relating to the case, the Council holds its own hearing for the institution. It is only after this second hearing that the Council makes its finding of violations, if any, and imposes a penalty. The principle controlling the type and severity of any penalty is that first set forth in 1963 by the Association's Long Range Planning Committee: "Penalties should be broad if there is a basic institutional pattern of nondeservance, narrow if violations are isolated and institutional dereliction is not involved." For example, a recruiting violation by a baseball coach, while it may lead to the baseball team being ruled ineligible for postseason competition, would not likely result in the football or basketball teams being ruled ineligible for television appearances.

Strengthening the Regulatory Function

The revised procedures for investigating and hearing cases again increases the burden on the NCAA Council. Inevitably, the whole procedure also raises questions from the membership regarding the fairness and working procedures of the Committee on Infractions. All of this prompts the Council, in August 1971, to appoint an ad hoc committee to review the Association's investigatory and enforcement process. This time, there is no tinkering with minor points and procedures. Instead, the work of this Special Enforcement and Reorganization Committee results in the most significant changes since 1952. In a series of recommendations delivered in October 1971 and April 1972, the special committee suggests major changes in the Association's constitution, bylaws and enforcement procedures. These recommendations are accepted by the Council and go before the Convention in 1973. But before presenting any of the specifics of this reorganization, the Council releases a statement that carries in its uncompromising sentences a strong measure of aidos: "With the planned increased emphasis on the enforcement program and the penalties which obviously will result, the Association undoubtedly will be subject to increased pressures, including legal action or the threat thereof, from parties directly involved. The Council will remain steadfast in its position that such pressures (or threats) will not deter the NCAA from adopting and applying governing legislation which is educationally sound in its purpose and in the best interests of intercollegiate athletics."

It is a strong statement of position, and it is followed by equally strong action by the membership as the Convention adopts constitutional, bylaw and procedural changes that will govern the Association's regulatory function into the 1980s. The major revisions are:

- The Committee on Infractions — not the Council — is now the initial penalty imposer, and the committee's decision is final unless the institution in question appeals to the Council.

- The Council now becomes a "court of appeals" only and therefore is freed of the excessive burden of having to be involved with every infractions case.

- The NCAA staff (which will soon be expanded) is to be the investigative arm of the enforcement program, charged with gathering and presenting evidence in infractions cases.

- The Committee on Infractions is to supervise all policies and procedures of the investigative staff.

By 1974, it is obvious that the NCAA investigative staff will need more manpower. A special committee recommends, and the Convention approves, an increase of six additional field investigators, bringing the Association's total to eight, or, in general point of practice, one investigator for each district.

The potential budgetary problem of such a sudden increase in staff is dealt with by Convention approval of a doubling of membership dues and by an annual assessment on football television revenue.

Even with more money and manpower and the backing of the Association's leadership and membership, the actual process of investigating alleged infractions remains a difficult one, particularly as regards the institution and people in question. To make these investigatory procedures as fair and as thorough as possible, the Committee on Infractions in 1977 asks the NCAA staff to codify all its policies and procedures regarding any investigation. In 1978, these procedures are defined meticulously in the section of the NCAA Manual entitled "The Official Procedure Governing the NCAA Enforcement Program." Reduced to their major steps and components, the investigative and enforcement procedures of the NCAA since 1978 work like this.

Investigative and Enforcement Procedures

A five-member Committee on Infractions (expanded to six members in 1981), appointed by the Council but including no Council members, is responsible for administering the NCAA enforcement program. This committee is charged with determining facts related to alleged violations and imposing penalties on members found to be in violation.

The Association's investigative staff, under the direction of the NCAA's assistant executive director for enforcement, reviews complaints filed with the NCAA.

Most complaints received fall into one of two categories: (1) complaints relative to a member's failure to maintain the academic and athletic requirements for membership, or (2) allegations of a member's violation of NCAA regulations or legislation, particularly those regulations controlling recruiting and financial aid.

Charges that are from "responsible sources" and are "reasonably substantial" (the wording of the guidelines) are received by the investigative staff, which conducts a preliminary inquiry to determine whether or not there is adequate evidence to launch an official inquiry. An institution that has received notice of a preliminary inquiry is notified of the status of the inquiry within six months.

Following the preliminary investigation, the staff may review cases of limited significance with the Committee on Infractions. If the committee determines that there has been a violation but not one of a serious nature, it may privately reprimand and censure an institution and may do so without a hearing. However, when the alleged offenses are serious enough to warrant an official inquiry, the NCAA's assistant executive director for enforcement notifies the chief executive officer, athletic director and faculty athletic representative of the institution involved, informing them of the charges under inquiry and requesting their cooperation in the further investigation. "Cooperation" specifically refers to an institution's full disclosure of all relevant necessary information and to the personal appearance of college representatives and student-athletes at a hearing if that is requested by the committee. A member that declines to meet with the committee forfeits its right of appeal.

The procedures to be followed at a hearing provide that the NCAA investigative staff first will present the information it has gathered in the case. The member then will present its explanation of the alleged offenses or questionable practices. Following these presentations, the rules provide that "questions and information may be exchanged between and among all parties."

After all presentations are made and the hearing is concluded, the Committee on Infractions excuses everyone from the room and proceeds to make its final determination of facts and violations. NCAA policies require that the committee "base its findings on information . . . which it determines to be credible, persuasive and of a kind on which reasonably prudent persons rely in the conduct of serious affairs."

If the committee decides that there has been a violation, it may proceed to impose any of several penalties available to it or it may take the more serious step of recommending to the Council the suspension or termination of an institution's membership. The committee's finding as to whether or not an institution is in violation is by majority vote.

After reaching its decision, the committee immediately must send a written report to the involved institution, which then has 15 days in which to appeal its case to the NCAA Council. After hearing a case on appeal, the Council makes a decision which, according to regulations, "shall be final, binding and conclusive and shall not be subject to further review by the Council or by any other authority."

Among the disciplinary measures now available — singly or in combination — to the infractions committee are:

- Reprimand and censure.
- Probation for one year.
- Probation for more than one year.
- Ineligibility for one or more NCAA championship events.
- Ineligibility for invitational and postseason meets and tournaments.
- Ineligibility for any television programs subject to the As-

sociation's control or administration.

- Ineligibility for the member to vote or its personnel to serve on committees of the NCAA.

- Prohibition against a team or teams participating against outside competition for a specified period.

- A reduction in the number of financial aid awards that may be given during a specified time.

- Requirement that an institution that has been represented in an NCAA championship by a student-athlete who was improperly recruited or subsidized shall return its share of receipts from such competition in excess of the regular expense reimbursement. Such school also may have individual or team awards stricken from the records or returned to the Association.

There also is a provision that the committee or Council may require a member institution that has been found in violation to show cause why further penalties should not be imposed if the institution does not take disciplinary or corrective action against individuals involved in the case.

In considering the rationale for this litany of penalties, the wording of the preamble to the enforcement procedures should be noted. Here, in large type and simple wording, is a straightforward philosophy of regulation that harkens back to former NCAA President Palmer Pierce's frequent early references to "the dignity and high purpose of education."

The preamble says that all involved in the coaching or conduct of intercollegiate athletics " . . . are, in the final analysis, teachers of young people. Their responsibility is an affirmative one, and they must do more than avoid improper conduct or questionable acts. *Their own moral values must be so certain and positive that those younger and more pliable will be influenced by a fine example. Much more is expected of them than of the less critically placed citizen.*" (Italics added.)

Academic Standards

From the day of its founding, the NCAA is an organization mainly composed of educators and scholars and is, therefore, an organization that sets a high priority on academic standards. The first Association Convention in 1906 includes a discussion of faculty control of athletics. This discussion leads to the adoption of the Association's first policy concerning academic eligibility:

> "No student shall represent a college or university in any intercollegiate contest who is not taking a full schedule of work as prescribed in the catalog of the institution."

This and other general rules of eligibility are set forth in the Association's constitution and bylaws from 1906 to 1938, even though the Association is without authority to enforce any such rule and both enforcement and interpretation are left to the discretion of the member institutions.

The Association manages to attain a degree of enforcement power over academic standards in 1939 when the Convention votes to establish eligibility rules for National Collegiate Championships and places in the hands of the Eligibility Committee the responsibility of determining eligibility of student-athletes taking part in postseason competition.

In 1946, the eligibility rules for the National Collegiate Championships begin to get more specific regarding academic eligibility. The rules include the requirement that a student-athlete must have been admitted to the institution under the published admission rules applicable to all students and that he must, at the time of competition, be registered for at least a minimum full-time program of studies as defined by his institution. Academic requirements get more specific in 1948 when eligibility requirements for National Collegiate Championships include a one-year residency rule for transfers, a three-year limit on varsity competition, restriction of competition to undergraduates only and ineligibility of freshmen for NCAA-sponsored events.

In 1952, the Association further broadens its perspective on academics by amending the provisions of Constitution 3 ("Academic Standards") to include the requirement that in order to be eligible for intercollegiate competition a student-athlete must have been making normal progress toward a degree as determined by the regulations of his institution.

The Association takes a step toward quantifying its academic standards in 1959 when Bylaw 4 ("Eligibility for National Collegiate Championships") is amended to require a student-athlete, at the time of competition, to be registered for at least a minimum full-time program of studies as defined by his institution but which could not be less than 12 semester or quarter hours. In the same year, an additional amendment to Bylaw 4 includes the requirement that a student-athlete complete his seasons of participation within 10 semesters or 15 quarters of residence from the beginning of the semester or quarter in which he first registers at his college.

In the early 1960s, the membership begins to consider the appropriateness of the NCAA extending its role in legislation to the area of admissions. After prolonged debate, the 1962 Convention votes to add the term "admissions" to Constitution 2-2, which now reads:

> "It is the fundamental policy of this Association that legislation governing the conduct of intercollegiate athletic programs of member institutions shall apply to basic athletic issues such as *admissions* (italics added), financial aid, eligibility and recruiting."

The 1962 Convention also defines a student-athlete's period of eligibility as being "five calendar years from the beginning of the semester or quarter in which he first registered at a collegiate institution, time spent in the armed forces or on compulsory church missions being excepted."

1.600 Rule

It is also in 1962 that the NCAA Executive Committee allocates funds to finance a study related to predicting academic success as a basis of awarding athletically related financial aid. The committee's concern with predicting academic success arises from a number of factors, among them a philosophy that intercollegiate sports are an integral part of the total educational pattern and that student-athletes representing an institution should be legitimate representatives of the student body in general. There is also at this time a public cynicism regarding the academic ability and achievement of some student-athletes that is countered by the desire of the majority of the NCAA membership to assure that, once a student-athlete is admitted and enrolled, he has a reasonable chance to achieve a degree.

The study is carried out in 1963 and 1964 under direction of the Academic and Testing Requirements Committee, chaired by James H. Weaver of the Atlantic Coast Conference. After analyzing the individual academic performances of 40,900 students at 80 member institutions, the committee produces in 1965 an "expectancy table."

The table is based on high school academic performance correlated with scores on one of the standard college entrance tests. Its purpose, as explained by committee member Laurence C. Woodruff of the University of Kansas, is to enable a college to "judge the probability that a student to whom we are granting an athletic scholarship will succeed academically in college and thus participate in the sport for which he is being considered."

After reviewing the study, the 1965 Convention adopts legislation commonly known as the "1.600 rule." This regulation (broadened in 1966 to limit practice and game competition along with the original 1965 limit on financial aid) provides that "A member institution shall not be eligible to enter a team or individual competitors in an NCAA-sponsored meet unless the institution: (1) limits its scholarship or (athletic) grant-in-aid awards and eligibility for participation in athletics . . . to incoming student-athletes who have a predicted grade-point average of 1.600 (based on a maximum of 4.000) as determined by demonstrable institutional, conference or national experience tables, and (2) limits its subsequent . . . awards and eligibility for participation to student-athletes who have a grade-point average, either accumulative or for the previous academic year, of at least 1.600."

The 1.600 rule becomes applicable January 1, 1966. In reporting on the rule's enactment, Sports Illustrated says of it, "The 1.600 rule is a long-overdue piece of legislation designed to guarantee that every student-athlete in all of the NCAA's . . . member schools maintains at least a C-minus average. A mark of C-minus amounts to a 1.600 on the 1.000-to-4.000 grading system."

In 1968, the membership strengthens the provisions of the 1.600 rule by passing a bylaw amendment to assure that members' prediction tables are representative of the student population involved and to require a minimum level of continuing academic attainment for members using tables less demanding than the NCAA's national tables.

However, it is also in the late 1960s that profound changes in the social structure of the nation begin to affect higher education. There is, in these years, a vast increase in Federally financed college-aid programs for disadvantaged students, and an increased number of colleges begin offering greater educational opportunities by adopting "open-door" admissions policies. In light of this, there arises a feeling among a growing number of the NCAA members that the 1.600 rule interferes with institutional autonomy and responsibility and that there are legitimate questions as to the validity of predictive tests. As a result, a proposal to rescind the legislation is made at the 1971 Convention. The proposal is defeated, but the rule is amended to modify the financial aid provisions for bona fide disadvantaged-student programs.

2.000 Rule

Nevertheless, member sentiment continues to grow against the 1.600 rule, though not against the principle of academic standards; and, in 1973, the membership abolishes the rule by a 204 to 187 vote and then adopts in its place new legislation known as the "2.000 rule." The new legislation does away with the prediction tables, requiring instead that athletic grants-in-aid be limited "to student-athletes who have graduated from high school with a minimum grade-point average of 2.000 ... for all work taken and certified officially on the high school transcript...." The rule also limits athletic grants-in-aid awarded after a student-athlete's freshman year to those "who meet the official institutional regulations governing normal progress toward a degree."

The same year that the 2.000 rule is adopted is also the year that an NCAA special Convention votes to reorganize the Association's legislative and competitive structure, creating three divisions (see Chapter Eleven). This reorganization permits voting by division; and, in the first such vote taken, Divisions II and III vote not to apply the 2.000 rule within their divisions, while Division I members vote to keep the rule in effect.

From the date of the elimination of the 1.600 rule and enactment of the 2.000 legislation, certain segments of the NCAA membership voice concern about the academic requirements affecting the first-year eligibility of student-athletes for participation and financial aid. Some members believe that a high school grade-point average of 2.000 is not significant and have made several unsuccessful attempts to strengthen the rule. Similarly, since 1973 there are several amendments aimed at reinstating the 1.600 rule, but all of these are defeated by Convention vote. Various other alternatives are at times suggested by the Academic Testing and Requirements Committee and the NCAA Council. It is a Council-sponsored bylaw amendment focusing on the issue of "satisfactory progress" that finally brings about a consensus. At the 1981 Convention, members in Divisions I and II (the amendment would not apply to Division III members, which do not award athletic grants-in-aid) approve a proposal that establishes quantitative standards defining satisfactory progress toward a degree; it further provides that such progress be measured before each term in which a season of competition begins. The proposal also requires member institutions to publish their satisfactory-progress requirements as a condition of NCAA membership.

But before the full effects can be felt of this more stringent satisfactory-progress regulation, results of a five-year study sponsored by the NCAA and conducted by the American College Testing Program show that the collegiate student-athlete is a more successful scholar than some cynics might allow. The study measures the performance of male students who entered college in the fall of 1975. The results show that 52 percent of the male athletes in the group had graduated by the spring of 1980 as compared with a nonathlete graduation rate of 41.5 percent. Of the athletes that had not graduated, 12.9 percent were still enrolled. Thus, 35.1 percent of athletes had dropped out or transferred as compared with a rate of 43.2 percent of nonathletes who dropped out or transferred.

Indeed, the intent of the NCAA's academic-standards legislation as defined by the Council — "to require student-athletes to meet a defined standard of academic progress in order to maintain eligibility" — is being fulfilled.

Recruiting and Financial Aid Regulations

What Pindar once referred to as the "secret gains" that steal away the spirit of *aidos* are today the variety of improper advantages that may accrue to a student-athlete, a member institution or both as a result of improprieties in the areas of recruiting and the awarding of financial aid.

"Recruiting," says NCAA Executive Director Walter Byers, "is the Achilles' heel of intercollegiate athletics."

Since 1952, the NCAA Committee on Infractions has been involved with more than 500 infractions cases, resulting in findings of either major or minor violations, the majority of such cases involving recruiting or financial aid irregularities.

It is unrealistic to think that any amount of regulation from any source can eliminate all abuses for all time. Or, to quote a delegate to the 1952 Convention, "There always will be an Institution X." However, the regulations and policies evolving through the years — most since the mid-1950s — seek to set common standards for the recruiting of student-athletes and the subsequent awarding of financial aid. These regulations have three purposes — to preserve the integrity of intercollegiate sport, to preserve the athlete's amateur eligibility and to protect the high school athlete who is being recruited.

The regulations take special aim at the three parts of the recruiting process — recruiter/prospect contact, player eligibility and the awarding of grants-in-aid.

Acceptance of the concept of athletic grants-in-aid comes in 1956 when the Convention votes to amend the constitution to include several Official Interpretations (O.I.s), the first of which states:

> "Financial aid awarded by an institution to a student-athlete should conform to the rules and regulations of the awarding institution and that institution's conference . . . but in the event such aid exceeds commonly accepted educational expenses for the undergraduate period of the recipient, it shall be considered 'pay' for participation."

The following year, this O.I. is amended to include a definition of "commonly accepted educational expenses" — these being recognized as tuition, fees, room, board, books and a maximum $15 a month for incidental expenses. At the same time, the Convention expands the constitution to stipulate that when unearned financial aid is awarded to a student and athletic ability is taken into consideration in making the award, such aid combined with other aid the student may receive may not exceed the commonly accepted educational expenses. The intent of the athletic grant-in-aid is to cover a student athlete's basic educational expenses and nothing more.

In the late 1950s, the NCAA also takes steps to protect the student-athlete through regulations that prohibit the arbitrary gradation or cancellation of aid based on injury or on team or individual athletic performance.

From this point through the 1960s, very little is changed in the basic NCAA constitutional provisions. But, beginning with the 1973 Convention, major changes in financial aid legislation reappear. Among the policies adopted this year is a constitutional provision that limits athletically related grant-in-aid awards to one-year duration. The membership also adopts Bylaw 5, which for the first time, sets limits on the number of financial grants-in-aid that may be awarded. In football and basketball, there is a limit on the number of awards that can be issued in each sport. In all other sports, there is a limit on the aggregate number of additional awards. These limits, though later modified and prescribed for each sport, remain in effect into the 1980s.

The Fight for Need-Based Aid

Clearly, the move to limit athletic grants-in-aid is a response to the rapidly rising costs of intercollegiate athletics and to the effects of accelerating economic inflation. But, in the meetings of the NCAA Financial Aid Committee, there is an even more profound philosophical shift toward the whole matter of athletic grants-in-aid. This is publicly evidenced as early as 1971 when, after a two-year study, the Financial Aid Committee, chaired by William J. Flynn of Boston College, releases a report recommending that future grants-in-aid be based on *need*.

"The term 'need,' " says the report, " . . . means that in determining the amount of aid to be granted, account is taken of the financial resources of the recipient and his parents . . . . "

This concept of need-based aid comes to a vote at the 1973 Convention, where it loses by a show-of-hands vote. However, the idea continues to gather momentum even after its initial defeat. Proponents argue that need-based scholarships not only will save money but also will remove a perceived inequity between athletic grants-in-aid and the need-based aid available to the generality of students. Opponents of the idea, generally those member institutions with large, revenue-producing football and basketball programs, contend that some of the savings are illusory and that many athletes still will qualify for full financial assistance.

A growing acceptance of the concept of need-based aid combined with the steady pressures of inflation and rising costs result in a modified need proposal coming before the Convention once again in 1976. This time, tuition and fees are exempted from the need criteria while room, board and books are to be subject to need. The proposal produces a lengthy and intense debate.

Stanley E. McCaffrey, president of the University of the Pacific, speaks in support of the proposal:

"I do not believe this (proposal) discriminates against the student-athletes. It is fair in its provisions. A student who has need and a student-athlete who has need will receive full support. A student-athlete, like other students, who does not have need will not receive room and board and book provisions but will receive tuition. Chancellor Young (Charles E. of UCLA) made the point — and I wish to reemphasize it — on campuses, university presidents know it is of the utmost importance that this is the single item that is most criticized by our students and by faculty. The athletes are granted special privileges and, thus, become a group apart; and that is difficult, if not impossible, to defend or to rebut. I believe it is entirely fair and possible to defend the granting of tuition, just as we grant tuition for other talented majors in drama, debate and music."

Edward M. Czekaj of Penn State speaks against the proposal:

"I speak in behalf of the 30 major independent Division I football schools. . . . . it was the unanimous position of this group to oppose this legislation. We firmly believe in granting aid based on athletic ability and not on need. We have lived with this philosophy a long time. It is a good philosophy and we prefer to keep it that way."

The proposal brings about the first roll-call vote in the history of the NCAA Convention. The vote is close, but, once again, the concept of need-based aid appears to be an idea whose time could be coming but has not yet arrived. It loses, 120 to 112.

The idea does not die with the 1976 roll call. A similar proposal sponsored by the NCAA Council calling for a need-based formula for room and board reaches the agenda of the 75th Convention in 1981. Once more, the lines of debate are drawn on the grounds of economy and philosophy. In columns voicing opposing points of view published in the October 31, 1980, NCAA News, UCLA Chancellor Young urges support of the proposal while University of Georgia President Fred C. Davison argues for its defeat.

Writes Young:

"It will save UCLA and those Divisions I and II public institutions with maximum allowable numbers of grants a very considerable sum . . . . It seems to me that universities, in providing scholarship assistance, are doing so to enable a student to receive an education. That is their mission. And while I recognize that a football player or basketball player at UCLA has demands upon him (or her) not expected of others, I also am aware of the nonfinancial awards the student-athlete is receiving as a result of his athletic experience. The educational rewards and character development are sufficient in my judgment to obviate the need or desirability for the income-sports participant receiving an extra bonus. Amateur athletics is still a viable and worthy ideal."

Writes Davison:

"Consider the morale of a star athlete from a family judged to be affluent. . . . The star player is bringing acclaim and perhaps financial support to the institution but is penalized. On a personal level, the athlete is not recognized for excellence in performance . . . . . If athletic scholarships were based on financial need alone, students eligible for partial support would be compelled in many cases to seek outside employment while enrolled. The time and effort required of athletes makes this nearly impossible, while the potential for abuse in job opportunities offered gifted athletes is obvious."

The idea of need-based athletic grants-in-aid once more encounters its major opposition from institutions sponsoring major football and basketball programs. In a lengthy speech just before the issue comes to a vote, Rev. Edmund P. Joyce, vice-president of the University of Notre Dame, says, "I predict that the need factor has less chance to be accepted in football circles than the ill-starred 18th amendment concerning prohibition, and the damage it could cause to the fragile fabric of sports honesty could be devastating."

While many delegates and journalists speculate before the Convention that this time the measure would pass, the votes show it failing once again, 148 to 101 in Division I and 72 to 47 in Division II.

Changes in Amateurism Regulations

While not opposed to professional athletics in the sense of being an adversary, the NCAA historically takes a strong stand for a line of demarcation between professional sport and its objective of gain and profit and amateur sport as a part of the educational process. Throughout the years, particularly through the 1960s and early '70s, the Association's Council receives a growing number of requests for waivers by active or potential student-athletes wishing to turn professional in one sport while maintaining amateur status in another or to regain a lost amateur standing or, in some cases, to accept a professional tryout before deciding to pursue an education or a professional career. The Council is consistent in rejecting such requests, but at the same time there arises a sentiment for applying amateur principles on a sport-by-sport basis rather than to all sports "across the board."

In 1970, the Council appoints an Amateurism Committee chaired by Marcus Plant of the University of Michigan and including ECAC Commissioner Robert "Scotty" Whitelaw and Pacific Coast Athletic Association Commissioner Jesse T. Hill. Later, Harry M. Cross of the University of Washington, John A. Fuzak of Michigan State and Howard Gentry of Tennessee State are added to the committee. The committee is charged with examining the issue of amateurism and with considering possible alternatives to the general principle that violation of amateur regulations in any sport renders a student-athlete ineligible in all sports.

After four years of meetings and discussions, the committee, now chaired by Cross, goes before the 1974 Convention with a proposal calling for sweeping changes in the amateurism rules. The proposed changes allow an athlete to compete as a professional in one sport while keeping his eligibility to compete in other intercollegiate sports. The proposed changes also allow a student-athlete to teach, coach and officiate sports except on a professional level and to accept a tryout with a professional team provided the amateur pays his own expenses and does not receive remuneration in any form.

"I think the guts of what we are addressing ourselves to," Whitelaw tells the Convention, "is that instead of making the amateurism principle apply across the board in all sports, to make it apply sport by sport."

The committee's proposal, in the form of constitutional amendments, passes with far more than the required two-thirds majority vote, as the membership clearly expresses itself in favor of the spirit of *aidos* but with such spirit supported by more realistic rules.

Recruiting Regulations

The number of recruiting regulations evolving over the past three decades is extensive, and many have as their general intent control of the type and frequency of recruiter/prospect contacts. As a general policy, a recruiter (who may be a coach, alumnus or any representative of an institution's athletic interests) is subject in Divisions I and II to a specific limit on in-person, off-campus contacts with a prospect; and none of these contacts may come before the conclusion of the prospect's junior year in high school. In football and basketball, regulations are adopted in 1981 to confine recruiting periods to specified time periods for Divisions I and II.

Association regulations permit a college to pay the cost of one on-campus visit for a prospect, provided the visit does not exceed 48 hours; transportation, if by air, tourist class, and any entertainment is "at a scale comparable to normal student life."

A prospective athlete is limited to accepting only six such expense-paid campus visits.

Activities forbidden by NCAA recruiting and financial aid regulations include:

- A college offering a prospect, his family or friends improper inducements to enroll. Forbidden inducements include cash, promise of a job after graduation, loans, jobs for relatives or friends, arrangements for professional or personal services or charge privileges, use of a car, transportation to or from a summer job, cosigning a loan or note and gifts of money or any tangible item (e.g. jewelry).

- A recruiter making more than the permissible number of in-person, off-campus recruiting contacts with a prospect or his family.

- A recruiter contacting a prospect at his high school without permission of the principal or his authorized representative.

- A prospect or high school coach making any television or radio appearance arranged by a recruiter.

- Any group or organization other than a college's athletic department spending any money to recruit a prospect.

- Company funds being spent to recruit a prospect.

- Tryouts arranged for the prospect to demonstrate his athletic ability in a sport.

- A recruiter paying transportation expenses for a prospect's relatives or friends to visit a college.

- A recruiter entertaining a prospect or his family on any occasion other than during the prospect's one on-campus visit.

- A college supplying a prospect with free tickets to its away games. (A prospect may receive three tickets to a home game.)

• A recruiter entertaining a prospect's friends, anytime, anywhere.

In 1978, the NCAA enforcement staff initiates a program called "Operation Intercept." As its name implies, Operation Intercept is aimed at heading off recruiting violations before they can occur. The program involves the use of all NCAA enforcement representatives to visit, prior to the signing of national letters-of-intent, with the country's top high school athletic prospects — primarily in the sports of football and basketball — and explain to them what they may and may not accept during the recruiting process.

The NCAA "Big Brother" program, begun by the enforcement staff in 1979, is similar to Operation Intercept in its preventative approach. But Big Brother begins even earlier in the recruiting process. In the summer before a major prospect's senior year, an NCAA enforcement representative holds the first of what will be a series of meetings with the prospect, his coaches and, on occasion, the prospect's family. The purpose of the visit is to get to know the athlete on a personal basis and to prepare him and those who will be advising him for the pressures of the recruiting process. This includes explanations of the kind of offers the athlete may accept and, conversely, the type of inducements that may represent violations of NCAA regulations. The enforcement representative checks back with the athlete several times during the recruiting period to clear up any ambiguities and, in the words of an enforcement representative, "to make sure there isn't any hanky-panky going on. We have had cases where athletes have alerted us to recruiting irregularities very early."

The idea behind Big Brother is to establish a personal, friendly relationship with the athlete early enough so he or she feels free to call the NCAA about any problems and is more apt to look at the NCAA as another adviser in the sometimes complicated recruiting process.

Manpower limitations mean the Big Brother program is restricted to the bluest of the blue-chip prospects, maybe the top 15 or 20 in basketball and football. However, the NCAA supplements the Big Brother program and Operation Intercept with an annual publication aimed at all college-oriented high school athletes. Since 1974, the Association has published the "NCAA Guide for the College-Bound Student-Athlete," a relatively easy-to-read summary of regulations governing transferring, recruiting, financial aid and eligibility. The booklet stresses the major (or most often violated) regulations and any new legislation enacted in the preceding year. It is published, in the words of its introduction, "with a view to avoiding involvement in a violation of NCAA legislation which might result in the loss of an individual's eligibility or disciplinary action against a member institution."

Simply put, the guide, Big Brother and Operation Intercept are several pounds of prevention forestalling what could prove to be the more disagreeable "cures."

"As a general rule," explains one of the Association's enforcement representatives, "we try to stress to athletes in all sports that they should look upon their own athletic ability as a way to get a good education and that they shouldn't let their heads get turned by flattery or by dreams."

Or by secret gains.

Theodore Roosevelt

Gang tackling of the early 1900s

President Theodore Roosevelt brought the seriousness of football violence to national attention when he called a special White House conference of football leaders in October 1905.

Concerned with football violence, Henry M. MacCracken, chancellor of New York University, called a special meeting of football-playing colleges. Thirteen colleges sent representatives. Three weeks later, 58 colleges were represented as the conference reconvened. From this General Convention of Colleges and Universities of 1905, the NCAA was born. Soon after, Amos Alonzo Stagg, legendary football coach at the University of Chicago, lent his influence to the fledgling organization.

General Convention of Colleges and Universities, December 29, 1905

Henry M. MacCracken   Amos Alonzo Stagg

The NCAA championships began in 1921 with the National Collegiate Track and Field Championships. Through the years, many great teams and individuals have displayed their talents. Jesse Owens stands alone in track and field annals as the only athlete to have won four individual titles in one year — and he did it twice, 1935 and 1936. In wrestling, Oklahoma State has won 27 of 52 team championships, beginning with the first NCAA wrestling championships in 1928.

Jesse Owens

Oklahoma State wrestling, 1928. Pictured third row, left, is E. C. Gallagher, coach of 11 NCAA championship teams.

1921 National Collegiate Track and Field Championships, Stagg Field, University of Chicago. 100-yard dash final (left to right): Ed Smith, Nebraska, third; W. D. Hayes, Notre Dame, second; L. T. Paula, Grinnell, first; Vic Hurley, Washington, fifth, and E. C. Wilson, Iowa, fourth.

First NCAA basketball championship, 1939

Four coaching greats

The NCAA basketball championship has become one of America's greatest sporting events. In action from the first NCAA championship game, John Schick (white jersey) tips in two points for Ohio State. It was not enough, however, as Oregon defeated the Buckeyes, 46-33. Many great coaches have led their teams to NCAA championships. Shown above (left to right) are Nat Holman, City College of New York, one title; Adolph Rupp, Kentucky, four; Henry Iba, Oklahoma State, two, and John Wooden, UCLA, 10.

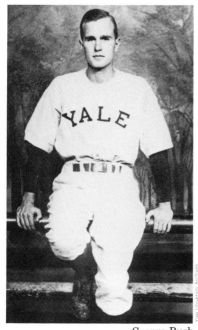

George Bush

Many prominent national leaders have participated in college athletics. In the first baseball championship in Kalamazoo, Michigan, in 1947, Yale University was captained by George Bush, later to become vice-president of the United States. In the mid-1930s, Gerald R. Ford played center on the Michigan football team. As President of the United States, Ford was the 1975 recipient of the Theodore Roosevelt Award, the highest honor the NCAA may confer on an individual.

Gerald R. Ford

Walter Byers

NCAA National Office, Mission, Kansas

Left to right: Walter Byers, Wayne Duke, Arthur J. Bergstrom

Asa S. Bushnell

The Association's national office structure began
to take shape in 1951 with the hiring of Walter
Byers as the first full-time executive director. By
1956, Wayne Duke and Arthur J. Bergstrom had
joined the staff as assistants to the executive director. Today, the staff of 85 is housed in the Mission, Kansas, national office building, completed
in 1973. At the same time as the NCAA began
hiring an executive staff, the Association implemented the first television plan in 1952, with
Asa S. Bushnell, commissioner of the Eastern
College Athletic Conference, serving as television
director from 1952 to 1970.

From the packed stadium on a Saturday afternoon to the one-on-one relationship of the National Youth Sports Program, the NCAA touches many aspects of America's society. College football was viewed by 35,540,975 fans in 1980, another record-setting year. More than 450,000 of the nation's neediest youngsters have been reached by the NYSP since its inception in 1969.

NYSP

College football on a Saturday afternoon

Dacia Schileru   Muriel Bower

Women's Swimming Committee Meeting

Involvement of women in the NCAA began in the 1970s and carried into the '80s. Dacia Schileru, a Wayne State University diver, became the first female to compete in an NCAA championship when she entered the College Division Swimming and Diving Championships in 1973. In that same year, Muriel Bower of California State University, Northridge, became the first female to serve as chair of an NCAA committee when she assumed the leadership of the NCAA Fencing Committee. As a result of decisions made at the 74th and 75th annual Conventions to sponsor NCAA championships for women, the first women's sports committees were formed in 1980. Gathering in November 1980, the Women's Swimming Committee was one of the first to meet. Shown above at that meeting (left to right) are Patricia W. Wall, MacMurray College (later NCAA); Ruth M. Berkey, NCAA, and Susan J. Petersen, chair, U.S. Merchant Marine Academy.

NCAA Presidents

Capt. Palmer E. Pierce
1906-1913, 1917-1929

Capt. Palmer E. Pierce was the first president of the NCAA and the leading voice in the early years of the Association. It was he who referred to the NCAA as "the voice of college sports."

LeBaron R. Briggs
1914-1916

Charles W. Kennedy
1930-1932

Maj. John L. Griffith
1933-1937

W. B. Owens
1938-1940

Phillip O. Badger
1941-1944

Wilbur C. Smith
1945-1946

Karl E. Leib
1947-1949

Hugh C. Willett
1950-1952

A. B. Moore
1953-1954

Clarence P. Houston
1955-1956

Frank N. Gardner
1957-1958

Herbert J. Dorricott
1959-1960

Henry B. Hardt
1961-1962

Robert F. Ray
1963-1964

Everett D. Barnes
1965-1966

NCAA
Presidents

Marcus L. Plant
1967-1968

Harry M. Cross
1969-1970

Earl M. Ramer
1971-1972

Alan J. Chapman
1973-1974

John A. Fuzak
1975-1976

J. Neils Thompson
1977-1978

William J. Flynn
1979-1980

James Frank
1981-1982

A listing of institutional affiliations of
NCAA presidents and
secretary-treasurers appears in
Appendix C.

NCAA
Secretary-Treasurers

Louis Bevier Jr.
1906-1908

W. A. Lambeth
1908
(Treasurer only)

Frank W. Nicolson
1909-1939

Maj. John L. Griffith
1940-1944

Kenneth L. Wilson
1945-1951

Earl S. Fullbrook
1952-1954

Ralph W. Aigler
1955-1956

Edwin D. Mouzon Jr.
1957-1958

Percy L. Sadler
1959-1960

NCAA
Secretary-
Treasurers

Rev. Wilfred H. Crowley
1961-1962

Everett D. Barnes
1963-1964

Francis E. Smiley
1965-1966

Ernest B. McCoy
1967-1968

William J. Flynn
1969-1970

Samuel E. Barnes
1971-1972

Richard P. Koenig
1973-1974

Stanley J. Marshall
1975-1976

Edgar A. Sherman
1977-1978

James Frank
1979-1980

John L. Toner
1981-1982

CHAPTER EIGHT

" 'That,' she said, 'is the legislative process.' "

Frigid arctic air sweeps into southern Florida on the morning of Monday, January 12, 1981.

"I woke up, put on running shorts and a T-shirt and headed for the beach. Three steps later, I'm back in my room putting on a sweater," says Bob Hartwell, athletic director at Babson College, Wellesley, Massachusetts, one of a record 1,314 delegates to the NCAA's 75th annual Convention at Miami Beach's famed Fontainebleau Hotel.

The record delegate turnout is due mainly to an agenda that includes several major questions, among them propositions and amendments that will require history-making votes on the issue of women's intercollegiate athletics and the NCAA.

The Convention must decide on whether or not to alter substantially the governance of the Association to accommodate representatives of women's sports, and it must decide whether or not to revise its championships format to provide national championships for women's teams in addition to those for all-male and mixed teams.

Hartwell is asked if he thinks debate on the issues might make the Convention itself unusually chilly.

"I think it might heat it up," he says.

It is still cold — record cold in some parts of the state — on Tuesday, the first day of the Convention's general sessions. The Grand Ballroom of the hotel is set with long, straight rows of tables and chairs, accommodations for the hundreds of delegates, guests, staff and media representatives expected for the debate and voting. Twelve microphones stand straight and silent in the ballroom's aisles. A head table sits high on the dais. Behind it is the NCAA seal bearing the symbol of the Association — hands laying the laurel wreath of victory on the slightly bowed head of an athlete. The athlete is male. The seal reads: "National Collegiate Athletic Association. Founded 1906."

In 1906, the Association was little more than a small reformist group called the Intercollegiate Athletic Association of the United States. If the 28 delegates attending that first Convention at New York City's Murray Hill Hotel were to walk into the Fontainebleau ballroom in 1981, they would be surprised not only at the growth of their little organization, but at the corresponding growth in college sports.

What no doubt would surprise the founders even more than the growth of their organization is a drawing unveiled for the media the day before the start of the 75th Convention. The drawing is a design for a new NCAA seal. It calls for the same circular design and the same wording, but the picture is different. The new seal shows two athletes, rather than one. The male athlete is still shown with the wreath being placed on his head. But now there is added a female athlete. The wreath is already on her head.

The issue at the time of the founding of the NCAA had been the violence of college football, and the big question was how the colleges were to work together to save this most popular of college sports. That the original organization succeeded where other groups failed was due perhaps less to idealism — ideally, all colleges opposed violence — than to the founders' administrative and diplomatic capacities. Where previous groups, most notably an organization called the Football Rules Committee, were made up of a small number of schools attempting to set rules, if not policy, for a larger number, the infant NCAA was more of an ad hoc organization open to all who wished to join. It was founded on two strong and enduring principles. The first was the sanctity of "home rule" — that each member is responsible for its own athletic program and is not to be dictated to; the second was that any organization purporting to represent college sports must, in the end, be a vehicle and a voice for its members. It must enact *the will of its members;* in effect, the Association must *be* its members.

It is these two principles, more than any other factors, that sustain the NCAA for three-quarters of a century, from 28 men at the Murray Hill Hotel in 1906 to more than 1,300 men *and* women at the Fontainebleau in 1981. Whether these two principles are enough to get the Association through the next two days is, on this cold Monday, a matter of some conjecture.

The Background

It is perhaps a measure of the progress of the long, slow swing of the social pendulum that an association founded 14 years before passage of the women's suffrage amendment is in 1981 ready and, in the main, eager to include women's athletics leaders in its governing structure and to sponsor national championships for women. And it is equally typical of the times and of the fast-advancing status of women that some organizations that have arisen in response to the growing interest in women's intercollegiate athletics — most notably the Association for Intercollegiate Athletics for Women (AIAW) — feel themselves threatened by these intentions of the NCAA. It is a situation reminiscent of that existing 75 years earlier, when the original Football Rules Committee casts a wary eye on the original Intercollegiate Athletic Association, though history would prove the two to be both compatible and productive.

The Grand Ballroom is quiet now, but it is about to ring with the amplified voices of those who will debate the role of the NCAA in women's athletics. It is a debate that will focus not only on women's intercollegiate sport, but on the governance and working procedures of the NCAA. In the end, this issue, perhaps more than any other question ever to confront the NCAA, can demonstrate the fidelity of the Association to its 75-year-old principle of institutional control and of enacting the will of its members. The debate will help decide if the NCAA remains what one of its founders and its first president, Capt. Palmer Pierce, once called " . . . the voice of college sports."

In the hotel's meeting rooms and coffee shop, pre-Convention activity takes a decidedly modern turn toward argument by lapel button. Several NCAA delegates wear pins reading, "The NCAA is for Women." Meanwhile, many visitors from the AIAW wear pins of their own, reading "NCAA, Make Love, Not War."

Had there been any lapel buttons handed out in 1906, they might have read, rather accurately, "The NCAA Is Not Against Women," this being the prevailing attitude of most college sports leaders toward women's athletics at the turn of the century. In fact, the Association shows itself early in its history at least to be aware of, if not involved with, women's athletics. On December 28, 1922, D. W. Morehouse, acting president of Drake University and an NCAA delegate, says in a speech to the NCAA Convention:

"Considerable agitation has been developed over the possibility of athletics for women. A large number of schools are giving
this branch of physical education very serious attention. At
Drake University, in addition to the regular floor work in the
gymnasium and basketball, hockey, tennis, hiking and swimming are outdoor sports which have found great favor among
the young ladies and are participated in by a remarkably large
number. The desirability of further encouraging such work was
stressed by (other college presidents)."

Morehouse's remarks come as the result of responses to a questionnaire on college athletics that he had circulated among college and
university presidents in his NCAA district. Morehouse's observation,
while interesting, does not prompt any action by the 1922 Convention. This is not surprising. It is the prevailing feeling of the era —
documented in history and literature — that while men and boys are
to be encouraged in the rough and tumble of athletics, a young
woman's place is on the sidelines. This attitude echoes in the words of
retired Yale football coach Walter Camp who, just a few hours after
Morehouse's observation, talks to the delegates of " . . . the early
beginning of the sporting spirit — man to man." That may have been
the beginning, but it is not to be the end.

Camp, of course, speaks primarily of varsity sports, particularly
football. But in other sports, and at other than the varsity level, the
sociological pendulum picks up speed. Morehouse and his fellow
college presidents are not the only ones to notice the increased interest in women's athletics. The members of the Basketball Rules Committee make several early observations as to that sport being particularly popular among women.

But it is not until the 1950s that the slow, steady growth of women's
athletics shows itself most clearly to the Association's membership.
In 1956 and 1957, the NCAA, responding to a suggestion by its
Committee on Youth Fitness, conducts the first nationwide study of
college athletics, a study designed to provide the membership and the
public-at-large with factual information regarding the role of higher
education in athletics, physical education and recreation. It is the
first such study of its type and scope. It is called "The Sports and
Recreational Programs of the Nation's Universities and Colleges,"
and it is published in 1958. Buried in its neat, tabular columns of
figures are the clear signs of coming trends. While the study confines

its research on varsity sports to "full-time undergraduate male enrollment," it makes no such sex distinction in its study of physical
education programs. Here, the figures show that of 395 member
colleges surveyed, 280 require physical education for women; of that
280, there are 208 colleges (74.3 percent) that require a two-year
physical education program. The study also shows that 38.7 percent
of all full-time undergraduate women are enrolled in a physical
education program. Women's sports, though not yet making much
impact at the varsity level, clearly are gaining strength at the grass-
roots level. Women are moving off the sidelines and onto the playing
fields.

The NCAA's first direct contact with women's athletics comes in
October 1963, when representatives of the Association accept an
invitation to participate with two women's sports groups in a national
institute for girls' sports held at the University of Oklahoma. Partially as a result of this conference and in response to a request made
by women college sports leaders, the NCAA Executive Committee, on
April 18, 1964, amends the Association's Executive Regulation 2 to
prevent women student-athletes at NCAA member institutions from
being eligible for NCAA championships.[11] A parenthetical note following the written report of this decision in the Association's 1964
Yearbook reads, "In taking this action, committee followed the recommendation of Dr. Marguerite Clifton, an officer of the Division of
Girls' and Women's Sports of the American Association of Health,
Physical Education and Recreation, and Mrs. Sara Staff Jernigan, a
member of the U.S. Olympic Committee's Women's Development
Committee." The day after the Executive Committee takes this action, the NCAA Council appoints a Special Committee on Women's
Competition "to serve as a liaison agency with all other interested
groups."

During the next three years, there arises a growing feeling among
the Association's members that for the NCAA to deliberately eschew
involvement in women's athletics is to renounce one of its mandates
— to supervise and promote all forms of intercollegiate athletics
among its members. Consequently, on October 24, 1967, the Council
appoints a committee "to study the feasibility of establishing appropriate machinery to provide for the control and supervision of wom-
en's intercollegiate athletics." In reporting this action to the membership, Council member Arthur W. Nebel of the University of Missouri says:

[11]The Association rescinds this rule in 1973 on advice of legal counsel.

"All of us are aware of women's important role in (society). They now are becoming more interested in intercollegiate athletics. NCAA championships are limited to male students. Also, the Association's rules and regulations governing recruiting, financial aid and eligibility apply only to the male student.

"It was recently brought to the Council's attention that an increasing number of NCAA institutions are sponsoring intercollegiate athletic activities for women. Some of these institutions have sought the advice of the Association as to the proper administrative procedures for an intercollegiate program for female students.

"As a result, the Council has appointed a committee to study the feasibility of establishing appropriate machinery to provide for supervision and administration of women's intercollegiate athletics. Let me say now, before there is any misrepresentation of the Council's action, that the committee appointed is strictly a study group and includes among its membership some of the leaders of the Division of Girl's and Women's Sports of AAHPER. This should not be misconstrued as an effort on the part of the NCAA to establish women's championships or extend present Association regulations to women's intercollegiate athletics. It is possible that this may be the eventual result. It is important to stress again, however, that at the present time, the Council is merely investigating this matter . . . . "

This committee, chaired by Ernest B. McCoy of Pennsylvania State University, meets in 1968 and 1969 with various leaders of women's intercollegiate athletics. Once again, the women ask that the NCAA not involve itself in developing a women's program and administrative structure. While these meetings go on at intercollegiate sport's highest levels, there is a continuing surge in women's athletics at the grass-roots level. The signs are abundant. For example, in academic year 1966-67, there are 15,727 participants in women's intercollegiate athletics at 577 NCAA member institutions. By the 1971-72 academic year, this number has more than doubled to 33,019 at 663 member institutions. Later research by the NCAA will show that women student-athletes account for more than 57 percent of the increase in number of participants in intercollegiate athletic programs for the period from 1971-72 to 1973-74. Perhaps the most straightforward and dramatic indicator of the growth of women's athletics is the increase in the sponsorship of women's sports. In

1966-67, 62 NCAA member institutions offer five or more intercollegiate sports for women. By 1971-72, the number of colleges offering five or more sports for women *triples* to 186, of these schools, 26 offer 10 or more sports for women.

Title IX

The wave breaks publicly in 1972. This is the year Congress passes a piece of legislation called the Education Amendment Act, Title IX of which is devoted to "nondiscrimination on the basis of sex in education programs and activities receiving Federal financial assistance." Briefly, this is a Federal law prohibiting sex discrimination in education. The law includes guidelines for its application to intercollegiate athletics and a provision that the U.S. Department of Health, Education and Welfare (HEW) is to be responsible for overseeing compliance with the new law. While the membership of the NCAA generally is sympathetic with the intent of Congress and of the legislation, the HEW-supervised compliance later will prove a bone of considerable contention. (See Chapter Ten.)

With the enactment of Title IX and the resulting increase in pressure for equality of opportunity for both sexes, it becomes increasingly clear that the NCAA no longer can delay in determining its role in the development of intercollegiate athletics for women. Pressure by women's groups for governmental and judicial intervention on behalf of women's rights in education and intercollegiate athletics heightens the need for the NCAA to act.

The first notable action actually takes place *before* passage of Title IX with the appointment in 1971 of a Special Committee on Women's Intercollegiate Athletics, chaired by David Swank of the University of Oklahoma. Between July 6, 1971, and October 10, 1975, this committee holds several meetings with the leaders of the National Association for Girls and Women in Sports (NAGWS) of the American Alliance for Health, Physical Education and Recreaction (AAHPER). The committee also meets with the leaders of the increasingly active AIAW, an affiliate of the NAGWS/AAHPER, after its formation in 1971. During these meetings, representatives of NAGWS and the AIAW consistently argue for separate but equal athletic programs and administrations. Meanwhile, beginning in 1971, the NCAA's legal counsel consistently reminds the Association's Council that NCAA rules and regulations pertaining to institutional membership, as they are written, relate to *all* varsity intercollegiate sports, that they do not differentiate between men and women and that the NCAA may be facing legal obligations to offer services and programs for female student-athletes as it traditionally has done for male student-athletes.

The path becomes clearer in 1975 when NCAA President John A. Fuzak of Michigan State University sends a report from the Council to the membership. The report reads, in part:

> "The Council recognizes that the moral obligation to provide meaningful services for the female student-athletes of its member institutions is greater today than ever before and that to temporize further is to deny the NCAA's own statements of 'Purposes and Fundamental Policy' contained in Article 2 of the NCAA constitution . . . . "

As it begins to develop its approach to women's athletics, the Council comes to three conclusions: (1) It is not feasible or desirable for the NCAA to confine future services and programs only to male student-athletes; (2) it is not possible under the provisions of the law to restrict application of NCAA rules only to male student-athletes competing on intercollegiate varsity teams, and (3) it is not permissible or plausible for the NCAA to enter into agreements with other organizations that, for example, would accord the NCAA exclusive authority over male intercollegiate athletics and accord a like monopoly position to an organization for control of women's intercollegiate athletics.

"Existing rules of law and NCAA policy," asserts the 1975 Council report, "contemplate that qualified females will participate on teams which formerly were exclusively male. *The NCAA cannot legally or practically limit its services and programs so as to exclude such qualified females.*" (Italics added.)

The Council also takes a dim view of the "separate but equal" programs approach, saying in its historic report:

> "While the argument may be made that it is legally possible to provide . . . programs through separate but equal facilities and staff, economy probably will dictate that there be a minimum of duplication of personnel and facilities. Furthermore, administrative necessity and the need for equitable eligibility requirements will require coordination and similarity not only at the institutional level, but also on a national level. Integrated or coordinated programs at the national level cannot be achieved if separate male and female national organizations are left to accomplish it through . . . bilateral agreements. Recent history

of NCAA efforts in this regard dramatizes the difficulty of reaching such accords in matters of the most preliminary nature .... "

The report concludes, bluntly:

"For the NCAA now to renounce its mandate to supervise and promote all forms of intercollegiate athletics among its members would be to deny services to women's intercollegiate athletics .... "

As deliberations go on within the NCAA and between the NCAA and the AIAW, the latter organization begins a period of growth and increasing influence. In 1973, the AIAW holds its first delegate assembly and begins sponsorship of championship events for women in badminton, basketball, golf, gymnastics, swimming, track and field and volleyball.[12]

With specific reference to its posture toward the AIAW, the Council reports in 1975 on the NCAA's intentions regarding women's intercollegiate athletics:

" ... (the NCAA) in no way suggests that the AIAW should abandon its program or that those NCAA member institutions which are AIAW members should not support and participate in programs of the AIAW/AAHPER and the NCAA, just as institutions are members and participate in the activities of both the NCAA and NAIA (National Association of Intercollegiate Athletics). The Council, however, does not believe it is practical or desirable to attempt to create exclusive arenas for the separate operations of men's and women's organizations and services, and to do so would deny NCAA services to the female student-athletes of 331 NCAA members (45.8 percent) which are not AIAW members."

The Council's report, in the form of a resolution to begin offering championships and support services for women's athletics, goes to the Convention floor in 1976. Perhaps typical of the uncertainty of the times, the plan is neither accepted nor rejected but is instead turned back to a committee of the Council for further study.

[12]Coincidentally, on March 15 of this same year, Dacia Schileru, a diver on the Wayne State University (Michigan) swim team, becomes the first female to compete in an NCAA championship, entering the College Division Swimming and Diving Championships.

Two years later, when the issue of women's sports again reaches the Convention floor, it arrives not as a resolution addressing the entire issue of women's athletics, but as a modest proposal sponsored by six Division II member institutions advocating the establishment of Division II championships for women in basketball, gymnastics and swimming.

The arguments advanced in support of the resolution illustrate the continuing evolution of the attitudes of the nation's intercollegiate athletic leadership toward women's sports. Thomas J. Niland Jr., delegate from Le Moyne College and one of the resolution's sponsors, rises first to speak to the motion:

"As a member of Division II and the College Division prior to that, we have participated in practically all NCAA postseason play-offs. We have undertaken a women's program in the last few years. It is the feeling of the members of our institution, both the men and the women in the athletic department, that we would like to follow suit and have our women compete in the postseason championships . . . . "

Other members speak in favor of the proposal, and delegate Edward S. Steitz of Springfield College addresses the problem of the AIAW's opposition to such a step by the NCAA. Says Steitz:

"As we all realize, no institution is compelled, nor is it mandatory, to participate in an NCAA championship. We have NCAA members, especially in Divisions II and III, that are not members of AIAW or any other predominantly female-dominated organization. The NCAA has both a moral and legal responsibility to provide women's championship competition for our colleagues who are in those positions. The NCAA legal counsel has told us so without any equivocation.

"We strongly believe the NCAA, or any other national organization to which we belong, has the responsibility to present as many opportunities and services to the membership as it can possibly provide, regardless of whether another organization to which we belong offers somewhat similar service.

"My institution is a charter member of the AIAW. We had a quality competitive program before Title IX or the AIAW came on the scene. We have hosted national championships for the AIAW . . . . We have poured in thousands of dollars and provided countless hours of leadership . . . .

"Our record speaks for itself. The reason I mention this, ladies and gentlemen, is because I hear rumblings that the spirit and intent of this motion is to do harm to another organization. Nothing, but nothing, Mr. President, is further from the truth.

"The only thing we seek in this motion is for the NCAA to provide a service to us in order to help meet the needs of our female student-athletes. Those of us who have held dual membership in the NCAA and NAIA recognize it is our institution's determination as to what championships we want to participate in."

The only opposition to women's championships centers not on the content of the resolution but on its timing and plans for implementation. It is best put by delegate Edward S. Betz of the University of the Pacific, then chairing the NCAA Committee on Women's Intercollegiate Athletics:

"If the Association believes that we must go into women's championships, then we will proceed to plan along those lines. (But) there has been no planning to bring women into the management of this program. The present Divisions I, II and III structures may not be appropriate at all for women. I think we are going into this a little rapidly and perhaps will foul up what we might do better at a later time."

The proposal is defeated by Division II voters, 31 to 44; but judging from the comments, it appears that here, early in 1978, the idea of sponsoring women's championships is reasonably well accepted. What remains to be done, however, is to involve women not only at the competitive level, but at the Association's highest governing levels as well. The "later time" Betz referred to is drawing ever nearer.

The step toward women's championships proposed in 1978 finally is taken in 1980, and it is a bigger step than originally was planned. At the 1980 Convention, the members of both Divisions II and III vote to conduct National Collegiate Championships in five women's sports — basketball, field hockey, swimming, tennis and volleyball — beginning in the 1981-82 season.

Governance Issue

The historic decision to begin women's championships is accompanied by a feeling among most NCAA members, and in particular among leaders of women's athletics at NCAA member schools, that women should be accorded a corresponding representation in the governing structure of the Association. The issue now moves from one of competitive opportunity to one of governance. Thus, immediately after passage of the proposal to begin Divisions II and III women's championships, the NCAA's Special Committee on Governance, Organization and Services (GOS) and the NCAA Council begin to consult with numerous women in athletics as they construct a plan that will call for extensive changes in the governance of the NCAA.

The final plan is completed in late 1980. It is, in the words of James Frank, then NCAA secretary-treasurer and chair of the GOS committee, " . . . in intent and in fact, designed to offer member institutions an alternative for women's competition and to involve women throughout the NCAA governance structure." Frank adds that the plan "does not force any institution to avail itself of NCAA-sponsored women's championships."

After several committee meetings and membership surveys — of which Frank later will say, "Never before in the history of the Association has such an effort been made to seek advice from so many different segments of the membership" — the "governance plan" is put in the form of four key proposals to appear on the agenda of the 1981 Convention. These proposals would:

1. Alter the administrative structure of the NCAA. Under terms of two of the proposals, the NCAA Council would be expanded from 18 to 22 persons, with a minimum of four positions allocated for women. The Executive Committee would be expanded from 10 to 12 members, with a minimum of two positions provided for women. The legislation also provides that certain women athletic administrators who do not serve as faculty representatives, directors of athletics or chief executive officers would still be eligible to serve on the Council or the Executive Committee.

2. Create the women's sports committees necessary to conduct the Divisions II and III championships, provide for representation of women on the NCAA general committees and establish a Women's Committee on Committees to appoint women's sports committees.

3. Allow a member institution to be eligible for NCAA women's championships from August 1, 1981, to August 1, 1985, either using NCAA rules or the formalized rules of any

recognized state, conference, regional or national organization under which the institution administered its women's athletic program before August 1, 1981.

4. Stipulate that an institution, effective August 1, 1985, could either place its women's program in the NCAA under NCAA rules in effect at that time or not affiliate its women's program with the NCAA, with no adverse effect on the men's program.

As James Frank intimated following publication of the governance plan, given the frequency of committee meetings and various pollings of the membership, the provisions for women's championships and the revisions in governance might accurately be said to have emanated from the membership more than from the leadership of the Association. In the final analysis, it is the membership that will decide the issue by its vote at the Convention. Says one delegate, "I don't see how you can get more democratic than this."

Before considering the voting on the issues of governance and championships, it is interesting to note the procedure by which a motion arrives on the Convention floor — the concept of access being as much a part of democracy as the actuality of voting expression.

According to the NCAA constitution and bylaws, amendments to either the constitution or bylaws require the sponsorship of only six active members to be put on the Convention agenda. Thereafter, an amendment to the constitution needs a two-thirds majority for passage; a change in the bylaws takes but a simple majority. The NCAA Council also is enabled to sponsor amendments, many of which are recommended by the Association's various committees. In the case of women's championships, the Council, meeting in Kansas City, October 15-17, 1980, specifically affirms a year-old policy of *not* sponsoring proposals to establish women's championships. These proposals are sponsored by member institutions. The amendments concerning governance are sponsored by the Council, as recommended by the GOS committee. As GOS Chair Frank says in a speech to the membership before the opening of the 1981 Convention:

"This is not a matter that can be or should be negotiated between or among national organizations; it must be decided by the member institutions themselves . . . . The colleges and universities of the nation must determine their approach to and solution for athletic problems. This is the appropriate forum for the membership of the NCAA to decide if it wants the Association to offer these programs and services. The NCAA, as a corporate expression of its membership, speaks and acts on athletic matters at the national level. In my view, there is not a superior democratic process available or proposed than this Convention . . . . "

Despite the myriad changes in college athletics, Frank's remarks may have been as appropriate in 1906 as they are in 1981.

However, the governance and championship plans are not without opposition, most notably from representatives of the AIAW.

On January 5, 1980, as the NCAA's committees are in the early stages of their work on governance and championships, the AIAW executive board adopts a resolution opposing the already-approved NCAA women's championships in Divisions II and III. The same board earlier had adopted a resolution asking the NCAA and the NAIA for a five-year moratorium "on efforts and plans to initiate championship programs for women." This latter action suggests, according to Frank, "that they did not want to talk or intend to talk about championships or governance for five years."

Donna Lopiano of the University of Texas, Austin, and 1981 president of the AIAW says her organization opposes the NCAA's planned actions because they would bring about "massive duplication" of women's championships (with the AIAW sponsoring its own women's championships) and because such actions could bring about an increase in the costs of recruiting due to the NCAA policy of permitting off-campus recruiting contacts between coach and prospect, whereas the AIAW does not permit off-campus contact.

However, several women athletic leaders publicly favor the plan.

"What we're asking for is simply a choice," UCLA delegate Judith R. Holland, a former AIAW president, told the Miami Herald. "We are trying to allow more options for women, the same type of opportunities men have."

Opponents of the governance plan also argue that the proposed Council and committee representation is discriminatory because it does not provide for precisely equal representation of men and women on all committees.

"On the contrary," says James Frank, "the plan is a very constructive, positive approach to enhancing women's roles in intercollegiate athletics management and policy development . . . . At NCAA member institutions, there are imbalanced ratios of male and female student-athletes, male and female coaches and male and female administrators . . . . The minimum allocations on the steering com-

mittees and the general committees were based . . . on a formula of
one-third allocated for women, one-third for men and one-third unal-
located and thus available to either. The one-third (is) based on
present participation ratios of approximately two men athletes to one
woman athlete. The proposed minimum allocations for women in the
NCAA administrative structure are hardly tokenism. Of the elected
positions on the NCAA Council and Executive Committee, women
would be assured of at least 20 percent of the positions and 30 percent
of the positions on the division steering committees."

To strengthen his point, Frank refers to action taken by the Association following the 1980 vote to establish women's championships in
Divisions II and III. "Of the first 38 individuals appointed to the
women's sports committees to administer the Divisions II and III
women's championships . . . 35 (92 percent) are women. All of the
chairs are women. If all portions of the governance plan were adopted,
approximately 215 women would be involved from the outset."

But while the tides of argument and counter-argument wash over
them, it is still the delegates, now seated in the ballroom, who are
about to make the final decision.

The Voting

At 8:04 a.m. on Tuesday, January 13, 1981, NCAA President William J. Flynn of Boston College bangs his gavel to call the Convention
to order, and immediately there is heard the crash of dinnerware as a
pile of plates falls to the floor of the hotel's kitchen.

"Is that an omen?" whispers one of the members of the media
covering the Convention.

There is a tentative collective laugh throughout the room as the
irony of that particular conjunction of events is not lost on the
membership.

Nevertheless, the Convention's business session begins quietly
enough with a virtually unanimous vote on what is known as the
"consent package," a group of 26 constitutional and bylaw amendments deemed to be noncontroversial. The amendments are packaged
together and voted on as one issue in order to speed up the legislative
process which, since 1906, has increased from less than one day to a
busy three days. A single objection to any of the "packaged" amendments is enough to single out that issue for a separate vote. Today
there are no objections.

While the first vote is not particularly interesting, there being no
issues to discuss, the voting process is interesting and somewhat

unusual. Whereas the Association's first president, Palmer Pierce, easily could determine the result of a voice vote or quickly count a show of hands, the growth of the Association and the establishment of three membership divisions have given rise to the "paddle system."

The paddle system works like this. Upon registering, each voting delegate (usually the chief executive officer, faculty representative or athletic director) receives a "voting paddle." Paddles are color-coded in order to facilitate voting by divisions, and a vote of the entire membership at once can be a colorful affair. Paddles for Division I members that are Division I-A in football are blue, Division I members that are Division I-AA in football get green paddles and all other Division I members get white paddles. Division II members use orange, Division III members have yellow and the voting paddles of unclassified members are the colors of the institution's preferred division and are marked by a stripe to assure that the institution votes only on constitutional proposals.

The 75th annual Convention moves easily through its first hours until it reaches agenda item No. 51, "Women's Athletics — Administrative Structure," this being the first major issue involving women's athletics to be brought to the floor. Basically, this is the plan that, if approved, will alter the administrative structure of the NCAA to place women on the Association's highest policy-making bodies — the Executive Committee, the Council and the division steering committees.

The Council, the 18-member body authorized to make policy decisions between Conventions, heretofore has been made up of the NCAA president and secretary-treasurer as ex officio members, the eight district vice-presidents and eight vice-presidents at large, all elected by the Convention. Under terms of the amendment, there will be 12 at-large vice-presidents, and the four additional positions on the Council will be taken by women.

While the Council is the policy-making body, it is the 10-member Executive Committee of the Association that is charged with overseeing the business transactions and the championships of the NCAA. The Executive Committee consists of the NCAA president and secretary-treasurer, once again acting as ex officio members, and eight additional members elected by the Council following the annual Convention. Under terms of the amendment, the two additional places reserved for women will be filled by vote of the Council.

Since the vote is on a constitutional amendment, it is to be a common vote of all divisions and one that will require a two-thirds majority for passage.

"Those in favor," intones Flynn in a pronounced New England accent, "raise your paddles."

The paddles go up. The vote is clearly more than half, but it may be questionable as to whether it constitutes two-thirds. Flynn looks slowly around the room, squinting through the glare of television lights.

"All right. Now, those opposed raise your paddles."

Again, the paddles go up.

Flynn looks around the room and hesitates.

"Again. Those in favor raise your paddles."

The paddles go up.

"Those opposed."

The paddles go up.

"It's too close; we need a count," Flynn declares.

There is a barely audible groan throughout the ballroom.

"Those in favor raise your paddles."

This time when the paddles go up, Flynn calls on members of the Voting Committee, who walk among the rows of tables making a paddle-by-paddle count of the vote and then pass the results to the Voting Committee chair to tally.

"Those opposed," says Flynn.

The paddles go up and the process is repeated. The slip of paper with the final count is given to Flynn.

"The vote," Flynn says, as only his voice and the whir of a camera are heard in the room, "is 369 in favor, 169 opposed. That is a 68.6 percent margin. The motion passes."

A call for a recount only succeeds in seeing the margin jump to 69.5 percent (383 to 168). Thus, for the first time since the NCAA's founding 75 years earlier, women athletics leaders are to be assimilated into the Association's decision-making structure.

While nearly 70 percent favored the governance amendments, the vote on women's championships is to be much closer.

Shortly after 5 p.m., the amendment to establish NCAA Division I women's championships in basketball, cross country, field hockey, gymnastics, softball, swimming and diving, tennis, outdoor track and volleyball comes to the floor for a vote. Since this motion amends a bylaw, as opposed to a constitutional change, it will require a simple majority vote, and that vote will be by Division I institutions only. In certain areas governed by bylaws (recruiting, playing seasons, financial aid and championships, among others), the NCAA permits each division to determine its own legislation.

Once again, the paddle vote is too close to call. In fact, this time even the count by the Voting Committee is too close to call. When President Flynn reads the totals, he announces a tie — 124 in favor, 124 opposed. When uncertainty develops over whether all the votes were counted in one corner of the room, Flynn orders a recount. This time the motion fails by the smallest possible margin — one vote, 128 to 127. Curious though it seems, it apparently is the will of the members that women are to be involved in NCAA governance and allowed to compete in Divisions II and III championships, but such are the NCAA checks and balances that it remains the right of Division I institutions to reject their own women's championships if they so choose.

The vote against establishment of Division I women's championships, however, is followed by a motion asking the membership to rescind the vote of the previous year's Convention and do away with the already-approved Divisions II and III women's championships. The motion is overwhelmingly defeated; and as the first day's business draws to a close, the NCAA is once again in the odd position of being directed by its members to implement national women's championships for some institutions but not for all. This apparent inconsistency and the wide margin of approval for Divisions II and III women's championships brings a call for reconsideration of the Division I women's championships proposal. (Under Robert's Rules of Order and NCAA regulations, any member voting on the prevailing side of a motion may request reconsideration.)

Before a vote can be taken on the issue, there must be a vote on the motion to reconsider. This vote passes easily, 141 to 105, as if foreshadowing a general change in the consensus of the Convention.

The Division I membership, in the final vote of the day, then votes again on the matter of Division I women's championships. This time the motion carries, 137 to 117.

Given the facts of constitutional democracy and government by open convention, the most appropriate comment on the issue may have come from Linda K. Estes, a Convention delegate and women's athletic director at the University of New Mexico, when asked by a writer for her thoughts had the membership rejected women's championships. "That," she said matter-of-factly, "is the legislative process."

It is also the legacy of the 28 men in the Murray Hill Hotel 75 years ago.

Assessing the impact of the votes on women's athletics, NCAA Executive Director Walter Byers says at a news conference at the close of the 1981 Convention that the votes on governance and championships constitute "a historic commitment by the NCAA to enhance opportunities for women." He says he expected the decisions to give "fresh and renewed impetus to intercollegiate athletics for women at all levels . . . . We're going to watch women's athletics rise to a new plateau," Byers predicts.

By late Wednesday morning, the Convention has worked its way through a 121-item agenda that, in addition to governance and women's championships, includes resolutions regarding broadcasting, recruiting, insurance, financial aid, academic standards, eligibility, postseason play and several other issues that undoubtedly would have surprised the Association's founders.

The Convention closes with the election of a new slate of officers, put forth by the Nominating Committee for approval by the membership. Outgoing President Flynn announces that the new NCAA presidential nominee is his secretary-treasurer, James Frank, the president of Lincoln University in Missouri. Frank is the first college president and the first Black ever elected president of the NCAA.

Outside the Fontainebleau, the wind has shifted to the southwest and temperatures are on their way from the high 30s to the low 70s. Babson College's Bob Hartwell walks through the lobby, pausing to look out a window toward the beach.

"Climate's a lot better now," he says.

CHAPTER NINE

" *. . . to determine the national intercollegiate champion."*

Competition may lie at the heart of sport and, indeed, at the heart of the American way of life, but in the beginning it lies rather far from the minds of the NCAA's founders.

The Association is not established in 1906 with any thought that it will administer sporting events; ironically, it is this very activity that, in the latter half of the century, most often will bring the Association to public attention. In fact, there is nothing in Article 2 ("Purposes") of the original constitution that empowers the NCAA to conduct sporting events.

It is not until 1919, with the NCAA already at the end of its 13th year, that President Palmer Pierce broaches the topic of National Collegiate Championships. He includes it almost as an afterthought at the end of a long address to the membership December 30, 1919.

"This" (Pierce has been speaking of American Expeditionary Force competitions in France during World War I) "brings to mind the fact that the college athletes of the United States possibly might meet in competition for the various national championships. Would it not be advisable for our Association to favor this . . . ?"

The Executive Committee takes up Pierce's idea and by December 1920, Pierce is able to tell the Convention:

> "Your Executive Committee has given careful consideration
> to the question of an annual field and track meet to be held at
> some central place in the country, as accessible as possible to all

our universities and colleges. It is considered that such a national contest would act as a stimulus to field sports and track events throughout the whole length and breadth of the land, and by actual competition determine the national championship. However, in this connection, there are many details to be thought of, such as the time, place and expense involved."

Later during the same Convention, the Executive Committee sponsors and the membership approves a motion "that a national intercollegiate field and track meet be held annually, under the auspices of this Association, to determine the national intercollegiate championship in the several events."

The three men named to the committee to arrange the details for the championship are Amos Alonzo Stagg, University of Chicago; Maj. John L. Griffith, University of Illinois, and Thomas E. Jones, University of Wisconsin.

The vote to hold such a meet is a historic one, but the *idea* of holding National Collegiate Championships is not new. Some intercollegiate championships predate the founding of the NCAA. The oldest of these is the National Collegiate Tennis Championships, first conducted in 1883 when Trinity College (Connecticut) hosts Harvard, Yale and Brown at Hartford, Connecticut. Sponsored by the U.S. Lawn Tennis Association, the tournament is held on grass courts on the grounds of an insane asylum.

Similarly, in 1897, the U.S. Golf Association, through its affiliate, the Intercollegiate Golf Association of America, begins sponsorship of National Collegiate Golf Championships. It is stretching the point, however, to describe these as true national intercollegiate championships since both tournaments are invitationals and both produce individual rather than team champions.

The NCAA's entry into the arena of national intercollegiate championships is not solely motivated by the members' desires to determine the national champion in a given sport. The Association's involvement is as much — perhaps more — the result of a prevailing philosophy among college sports leaders that intercollegiate athletics should be sponsored, administered and controlled by the colleges themselves, rather than by outside organizations.

The first true National Collegiate Championship (under this name) takes place in June 1921 at Stagg Field on the University of Chicago campus. The site is chosen for its convenient geographical location, though it also is appropriate because Amos Alonzo Stagg is the driving force behind the organization of this historic meet. Track and field athletes from 62 colleges and universities are represented at this first meet. According to tournament committee member Griffith, "A large number of other institutions have assured the committee that if this Association decides to continue the meet, they will be represented."

The meet itself is aimed primarily at determining individual champions, but there is a team championship award. There also is a special award given to mark what NCAA members sense is the historical significance of the meet. Says Griffith in his report to the Association:

"Believing that this meet was one of historical significance and feeling that everyone who competed in it would look back with pleasure to his competition, the committee had bronze medals in commemoration of the event struck off and presented them to all of the contestants who had not won any prizes."

Financial solvency, while desirable, is not a determining factor in the launching of the first national championship, nor, in later years, in the establishment of any National Collegiate Championship. However, financial return from the first National Collegiate Track and Field Championships is gratifying, if modest. The Association nets $146 on a gross of $4,000, such return allowing the committee to refund two-thirds of the traveling expenses of the competing teams. The committee — Stagg, Griffith and Jones — probably does not realize it as yet, but its practice of paying the travel expenses of the competitors will become a firm and enduring policy of the NCAA in the conduct of its future championships.

That the first NCAA-sponsored championship should occur in the early 1920s is as much due to forces outside the Association as it is to forces within. There is a nationwide sports boom following World War I, a relatively prosperous period during which colleges and high schools around the country begin building new and larger tracks, stadiums and gymnasiums — forerunners of the magnificent sports structures that will be found on many college campuses by the 1970s. With added interest in athletic competition and with creation of good facilities, it is only natural that there arises a desire to extend competition beyond regional lines. The inauguration of the first NCAA championship is, in part, a natural byproduct of this national development.

The pattern of the establishment of most early NCAA championships, during and after the 1920s, is that the Association usually acts not upon its own initiative, but upon a recommendation to a rules committee from the coaches association of the sport involved. A typical case in point is the first National Collegiate Swimming Championships.

Buoyed by the success of the first track and field meets and by a phenomenal growth in intercollegiate swimming (12 NCAA member institutions sponsor swimming in 1914; by 1924, this number is more than 100), F. W. Luehring, chair of the NCAA Rules Committee for Swimming and Water Sports, reports to the membership in 1923:

"Another important suggestion made by the Swimming Coaches Association and which has the unanimous approval of the committee is a recommendation that the NCAA foster a national collegiate swimming meet at the close of the various leagues, similar to the present track and field meet . . . . It is also suggested that possibly this year the meet might be considered one of the official Olympic tryouts, similar to the arrangement in track."

Following Luehring's report, the membership votes to authorize the committee to conduct a swimming meet along the lines of the track and field meet. The U.S. Naval Academy agrees to host the meet, and the American Olympic Committee responds favorably to the rules committee's request and designates the meet an official Olympic tryout.

Fifty swimmers from 14 colleges attend the meet. There undoubtedly would be more entries if the committee had not had the foresight to restrict the meet to first-place winners in the various conferences and swimming leagues. As if literally to mark the event with its stamp, the NCAA has struck gold, silver and bronze medals bearing the Association's name to be awarded to the top finishers in each event.

Like its track and field predecessor, the NCAA swimming championship is widely acclaimed a success. There is, however, one important aspect in which the swimming championship differs from the track and field meet. The swimming committee decides not to hold the meet at the same site each year, as is the case with the track and field meet at Stagg Field, but to move it to various campuses in different parts of the country. "An ideal arrangement," reads a committee report published after the first meet, "would be to have the meet alternate in different sections of the country. Plans now are under way to hold the championship in the Middle West at the close of the present season."

The decision to hold a championship at a fixed site or to move it about the country is a choice that, sooner or later, will be faced by all the sports committees. While consideration of distance and traveling time are major factors, particularly in the days of train travel, it will remain one of the inexplicable facts of the collegiate championships that, while some championships build a following and thrive at a fixed site (e.g., baseball), others will do better when moved to different locations (e.g., basketball).

In 1928, the first National Collegiate Wrestling Championships are held. The establishment of this meet, like that of its predecessors, results from action taken by the sports committee (the NCAA Wrestling Rules Committee) and the advice of the sport's coaches.

At a midyear meeting in 1927, the Wrestling Rules Committee decides to hold the first National Collegiate Wrestling Championships March 30-31 of the following year on the campus of Iowa State College (now Iowa State University). The meet attracts 40 wrestlers representing 16 colleges. Again, as in swimming, the list of entries would be much longer were it not for the committee's stringent eligibility rules, including a one-year residency requirement and a three-year participation rule. Nearly all contestants at the meet are conference or sectional champions; and such is the caliber of wrestling that the AOC recognizes the meet as a sectional Olympic tryout, meaning that the first- and second-place winners qualify for the final Olympic tryouts. While not as successful as the track and field meet, the wrestling event is able to generate enough revenue that the committee is able to reimburse contestants for more than one-half of their train fare.

The establishment of these first three National Collegiate Championships, all within a seven-year time span, is followed by a period of consolidation that sees the three existing championships firmly entrenched. Eventually, this beginning leads to another burst of championship activity by the Association in the late 1930s.

While the founding of each of the original championship events constitutes a story in itself, it is common to all of them, and should not be lost sight of, that they owe their founding and success perhaps as much to *individual* energies and impetus as to the subsequent collective support of the NCAA. As retired NCAA Controller Arthur J. Bergstrom writes in his report on the championships, "The success of the Association's championships can be traced to the foresight and diligent labors of many dedicated individuals who were willing to devote long hours of tedious work and to institutions that were willing to spend considerable money to launch and build these events." Stagg and the track and field championships immediately come to mind.

"Hard work and the willingness to adjust to abnormal conditions were responsible for keeping the championship series alive during World War II," reports Bergstrom. "Schedules were modified to shorten time of competition, and meets and tournaments were located in areas where availability of transportation was less than a major problem."

The series survives World War II and, as we shall see in our examination of the individual sports, becomes more popular as time goes on.

College Division and Divisions II and III Championships

As the NCAA membership grows, many institutions with outstanding teams but playing less than major schedules are denied the opportunity to participate in national competition. Consequently, the membership votes to establish national competition for College Division institutions, beginning with a basketball tournament. The first National College Division Basketball Championship finals are hosted by the University of Evansville in 1957. The tournament format provides for a 32-team bracket; most of these teams would not otherwise have enjoyed the opportunity for postseason championship play.

In 1973, the Association takes another step toward the better accommodation of the smaller institutions when it establishes three divisions within the Association, an action that immediately stimulates the inauguration of additional national championships in 18 sports. At this point, the NCAA offers 41 championships — 17 are classified as National Collegiate Championships, 13 as National Collegiate Division II Championships and 11 as National Collegiate Division III Championships. In those events in which there is only one national championship meet or tournament, the Association rules that all members may be eligible to participate. Despite the three-division championship structure, interest in the National Collegiate Championships will become so strong through the 1970s that it will be necessary for the various sports committees to establish qualifying standards as a means to entry in certain championships, notably those involving individual events.

Women's Championships

Next to the decision to go ahead with the 1921 track and field meet, perhaps the most important decision on the conduct of intercollegiate championships will concern women's athletics.

In January 1980, the Convention votes to conduct women's championships in five sports in Divisions II and III, beginning in 1981-82. But before any of these championships are held, the 1981 Convention reaches its historic decision in favor of the NCAA conducting Division I women's championships in nine sports: basketball, cross country, field hockey, gymnastics, softball, swimming and diving, tennis, outdoor track and volleyball, and National Collegiate Championships (all three divisions) in fencing, golf and lacrosse. These championships also are scheduled to begin in the 1981-82 academic year. (See Chapter Eight.)

These decisions to proceed with women's championships lead directly to passage of the 1981 governance plan which, as we have seen, brings significant numbers of women into the NCAA's governing structure and also leads to an increase in the Association's administrative staff, including the appointment of Ruth M. Berkey as the first director of women's championships.

Berkey, former director of athletics at Occidental College, is charged not only with assuring the success of the women's championships, but also, as Executive Director Walter Byers says in making the appointment, "for representing women's sports interests in all facets of NCAA operations."

Like most decisions affecting sport, the major impact of the women's championship series is expected to be most in evidence in the games and contests where increased competitive opportunities should lead to improvement in the quality of coaching available to women and, eventually, in steadily improving athletic performance. Looking ahead one decade, NCAA President James Frank says in 1981, "In the years leading up to 1990 . . . women will continue to make sizable gains both in terms of financial support for the women's programs and attention to their cause. Factual equity for women's sports will be almost complete."

From the beginning, all the NCAA-sponsored championships are administered by sports committees appointed to serve a particular meet or tournament, with member institutions serving as host institutions, assisted by the respective committees and the national office staff. In those events in which all teams are not selected automatically, the sports committees are assisted by regional advisory committees, thus assuring the inclusion of the most outstanding teams in the championships.

But to get back to the championships themselves, in the five-year period from 1937 to 1941, the NCAA inaugurates seven national meets and tournaments as the administration of championships now becomes a major part of the Association's work. Let us look at these and subsequent championships in the order in which they arise.

Boxing

In 1932 and 1936, there are national collegiate boxing tournaments — not properly championships — held as qualifying matches through which college boxers can gain entry to the Olympic trials. The first NCAA-sanctioned National Collegiate Boxing Championships are held in 1937 in Sacramento, California. The event hereafter is continued annually (with the exception of the war years, 1944-1946) until 1960, at which time the Association, meeting at its 55th annual Convention, votes to discontinue the boxing championships. This decision is based on the apparent lack of interest in intercollegiate boxing by a majority of the membership, the scarcity of competent college-oriented coaches and the fact that few high schools in the country sponsor interscholastic boxing.

The boxing championships, however, do enjoy an era of popularity with spectators and participants. The three-day tournament in Madison, Wisconsin, in 1949 attracts 49,800 spectators; two years later, the 1951 championships attract boxers from a record 31 member institutions.

Gymnastics

The first National Collegiate Gymnastics Championships are held April 16, 1938, at the University of Chicago, with the host team emerging as the first national champion over runner-up Illinois. At first, interest is modest among competitors and spectators; but the event gradually becomes more popular until, in 1965, the Gymnastics Committee finds it necessary to establish qualifying meets to assure that the number of contestants in the championship itself is not unwieldy and that the athletes competing are, in fact, of championship caliber. By 1973, there are nine such qualifying meets in various sections of the country. The gymnastics championships are held annually with the exception of the war and postwar years, 1943 through 1947.

To relieve further the pressure of entries in the Division I championships and to compensate for the fact that by the 1960s it is extremely difficult for a College Division gymnast to qualify for the national championships, the Association in 1968 inaugurates the National Collegiate College Division Gymnastics Championships to provide national competition and recognition for College Division gymnasts. Northridge State wins the first championship.

Among those achieving prominence in the National Collegiate Gymnastics Championships are Penn State coach Gene Wettstone, whose squads have won a record nine team championships; Olympian Kurt Thomas of Indiana State, who won three individual championships (horizontal bar, parallel bars, best all-around) in the 1979 tournament; Bart Conner of Oklahoma, runner-up to Thomas by just three-quarters of a point in the 1979 event, and Jim Hartung of Nebraska, a two-time winner of the all-around title, 1980 and 1981.

Tennis

As we have seen, it is the U.S. Lawn Tennis Association (USLTA) that sanctions what generally, if loosely, is referred to as the first intercollegiate championship meet at Trinity College (Connecticut) in 1893. The USLTA continues to sponsor this invitational meet until 1938, when it agrees to conduct the meet as a national championship under joint sponsorship with the NCAA. This sponsorship arrangement continues until 1941, when the NCAA assumes complete responsibility for the conduct of the championships.

The tennis championships actually are individual, rather than team, championships until 1946, when the Association also recognizes a team champion. In this instance, it is Southern California over runner-up William and Mary.

The caliber of intercollegiate tennis improves so fast through the 1950s, '60s and early '70s that prior to 1976 the Tennis Committee asks member institutions to limit their championship entries to players whose regular-season performance would indicate a chance to score points in the championships. In 1976, the national committee takes over the selection process, choosing the top 128 singles and 64 doubles players for entry in the tournament. In 1977, the tournament format is again revised; now the committee selects the nation's top 16 college *teams* to compete in the team championship and then selects the top 64 singles and 32 doubles players to compete for individual titles.

In 1963, the Division II championships begin with Los Angeles

State winning the title. The Division III tournament is added in 1976 and is won by Kalamazoo.

Among the famous players to have competed in this tournament are Arthur Ashe and Jimmy Connors of UCLA; Francisco "Pancho" Segura, Dennis Ralston and Stan Smith of Southern California, and John McEnroe of Stanford. Coach George Toley of Southern California has established himself as one of the premier college coaches, taking his teams to 10 National Collegiate Championships between 1955 and 1976. UCLA's J. D. Morgan won seven championships before going on to become a nationally recognized athletic director at the Bruin campus.

Cross Country

The National Collegiate Cross Country Championships evolve from the Central Intercollegiate Conference meet, which begins in 1926 and by the 1930s achieves a sort of national character despite its not being an official national championship. The first running of the NCAA-sponsored national championships takes place in 1938 in East Lansing, Michigan. Michigan State University is the host as Indiana edges Notre Dame for the team championship.

With the exception of the war-cancelled 1943 meet, Michigan State continues as annual host through 1964. Since then, the committee has moved this championship to various sites around the country.

Beginning in 1945, the Earle C. "Billy" Hayes Trophy is awarded annually to the institutional winner in the National Collegiate Cross Country Championships. This traveling trophy honors the former Indiana University coach who was one of the organizers of the meet and who helped found the U.S. Cross Country Coaches Association. Hayes' Hoosiers won the team title in 1938, 1940 and 1942. Individual runners gaining national recognition in recent years include three-time meet winners Gerry Lindgren of Washington State (1966, '67, '69), Steve Prefontaine of Oregon (1970, '71, '73) and Henry Rono of Washington State (1976, '77, '79).

The Association initiates the College Division (now Division II) championships in 1958; Northern Illinois wins the first title. In 1973, the newly created Division III operates its championships in conjunction with Division II and then becomes a separate entity in 1974. Ashland is the first Division III champion.

Cross country is a nonincome sport, and all of this sport's championships operate with deficits, the exception being 1968 when the meet receives $10,000 as a television rights fee. However, revenue is not a factor in a sport such as cross country, which the NCAA membership consistently views as an integral part of most good intercollegiate athletic programs.

Basketball — Division I

As early as 1909, when what we know as the NCAA is still calling itself the Intercollegiate Athletic Association of the United States, R. B. Hyatt of Yale, chair of the Collegiate Basketball Rules Committee (a committee that predates the Association), tells the third annual Convention: "Basketball without a doubt is here to stay. Outside of college, it is immensely popular; more so, in fact, than it ever will be in college."

Hyatt unquestionably is right about the longevity of basketball; but his assertion that the sport will become more popular outside the college ranks is open to some debate, particularly by anyone who will ever see the tournament that has come to be called — simply and accurately — "The Classic."

The word "classic" is applied to the National Collegiate Basketball Championship right from the beginning. The tournament is established in 1939. Writing in the 1939-40 basketball guide, NCAA President William B. Owens of Stanford University says, "It is entirely fitting that the prestige of college basketball should be supported and demonstrated to the nation by the colleges themselves, rather than this be left to private promotion and enterprise. . . . . The National Collegiate Athletic Association basketball tournament should become a *classic* (italics added), a fitting annual climax in the program of this great American sport."

As with most of the other championships, the basketball tournament comes about as the result of a recommendation by the coaches association (the National Association of Basketball Coaches) to the Executive Committee of the NCAA that such a tournament be established. The Executive Committee and, later, the NCAA Convention approve.

The first championship is a three-round affair involving one representative team from each NCAA district. Teams representing Districts 1 through 4 meet in Philadelphia and those from Districts 5 through 8 meet in San Francisco to determine the East and West champions. The winners — Ohio State and Oregon — meet at Northwestern University on March 27, 1939, to play for the national championship. Oregon wins, 46-33, to emerge as the first National Collegiate Basketball Champion.

The original tournament format remains in effect until 1951, when the basketball tournament enters an era of expansion that is to continue into the 1980s. In 1951, the format changes to award 10 conferences automatic qualification for the championship, with the basketball committee then responsible for selecting six at-large teams to round out the 16-team field.

In 1952, the number of regional sites is increased from two to four, with the four winners advancing to the finals. This is the format still in use in the 1980s.

The tournament bracket is increased from 16 to 22 teams in 1953, with 14 conferences receiving automatic qualification; and the growth continues into 1954, when the bracket is expanded to 24 teams, with 15 conferences receiving automatic qualification.

So great is the tournament's popularity in the early and mid-1950s that the 1954 finals are televised nationally. LaSalle defeats Bradley, 94-76, in this historic sports telecast.

During this period of expanding brackets, growing public popularity and media attention, the tournament is developed and guided by a committee chaired from 1948 to 1960 by Arthur C. "Dutch" Lonborg of the University of Kansas.

The tournament field remains stable at 23 to 25 teams per year (usually 15 automatic qualifiers and nine to 11 teams selected by the committee) through the 1960s as both attendance and media coverage continue to grow. In 1973, the committee, chaired by Tom Scott of Davidson College, announces that effective in 1975 the tournament will once again expand, this time to a 32-team bracket. This is done partly to allow the Division I Basketball Committee to select a second conference team as an at-large entry. In the first year of the new system, the 1975 tournament field consists of 16 conference champions, four Eastern College Athletic Conference (ECAC) regional champions receiving automatic qualification, five independents and seven additional conference teams receiving at-large berths. The purpose of the larger, even-numbered bracket is to allow more member institutions to participate in the tournament and to eliminate all byes to assure that each team begins play in the first round.

In 1978, the basketball committee once more expands the tournament, this time to a 40-team bracket. Twenty conference champions and three regional champions from the ECAC automatically qualify, with the committee selecting the other 17 teams.

The tournament grows again, this time to a 48-team bracket, in 1980 and 1981. At the Association's 75th annual Convention in 1981, the championship takes a step into the computer age with the tournament committee's announcement that it will use a computer-ranking system to assist in determining its at-large selections. The computer system is designed to take account of Division I winning percentage, road success, opponents' success and opponents' strength of schedule to produce a Ratings Percentage Index (RPI). The tournament format specifies that, by 1983, not more than 50 percent of the bracket may be made up of conferences receiving automatic-qualifying berths, thus leaving the committee the task of choosing at least 24 teams. Committee Chair Wayne Duke of the Big Ten emphasizes, however, that the actual selections will be made by the committee, not the computer, and that the RPI is to be "an aid . . . for each committee member to use in evaluation of the teams available for the tournament." To which he wryly adds, "We'll still hear from the 49th-rated team, I'm sure."

In the course of his remarks, Duke refers to the tournament as "one of the greatest athletic spectacles in all of sports." Public interest, as demonstrated by attendance and television revenues, seems to support the statement. More than 4.7 million spectators attend the tournament games during the first 38 years, including a record 63,313 for the 1970 finals at the Houston Astrodome. Tournaments being sold out becomes an annual occurrence. There are no complimentary tickets to the National Collegiate Basketball Championships, and those tickets available for public sale are awarded by means of a drawing from among hundreds of thousands of applicants. So intense is the demand for tickets that the tournament committee has decided that beginning in 1983 the facility selected for the final round must have a minimum of 17,000 seats.

Predictably, television has been eager to bring the games to those who cannot attend, and television rights fees have climbed from $180,000 in 1966 to $18 million for each of the tournaments in 1982, '83 and '84.

In 1969, net income from the tournament exceeded $1 million for the first time (approximately half from television fees); tournament income exceeded $2 million by 1973. By 1981, the National Collegiate Basketball Championship had produced cumulative income of $65.6 million.

Few tournaments in any sport have been graced by the presence of as many outstanding athletes as the National Collegiate Division I Men's Basketball Championship. Among those basketball stars whose names would become household words during and after their appearance in the tournament are David Thompson, North Carolina State; Elvin Hayes, Houston; Bill Bradley, Princeton; Elgin Baylor, Seattle; Oscar Robertson, Cincinnati; Jerry West, West Virginia; Magic Johnson, Michigan State; Larry Bird, Indiana State; Bill Russell, San Francisco; Lew Alcindor, UCLA; Jerry Lucas, Ohio State, and Wilt Chamberlain, Kansas.

The tournament also has helped produce at least one coaching legend, that of UCLA coach John Wooden, the "Wizard of Westwood." From 1964 to 1975, Wooden's teams won a record 10 national championships, including seven in a row from 1967 to 1973. Included in the list of outstanding coaches who have taken their teams to national titles are Henry Iba, Oklahoma State; Adolph Rupp, Kentucky; Bobby Knight, Indiana, and Al McGuire, Marquette.

Basketball — Division II

It is understandable that many smaller NCAA members with outstanding basketball teams encounter difficulty through the years in qualifying for the National Collegiate Basketball Championship because their schedules include few of the so-called "major" teams. The matter is complicated further by the sheer number of colleges playing basketball and particularly by the rapid rise of the sport's popularity in the College Division segment of the Association. In view of this, the NCAA in 1957 institutes the College Division (later Division II) championship. It is the first NCAA-sponsored championship designed to provide national competition for College Division institutions. Wheaton earns the distinction of being the Association's first College Division champion by defeating Kentucky Wesleyan, 89-65.

The 1957 format calls for 16 first-round and eight second-round games to be played on the campuses of participating institutions, with the eight winners proceeding to the finals. This format is abandoned a year later, when eight four-team regionals are held with the eight winners advancing to the finals. The regional format remains in effect, though it later is modified to have the eight regional winners play quarterfinal games to determine four finalists. As is the case with the Division I championship, the Division II tournament provides automatic qualification for the champions of certain conferences.

It is a significant measure of the popularity of intercollegiate basketball that the Division II championship ranks fifth among all NCAA championships in revenue, having netted $1,234,292 from

1957 to 1981.

This tournament also has served to showcase some of basketball's nationally recognized talents, including Earl Monroe of Winston-Salem State and Jerry Sloan of Evansville.

Basketball — Division III

Like its Division II counterpart, the Division III tournament is designed to provide national competition for another segment of the Association's membership. The tournament's 32-team bracket and preliminary regional format are similar to that in effect in Division II. The first National Collegiate Division III Basketball Championship is held March 15, 1975, at Albright College, Reading, Pennsylvania, where LeMoyne-Owen defeats Glassboro State, 57-54.

Golf

As we have seen, the first intersectional collegiate golf championships begin as an invitational tournament conducted by the Intercollegiate Golf Association of America (in reality, the U.S. Golf Association). It continues to be conducted under USGA auspices from 1897 until 1939 (no tournaments were held in 1900, 1917 and 1918), when the NCAA inaugurates its National Collegiate Golf Championships.

Not surprisingly, the early competitions are dominated by Ivy League schools — Yale wins seven of the first 11 tournaments, Harvard wins the other four. It is not until Michigan's win in 1934 that a non-Ivy League school takes the title.

Stanford wins the first NCAA-sponsored championship in 1939, taking the team title by edging Northwestern by two strokes.

As is the case in tennis and some other sports, rapid improvements in the caliber of play result in increased interest in the National Collegiate Golf Championships. Most of the nation's (and some of the world's) best golfers gained recognition in the National Collegiate Golf Championships, including Arnold Palmer of Wake Forest, Jack Nicklaus of Ohio State, Tom Watson of Stanford, Ben Crenshaw of Texas and Hale Irwin of Colorado. Leading coach in the tournament is Houston's Dave Williams, whose teams won 10 titles from 1956 to 1977.

Division II (1963) and Division III (1975) national championships are established by the NCAA for the customary purpose of providing competition for all member institutions. Southwest Missouri State is the first Division II champion while Wooster takes the initial Division III title.

Fencing

The National Collegiate Fencing Championships come about in 1941 as the result of an NCAA survey showing ample membership interest in holding such an event. The first meet is hosted by Ohio State University and won by Northwestern. Since then, the fencing championships have been held every year with the exception of the war years, 1943-1946.

The fencing championships are among those NCAA tournaments operating at a deficit, but they generally are considered to be meets of artistic success providing the best in intercollegiate competition for those individuals and institutions interested in this sport of specialists. One of the more prominent names in the history of this tournament is that of New York University coach Hugo Castello, whose teams won 10 championships from 1954 to 1974.

Baseball

The College World Series is the way people commonly refer to the National Collegiate Baseball Championship, an event which has progressed from inauspicious beginnings to assume a place among the most prestigious of the Association's championships and the most important amateur baseball event in the country.

The College World Series begins with a recommendation in 1947 by the American Association of College Baseball Coaches to the NCAA's Executive Committee that the Association begin sponsoring a baseball championship.

The first tournament is held June 27-28, 1947, on the campus of Western Michigan University in Kalamazoo. The original format provides for the selection of one team from each NCAA district to play in two single-elimination regionals (East and West), with the winners advancing to the finals for a best-two-out-of-three play-off. California wins the first championship by sweeping Yale, 17-4 and 8-7.

In 1950, the College World Series takes its place among those few national championships operated annually at the same site. A helpful and forward-looking civic group in Omaha, Nebraska — the Omaha Baseball Committee — invites the NCAA to adopt Omaha as a permanent site for the championship. The committee's confidence in the potential of college baseball is sorely tested before it is vindicated. From 1950 until 1962, there are only two championships that operate in the black, and the Omaha Baseball Committee finds itself absorbing deficits in the amount of $38,173. Since 1962, however, the baseball championship has operated at a surplus, providing a financial return to the participating institutions, the NCAA and the Omaha sponsors, who in 1981 are operating as College World Series, Inc.

In 1954, the NCAA Baseball Committee revises the tournament format to one similar to that used in basketball; that is, there is automatic qualification for the champions of certain conferences, with the rest of the field made up of outstanding independent teams selected by the committee. The winners of the eight district competitions advance to the finals.

There is another format change in 1975, when the Baseball Committee is given the authority to select more than one team from an automatically qualifying conference. This change comes about as a result of the growth of college baseball and the development of many more outstanding college teams. In 1976, a field of 34 teams begins the quest for the national championship.

More than a few modern-day baseball stars have participated in the College World Series, among them Reggie Jackson, Bob Horner and Sal Bando of Arizona State; Fred Lynn and Steve Kemp of Southern California; Mike Schmidt of Ohio; Burt Hooton of Texas, and Dave Winfield of Minnesota. United States Vice-President George Bush played for Yale in the 1947 and 1948 championships.

While he may not be as well known as many of his players, Southern California coach Rod Dedeaux is the tournament's most successful coach, with 10 College World Series championships between 1958 and 1978, including five in a row (1970-1974).

The first National College Division (later Division II) Baseball Championship final is hosted by Southwest Missouri State College (now Southwest Missouri State University) in Springfield June 5-7, 1968, and is won by Chapman. This tournament is held in Springfield, Missouri, until 1971, when it moves to Springfield, Illinois, where it stays through 1979. The University of California, Riverside, hosts the 1980 and 1981 championships.

The Division III Baseball Championship is launched June 4-6, 1976, at Marietta College, Marietta, Ohio, with Stanislaus State of California as the first champion. Marietta College has hosted the championship each year.

Ice Hockey

The Broadmoor, a famous resort in Colorado Springs, Colorado, becomes the site for the first 10 National Collegiate Ice Hockey

Championships beginning March 18-20, 1948, with Michigan defeating Dartmouth, 8-4, for the first national title.

In 1958, the Ice Hockey Committee selects the tournament site from among those cities and institutions interested in hosting the championship. The general pattern is for the committee to schedule the championship in the East one year and in the West or Midwest the following year, although from 1972 to 1974 the venerable Boston Garden is the tournament site.

Until 1981, the tournament format calls for four teams to compete at the finals site, with the champions of the Western Collegiate Hockey Association (WCHA) and the ECAC enjoying automatic qualification. The two remaining teams may be selected by the committee or determined through first-round games. In the East, the committee has the discretion of holding first-round competition or selecting a representative. In the West, there is a mandatory first-round game between a team from the WCHA and a team from the Central Collegiate Hockey Association (CCHA) or from the independent ranks.

Beginning in 1981, the championship format is expanded to include eight teams, four from the West and four from the East. Automatic qualification is granted to the champions of the ECAC, WCHA and CCHA. The remaining five teams are selected at large, two from the West and three from the East.

Several members of the 1980 U.S. Olympic team, the famed "Miracle on Ice" gold-medal champions, earlier in their careers demonstrated their considerable talents in the National Collegiate Ice Hockey Championships. They include Neal Broten of Minnesota, Mark Johnson of Wisconsin and team captain Mike Eruzione and three of his Boston University teammates, Jim Craig, Jack O'Callahan and David Silk. Olympic team coach Herb Brooks, who gained world acclaim during the Olympics, is no stranger to the National Collegiate Ice Hockey Championships. His Minnesota team won the tournament three times — 1974, 1976 and 1979. Other collegians who played in the tournament before going on to professional stardom include Keith Magnuson of Denver, Ken Dryden of Cornell and Lou Angotti and Tony Esposito of Michigan Tech.

A nationwide increase in youth hockey in the 1960s leads to an increase in intercollegiate hockey in the 1970s and eventually brings about the establishment of a Division II Ice Hockey Championship. The first tournament is held at American International College March 16-18, 1978. Merrimack wins the initial championship by defeating Lake Forest, 12-2.

Skiing

The National Collegiate Skiing Championships begin as a trial meet held in Reno, Nevada, March 4-7, 1954. Denver wins the first national title. It is the first of 13 national championships won by coach Willy Schaeffler's teams.

The first meet proves successful, if not from a financial standpoint, at least from the enthusiasm of the teams and their followers; and, in January 1955, the Convention votes to hold the meet on a permanent basis. As is the case with ice hockey, the skiing championships are held at a different site each year and generally alternate between western and eastern locations.

Soccer

Soccer, long a popular participation sport in American colleges, sees its first National Collegiate Championship established in 1959. Eight teams are chosen for the tournament played in single-game elimination format — first round, semifinals, finals. The University of Connecticut hosts the first finals, won by St. Louis, 5-2, over Bridgeport. This will be the first of 10 national titles won by the Billikens during the tournament's first 15 years.

In 1963, the Soccer Committee expands the tournament to include 16 teams participating in four regional play-offs, with the winners advancing to the finals. In 1969, the field expands once again, this time to 24 teams, all playing regional qualifying matches to determine the four teams entering the championship round.

Dan Counce of St. Louis, Angelo DiBernardo of Indiana and Christian Nwokocha of Clemson are three well-known soccer stars who participated in the National Collegiate Soccer Championships.

The College Division Championship (now Division II) is first held in 1972, with Southern Illinois-Edwardsville winning on its home field, 1-0, over Oneonta State. Three years later, Southern Illinois-Edwardsville will be the national second-place finisher in Division I.

With the inauguration of the Division III championship in 1974, both Division III and Division II become 16-team tournaments — regional play-offs followed by final rounds-of-four. Brockport State wins the first Division III title, defeating Swarthmore, 3-1.

Wrestling

We saw earlier how the National Collegiate Wrestling Championships, introduced in 1928, are among the first tournaments to be conducted by the Association.

The first 25 years of championship competition are dominated by Midwest institutions, primarily Oklahoma State, which eventually will win 27 of the first 45 NCAA wrestling championships, including seven in a row from 1937 to 1946 (there are no championships in the war years, 1943-1945). Eleven of these titles are won under the tutelage of coach E. C. Gallagher. In 1953, Penn State becomes the first team outside the Midwest to win the national title.

Steady improvement in the abilities of intercollegiate wrestlers makes it necessary for the Wrestling Committee to establish stringent qualifying standards in order to limit the number of entries in the championships. Automatic qualification is awarded to a fluctuating number of participants (ranging from one to four in each weight class) from the wrestling tournaments of selected conferences. The Wrestling Committee holds annual reviews of the wrestling programs in these selected conferences and forwards its recommendations for automatic qualification to the NCAA's Executive Committee, which approves automatic qualifiers in each appropriate sport.

Outstanding performers in the wrestling championships include Oklahoma's Dan Hodge, a three-time champion and two-time outstanding wrestler award winner, and Iowa State's Dan Gable, a collegiate and Olympic champion who later goes on to coach at Iowa, leading the Hawkeyes to four consecutive titles — 1978-1981.

Oklahoma State coach Myron Roderick follows a similar course, winning three titles as a wrestler at Oklahoma State (1954, '55, '56) and, as a coach, leading his teams to seven championships from 1958 to 1968.

The Divisions II and III Wrestling Championships are established in 1963 and 1974, respectively, and are conducted in formats similar to that used in Division I. Western State (Colorado) wins the first Division II championship while Wilkes gains the first title in Division III. Coach Vaughan Hitchcock of Cal Poly-San Luis Obispo brought his teams to national prominence in Division II, winning eight team titles in nine years from 1966 to 1974.

Outdoor Track

Outdoor track and field is the oldest of the Association's championships, with its origins dating back to that historic first meet in 1921 at Stagg Field on the University of Chicago campus, where Illinois defeats Notre Dame, 20-16, for the first team title.

It is appropriate and historically significant that the University of Chicago also becomes the site of the first Division II Outdoor Track Championships in 1963 and the third Division III Outdoor Track Championships in 1976. Maryland State (now Maryland-Eastern Shore) wins the first Division II meet, and Ashland wins the first Division III meet at Eastern Illinois University in Charleston, Illinois, in 1974.

Southern California has turned in strong performances in the national championships, winning a record 26 team titles. Twelve of them, including nine in a row (1935-1943), come under coach Dean Cromwell.

While his Villanova team only wins one outdoor national championship (1957), the popular and widely respected coach, James "Jumbo" Elliott, gained national recognition coaching 14 sub-four-minute milers, including three-time NCAA mile champ Marty Liquori. The Division I Outdoor Track Championships also have helped develop many world-class athletes, including Jesse Owens of Ohio State, Jim Ryun of Kansas, Steve Prefontaine of Oregon, Dave Wottle of Bowling Green and Ralph Metcalfe of Marquette.

The Divisions II and III championships also have showcased outstanding athletes — among them are Larry Myricks of Mississippi College and Rod Milburn of Southern-Baton Rouge, both Division II members, and Edwin Moses of Morehouse, a Division III member.

Indoor Track

The National Collegiate Indoor Track Championships are established in 1965 and quickly rise to prominence as the nation's premier indoor track event, annually attracting capacity crowds to Detroit's Cobo Hall. Missouri wins the first meet, 14-12, over runner-up Oklahoma State.

The natural limits of an indoor facility make it necessary for the committee to establish strict qualifying standards for this meet. Only the best collegiate athletes gain entry.

Understandably, many of the same teams, coaches and athletes participating in the outdoor event also compete in the indoor championships, although some athletes tend to turn in their better performances indoors. Among them are Jim Ryun, who won the indoor mile three consecutive years (1967-1969), and Maryland hurdler Renaldo Nehemiah, who won the 60-yard high hurdles in 1978 and 1979.

Other outstanding performers include long-jumper Bob Beamon of Texas-El Paso and high-jumper Dwight Stones of Long Beach State.

In 1981, Carl Lewis of Houston becomes the first NCAA indoor performer to win titles in both a track event and a field event (long jump and 60-yard dash).

Football

While most NCAA championships begin in what is now Division I and only later are inaugurated for the Divisions II and III schools, football takes an opposite tack. By their own choice, there is no official championship game or tournament among the approximately 140 Division I-A football-playing institutions, and the still-mythical "national championship" remains to the speculation of journalists and pollsters. There is national championship competition, however, in Divisions I-AA, II and III.

Disenchanted at not enjoying postseason opportunities, College Division institutions request in the early 1960s that the NCAA inaugurate some form of championship event. As a result, the Association establishes four two-team regional play-offs in 1964, with East Carolina (East), Middle Tennessee (Mideast), Northern Iowa (Midwest) and Montana State (West) emerging as regional champions. These competitions are considered "bowl games" and are so named — Tangerine and Boardwalk (East), Grantland Rice (Mideast), Pecan and Pioneer (Midwest) and Camellia (West). But, satisfying as these contests are to the participating institutions, they still do not result in a national champion in any division until 1973, when the play-off format is expanded and restructured to include four first-round games, two semifinals and a championship final. The winner is declared the National Collegiate Division II Football Champion. Louisiana Tech wins the first football championship, 34-0, over Western Kentucky.

The Division III football championship, like that of Division II, begins with regional "bowls" in 1969, the first winners of which are Randolph-Macon (Knute Rockne Bowl) and Wittenberg (fittingly, the Amos Alonzo Stagg Bowl). In 1973, these regional games are superseded by a format calling for first-round, semifinal and championship final games. Wittenberg wins the first Division III championship, 41-0, over Juniata.

The most recent NCAA-sponsored football championship — again, one founded with a view toward providing more opportunities for more members — is the National Collegiate Division I-AA Football Championship. This event traces its origins to a decision by the membership in January 1978 to realign Division I football into Division I-A and Division I-AA. The former includes more than 130 teams generally considered as the "major powers" in college football; the latter involves more than 40 other Division I institutions, most of which previously classified their football programs in Division II.

To earn and retain Division I-A status, an institution must sponsor at least eight varsity sports for men (all in Division I), schedule at least 60 percent of its football games against others classified Division I-A and meet certain minimums for home-game attendance and stadium seating capacity. An important exception permits an institution to bypass the attendance and stadium requirements by sponsoring at least 12 men's sports. In Division I-AA, meanwhile, the member has only to sponsor eight men's varsity sports and play more than 50 percent of its football games against I-A or I-AA opponents.

On December 16, 1978, Florida A&M becomes the first National Collegiate Division I-AA Football Champion with a 35-28 victory over Massachusetts in the Pioneer Bowl at Wichita Falls, Texas.

Despite the absence of any formally recognized football championship among the nation's leading football powers, no intercollegiate sport has ever produced as many nationally recognized names — players and coaches — as has college football. There are Jim Thorpe of the Carlisle Indian School, Red Grange of Illinois, Doak Walker of Southern Methodist, Felix "Doc" Blanchard of Army, Roger Staubach of Navy, Jimmy Brown of Syracuse, O. J. Simpson of Southern California and hundreds of others who dominated the nation's sports pages as they starred on the collegiate gridirons. Coaches, too, became football legends — Walter Camp of Yale, Amos Alonzo Stagg of Chicago, Knute Rockne of Notre Dame, Paul "Bear" Bryant of Alabama and Charles "Bud" Wilkinson of Oklahoma, just to name a few of the men whose careers lend dignity as well as fame to the role of college coach.

Water Polo

November 28-29, 1969, marks the beginning of the National Collegiate Water Polo Championship. The tournament results generally reflect the state of water polo as a West Coast-dominated sport. UCLA wins the first championship, 5-2, over California in a match hosted by Long Beach State. UCLA will go on to win three of the first four national championships, with California coming on to capture four of the first nine.

The tournament format, established by the Water Polo Committee

in 1976, calls for single-elimination play, with the committee selecting eight teams from among all institutions sponsoring water polo
and signifying their availability for this postseason event.

Volleyball

The first National Collegiate Volleyball Championship is held
April 24-25, 1970, at UCLA. The host Bruins win the first of three
consecutive championships, 3-0, over Long Beach State. Coach Allen
Scates' UCLA teams go on to win eight of the first 12 championships.

Participating teams are selected by the Volleyball Committee on
the basis of regular-season records, with the tournament format
requiring that there be one representative each from the East, West
and Midwest regions and one at-large team. Despite the geographical
balance, the volleyball championships are dominated by California
schools.

Lacrosse

Although it is one of the oldest games played in the United States
— indeed, it is a game that traces its origins to the North American
Indians — lacrosse as an intercollegiate sport, and especially as a
national championship event, is a relative newcomer.

The first National Collegiate Lacrosse Championship is played
June 5, 1971, at Hofstra University in Hempstead, New York, and is
won by Cornell, 12-6, over Maryland. As water polo and volleyball
tend to be West Coast sports, lacrosse is generally an East Coast
sport, with pockets of high interest among institutions in New England, upper New York State and the Middle Atlantic States, especially the Baltimore area. Johns Hopkins of Baltimore wins four
championships and records four second-place finishes in the tournament's first 10 years.

The tournament format calls for four first-round games, two semifinal games and one championship final.

A Division II Lacrosse Championship begins on May 25, 1974, at
Cortland State University, Cortland, New York, where Towson State
defeats Hobart, 18-17, in overtime. Since establishment of a Division
III championship in 1980, Hobart has won both titles.

Swimming

As we have seen, postseason intercollegiate swimming begins in
1924 at an NCAA-sanctioned meet held at the U.S. Naval Academy.
But, from this year through 1936, there are no formally recognized

team championships and entries are not national in scope.

The swimming championships enter a second era in 1937 when the first official National Collegiate Swimming Championships are held at the University of Minnesota and won by Michigan over runner-up Ohio State. Michigan, Ohio State and Yale will dominate the championships, winning all team titles through 1959. Ohio State, under coach Mike Peppe, will win a record 11 titles. This succession ends in 1960 when Southern California wins the championship, marking the beginning of a 17-year period in which Southern California, coached by Peter Deland, and Indiana, coached by James Counsilman, will win all but three team titles. Southern California wins nine championships and Indiana wins six, all in a row (1968 to 1973).

Outstanding collegiate champions who will later go on to gain world fame as Olympians include Indiana's Mark Spitz, a winner of seven gold medals at the 1972 Olympics; Southern California's John Naber, who holds a record 10 individual NCAA titles; UCLA's Brian Goodell, a holder of nine individual NCAA titles and two Olympic records, and Yale's Don Schollander, a winner of four gold medals at the 1964 Olympics.

The College Division (later Division II) championships are established in 1964 with Bucknell the winner over runner-up East Carolina. The Division III championships begin in 1975 with Chico State winning and Johns Hopkins finishing second. But, even with three national championships, it is necessary for the NCAA Swimming Committee to establish increasingly stringent individual performance standards for entry.

Rifle

Unlike most other NCAA championships, the rifle championships begin as a test or so-called "pilot" event in 1980. This temporary provisional status results from a vote at the 1979 Convention where Division I members approve the championships (it is defeated in Divisions II and III) but then discover that there are fewer than the constitutionally required 45 schools sponsoring rifle teams.

Arguments in favor of holding a rifle championship are that riflery is an Olympic sport, that many NCAA member institutions with ROTC programs already have rifle teams and that riflery is a coeducational sport where women compete on equal terms with men.

The pilot championships are held April 4-5, 1980, at East Tennessee State University, with Tennessee Tech — led by individual high scorer Rod Fitz-Randolph — defeating runner-up West Virginia. A woman, Tennessee Tech's Elaine Powell, is second highest individual scorer. The event is an individual and team championship, with the top 10 teams and top 40 individual performers in each event (small-bore rifle and air rifle) invited to compete.

In 1981, the pilot program having proved successful, riflery takes its place with other sports in the National Collegiate Championship series. The 1981 National Collegiate Rifle Championships are held at the U.S. Military Academy, where Tennessee Tech makes it two titles in a row, again edging West Virginia.

One of the beliefs underlying the founding of any NCAA-sponsored championship is that, while financial return may be desirable, it never is the determining factor. In fact, many meets and tournaments begin with deficits and only with time develop into events providing substantial financial return. This course of development is dramatically illustrated by the National Collegiate Basketball Championship. The inaugural 1939 tournament records a deficit of $2,500. But in 1981, the championship nets $13,153,041, including more than $10 million in television rights fees.

Revenue from the various championships has become increasingly important to the NCAA, to a point where such revenues make up three-quarters of the Association's 1981 budget. Projected revenue for the 1980-1981 academic year shows a total of $15.3 million, or 68.2 percent of all revenues, coming from Division I championships, $902,000 (four percent) from Division II championships and $320,000 (1.4 percent) from Division III championships. Because the NCAA is incorporated as a nonprofit association, funds realized by the Association from its championships immediately are plowed back into membership services and used to reimburse travel and per diem expenses of participating member institutions.

Taking account of inflation and the continuously increasing costs of conducting a championship, the Association's Executive Committee in 1974 abandons its long-established policy of offering no guarantee against financial loss to either the host or the participating institutions of a championship. Instead, the committee creates a championship reserve fund, from which a host institution may be reimbursed for losses up to the amounts of previously approved budgets.

This policy is liberalized in 1976-77 to include at least an 80 percent guarantee of payment of the travel expenses of teams and individual medal winners. In 1978-79, this policy is expanded once more to include a guarantee of all travel and per diem expenses for all participants.

The policy first adopted in 1978-79 is revised by the Executive Committee in 1981 to meet the needs of women's championships. Transportation expenses are guaranteed for all men's and women's championships; and in those championships that generate net receipts, those receipts are to be used to pay per diem expenses, all or in part, for the competing teams and individuals.

Beyond their size and scope as measured in dollars and cents, the championships and the season-long competitions leading up to them make up the foundation of the NCAA and of college sports. Says NCAA Executive Director Walter Byers, "There's going to be intercollegiate athletics as long as young people want to play the games. That's how it started, and it will always be there."

CHAPTER TEN

" ... and guides the Association in its efforts in Washington, D.C., and state capitals."

It might properly, if wryly, be said that the U.S. government addresses itself to the NCAA even before the NCAA exists. In fact, the absence of any national collegiate athletic organization is part of the problem in 1905 when President Theodore Roosevelt calls representatives of Harvard, Yale and Princeton to his White House office to see what can be done to reform the brutal sport of college football.

As we saw in Chapter One, the challenge posed by Roosevelt to the colleges — clean up football or see it abolished — is taken up by the then established but rather ineffective Intercollegiate Football Rules Committee. As it becomes evident that the committee is unable or unwilling to solve the problem, New York University Chancellor Henry M. MacCracken, acting on his own initiative and out of concern for college football, calls an informal meeting of college athletic leaders. Thirteen institutions send representatives to MacCracken's little gathering, out of which is formed the Intercollegiate Athletic Association of the United States, forerunner of the NCAA.

It is with considerable historical support, therefore, that the NCAA can trace its origins to the Roosevelt Administration. But this is not the last time that matters concerning intercollegiate athletics will reach Washington.

From its beginnings, the NCAA concerns itself with only those athletic issues that spread across regional lines. This concern for common, rather than individual, problems, along with the fact that the NCAA very early is made up of institutions from all parts of the nation (in the words of its first president, Palmer Pierce, "an organization national in character"), makes it inevitable that the Association occasionally will have to deal with national issues involving the Federal government. These involvements frequently are cooperative, as in the case of the colleges' support of the World Wars I and II defense efforts and the later cooperation of the Association and many of its member institutions in the formation of the National Youth Sports Program. On the other hand, some governmental relationships are unavoidably strained, as in the controversy surrounding the Department of Education's compliance procedures for Title IX legislation and the 1978 House of Representatives inquiry into the Association's enforcement procedures, which we shall examine later in this chapter.

Opposition to Federal Admissions Tax

The Association's first major involvement with the government — other than the football crisis of 1905 — comes in the form of a lobbying effort that begins in 1917 and ends successfully two years later. The object of the Association's concern is a Federal tax that is being levied on admissions to college athletic events. Colleges, as nonprofit institutions, generally are tax exempt; and it is to reinforce this tax-exempt status, as well as to have the financial burden itself lifted, that the NCAA appoints a special committee chaired by Maj. John L. Griffith of the University of Illinois to lobby for repeal. "Such taxes," charges Palmer Pierce, "(are) being collected contrary to the intentions of the framers of the law."

The success of this lobbying effort is attested to by Pierce at the 1919 Convention, when he tells the membership, " . . . two years ago, this Association inaugurated a movement to secure such revisions of the revenue laws as would abolish the Federal tax on admission to intercollegiate contests, and the thanks of the collegiate world are due to Maj. Griffith for his successful efforts in relieving the colleges of this burden."

The Association's second involvement with a national issue is equally successful, though in this instance the Association's members are more inclined to offer a service to the country rather than to remove a "burden."

In Support of Physical Education

The shocking result of the World War I-induced military draft is that approximately one-third of the draft-age male population of the country is found to be physically unfit for military service. This figure alarms the country's military leaders — as well it might — and arouses the concern of the nation's physical educators and athletic leaders, including many representatives of NCAA member institutions.

In 1918, in response to a speech given a year earlier at the NCAA Convention by Dr. Thomas A. Storey, New York state inspector of physical training, the Association formally places its weight behind a movement to secure Federal and state legislation for universal physical education. In supporting this legislation, the NCAA is allying itself with the U.S. Commissioner of Education, the National Committee of Physical Education and the Playground and Recreation Association of America. The Association, acting through its Special Committee on Universal Physical Training, does not mince words regarding its intentions in this relatively new area of governmental relations. Dr. Storey chairs the special committee, and he reports to the membership in 1919 that the committee will make "persistent efforts to influence state boards of education . . . in all the states to make it their effective rule that . . . no applicant may receive a license to teach any subject in any school who does not first present convincing evidence of having covered in a creditable manner a satisfactory course in physical education in a reputable training school for teachers."

And the efforts of the committee will not end at the state level, as Storey explains: "Your committee made every reasonable effort to influence *Congress* (italics added) . . . to enact laws providing for the effective physical education of all children of all ages in elementary and secondary schools."

The point here is not so much that the NCAA takes specific action on a national issue, but that while the NCAA was not founded and has never existed as a lobbyist group, it also has never been loath to man the legislative or political front when such action seemed called for. In the words of Storey, the Association must be willing "to assist and cooperate with all agencies actively concerned with influencing state and national legislation that will develop and conserve character, vigor and health in the youth of the land."

Lobbying for the Fess-Capper Bill

The NCAA, in the persons of four representatives of its member institutions, makes its first appearance in the chambers of Congress in 1921, when Joseph E. Raycroft, R. Tait McKenzie, J. H. McCurdy and C. W. Savage appear before the Congressional Committee on Education and Labor to speak in support of the Fess-Capper Bill, proposed legislation that would provide $10 million in matching Federal funds for state physical education programs.

While the Fess-Capper Bill lingers in Congress, lobbying efforts by the NCAA and other groups at the state level are more successful. By 1920, 16 states pass legislation calling for mandatory physical education courses for students and prospective teachers. But this will be the last legislative involvement by the Association for some time.

Throughout the 1920s and into the 1930s, the NCAA has little contact with the executive or legislative branches of the government. As we have seen (in Chapter Five), however, the growing jurisdictional dispute among the NCAA, Amateur Athletic Union and American Olympic Association (later Committee) generally finds the NCAA allied with the Army, Navy and Marine Corps. This is the case in 1926 when all four of these organizations withdraw from the American Olympic Association because of their collective minority representation as compared with the dominance of the Amateur Athletic Union.

In Support of National Defense

The outbreak of World War II finds the NCAA once again lending support to the war effort, this time to an even greater degree than was the case in World War I. During World War I, the Association votes to abolish preseason practices, restrict schedules and generally cut back on costs and activities, "to the end that athletics be made subservient to the demands of military preparation," in the words of the resolution. But in December 1942, as the United States is drawn deeper into the global fighting, the NCAA formally advocates use of the athletic facilities of member institutions by the armed services to maintain active sports programs. Besides bringing the soldier to the campus, the NCAA also cooperates in a unique military training plan that brings some of the campus to the soldier, in this case to naval aviators.

This defense program is called the Physical and Military Training Program or, more simply, the Naval Air V-5 program. The idea comes from former U.S. Naval Academy football coach Thomas J. Hamilton, who, in 1940, is serving as a lieutenant commander and pilot in the Navy. After getting permission from naval authorities, Hamilton attends the 1941 NCAA Convention, where he speaks to a joint meeting of the NCAA and the American Football Coaches Association, persuading each group to permit some of its coaches to serve as physical education instructors and coaches at various naval preflight and war-training schools. Recalls Hamilton, "The idea was that competitive athletic training would produce and enhance qualities needed in combat aviation, things like coordination, good reflexes, aggressiveness, teamwork and so on."

More than 2,500 college and high school coaches take part in the V-5 program during the war years, offering instruction in 11 sports at 37 naval air bases around the country.

"I think the Navy's acceptance of the program is testimony to the far-reaching value of organized athletics," says Hamilton.

The NCAA also lends support to the war effort when on April 20, 1945, in cooperation with the Office of Defense Transportation, the membership endorses a 15-point plan designed to curtail athletic travel. Included in the resolution are policies reducing the size of traveling teams, discouraging most postseason competition and discouraging student attendance at away games.

Opposition to the
Second Federal Admissions Tax

Other than in its ongoing difficulties with the AAU and a judicial question as to whether the Association's limited and controlled television program — or, for that matter, any such television program — was in restraint of trade (it was not, see Chapter Six), the Association has little contact with the government until 1954, when, once again, the NCAA finds itself seeking elimination of another Federal admissions tax on college sports. On January 9, 1954, the Convention approves the establishment of a Special Committee on Federal Admissions Tax to lobby for elimination of the tax.

The Association makes its point quickly this time. By March, President Dwight D. Eisenhower signs a new Federal excise tax bill providing that the Federal admissions tax "shall not apply in the case of any athletic event between educational institutions held during the regular athletic season for such event, if the proceeds therefrom inure exclusively to the benefit of such institutions."

The admissions tax remains on tickets to professional games, however; and the 1954 revision is among several Federal decisions acknowledging the fundamental differences between professional and amateur sport. Another such decision occurs on September 30,

1961, when Congress enacts legislation prohibiting the telecasting of professional football games on Friday evenings and Saturdays from a telecasting station located within 75 miles of an intercollegiate football game.

Antibribery Legislation

A year later, on October 1, 1962, the NCAA and all of organized sport receive an additional measure of government protection and support when the U.S. Senate enacts a law making it a Federal offense to attempt to influence the outcome of any sports contest by means of a bribe. The NCAA Council, which since August 1956 has expressed concern about a reported increase in basketball gambling, publicly supports such a law; and the Association's officers urge the district vice-presidents to carry the campaign further by making every effort to bring about development of antibribery laws at the state level. By the end of 1962, the officers of the Association report that there are only 16 states in the nation without antibribery legislation, and seven of these are in the process of drawing up or enacting antibribery laws. By 1964, after urging from the NCAA's Legislative Committee and from spokesmen for several member institutions, both the House and Senate pass, and President Lyndon B. Johnson signs, a Federal antibribery sports bill.

This mutually supportive relationship between the colleges and the government — a far cry from the days when Teddy Roosevelt seemed to be reaching into the closet for his big stick — gathers momentum through the 1960s and into the 1970s.

The Theodore Roosevelt Award

On January 11, 1966, at its 60th annual Convention, the NCAA holds the first of what will become an annual honors luncheon. Honorees are 50 members of the executive and legislative branches of the government, all former college varsity-letter winners. Four months later, the Executive Committee of the Association votes to go one step further in its recognition of the leadership value of college sports. The committee establishes the Theodore Roosevelt Award "to honor a distinguished citizen of national reputation and outstanding accomplishment who earned a varsity athletic award in college and has demonstrated a continuing interest in physical fitness and intercollegiate athletics." The award — informally known as the "Teddy" — also recognizes Roosevelt's role in the birth of the Association.

President Eisenhower is named recipient of the first annual Theodore Roosevelt Award on January 10, 1967. Since then, prominent individuals from all walks of life have received a "Teddy." Among those recipients associated with the government are Sen. Leverett Saltonstall of Massachusetts (1968), Supreme Court Justice Byron R. "Whizzer" White (1969), National Aeronautics and Space Administration Director Christopher C. Kraft Jr. (1971), U.S. Ambassador to Sweden (and former NCAA Council member from Hampton Institute) Jerome H. Holland (1972), Gen. Omar N. Bradley (1973), President Gerald R. Ford (1975) and Rear Adm. Thomas J. Hamilton, originator of the V-5 program (1976).

The National Youth Sports Program

Perhaps the high point of NCAA governmental cooperation comes about in 1969 with creation of the National Summer Youth Sports Program, later to become the National Youth Sports Program (NYSP), a year-around activity. In March 1969, following the disturbances and racial unrest of the previous two summers, the NCAA and the President's Council on Physical Fitness announce initiation of the jointly sponsored NYSP to provide on-campus sports activities, medical examinations and a lunch program for underprivileged boys and girls. One hundred NCAA member institutions take part in the program that, in its first year, enrolls more than 43,000 youngsters between the ages of 12 and 18 in the country's 25 largest cities. The dollar commitment of the NCAA and its cooperating member institutions comes to more than $2 million in personnel, administrative support, legal counsel, printing, travel costs and the services of a national program director. The colleges' contributions are matched by $3 million in Federal funds.

Development of the NYSP quickly moves beyond the swimming pools and athletic fields to encompass personal counseling, career guidance and drug and general health education. By 1980, the NYSP has reached 483,581 of the nation's neediest youngsters.

But in spite of the NYSP's acknowledged efficiency and success, as well as the fact that half of the program's support is in non-Federal contributions and only two percent of the Federal funding goes for administrative expenses, the directors of athletics and other officials of several NCAA member institutions nevertheless find themselves involved in several lobbying efforts to preserve Federal funding. Five times, from 1971 to 1981, the colleges participating in the NYSP successfully persuade Congress to maintain its financial support of the program.

A similar cooperative NCAA/government venture takes place in the summer of 1970, when the NCAA joins with the U.S. Department of Defense in sponsoring the first Vietnam tour by some of the country's better-known student-athletes.

Actions Regarding Federal Control of Amateur Sports

While cooperative efforts such as the NYSP continue through the 1970s, relationships between the Association and the government occasionally move back into the legislative arena. Such is the case in August 1973, when the Association and the National Federation of State High School Associations, along with other amateur sports organizations, join to oppose Senate Bill 2365. That bill, if passed, would put some phases of intercollegiate and high school athletics under jurisdiction of a Federal board of control. The arguments of the NCAA and of almost all of amateur sport prevail, and the Senate returns the bill to the Commerce Committee in a move generally interpreted as emphasizing the government's reluctance at this point to create any Federal control over United States amateur sport.

Governmental involvement in *international* sport, however, seems necessary, if not desirable, in view of the continuing difficulties among the NCAA, AAU and U.S. Olympic Committee. On May 5, 1974, the NCAA Council adopts a resolution supporting U.S. Senate Bills 1018 and 3500, which would provide Federal review procedures of the administration of amateur international athletic competition. This proposed legislation — S. 3500 was adopted by the Senate, but not the House — and the growing concern of the government over the conduct of the United States program in international amateur sport eventually will lead to the enactment of the Amateur Sports Act of 1978 (see Chapter Five).

Unfortunately — but perhaps predictably — relations between the NCAA and the Federal government are not always harmonious. Serious friction between these two bodies occurs in the early 1970s.

Title IX Implementation

The legislative controversy that is to dominate the 1970s is that concerning the implementation of Title IX of the Education Amendment Act of 1972. This is a Federal law prohibiting sex discrimination in education (see Chapter Eight). The law includes guidelines for its application to intercollegiate athletics and a provision that the

U.S. Department of Health, Education and Welfare (HEW) is to be responsible for overseeing compliance with the new law. While the membership of the NCAA is generally sympathetic with the intent of Congress expressed in the legislation, the HEW-supervised compliance is another matter.

One of the Association's chief objections, in the words of an NCAA Council report given to HEW in 1974, is that "the proposed regulations are unreasonably vague, ambiguous and lacking in specific standards." The Council predicts to HEW that, as a consequence of this ambiguity, "confusion, conflict and controversy will characterize efforts to comply. Solely because of the vagueness of proposed (guidelines), and not because of the merits or demerits of their athletic programs, virtually no coeducational institution of higher learning in this country can possibly be assured that it is in compliance with the regulations ... and no such institution can tell what it should do to attempt to comply or even whether the greatest good-faith effort on its part would suffice."

The Council cites numerous examples of vagueness and lack of specific standards, such as a section of the legislation requiring "affirmative efforts to provide athletic opportunities (in such sports and through such teams) as will most effectively equalize such opportunities for members of both sexes."

There are numerous other examples, but the central questions remain: What does Title IX mean specifically? And what, specifically, constitutes compliance?

To attempt to clarify the matter, HEW in 1975 promulgates a list of regulations as to what will constitute Title IX compliance. However, the regulations are, according to NCAA Government Relations Committee Chair Ferdinand A. Geiger of the University of Pennsylvania, "inexact and seemingly contradictory." All of this confusion leads HEW in 1977 to appoint a work group charged with drafting specific enforcement principles, prompting Geiger to note, wryly, that the principles "would explain the guidelines which had been written to explain the regulations."

In response to continuing queries by the NCAA and many of its members, HEW, on December 6, 1978, releases its interpretations of Title IX implementation regulations. At first, HEW states its essential criterion of compliance as being an equal per-capita expenditure test. However, this is modified a year later when compliance criteria issued by HEW in December 1979 set aside insistence on per-capita expenditure, substituting instead a "financial-proportionality" standard as the principal test of compliance. "In other words," explains HEW Secretary Patricia Harris, "if 70 percent of a school's athletes are male, they are entitled to 70 percent of the financial aid their school makes available." The criteria also establish "equivalency tests" for 11 aspects of athletic programs other than financial aid; among these are travel allowances, scheduling, compensation of coaches and the availability of equipment.

In May 1980, the responsibility for administration of Title IX passes from HEW to the newly created Department of Education, the body that will conduct on-campus compliance reviews and investigate complaints. Still concerned about specific interpretations of Title IX regulations, the NCAA submits 45 questions to the Department of Education. The department agrees to answer the questions, giving its specific interpretations of the regulations. The NCAA in turn makes the replies available to its members by publishing the questions and answers verbatim in the NCAA News. The following fairly typical example concerns the department's interpretation of the proportionality requirement:

"Question: If an institution treats its male and female basketball teams equivalently in all respects and decides to increase the amount of athletic financial assistance provided to basketball players of one sex, must it proportionately increase the amount of financial aid provided to basketball players of the other sex?"

"Answer: No. Institutions must award substantially proportionate amounts of athletic financial assistance (scholarship aid) to the men's and women's intercollegiate athletic programs based on the participation rates of men and women in the *overall* intercollegiate athletic program. There is no requirement that proportionately equal amounts of scholarship aid be awarded to comparable or similar men's and women's sports. Institutions are free to award differing amounts of scholarship assistance to their various men's and women's teams as long as, overall, the amount of scholarship assistance provided to male and female athletes, as a group, is substantially proportionate to their rates of participation in intercollegiate athletics."

Meanwhile, removed from the furor surrounding compliance provisions and regulations, women's intercollegiate athletics continues an era of rapid expansion in interest and participation, a period that reaches a high point in 1981 when the NCAA membership votes to inaugurate its program of women's championships and to incorporate women into the NCAA's governing structure. Reflecting on the Title IX controversy in the November 15, 1980, NCAA News, then NCAA Secretary-Treasurer James Frank of Lincoln University writes, "From this exhausting and rigorous exercise will come a great deal of growth and understanding and, finally, a better program for all parties."

The NCAA group monitoring the progress of Title IX compliance procedures and of other state and Federal legislation apt to affect college sports is the Governmental Affairs Committee. This committee is reorganized by the NCAA Council in 1979, when it is expanded from three to five members, with each post required to be filled by a member of the Council. It is this committee which, in the words of 1979 Chair James Frank, "keeps abreast of state and Federal legislation and recommends policies that help guide the Association in its efforts in Washington, D.C., and state capitals."

Congressional Hearings on Enforcement Procedure

Another serious confrontation between the Association and the government occurs in the late 1970s and involves the always sensitive and controversial areas of the Association's regulation and enforcement procedures.

As we saw in Chapter Seven, actions by the membership in the 1960s and 1970s lead to the expansion and strengthening of the NCAA's regulatory function and enforcement procedures. The inevitable result is that more member institutions are investigated by the Association and there is a corresponding increase in disciplinary actions taken by the Committee on Infractions. A number of cases involving patterns of widespread violations lead to severe penalties.

A much-publicized case occurs in 1977 when, acting on evidence compiled by the NCAA enforcement staff, the Committee on Infractions finds the University of Nevada, Las Vegas, and its basketball coach, Jerry Tarkanian, guilty of 36 violations of NCAA rules and, accordingly, places the university on probation.

In angry reaction to the committee's decision, U.S. Rep. James Santini of Nevada, an avid Nevada-Las Vegas basketball fan, voices his objections to the Association's investigatory procedures to U.S. Rep. John Moss of California, chair of the House Subcommittee on Oversight and Investigation of the Committee on Interstate and Foreign Commerce. Through Moss, Santini is able to bring about hearings by the subcommittee into the enforcement procedures of the Association.

The hearings begin in February 1978 and continue to July 1979. But it is not until September 27 and 28, 1978, that the Association is afforded an opportunity to testify or otherwise defend itself against a series of sensationalized charges. Among the more serious is that of "selective investigation" — that the Association's enforcement staff is more likely to investigate the smaller or less influential members of the NCAA than the major athletic powers. As it is later pointed out at the hearings, however, the list of member institutions disciplined by the Committee on Infractions includes some of the largest and most influential colleges in the country, among them several institutions whose representatives have served as officers of the NCAA (one was president while his university was under investigation) or whose alumni actually are members of the Association's enforcement staff.

The hearings begin in what Sports Illustrated senior writer John Underwood describes as an atmosphere of "threats and anger" and, according to Underwood, "never really (lose) the bitter tone of these early prejudices."

When at last the NCAA is given an opportunity to testify, its spokesmen are Walter Byers; J. Neils Thompson, NCAA president; Edgar A. Sherman, NCAA secretary-treasurer; William B. Hunt, assistant executive director for enforcement; S. David Berst, director of enforcement, and the five members of the infractions committee, including William L. Matthews Jr. of the University of Kentucky. Matthews, in explaining to Moss and his subcommittee the Association's investigative procedures, points out that the system is designed as a means for the college sports community to police itself in "a cooperative principle of administrative law." He goes on to point out that for the NCAA to revert to a system of criminal proceedings and a real "adversary" procedure would require subpoena powers and an enforcement staff 100 times the size of the present staff (eight field investigators at that time) and would result in a climate so unsavory that most institutions "would as soon give up athletics as operate it."

However, Moss, according to Underwood's published reports, is "never once swayed from his antagonism toward the ... NCAA enforcement process, even as it became evident that he did not always understand it or wish to."

The hearings end without the House subcommittee being able to substantiate any allegations that the office of the executive director of the NCAA exerts any insidious influence over the "justice branch" (i.e., the enforcement staff) of the NCAA.

The net result of the hearings is that the House subcommittee makes some 46 suggestions — never reviewed by the full House and not binding upon the NCAA — for changes in the enforcement procedures. This is a "laundry list" of ideas from all witnesses. All suggestions are reviewed by the NCAA membership; some are adopted, some are adopted in part and with revisions and some are rejected as impractical or even damaging.

Some suggestions are approved by the membership at the 1979 Convention. Basically, approval is given to proposals that clarify existing legislation. They include proposals:

• To emphasize that the Committee on Infractions establishes investigative guidelines that are to be implemented by the investigative staff in conducting investigations.

• To remove the Committee on Infractions from the role of reviewing the general scope of an infractions case prior to authorizing an official inquiry. As committee Chair Charles Alan Wright, University of Texas, Austin, says of these two proposals, the committee intends "to make it clear that the Committee on Infractions has no role in the investigatory stage of infractions cases."

• To clarify present Committee on Infractions procedures. As Wright says, " . . . to make it clear that the committee does not receive ex parte information dealing with violations."

• To clarify obligations to collect and provide full information to the Committee on Infractions.

• To clarify the definition of a representative of the institution's athletic interests. As Wright says, " . . . this proposal is an attempt to make clearer a portion of our Manual that has given a number of our members a great deal of difficulty."

The matter concludes on July 12, 1979, with testimony by NCAA officers before a panel chaired by Rep. Bob Eckhardt of Texas (who has succeeded Moss). Eckhardt closes the lengthy affair with the observation that "the inquiry has had a salubrious effect in general."

Indeed, even some of the Association's most difficult relationships with the government have concluded with favorable results for intercollegiate athletics, and Eckhardt's words echo with historic irony as they ring back through 75 years to the Roosevelt White House.

CHAPTER ELEVEN

"Organization is as necessary as in any business effort . . . "

"Organization is as necessary as in any business effort . . . " says Association President Palmer Pierce in a speech to the 1907 Convention. In full context, the statement contains Pierce's realization that it will take more than noble intentions for this small group one day, in his words, to "raise college sports to a higher level and keep them there."

Still, a dream etched with Pierce's practicality strikes us as a fanciful vision for a two-year-old organization that represents a minority of the nation's sports-playing colleges. It seems an almost laughable hope when we look at the funds available to the Association's founders. There is little money to apply to any grandiose schemes. On the same day as Pierce's speech, Association Secretary-Treasurer Louis Bevier Jr. reports "total receipts of $1,453.82, of which $1,346.62 (has) been paid out to meet the expenses of administration and the personal expenses of members of the Executive and Football Rules Committees, leaving a balance in the treasury of $107.20."

Lest $107.20 of uninflated 1907 currency seem a great amount, we note later in Bevier's report that the Association has unpaid bills in the amount of $100, leaving Pierce and his membership with precisely $7.20 in discretionary funds with which to put a foundation under what appears to be a castle in the air.

But from these modest beginnings, and after three-quarters of a century of expansion, the NCAA of 1981 embraces 881 member institutions and organizations and shows a balanced operating budget of $22.4 million.

We thus far have examined most of the major issues faced by the Association on its long march from an ad hoc group of football reformists to its stature as an organization through which the colleges and universities of the country speak and act on athletic matters. We have seen the Association progress from the voice of reform to the voice of college sports.

This growth seems brought about as much, perhaps more, by circumstance as by design. "This organization was born of necessity," Palmer Pierce says several times in the early years of his administration. One of these "necessities" was, and remains, the need to maintain sound educational standards in the administration and conduct of intercollegiate athletics. But need and good intentions are not enough to insure organizational survival and growth for 75 years. Seven dollars and 20 cents can take you only so far. For most of its history, and for all of its first 50 years, the strength of the NCAA lies in its influence, not in its wealth.

Early Financial Growth

The founders seem to be acknowledging the importance of a large membership over a large bank balance when, in 1912, the Convention votes a reduction in dues for the sole purpose of increasing membership. This is a particularly idealistic move when we consider that for its first 14 years, the NCAA receives no income other than member dues. The first nondues income, received in 1920, amounts to the less-than-princely sum of $20.25 from the interest on two Liberty Bonds.

The picture brightens somewhat in 1921, when the Association realizes a surplus of $146 from the first National Collegiate Track and Field Championships; there is a more lucrative financial diversification noted in 1924, when Joseph E. Raycroft, chair of the Committee on Publication of the Rules, reports that the Association has netted about $10,000 from 1920 to 1924 on its royalties of two cents per issue on the sale of rules books for football, basketball, swimming, soccer, track and volleyball.

However, financial growth remains slow. The NCAA is mainly a dues-supported organization until 1940, this being the first year that income from meets, tournaments and the sale of rules books exceeds that from membership dues. But total revenues remain modest, and it will not be until 1947 that the Association's general revenue will exceed $100,000.

The National Collegiate Athletic Bureau

For many years, the slow-but-steady financial growth of the NCAA lags behind the educational and social influence of the Association, which is administered through those years solely by volunteer leaders and committee members. For 40 years, the NCAA operates without any paid staff, relying entirely on the efforts of its member-volunteers. It is not until 1946 that the Association, indirectly, hires some help. At a meeting in Chicago on July 23 of that year, the Executive Committee votes "that a sum of $5,000 from football royalties be placed at the disposal of the National Collegiate Athletic Bureau, New York City, under Homer F. Cooke Jr.; . . . (the bureau is) constituted as an official agency of the Association for an in-season program of statistics compilation and distribution in various sports and for other record services."

Three years later, at a June 1949 Executive Committee meeting, Cooke reports that he has investigated the possibility of having the National Collegiate Athletic Bureau (NCAB) publish the various guide books, heretofore produced mainly by A. S. Barnes and Company, Inc., of New York. Cooke states his conviction that the NCAB can be more than a statistical service and, in fact, could produce the guide books at a profit, with the NCAA acting as publisher. Cooke prevails and the Executive Committee gives its approval "for the NCAB to publish the guides, making use of the funds of the Association for this purpose."

The original working agreement with the NCAB and the expansion of its activities into the area of publishing bring to reality one of Palmer Pierce's earliest visions, first expressed at the Convention of 1907 — that the NCAA "may become a clearinghouse of athletic (information)" and that it one day may become involved in the writing and dissemination of "circulars and other published literature."

An Executive Director

At the same June 1949 meeting at which the NCAB is given publishing responsibilities, the Executive Committee, after more than four decades of reliance on volunteer support, at last begins to consider ways and means of financing a separate central office. NCAA Secretary-Treasurer Kenneth L. "Tug" Wilson brings the suggestion before the committee. Wilson also is commissioner of the Big Ten Conference; and it is evident to him, as it is becoming evident to others, that the size of the Association and its rapidly diversifying range of commitments points clearly to the need for a full-time executive. Association President Karl E. Leib appoints a special subcommittee to recommend a plan for creating a central office, the operation of which is to be financed entirely by member dues.

Two years later, on October 1, 1951, the Executive Committee selects Walter Byers, 29, as the first full-time executive director of the Association. It is a logical choice — Byers had been serving as part-time executive assistant of the Association and full-time assistant to Big Ten Commissioner Wilson. Byers receives strong support from Wilson, who says of him, "He was tailor-made for administrative assignments, and he did his job superbly." He adds, following Byers' NCAA appointment, "I hated to let the Big Ten lose him, but I'm glad it was the NCAA that got him."

Byers comes from an athletic background. He was an all-city football center for Westport High School in Kansas City, Missouri, in the late 1930s, played American Legion baseball and later played college baseball at the University of Iowa, where he majored in English and journalism. Upon leaving Iowa in 1943, he quickly combines his sports interests with his professional training by becoming a sportswriter and editor with United Press (now United Press International). He serves first as a general assignment reporter, then as Midwest sports editor in Chicago and later as foreign sports editor in New York. In 1947, he joins Wilson and the Big Ten.

"I wanted this job," Byers says of his NCAA appointment, "because of my very deep conviction in the value of intercollegiate athletics ... I envisioned the NCAA as an organization totally responsive to its membership."

Later, in recalling his meetings with the Executive Committee during the time he was being considered for the job, Byers will say, "I wrote (in a memo to the committee) that the NCAA should operate, in my opinion, on the committee system so that those people most familiar with a particular subject would have the most to do with setting policy on that subject." He adds an observation that clearly echoes the organizational philosophy of Palmer Pierce and the Association's founders: *"I said the director's office simply would implement the will of the organization* (italics added). And that's how it has turned out. The Convention itself is the supreme authority for NCAA action. The executive director and staff exist to execute policy, not to formulate it."

Besides his adherence to the "will-of-the-members" administrative philosophy, Byers also appears to be inclined toward what has always been the decided academic bent of the Association. In 1965, in his 14th year as executive director, Byers will point out, with some pride, that the NCAA's "voting delegates are college presidents, faculty athletic representatives and athletic directors, with the preponderance being faculty representatives who do not receive any compensation whatsoever for their services in the athletic field."

When Byers assumes office, the NCAA headquarters are located in Chicago. On July 28, 1952, the offices are moved to Kansas City, Missouri, the largest metropolitan area nearest the exact geographical center of the country. Beyond the practical matters of office rental and travel logistics, it perhaps is significant that the move southwestward reflects the broadening base of the NCAA as a truly national organization. The Association was founded in the Northeast, drew much of its early support from that sector of the country and held nearly all of its early Conventions in New York City. But in taking up a permanent location in the center of the country, the Association gives indication that it belongs as much to the newer colleges of the West and South as to the older and historically more influential colleges of the East and North.

Strengthening the "Shoestring"

One of the earliest management principles governing NCAA operations is the belief that any surplus funds be plowed back into member services or set aside in an emergency cash reserve. However, for 50 years the NCAA's influence so far exceeds the meager power of its checkbook that the main financial concern is to assure each year that the modest receipts from dues and championships are sufficient to cover the staff salaries, committee expenses and costs of the NCAB to which the Association is committed. Says Secretary-Treasurer Ralph W. Aigler in his report in 1956:

"Through the years, the NCAA has been operating on a shoestring; and I, for one, can well remember past Executive Committee meetings when we never were sure we were going to have the finances to underwrite projects to which we already were committed."

But the "shoestring" never breaks; and in 1955, as the NCAA readies for observance of its 50th anniversary, the string is strengthened so substantially that for the first time it puts the Association on a secure financial footing. The windfall comes from television, though not, as we might expect, from rights fees or any major contract. Instead, ABC defaults on part of its 1954 contract to televise certain NCAA football games, for which default it is required to pay $200,000 to the Association.

"It is the largest amount of money that the Association has had to deal with at any one time, and I think it takes on, for that reason, a peculiar significance," reports Aigler to the 1956 Convention. Aigler's report makes it clear that the Executive Committee's handling of the funds is to be at once farsighted and conservative:

"It was the opinion of the Executive Committee that this money should be maintained for long-range investment purposes and, accordingly, the sum was invested in U.S. Government bonds, with approximately one-half of the amount in short-term bonds and the balance in long-term bonds. Your Executive Committee recognized that investments in common and/or preferred stocks would yield a greater income .... If the money had been put into a reasonably well-selected lot of common stocks ... we would have netted by now a considerable profit, but the committee felt it was not, should not be, its function to expose the assets of this organization to the ups and downs of the stock market."

In this same year, and with similar farsightedness, the Association goes a step further in securing its financial future with establishment of a funded cash reserve. The rather traditional philosophy governing the handling of these funds and all NCAA finances is put forth directly by Aigler at the close of his speech to the 1956 Convention:

"It has been (our) aim to put our financial house in order and in such shape that the coming of the lean years will not cause us the embarrassment ... that would come if we did not have some provision made.

"I think we all recognize that nationally we are in the midst of what people refer to as a lush period .... The purpose of this funded cash reserve is to put aside some of that income against the need of days when the income may not be so lush."

Publications, Communications and Public Relations

As the NCAA moves onto firm financial ground, it is better able to support what, since Palmer Pierce's day, has been an important, if occasionally neglected, facet of intercollegiate athletics — communications. While the communications function will be called everything from "propaganda" to "sports information" to "public relations," the NCAA in the 1950s begins doing more to communicate to the general public and to the college community the full impact of intercollegiate athletics. In speaking of this emphasis on communication, Aigler, representing the Executive Committee, says of the NCAA's $200,000 windfall, "The interest to be derived from this investment is to be used for general services of the Association, with particular earmarking for the budding NCAA public relations program."

One of the earliest manifestations of this commitment to public communication is the first in a series of special reports, published September 30, 1958, and entitled, "The Sports and Recreational Programs of the Nation's Universities and Colleges." The document presents, for the first time, a detailed and graphic picture of athletic participation among NCAA members and depicts the scope and resources of their athletic and physical education programs.

The study, based on questionnaires sent to those four-year colleges and universities that are members of the NCAA, shows the 476 member institutions spending more than $81 million to provide athletic, physical education and recreational programs for 1,082,635 students.

In making public the report, the NCAA's Committee on Youth Fitness also announces its intention to conduct and publish follow-up studies designed "to measure the progress the colleges have made during the intervening years." Similar reports are published in 1963, 1969, 1974 and 1978, with the latest report showing more than four million individuals engaged in sports and related recreational activities at NCAA member institutions.

Another significant step toward better informing the general public, as well as toward providing improved member services, occurs August 27, 1959, when the Executive Committee votes that the NCAA should assume ownership of the National Collegiate Athletic Bureau in New York. Since 1950, the NCAB has served as the publishing agency for the NCAA, and since 1940, it has served as the statistical bureau for the nation's sports-playing colleges and universities. Under the new arrangement, the NCAB is to become, in the words of Executive Committee member Jefferson J. Coleman of Alabama, "a wholly owned and operated subunit of the Association under the direct supervision of the Executive Committee and the executive director."

The move more than doubles the NCAA staff since there are 10 persons employed at the NCAB as compared to only six full-time staff members at the NCAA headquarters in Kansas City. Acquisition of the NCAB also represents a major financial commitment by the Association because the NCAB will require a $120,000 budget, compared to $204,000 for all of the Association's other activities. Nevertheless, the Executive Committee, according to Coleman, "is confident that acquisition of the bureau will serve to better promote intercollegiate athletics and represents an important step forward in expanding services to an ever-increasing membership."

Within five years of the acquisition of the NCAB, the Executive Committee realizes that the statistics and publishing functions have expanded to the point where each makes up a major activity. Thus, the committee votes to divide the responsibilities of the NCAB into publications and public relations (including statistics compilation). The publishing branch is named the College Athletics Publishing Service and is established by Homer Cooke as a separate entity in Phoenix, Arizona. The New York office of what was the NCAB later is renamed National Collegiate Sports Services.

Offices in New York, Kansas City and Phoenix begin to give the once shoestring-budgeted NCAA something of the aura of a corporate conglomerate, at the same time imposing obvious logistical and administrative limitations. Eventually, both services will be moved to the main offices in Kansas City, the College Athletics Publishing Service moving from Phoenix in December 1973 and being renamed NCAA Publishing Service and National Collegiate Sports Services being moved from New York in July 1975, renamed NCAA Statistics Service.

National Office Building

This consolidation and the permanent location of the NCAA offices in Mission, Kansas — a suburb of Kansas City — is made possible by a 1969 Executive Committee decision to appoint a special Investment Study Committee charged with examining the Association's finances and studying the feasibility of constructing a headquarters building in the Kansas City area. "The Executive Committee believes that such a project is in the best interest of the Association financially and administratively," says Executive Committee member Jesse T. Hill of the University of Southern California, " . . . we hope the NCAA will have its own building by 1973 or 1974.

The committee's hope is realized somewhat ahead of Hill's schedule. The Investment Study Committee recommends in favor of such a central office; on April 26, 1970, the Council approves an earlier action by the Executive Committee to acquire 3.36 acres of land in Mission, Johnson County, Kansas, and to proceed with architectural plans for a headquarters building. The Association breaks ground for construction February 25, 1972; the three-story building is dedicated 14 months later on April 28, 1973. It is a tribute to the Investment Study Committee's business acumen that the total cost of the building is $1,535,851 — within one percent of the estimated cost. The building is financed by means of a loan of $1,101,604. It is secured for a term of 15 years, but the Association pays it off October 1, 1976.

One of the first occupants of the original building is the relocated NCAA Publishing Service. At this time, the publishing function of the NCAA has grown to the point where the Association is producing more than 200 printed items each year, with at least 40 of these being of sufficient size to be classified as books or booklets. One measure of the NCAA's broadening view of its public relations responsibilities is that the single largest press run of any item in the history of the Association is one million copies of a 1971 folder on drug education.

But such is the expansion of the NCAA's activities through the 1970s that, by 1981, the Association finds itself back in the position of having to rent commercial office space to accommodate part of its communications department and to relieve some of the overtaxing of the main building caused by additions to the championships department, necessary for administration of the 29 women's championships to begin in 1981-82.

Again faced with a rent-or-build question, the Executive Committee turns the problem over to its Investment Committee, chaired by William H. Baughn of the University of Colorado, and a special committee to review office-space needs, chaired initially by James Frank (later to become NCAA president) of Lincoln University (Missouri) and then by John L. Toner of the University of Connecticut, who becomes secretary-treasurer when Frank is elected president. Repeating the choice of a decade earlier, the committees decide that the Association should own rather than rent. In April 1981, the Executive Committee votes to construct a second office building encompassing about 16,000 square feet on property already owned by the Association and located across a street from the main building. Rather than finance the building from current income sources, nearly all of which are needed to fund the Association's programs, the Executive Committee decides to liquidate approximately $600,000 in assets to invest in the undertaking, with financing through bonds and rental income expected to satisfy the remainder of the estimated $1.2 million cost.

Administrative Organization

Under the NCAA's administrative organization, the national office staff is divided into five departments, each with clearly defined responsibilities for providing services requested by the membership. Each department is under the supervision of an assistant executive director who reports directly to the Association's executive director. It is the Executive Committee that holds the constitutional authority to employ an executive director and "such other persons as may be necessary to conduct efficiently the business of the Association."

The general administration department is responsible for all of the Association's increasingly wide-ranging business affairs, including finances, investments, membership insurance, employee benefits, computerized accounting procedures and all other fiscal and personnel policies. This department also conducts Association research projects, maintains the NCAA library, oversees administration of the Association's numerous committees, arranges the annual Convention and administers the National Youth Sports Program and drug education programs. The department is under the supervision of NCAA Controller Louis J. Spry and Assistant Executive Director James H. Wilkinson.

The championships department primarily is responsible for administration of the Association's 72 national championship meets and tournaments in 21 sports, including the 29 championships for women. Dates and sites for the championships are approved in advance by the Executive Committee, after which championships department personnel are responsible for checking financial reports against proposed budgets, securing team expense reports, providing the host institution with all eligibility forms and administrative handbooks and maintaining liaison with the sports committee involved in a particular championship. The department is under the supervision of Assistant Executive Director Thomas W. Jernstedt.

Communications, in the earliest days of the Association, consisted of the NCAA secretary-treasurer reprinting various Convention speeches and mailing them to the nation's sports editors. From that haphazard system has evolved a modern communications department, the activities of which include electronic as well as print media. The communications department is responsible for all media relations, monitoring of governmental activity on the state and national level, administration of the NCAA football television program, promotion of the various championships and the administration of NCAA Productions, which films and televises championships and other NCAA activities. This department also compiles collegiate records and statistics in football, basketball and baseball via its

A Management Philosophy and the Art of Saying "No"

In remarks to an NCAA delegates briefing session in 1972 at Hollywood, Florida, Executive Director Walter Byers reflects on the operating philosophy guiding most of the Association's work, particularly in the difficult and sensitive area of regulation and enforcement.

"The NCAA is more or less a two-way organization. On the one hand, we attempt rather diligently to provide quality services, pleasantly and promptly, where they have to do with the official playing rules and the ... conduct of the various National Collegiate and College Division Championships for which we are responsible, and in other areas of service, such as the postgraduate scholarship program and devices we use in electronic media. Whatever it may be, it is our philosophy to try to perform with some distinction and do it with some efficiency.

"On the other hand, we are a regulatory and disciplinary body. By letter and by telephone, constantly we are saying 'no' to member institutions who want to do something they feel they are compelled to do or they would like to do for the advancement of their own interests and their own programs.

"For example, in a single day Warren Brown (then assistant executive director for enforcement) answered 36 telephone requests for interpretations. I didn't ask him how many times he said 'yes,' but I suspect he said 'no' 36 times.

"The constant regulatory function of our staff does put a strain on

statistics bureau, NCAA Statistics Service. Other departmental responsibilities include administration of the marketing and licensing program, including the licensing of firms to produce and market merchandise bearing the NCAA name, and administration of the Theodore Roosevelt Award and the annual College Athletics Top Ten Awards. The department is under the supervision of Assistant Executive Director Thomas C. Hansen.

As we saw in Chapter Seven, the Association's membership in 1952 creates the enforcement machinery to increase observance of its governing legislation. Thus, the NCAA enforcement program is basically a cooperative undertaking by member colleges and allied

our relations with the membership from time to time, even though we merely are carrying out the decisions reached by . . . the Association's Council.

"From our own family experiences, I am sure we all often are aware of the strain placed on family relations and the members of the families. It doesn't take much imagination to project that situation to the broader aspect of the NCAA regulatory function, which is carried out in public when the penalty and treatment are published in the town newspaper. That is the way it has to be done.

"The NCAA has performed these dual functions for many years, and we suggest no change in the pattern. But we must try to have a better understanding of those functions.

"As far as the administrative philosophy is concerned, our staff is totally conscious of its responsiveness. The membership's decision is reached in annual Convention, and those decisions are implemented and interpreted by the NCAA Council, Executive Committee and our staff in Kansas City. The principle we try to instill in our office is one of impartiality and fairness. If there is anything I have attempted to stand for in the several years I have been in this position, it is that we will treat each institution, black or white, rich or poor, the same way. Whether we are talking of regulation or discipline, whether it is a small institution or a major university, each member will get the same answer to the same question, and there will be no partiality or favoritism. I hope we have carried that philosophy to the point where — even though you may disagree with the answer you get to a question, or there may be some irritation in the disciplinary and enforcement area — this continuing philosophy of fairness has earned for our staff the reputation of impartiality."

conferences, designed to insure compliance with legislation adopted by the membership. The purpose of the enforcement *department* of the NCAA, as part of the larger enforcement *program*, is to investigate and process reports of alleged violations of NCAA legislation. The enforcement department reports the results of its investigations to the Committee on Infractions, a nonstaff body which has the authority to make findings of fact and to impose appropriate penalties based upon those findings. Actions taken by the Committee on Infractions are subject to appeal to the NCAA Council upon request of the involved member institution. The department was under supervision of Assistant Executive Director Warren S. Brown from 1966 to 1977 and under Assistant Executive Director William B. Hunt since 1977.

Since the relocation of the NCAA Publishing Service, or the publishing department, from Phoenix to Kansas City, the department has grown to a rate where, in 1981, it is overseeing the printing, distribution and sale of more than 275 printing jobs per year. Included in these are the NCAA News, published 18 times each year; the official rules books for 12 sports; fact books for seven sports; records books for football and basketball, and all of the Association's membership publications, including the NCAA Manual, National Collegiate Championships records book and championships handbooks. In addition to its publishing and printing responsibilities, the department maintains the Association's membership mailing lists. With the relocation of the NCAA Publishing Service in 1973, Ted C. Tow replaces the retiring Homer F. Cooke Jr. as director of publishing and later is accorded senior staff status as assistant executive director.

The Changing Budget

Beginning in the mid-1950s and continuing through the 1970s, the Association is to see an ever-accelerating flow of revenue. Money is coming in and going out at record rates and for purposes the founders would not have imagined.

While it takes 41 years (1906-1947) for the Association's general revenue to exceed $100,000, only 20 years after that the Association exceeds the $500,000 mark (1967). Only four years later (1971), NCAA revenues top $1 million for the first time. After 75 years of growth, most of it slow, the Association's annual budget for its diamond anniversary year stands at a record $22,429,000. But what would surprise the founders most is that less than one percent of this amount comes from member dues.

Key contributors to this dramatic financial growth are increasing revenues from the various National Collegiate Championships, particularly the Division I Men's Basketball Championship, and an increase in returns from television assessments. The most important of these is the championships.

Sixty years after the Association netted $146 on its National Collegiate Track and Field Championships in 1921, the combined revenues from all NCAA Division I championships come to $15,300,000, or 68.2 percent of the 1980-81 NCAA budget. An additional $1.2 million is realized from Divisions II and III championships, thus making the various championships account for nearly three-quarters (73.6 percent) of all NCAA revenues. Consistent with longstanding NCAA policy, most of this money is returned to members, not in the sometimes amorphous guise of "services" but in actual cash. For example, NCAA member institutions will receive $13.5 million in distributions from the $16.5 million receipts from all 1980-81 championships. Nearly all of this money will be in the form of travel and per diem allowances for participating student-athletes or as distributions of net receipts to competing institutions. In the case of the Division I championships, the NCAA will return $10.7 million of the $15.3 million in total revenue, while in the case of Divisions II and III championships, the balance will tip even more. For Division II championships, the Association will return $1.6 million while realizing only $902,000; in Division III, the Association will return $1.1 million on revenues of $320,000.

While the return from television assessments is substantial at $2.3 million, or 10.4 percent of the NCAA's total annual revenue for fiscal 1980-81, it remains a basic tenet of all NCAA television plans (see Chapter Six) that more than 90 percent of the rights fees from television broadcasts is returned directly to the participating institutions. The Executive Committee determines the assessment made upon football television receipts. This amounts to a fairly typical eight percent for a recent two-year period of the television plan, with such monies earmarked to meet the expenses of administering the TV plan, funding the postgraduate scholarship program, and, according to the provisions of the TV plan, advancing "the interests of intercollegiate football (and) intercollegiate athletics in general."

Competitive and Legislative Reorganization

For more than 50 years, the NCAA exists without divisions of any kind. It isn't until 1957 that the Association inaugurates its College Division championships in basketball and cross country, doing so in consideration of the reality that it is getting increasingly difficult for member institutions with small enrollments to compete on even terms with teams from the nation's largest universities.

The principle of competition by division is expanded in the 1972-73 academic year as the NCAA conducts 10 National College Division championships and six regional football bowl games for College Division members, again with the aim of providing more opportunities for more student-athletes.

This division along competitive lines actually is formalized in 1968 when NCAA members are required to designate their entire athletic programs as being either University or College Division. There is, however, no distinction between University Division and College Division on any sort of legislative basis. Bylaws and regulations applying to the largest university apply equally to the smallest college, and all legislation is voted on by all members meeting at the annual Convention.

As it becomes more obvious that an increasing number of issues and proposals concern one division of the membership while affecting the other hardly at all, the Association in 1971 adopts a concept called "conscience voting." This is not binding upon members but is a request for delegates to the Convention to abstain from voting on any issue that does not affect that delegate's school.

But it is also in 1971 that the Association takes a more concrete step in the direction of formalized legislative divisions when the Council appoints a Special Committee on Reorganization, charged with studying the Association's membership and determining what, if any, need exists for reorganization. David Swank, professor of law at the University of Oklahoma, is appointed chair of the seven-man committee, which is selected to represent a cross-section of the Association's membership.

After nearly two years of work, the committee goes before the 1973 Convention with a proposal that, for the first time, suggests dividing the NCAA membership into two groups for legislative as well as for competitive purposes. Under the proposal, the existing University and College Divisions are to become Division I and Division II, with the basic requirement for Division I membership being a broad range of sports sponsorship and a major program in at least two sports, one of which must be football or basketball. Each Division I institution is also to be required to sponsor a varsity program in at least eight of the 17 sports in which the NCAA sponsors championships. Very simply, those members who do not opt for Division I will be placed in Division II.

The proposal's legislative provisions do not call for any changes in voting on constitutional amendments (i.e., votes on constitutional matters will still require a two-thirds majority of all Convention delegates present and voting, regardless of division) but do allow for voting by divisions on bylaw changes.

While the plan enjoys a good deal of support as representing a step in the right direction, it also meets opposition from those who regard the step as stopping short of the mark. Among the proposal's opponents are many members of the 200-member Eastern College Athletic Conference, the largest conference within the Association, whose main objection is that the reorganization does not allow sufficient self-determination by the various colleges as to which division they will be in. There are also objections raised on the grounds that two divisions are not enough and that the membership might more logically be divided into three divisions. Says delegate James Bedell of Adelphi: "It seems to me the very first step ... is to establish a realistic division of interest groups within the NCAA. I don't believe Divisions I and II, which are little more than an elaboration of the College and University Divisions, will do it. I think there are more interest groups than that."

Though he favors passage of the reorganization plan as an important first step, Edgar A. Sherman, athletic director at Muskingum College, predicts " ... there are going to be three divisions within this organization before very long. We are leaning that way."

The vote is close, 218 to 224, but the reorganization proposal fails. Following the proposal's defeat, the Council, in a unanimous and historic decision, votes to hold a special Convention to reconsider the question of reorganization. At the same time, the Council appoints an 11-man committee, chaired by Sherman, to draft a new proposal. The new committee, like its predecessor, has broad geographical representation and, perhaps more important in the long run, reflects a competitive distribution of large, medium and smaller institutions. In addition to Sherman, the committee members and their institutions are Richard T. Bowers, University of South Florida; Harvey C. Chrouser, Wheaton College; Edward M. Czekaj, Pennsylvania State University; Ferdinand A. Geiger, Brown University; Wiles Hallock, Pacific-Eight Conference; Charles D. Henry, Grambling College; Franklin A. Lindeburg, University of California, Riverside; Max O.

Schultze, University of Minnesota, Twin Cities; Ross H. Smith, Massachusetts Institute of Technology, and David Swank, University of Oklahoma.

The special committee meets in February and March 1973, eventually emerging with a proposal that the NCAA reorganize into three competitive and legislative divisions.

"We believe our proposal will enable each NCAA member to seek the level of competition it desires and will permit each division, within certain limits, to determine its own legislative destiny," says Sherman.

The main points of the proposal are:

• Those institutions classified as "major" in the sport of football are to remain intact and may vote as a group on restrictive bylaw legislation pertaining only to them in the sport of football.

• The membership will be divided into three categories, Divisions I, II and III, with the NCAA Council empowered to decide which legislation will be subject to voting by divisions.

• Each institution is to be given the prerogative of deciding in which division it wishes to vote and participate, exclusive of football.

• By the 1975-76 academic year, there are to be 39 national championships to be sponsored by the NCAA, with a minimum of 10 of these championships to be conducted in each of the three divisions.

• The NCAA Council and the Executive Committee are to be restructured, with each of the three divisions being guaranteed representation on each group.

Regarding the labeling of the divisions, Sherman says, "The committee started out by suggesting maybe we could call (the divisions) by colors or names to try to avoid the one, two, three implication; but as we progressed, the discussion always got back to designating them one, two and three. People who wrote in with suggestions and comments also termed them to be one, two and three. I guess rather than fight, we gave in to it, and those are the names given . . . . "

The plan allows for a large measure of self-determination by member institutions. "How do you get into a division?" says Sherman. "If for a moment you could pretend you didn't have a football program, each institution shall select its division through a process of self-determination."

The proposal also provides for self-determination in a larger sense, stipulating that members of each division may establish the criteria for membership in that division.

The first special Convention in the history of the NCAA takes place August 6-7, 1973, in Chicago. From the beginning, it is apparent that the Sherman committee's reorganization proposals have satisfied the objections of those who earlier in the year had opposed the two-division plan. Says Ross Smith of the Massachusetts Institute of Technology, an opponent of the two-division plan but, as a member of the second reorganization committee, one of the architects of the three-division plan: "There was a lot of long, hard soul-searching within our own reorganization committee before we finally arrived at a position of unanimity. I would say, even though there wasn't complete agreement, we feel that the package that you see is one that does assure a voice for all the segments of the three divisions."

The specifics of the representation Smith refers to is a call for a restructuring of the Council, which is to have six at-large members along with the eight district vice-presidents. Of this 14-member Council, eight members must be from Division I, three from Division II and three from Division III.

The Executive Committee is to total eight members, five from Division I, with Divisions II and III being guaranteed at least one member each.

This time there is little opposition to the proposal. The membership — meeting for less than a full day — votes overwhelming approval of the reorganization plan, prompting Association President Alan J. Chapman of Rice to say at the conclusion of the Special Convention: "The approval of reorganization will make the NCAA an even more viable force in intercollegiate athletics. Reorganization will enable our members to enact rules that pertain to their own competition."

And it is this competition and the interests of the student-athletes that lie at the heart of the Association's new structure. "One of the points that should be underscored," says 1973 Association Secretary-Treasurer Richard P. Koenig of Valparaiso, "is the creating of more championships. More championships mean more competition for the student-athletes."

Final alignment into conferences shows most institutions — 237 — casting their lot with Division I, 194 choosing Division II and 233 choosing Division III.

Besides the 126 "major" football-playing institutions at the time, Division I is made up of 111 schools with major programs outside of football. In addition to the 237 Division I members, 40 institutions from Divisions II and III choose to participate in Division I in one sport, 11 choosing soccer and 10 outdoor track. As predicted, reorganization offers members flexibility in choosing the level at which they wish to compete, vote and conduct their athletic programs.

A Consistent Constitution

Through all of its growth and changes, particularly during the 1960s and '70s, the NCAA continues to be guided by the constitutional principles first evoked in 1906, especially the fundamental beliefs of institutional control and the need for the colleges to maintain ethical standards.

Growth inevitably begets constitutional amendments and bylaw changes. But even a complete recodification of the NCAA constitution and bylaws by the Council in 1970, while producing documents far more comprehensive than the 1906 versions, leaves the Association's fundamental beliefs virtually unchanged. Henry M. Mac-Cracken, Palmer Pierce, Louis Bevier and the other founders of the NCAA agreed in 1906 (as stated in Article 2 of the original constitution) that the Association's "object shall be the regulation and supervision of college athletics throughout the United States, in order that the athletic activities in the colleges and universities ... may be maintained on an ethical plane in keeping with the dignity and high purpose of education .... "

Seventy-five years later, we are to find the wording of Article 2 changed only slightly and the intent changed not at all. In 1981, that article reads, in part: "The purposes of this Association are: ... To initiate, stimulate and improve intercollegiate athletic programs for student-athletes and to promote and develop educational leadership, physical fitness, sports participation as a recreational pursuit and athletic excellence." The article goes on to "uphold the principle of institutional control" and to "encourage its members to adopt eligibility rules to comply with satisfactory standards of scholarship, sportsmanship and amateurism."

The welfare of the student-athlete, the autonomy of the colleges and universities, the principles of amateurism and the integrity of athletic competition remain, for three-quarters of a century, the essential concerns of the NCAA. In their behalf has the voice grown stronger. It has not wavered, nor has its message changed.

APPENDICES

APPENDIX A

THE NCAA THROUGH THE YEARS
1905-1981

The National Collegiate Athletic Association's first 75 years have been marked by phenomenal growth and expansion. A chronology of the events that have gone into the making of the present NCAA follows.

1905-1909

December 9, 1905 — Conference of colleges called by Chancellor MacCracken of New York University to decide whether to abolish football or reform the game. Thirteen Eastern institutions attended the meeting. It was decided to reform the game, and a second conference was called to implement the decision.

December 28, 1905 — The football conference convened with 62 institutions in attendance. A Football Rules Committee of seven was appointed and an amalgamation with the old American Football Rules Committee was accomplished to form a single rules committee. At the same conference, the Intercollegiate Athletic Association of the United States was formed. This body was conceived as an educational body without legislative authority.

March 31, 1906 — Adopted constitution and bylaws for the permanent government of the Association.

December 29, 1906 — First annual Convention of the Intercollegiate Athletic Association held at Murray Hill Hotel, New York City. Capt. Palmer E. Pierce, United States Military Academy, president of the Association, presided. Twenty-eight of 38 member colleges and universities sent representatives.

December 29, 1906 — First report of Football Rules Committee presented to Convention.

December 29, 1906 — Assumed publication of Official Football Guide.

December 28, 1907 — Authority granted Executive Committee to form representative Basketball Rules Committee.

December 28, 1908 — Provided joint membership, a provision for conferences to join the Association.

December 28, 1908 — Assumed publication of Official Basketball Guide, published since 1894 by the YMCA and AAU.

December 28, 1909 — Membership numbered 69 universities and colleges.

December 28, 1909 — Granted authority to form Track and Field Rules Committee.

December 28, 1909 — Created associate membership classification.

1910-1914

December 29, 1910 — Adopted present name, the National Collegiate Athletic Association.

December 29, 1910 — Divided membership into seven geographic districts.

December 29, 1910 — Voted to expand Executive Committee, governing body of Association, to include one representative from each athletic conference consisting of seven or more members.

December 28, 1911 — Divided membership into eight geographic districts.

December 28, 1911 — Appointed committee to promote and regulate association football (soccer).

December 30, 1913 — Appointed rules committee for swimming and water sports.

December 30, 1913 — Assumed publication of Official Soccer Guide.

December 30, 1913 — Appointed committee to determine methods of athletic regulation and control in other countries.

December 29, 1914 — Recommended that basketball, swimming and track committees be empowered to cooperate with other national organizations to develop common playing rules for each sport.

1915-1919

December 28, 1915 — Appointed Committee on Publication of the Rules as standing committee.

December 28, 1915 — Originated Official Swimming Guide.
December 28, 1915 — Walter Camp of Yale University, for 30 years associated with the formulation of football rules, resigned from Football Rules Committee.
December 28, 1915 — Voted to recommend that an advisory committee be appointed to assist in the adjustment of athletic differences between institutions.
December 28, 1916 — Adopted resolution to petition a large foundation to survey intercollegiate athletics. (Carnegie Foundation published a study of "American College Athletics" in 1929.)
December 28, 1916 — The Football Rules Committee came completely under NCAA jurisdiction.
December 28, 1916 — Divided membership into nine geographic districts.
December 28, 1917 — Appointed Wrestling Rules Committee.
December 28, 1917 — Recommended adoption of military rifle shooting as an intercollegiate sport.
December 27, 1918 — Appointed Volleyball Rules Committee.
December 27, 1918 — Voted that tennis be given recognition equivalent to other sports.
December 27, 1918 — Recommended that the department of physical training and athletics be recognized as a department of collegiate instruction directly responsible to the college or university administration and that each college faculty make adequate provisions in students' schedules for physical training and athletics.
December 27, 1918 — Recommended that hiring of seasonal coaches, scouting, training tables and organized coaching or training in the summer months be considered detrimental to the good of football.
December 28, 1918 — In recognition of war conditions, adopted resolution which called for abolition of preseason coaching, preseason practice, scouting and training table; reduction of number of officials; improvement of intramural program, and restriction of schedules to the end that athletics be made subservient to the demands of military preparations.
December 30, 1919 — Appointed a special committee on boxing rules.

1920-1924
December 29, 1920 — Voted special committee on boxing rules be made a standing committee.
December 29, 1920 — Requested member institutions to declare ineligible any undergraduate who either in vacation or during the regular college year represented any other athletic organization without the permission of his institution.
June 17-18, 1921 — First National Collegiate Track and Field Championships held at the University of Chicago, marking first time a national intercollegiate championship was held under the auspices of the Association. Forty-five colleges and universities competed, with 31 winning team points.
December 29, 1921 — Appointed rules committees for ice hockey, lacrosse, gymnastics and fencing.
December 29, 1921 — Added Official Track and Field Guide to NCAA guide series as annual publication following publication of single volumes in 1911 and 1916.
December 29, 1921 — Created allied membership classification for athletic conferences.
December 29, 1921 — Voted that a Council be elected at each annual Convention.
December 29, 1921 — Appointed special committee to study college baseball and methods to improve the game.
December 29, 1921 — Approved organization of the American Football Coaches Association.
November 22, 1922 — Assumed membership in the American Olympic Association.
December 28, 1922 — Created 10-point code and urged members to organize sectional conferences, abide by amateurism as defined by the Association, adopt the freshman rule, adopt strict rule against participation by members in professional football, limit participation to three years only, eliminate participation by graduate students, maintain absolute faculty control of athletics, suppress betting, prohibit participation on noncollege teams.
December 28, 1922 — Dropped joint memberships since allied memberships were created to allow conferences representation in the Association.
December 28, 1922 — Council replaced Executive Committee as policy body of Association. Council reorganized to include one representative from each geographic district, five members at large and officers.
December 28, 1923 — Instituted office of district vice-president, such officer to be district representative on Council. Offices of secretary and treasurer combined and office of single vice-president eliminated.
December 28, 1923 — Appointed Ice Hockey Rules Committee.
April 11-12, 1924 — First National Collegiate Swimming Championships held at the United States Naval Academy, Annapolis, Maryland.
December 30, 1924 — Membership numbered 135, including 123 active members, six associate members and six allied conferences.
December 30, 1924 — Reorganized membership into eight geographic districts.

1925-1929
December 30, 1925 — Advocated elimination of football practice prior to opening of college year.
December 30, 1925 — Declared that contests that had primarily commercial setting and motive were detrimental to the best interests of amateur sport.
December 30, 1925 — Appointed special committee to study: (1) overemphasis of football and (2) effect of professional football on the intercollegiate game.

December 30, 1926 — Recommended preseason football practice be limited to three weeks before opening game and all such practice be held on college grounds.

December 30, 1926 — Originated Official Lacrosse Guide.

December 29, 1927 — Originated Official Wrestling Guide following publication of rules during the preceding year.

December 29, 1927 — Appointed Gymnastics Rules Committee.

December 29, 1927 — Appointed Baseball Rules Committee.

March 30-31, 1928 — First National Collegiate Wrestling Championships held at Iowa State College, Ames.

December 28, 1928 — Approved organization of advisory committee to NCAA Football Rules Committee, composed of members of the American Football Coaches Association.

December 28, 1928 — Originated Official Ice Hockey Guide, following publication of rules in booklet form in 1926-27 and 1927-28.

1930-1934

January 1, 1930 — Instituted multiple-year terms for members of Football, Basketball and Track and Field Committees to provide continuity of membership.

January 1, 1930 — Voted representation of National High School Federation on NCAA Track and Field Rules Committee.

December 31, 1931 — Inaugurated "round-table conferences" at time of annual Convention.

July 29, 1932 — Special meeting held in Pasadena, California, at time of Olympic Games.

July 29, 1932 — Granted National High School Federation active representation on Basketball, Swimming, Track and Field and Wrestling Rules Committees, advisory representation on Football Committee.

December 30, 1932 — Appointed standing committee for Olympic Games with special regard to fund raising.

December 30, 1932 — Discontinued Baseball Rules Committee.

December 30, 1932 — Appointed special committee to study athletic injuries.

December 30, 1932 — Discontinued Volleyball Committee and organized Fencing Rules Committee.

April 8, 1933 — Formed National Basketball Committee of the United States and Canada to formulate playing rules for basketball.

December 30, 1933 — Appointed special committee to study recruiting and subsidization, with particular regard to conference regulations.

December 28, 1934 — Adopted code on recruiting and subsidizing of athletes with implementation by local conferences and associations.

December 28, 1934 — Established Eligibility Committee.

1935-1939

December 27, 1935 — Appointed special committee to study effect of radio broadcasting on attendance at intercollegiate athletic contests.

December 27, 1935 — Established standing committee on golf.

December 28, 1936 — Instituted Official Boxing Guide, bringing to nine the number of official rules books and guides published by the Association.

April 2, 1937 — First National Collegiate Boxing Championships held at California Agricultural College, Davis.

December 29, 1937 — Established standing committee on tennis.

December 30, 1937 — Established College Committee to consider and bring to attention of Association by its recommendations any athletic matter of common interest to smaller colleges in Association and in particular to be responsible for arranging and conducting the program of that session of annual Convention devoted to athletic interests of smaller colleges.

April 16, 1938 — First National Collegiate Gymnastics Championships held at the University of Chicago.

July 4-9, 1938 — Annual Intercollegiate Tennis Championships of the United States held under auspices of the NCAA for the first time at Marion Cricket Club, Haverford, Pennsylvania.

November 22, 1938 — First National Collegiate Cross Country Championships held at Michigan State College, East Lansing.

March 27, 1939 — First National Collegiate Basketball Championship held at Northwestern University, Evanston, Illinois.

June 24-29, 1939 — Annual Intercollegiate Golf Championships of the United States held under auspices of NCAA for first time at Wakonda Country Club, Des Moines, Iowa.

December 29, 1939 — Revised constitution, establishing certain standards for membership, and adopted executive regulations.

December 29, 1939 — Frank W. Nicolson, Wesleyan University, resigned after serving the Association as secretary-treasurer since 1909.

December 30, 1939 — Created affiliated membership classification.

1940-1944

December 31, 1940 — Added investigative and judicial proceedings to the legislative functions voted at the 1939 Convention.

March 29, 1941 — First National Collegiate Fencing Championships held at Ohio State University, Columbus.

December 31, 1941 — Awarded grant to National Association of Basketball Coaches for publications and research projects.

December 30, 1942 — Advocated use of college and university athletic facilities by armed services to maintain active sports program, urged members to continue their own programs.

December 29-30, 1944 — Officers, Executive Committee and chairs of rules committees met in New York in lieu of annual Convention.

1945-1949

January 5, 1945 — Membership numbered 210 active members, one associate, 17 allied and one affiliate.

April 20, 1945 — Endorsed 15-point program designed to curtail travel in cooperation with the purposes of the Office of Defense Transportation.

October 23, 1945 — Voted that as of September 1, 1947, the special war emergency provisions attached to eligibility provisions be eliminated, except as the eligibility rules were modified in their application to service veterans.

January 8, 1946 — Voted to add Swimming Rules Committee to those based on a district rotation plan. Other committees already using rotation plan were Track and Field, Basketball and Football.

July 22-23, 1946 — Conference of Conferences held in Chicago, resulting in first draft of "Principles for the Conduct of Intercollegiate Athletics." Questionnaire sent to members to determine extent principles accepted.

July 23, 1946 — Granted $5,000 to the National Collegiate Athletic Bureau, New York City, under the direction of Homer F. Cooke Jr., for statistics compilation and other record services.

January 6, 1947 — Voted $2,000 for research study of head and spinal football injuries by Dr. Floyd Eastwood.

January 8, 1947 — Adopted in principle five points of the recommendations stemming from Conference of Conferences: (1) Principle of Amateurism; (2) Principle of Institutional Control and Responsibility; (3) Principle of Sound Academic Standards; (4) Principle Governing Financial Aid to Athletes; (5) Principle Governing Recruiting.

June 20-21, 1947 — First National Collegiate Baseball Championship held at Kalamazoo, Michigan, with Western Michigan College as host institution.

July 26, 1947 — Executive Committee voted to finance the National Collegiate Athletic Bureau football statistical service for 1947.

January 7, 1948 — Extended statistical service to basketball.

January 10, 1948 — Adopted as permanent legislation five "principles" provisionally adopted January 8, 1947. These regulations commonly referred to as "Sanity Code."

January 10, 1948 — Appointed Constitutional Compliance Committee of three members.

March 18-20, 1948 — First National Collegiate Ice Hockey Championship held at the Broadmoor Ice Palace, Colorado Springs, with Colorado College as host institution.

January 8, 1949 — Endorsed following recommendations of Bowl Games Committee: (1) study to be continued with attention to establishment of criteria regarding sponsorship, management, participation and promotion of games; (2) study of criteria with regard to applying them to sports other than football; (3) requirement that no member institutions make bowl commitments until further action taken.

January 8, 1949 — Membership numbered 302, including 265 colleges and universities as active members, 26 allied conferences, three associate institutions and eight affiliated associations.

June 10, 1949 — Executive Committee voted to publish guides through the National Collegiate Athletic Bureau.

June 18, 1949 — Executive Committee voted $5,000 for a survey of the effect of television on football attendance.

1950-1954

January 6, 1950 — Executive Committee approved standard awards for athletes placing in National Collegiate Championship competition.

January 14, 1950 — Adopted Bowl Games Committee's recommendations governing postseason contests (now Article 2 of bylaws).

January 14, 1950 — Failed to meet required two-thirds majority (vote: 111-93) on motion that seven institutions be suspended for noncompliance with Sanity Code.

January 14, 1950 — Adopted so-called "Byrd Resolution" (named after H. C. Byrd, president, University of Maryland) that special committee be appointed to make complete survey of practices of member institutions in intercollegiate athletics to end that all institutions of comparable size shall adopt and maintain similar standards.

January 18, 1950 — Officers ruled seven institutions cited for noncompliance "not in good standing" since Convention majority supported finding.

April 4, 1950 — Executive Committee approved revised basketball tournament plan that expanded field from eight to 16 teams, 10 of which would automatically qualify by winning conference championships.

September 18, 1950 — Executive Committee authorized solicitation of funds from member institutions to enable NCAA to participate with television industry in survey to measure effect of live television on football attendance. The Association and its members provided one-half total survey cost.

January 12, 1951 — Voted 161-7 to declare moratorium on live telecasting of college football games for 1951; resolution called for cooperation of member institutions in experimental television and formation of a television committee to direct the project.

January 12, 1951 — Revised Sanity Code, dropping provision governing financial aid to athletes and abolishing enforcement machinery composed of Constitutional Compliance Committee and Panel.

March 1, 1951 — Council voted any member institution not observing the television resolution adopted by the 45th annual Convention shall be ruled member not in good standing.

June 7, 1951 — Officers ruled a member institution not in good standing as a result of its stated intention not to comply with television resolution.

July 13, 1951 — Officers declared the member institution to be in good standing upon its acceptance of provisions of television resolution.

August 29, 1951 — Council advanced 12-point program to deal with pressures connected with intercollegiate athletics. Program forwarded to the presidents of member institutions requesting presidents' reactions as basis for future legislation.

October 1, 1951 — Walter Byers, who had served as part-time executive assistant since August 1947, assumed duties as executive director of Association.

January 11, 1952 — Adopted provisions for enactment of temporary legislation through resolutions.

January 11, 1952 — Voted 163-8 that NCAA adopt program of limited live television for 1952, controlled and directed by the NCAA with the following objectives: (1) to minimize the adverse effects of live television upon attendance at college and high school football games; (2) to spread television, within the limits of such controlled plan as ultimately may be adopted, among as many colleges as possible; (3) to provide television to the public to the extent consistent with the first two objectives. Agreed detailed plan be submitted to membership in mail referendum, requiring approval by two-thirds of members voting.

January 12, 1952 — Adopted constitution and bylaw legislation dealing with academic standards, financial aid, ethical conduct and out-of-season practice in football and basketball, said legislation stemming from the response to the Council's 12-point survey.

January 12, 1952 — Voted that the Extra Events Committee make extensive survey of all postseason contests and propose such legislation as it might deem necessary to the 47th annual Convention.

January 12, 1952 — Established and appointed a five-man committee to conduct a survey on the number of games, length of playing seasons and length of accompanying practice sessions in all intercollegiate sports and recommend such legislation it might deem necessary as a result of its findings.

January 12, 1952 — Established Membership Committee to consider complaints filed with the Association charging the failure of a member institution to maintain the academic or athletic standards required for membership or the failure of a member to meet the conditions and obligations of membership; also created Ethics Committee.

April 6, 1952 — Council created operating procedure for the Membership Committee and its Subcommittee on Infractions.

June 13, 1952 — Adopted 1952 Television Plan by mail referendum, 185-15.

July 28, 1952 — The NCAA national office was moved from Chicago, Illinois, to Kansas City, Missouri.

September 1, 1952 — One hundred twenty-one member institutions enrolled in inaugural NCAA Intercollegiate Athletic Group Insurance program, a plan approved by NCAA Insurance Committee to provide catastrophe medical coverage for athletes engaged in intercollegiate athletics.

October 15, 1952 — Council voted to recommend to the 47th annual Convention that disciplinary action be taken against three member institutions for violations of NCAA rules and regulations.

December 9, 1952 — Council forwarded to membership 10-point plan to strengthen enforcement machinery of the NCAA and allied conferences.

December 23, 1952 — Published "A Survey of Postseason College Athletic Events," by the Association's Extra Events Committee, Wilbur C. Johns, UCLA, chair.

January 9, 1953 — Adopted disciplinary action as advanced by the Council relative to infractions by three member institutions.

January 9, 1953 — Delegated certain enforcement powers to Council by authorizing that body to take disciplinary actions, other than termination or suspension of membership, between Conventions.

January 9, 1953 — Established Skiing Rules Committee.

January 9, 1953 — Established Cross Country Meet Committee.

January 9, 1953 — Voted 172-13 that NCAA continue a limited live-television program for 1953, such program to be drawn up by a Television Committee and submitted to the membership in a mail referendum requiring approval by two-thirds of members voting.

January 10, 1953 — Adopted Council's proposed resolution that the Football Rules Committee be urged to amend the free-substitution rule to eliminate so-called two-platoon system.

January 10, 1953 — Adopted revisions in plans for the 1953 basketball tournament designed to shorten the basketball season, restrict members to one postseason tournament, increase automatic qualification for conferences and expand the tournament bracket.

February 7-8, 1953 — Conference of Conferences held in Chicago to solidify plans for investigation and enforcement cooperation between conferences and NCAA.

May 7, 1953 — Adopted 1953 Television Plan by mail referendum, 157-12.

August 12, 1953 — Executive Committee approved expansion of 1954 National Collegiate Basketball Championship to a 24-team field, 15 teams of which would automatically qualify as conference champions and nine as at-large entrants.

August 15, 1953 — Published "A Survey of Playing and Practice Seasons," by a special committee appointed by the Council, Paul J. Blommers, State University of Iowa, chair.

August 17, 1953 — Council, in accordance with authority delegated it by 47th annual Convention, adopted disciplinary action against three members.

August 17, 1953 — Council authorized president to appoint Public Relations Committee to be representative of Association as a whole.

January 4, 1954 — Executive Committee approved reorganization of National Collegiate Baseball Championship so as to expand tournament to 32-team bracket, institute automatic qualification of certain conference champions and provide for a final championship field of eight teams with double-elimination tournament to decide winner.

January 8, 1954 — Established office of vice-president at large, such officer to represent interests and viewpoints of smaller institutions of the Association, and reorganized College Committee on district representation basis.

January 8, 1954 — Voted 172-9 that NCAA continue limited live-television coverage of college football for 1954, such plan to be prepared by a Television Committee and submitted to the membership in mail referendum requiring approval by two-thirds of members voting.

January 8, 1954 — Reorganized Association's enforcement machinery to speed processing of cases. Membership Committee was eliminated and name of Subcommittee on Infractions changed to Committee on Infractions.

January 8, 1954 — Adopted proposal to establish permanent nine-man NCAA Olympic Committee to be responsible for planning and directing Olympic activities of members.

January 8, 1954 — Adopted amendments to the bylaws limiting the length of playing and practice seasons in football and basketball.

January 8, 1954 — Received report of Special Committee on Basketball Television, which recommended that continuing study be made.

January 8, 1954 — Voted that national meets and tournaments conducted by the Association be officially known as "National Collegiate Championship(s)."

January 8, 1954 — Received resolution of American Football Coaches Association citing that group's intentions to assist in the implementation of the NCAA enforcement program.

January 9, 1954 — Appointed Special Committee on Federal Admissions Tax to seek elimination of Federal admissions tax on college sports.

February 15, 1954 — Published first edition of "National Collegiate Championships" records book, containing the history and records of the 13 National Collegiate Championships conducted by the Association.

March 4-7, 1954 — First National Collegiate Skiing Championships held at the University of Nevada, Reno.

March 31, 1954 — President Eisenhower signed new Federal excise tax bill, which provided that Federal admissions tax "shall not apply in the case of any athletic event between educational institutions held during the regular athletic season for such event, if the proceeds therefrom inure exclusively to the benefit of such institutions."

April 14, 1954 — Adopted 1954 Television Plan by mail referendum, 184-26.

May 7, 1954 — Council initiated Certification of Compliance program, requiring certification of compliance by the chief executive officer of each member institution.

August 15, 1954 — The Executive Committee adopted the 1954-55 general operating budget in the amount of $138,160.

December 2, 1954 — Thirteen agencies and institutions sponsoring invitational athletic events joined in NCAA "cooperative boycott" program, whereby institution ruled ineligible for National Collegiate Championships also would be ineligible for said invitational events.

1955-1959

January 4, 1955 — Voted that a section entitled "Recommended Policies and Practices for Intercollegiate Athletics" be appended to the regulations of the Association, this section to contain recommendations adopted by the Council from time to time.

January 7, 1955 — Voted for the eighth consecutive time to retain the principle of controlled telecasting of collegiate football games.

March 25, 1955 — Voted, 193-27, to adopt 1955 Football Television Plan as submitted by Television Committee.

April 24, 1955 — The NCAA received, and eventually invested, $200,000 from ABC-TV for the network's failure to complete obligations regarding televising certain NCAA events.

April 26, 1955 — Council, following consideration of first case presented it by the Association's Committee on Ethics, adopted disciplinary action against member of the coaching staff of a member institution.

October 25, 1955 — The chief executive officers of 391 of the 398 NCAA member institutions had signed forms indicating compliance with NCAA rules and regulations.

January 7, 1956 — Minor League Baseball rejected the College Player Rule, an action that caused professional baseball to consider rescinding the major leagues' prior acceptance of the rule.

January 10, 1956 — The treasurer reported to the Convention that for the first time in its history, the NCAA was in a reasonably stable financial condition.

January 10, 1956 — The 50th annual Convention voted to prohibit any employee of a member institution from participating, in any way, in the promotion and administration of high school all-star games; supported the College Committee's recommendation by voting to initiate the first College Division event, a national basketball championship to be held in March 1957; voted to abolish out-of-season basketball practice and establish October 15 as the date for opening basketball practice.

May 2, 1956 — The Committee on Infractions recommended to the Council that in some infractions cases, the identity of staff members causing violations be disclosed.

August 21, 1956 — The Council expressed serious concern about the reported increase in basketball gambling and the fact that some institutions were permitting their players to participate in highly organized competitive summer basketball; accordingly, the Council voted to circularize the membership underscoring the dangers and the institutional responsibilities in these areas.

January 7, 1957 — The Executive Committee voted that the finals of the first College Division national basketball championship be held March 13-15, 1957, with Evansville College as host.

January 11, 1957 — The 51st annual Convention voted to include governmental grants for educational purposes (GI Bill) in determining the maximum amount of financial aid for which a student-athlete could be eligible; resolved to provide strong support to President Eisenhower's Youth Fitness Program; commended the objectives and purposes of the National Football Foundation and Hall of Fame.

October 15, 1957 — The Committee on Infractions reported to the Council regarding abuses present in organized summer baseball and submitted a proposal designed to reduce them.

January 8, 1958 — The 52nd annual Convention voted to support the Council's proposed policies governing organized summer baseball involving NCAA student-athletes; adopt the rotation principle in making committee appointments; adopt legislation requiring sponsorship of at least four sports, one in each of the traditional sports seasons, for eligibility for active membership, effective September 1, 1958.

May 19, 1958 — The Association's officers expressed serious concern to the membership about the impact on college football as a result of the National Alliance's attempt to persuade a segment of four-year colleges to play under National Alliance (high school) rules.

May 19, 1958 — The Council authorized the officers to forward reports of certain infractions cases to the appropriate regional academic accrediting agencies.

September 30, 1958 — The Association published the first report on "The Sports and Recreational Programs of the Nation's Universities and Colleges." This report presented a graphic and detailed story of athletic and game participation among NCAA members and depicted the scope and resources of their athletic and physical education programs.

October 22, 1958 — The three U.S. service academies reported to the Council in regard to the relationship between their preparatory education programs and NCAA eligibility rules.

November 15, 1958 — First National College Division Cross Country Championships held at Wheaton College, Wheaton, Illinois.

January 7, 1959 — The Council reaffirmed the criteria governing the Association's summer baseball certification program.

January 9, 1959 — The 53rd annual Convention adopted legislation requiring member institutions to provide to student-athletes a written description of financial aid awarded them and prohibiting athletic staff members from receiving compensation from professional sports organizations for scouting, evaluating talent or negotiating professional sports contracts.

June 12, 1959 — Acting upon a recommendation by the Executive Committee, the Council appointed a subcommittee to study and recommend ways and means to control recruitment of alien student-athletes.

June 12, 1959 — Based upon a report of the survey taken by the Special Committee on Junior Colleges, the Council voted not to recommend at the time the establishment of a junior college NCAA membership classification.

August 27, 1959 — Guided by the recommendation of a special committee, the Executive Committee voted that the Association should assume ownership of the National Collegiate Athletic Bureau in New York City.

November 28, 1959 — First National Collegiate Soccer Championship held at the University of Connecticut, Storrs.

1960-1964

January 6, 1960 — The Council referred to the Joint Committee on Amateurism the NCAA-AAU Articles of Alliance with the hope that a mutually satisfactory amateur rule could be developed.

January 9, 1960 — The Council referred to the NCAA Track and Field Rules and Meet Committee the problem regarding participation by alien student-athletes in the National Collegiate Track and Field Championships when that event was designated to serve as an Olympic Trials qualifying event.

January 9, 1960 — Holding the measure to be discriminatory, the 54th annual Convention voted down an amendment to place age limitations on alien student-athletes.

March 8, 1960 — The Council circularized to the membership a recommended financial aid form constructed to comply with NCAA legislation governing the award of financial aid.

April 24, 1960 — The Executive Committee reaffirmed its position that allied conferences enjoying automatic qualification for the University Division basketball tournament should permit their teams to compete only in the NCAA tournament; further, at-large teams owe their first allegiance to the NCAA tournament.

April 27, 1960 — Dissatisfied with AAU administration and policies, the Council cancelled the NCAA-AAU Articles of Alliance.

June 6, 1960 — Citing the inconsistent rules administration by the organization, the Council declined to enforce suspensions of college athletes by the AAU; further, the Council appointed a special committee to plan a long-range international sports exchange program for college student-athletes.

June 6, 1960 — Professional baseball requested and the Council agreed that a committee be appointed to work out an equitable rule to eliminate the indiscriminate signing of college baseball players.

August 8, 1960 — The Committee on Recruiting and Financial Aids recommended and the Council voted to support an amendment to provide a preregistration (letter-of-intent) program.

August 13, 1960 — The Executive Committee directed that the present scope of intercollegiate boxing be determined with a report and recommendation being made to the next Convention.

August 13, 1960 — The Executive Committee adopted 1960-61 operating budgets, as follows: NCAA, $215,200; National Collegiate Athletic Bureau, $123,500.

October 26, 1960 — The Council requested the commissioner of the American Football League to specify that organization's plans for drafting and signing college football players.

January 1, 1961 — Attendance at 1960 college football games involving 620 members was a record 20,400,000.

January 11, 1961 — The 55th annual Convention voted to abolish the National Collegiate Boxing Championships; reject a preregistration program; adopt a new policy statement extending the Association's legislative jurisdictions; adopt legislation requiring a student-athlete to complete his seasons of eligibility within five years from first college matriculation date; adopt legislation under which all-star high school games could meet NCAA requirements and be certified; adopt legislation governing the eligibility of alien student-athletes, and permit, under certain restrictive conditions, tryouts with professional sports teams.

April 26, 1961 — The Council extended exceptions to the preparatory education rule, previously granted to the United States Military Academy, United States Naval Academy and United States Air Force Academy.

August 15, 1961 — The officers submitted a preliminary report to the Executive Committee concerning the basketball gambling conspiracy, with the final report to be made to the Council during the October meeting.

September 30, 1961 — Congress enacted legislation prohibiting telecasting professional football on Friday evenings and Saturdays from a telecasting station located within 75 miles of an intercollegiate football game.

October 25, 1961 — The Executive Committee recommended and the Council approved the NCAA's participation in formation of the Basketball Federation of the United States.

October 25, 1961 — The Council authorized the officers to appoint a committee to study the problem of advanced football scheduling.

November 28, 1961 — The executive regulations were amended to prohibit holding NCAA meets and tournaments on Sunday.

January 10, 1962 — The Executive Committee voted to support the organization of federations in the sports of basketball, gymnastics and track and field; further, the committee adopted an NCAA employees' retirement program.

January 13, 1962 — The 56th annual Convention rejected an amendment to provide a preregistration program; established a committee to administer the Association's legislation related to all-star high school games; voted to prohibit outside basketball competition, with certain exceptions; voted to support the minimum college-level physical fitness program recommended by the President's Council on Fitness; supported the federation concept and organization of federations in the sports of basketball, gymnastics and track and field.

April 27, 1962 — The Council authorized the officers to appoint a Long Range Planning Committee to study and plan the future organizational structure, legislative philosophy and legislative procedures of the Association.

May 8, 1962 — The Special Committee on Basketball Television reported televising college basketball games did not have an adverse effect on attendance and did not constitute a national problem.

July 23-24, 1962 — The first meetings of the United States federations in basketball and track and field were held.

October 1, 1962 — The officers reported that the United States Senate had enacted legislation making it a Federal offense to attempt to bribe the outcome of any sports contests; further, the officers urged the Association's vice-presidents to make every effort to develop antibribery laws in their states.

October 24, 1962 — The AAU, although invited to join the new sports federations, rejected all invitations. NCAA colleges were urged to withdraw from membership in the AAU.

November 12, 1962 — Urged personally by the U.S. attorney general, the United States Track and Field Federation and the AAU agreed to the adoption of the Olympic House Coalition. Meeting December 1, 1962, the AAU rejected the coalition agreement.

December 8, 1962 — The officers reported that 16 states were without antibribery legislation; however, efforts by member institutions had resulted in the enactment of a law in one state, development of bills in three and progress toward enactment in three others.

January 5, 1963 — The Council voted support of President John F. Kennedy's decision to appoint General Douglas MacArthur to serve as arbitrator in the AAU-USTFF dispute.

January 5, 1963 — Based upon the report by the Special Committee on Advanced Football Scheduling, the Council voted to propose no legislation to the 57th annual Convention.

January 8, 1963 — The 57th annual Convention received a report to the effect that three major conferences had adopted an interconference letter of intent and five others had endorsed the principle of the plan.

January 9, 1963 — The 57th annual Convention clarified the committee membership rotation principle, strengthened the junior college transfer rule; resolved to support fully the federation movement and federation meets and tournaments by entering student athletes and providing coaches and use of institutional facilities.

March 15-16, 1963 — First National College Division Wrestling Championships held at the University of Northern Iowa, Cedar Falls.

April 27, 1963 — The Council approved on a one-year trial basis the summertime program of the newly organized Baseball Foundation, with the condition that all funds contributed to the foundation be channeled through the United States Baseball Federation.

June 6-8, 1963 — First National College Division Tennis Championships held at Washington University, St. Louis, Missouri.

June 7-8, 1963 — First National College Division Outdoor Track Championships held at the University of Chicago.

June 12-14, 1963 — First National College Division Golf Championships held at Southwest Missouri State College, Springfield.

August 13, 1963 — The executive regulations were amended to provide for Sunday competition in NCAA meets and tournaments in the event of emergency situations, but only with the approval of the competing institutions.

October 1, 1963 — Professional baseball established a new college player (draft) rule.

October 11, 1963 — The officers reported that both houses of Congress had introduced antibribery legislation. (As of November 11, 1963, the Senate had passed its bill.)

October 22, 1963 — The Long Range Planning Committee recommended and the Council supported a reaffirmation of the Association's enforcement policy: Penalties should be broad if there is a basic institutional pattern of nondeservance; narrow if violations are isolated and institutional dereliction is not involved.

December 5, 1963 — The Association published and circularized the second five-year study of "The Sports and Recreational Programs of the Nation's Universities and Colleges."

January 4, 1964 — The Council approved proposals that University Division events be known as National Collegiate Championships and College Division events as National College Division Championships.

January 4, 1964 — The NCAA and National Federation of State High School Athletic Associations joined in an effort to gain Federal prohibition of the telecast of professional football games on Friday nights in locales in which high school games were being played.

January 5, 1964 — Jay-Ehret Mahoney, president, and Col. Donald F. Hull, executive director, of the AAU, met with the Council and Executive Committee to discuss key issues in the track and field dispute. Although acknowledging that international rules did not prohibit dual sanctioning of track and field events, the AAU denied the right of educational institutions to sanction domestic track and field meets involving college students.

January 8, 1964 — The 58th annual Convention strengthened the junior college transfer rule; voted that all NCAA meets and tournaments be conducted under NCAA playing rules; increased numbers on various rules committees to accommodate College Division and junior college representatives; voted that any season-end elimination tournament played to determine a conference's representative in an NCAA basketball tournament would be considered one game in determining the permissible 26 contests.

March 20-21, 1964 — First National College Division Swimming Championships held at Grove City College, Grove City, Pennsylvania.

April 18, 1964 — Acting upon the request of female college sports leaders, the NCAA Executive Committee amended the executive regulations to limit participation in NCAA championships to undergraduate male students.

April 18, 1964 — The Executive Committee established 32 $1,000 scholarships for postgraduate and professional study by deserving varsity letter winners, the program to be financed from the Association's share of football television rights fees.

April 19, 1964 — The Council appointed a Special Committee on Women's Competition to serve as a liaison agency with all other interested groups.

July 21, 1964 — The NCAA Conference of Conferences met to discuss problems in the administration of international sports competition, letter of intent, principles of amateurism and educational objectives in intercollegiate athletics.

July 21, 1964 — Urged by NCAA institutions across the country and the Association's Legislative Committee, both houses of Congress passed and President Lyndon B. Johnson signed an antibribery sports bill.

September 11, 1964 — Col. Donald F. Hull, AAU, charged that the NCAA's permissible grant-in-aid program created an employee-employer relationship and threatened ineligibility for international competition for those athletes participating in the program.

November 4, 1964 — The NCAA Council again affirmed the Association's strong support of the sports federation movement in the United States and received a report that the United States Baseball Federation completed a most successful baseball tour to Japan.

December 4, 1964 — First College Division Regional Football Championship games held at Sacramento, California; Abilene, Texas; Murfreesboro, Tennessee, and Orlando, Florida.

December 21, 1964 — In light of the poor showing by United States wrestlers and mismanagement of their affairs, an organizing committee convened to form the United States Wrestling Federation.

1965-1969

January 12, 1965 — The 59th annual Convention adopted the so-called "1.600 rule," which required an academic floor for the award and retention of financial aid if an institution was to be eligible for National Collegiate and National College Division Championships; strengthened the junior college transfer rule.

March 1, 1965 — The NCAA Extra Events Committee initiated the Association's certification program in gymnastics and track and field. The AAU immediately rescinded sanctions previously granted to meets certified by the NCAA and threatened ineligibility of any athlete participating in meets not sanctioned by the AAU.

March 12-13, 1965 — First National Collegiate Indoor Track Championships held at Cobo Hall, Detroit, Michigan, and hosted by the University of Michigan.

April 10, 1965 — By resolution, the membership overwhelmingly supported the policy prohibiting athletic staff members from receiving compensation from professional sports organizations for scouting athletic talent or negotiating talent contracts.

August 20, 1965 — The Executive Committee voted to increase the number of postgraduate scholarships from 32 to 50; also, the committee adopted 1965-66 general operating budgets, as follows: NCAA, $355,300, and National Collegiate Athletic Bureau, $125,500.

September 1, 1965 — The NCAA agreed to cooperate with the United States Senate Commerce Committee in its call for binding and continuing arbitration in the track and field dispute. NCAA President Everett D. Barnes proposed that a new national commission be organized to administer United States track and field.

January 11, 1966 — The 60th annual Convention celebrated the Association's 60th anniversary by initiating the NCAA honors luncheon. During this first luncheon, 50 distinguished members of the executive and legislative branches of the Federal government were honored, all of them former varsity letter winners. Among those honored were three cabinet members, 17 senators and 30 congressmen.

January 12, 1966 — The 60th annual Convention rejected legislation to weaken, delay or eliminate the 1.600 legislation and voted to make freshmen at institutions of less than 1,250 male undergraduate enrollment eligible for National College Division Championships.

January 24, 1966 — The NCAA Media Seminar was inaugurated, with the University of Arizona serving as host to 14 news media representatives from all parts of the nation.

April 1, 1966 — Of the 571 active members, 493 (86.3 percent) declared their procedures in compliance with the provisions of Bylaw 4-6-(b), the 1.600 rule.

April 23, 1966 — The Executive Committee voted to divide responsibilities of the National Collegiate Athletic Bureau, separating functions into publications and public relations. The publishing branch was named College Athletics Publishing Service and moved to Phoenix, Arizona.

April 23, 1966 — The Executive Committee voted to establish the Theodore Roosevelt Award to honor a distinguished citizen of national reputation and outstanding accomplishment who earned a varsity award in college and has demonstrated a continuing interest in physical fitness and intercollegiate athletics.

June 15, 1966 — Vice-President Hubert Humphrey's arbitration board directed the AAU to take no action (declaration of ineligibility) against the 300 athletes who participated in the USTFF meets; further, the board recognized the USTFF as a separate, independent entity and invited it to be represented at the arbitration meetings.

November 1, 1966 — During the period September-November, the NCAA and the National Federation of State High School Athletic Associations intensified their efforts to defeat Senate Bill 3817, which would permit professional football to telecast individual games (apart from league package) against Friday night high school games as well as Saturday afternoon high school and college games.

January 1, 1967 — Attendance for 1966 college football involving 616 members was a record 25,300,000.

January 10, 1967 — Dwight D. Eisenhower was named recipient of the first annual Theodore Roosevelt Award. In addition, those receiving NCAA honor awards were 12 astronauts (former varsity letter winners at NCAA member institutions) of the National Aeronautical and Space Administration Manned Space Program. Among the 12 were Maj. Edwin E. Aldrin, Capt. Alan

B. Shepard, Col. Edward H. White and Capt. Alfred M. Worden.

January 11, 1967 — The 61st annual Convention voted to exclude payments under the GI Bill of Rights from the financial aid computations otherwise specified under the constitution; took action to strengthen and support the 1.600 legislation, and voted to strengthen extra events and enforcement procedures.

May 5, 1967 — Reporting compliance with the provisions of the 1.600 legislation were 550 institutions, or 93.5 percent of the membership. Of these 550, 347 used national academic prediction tables, 112 utilized institutional tables and 91 used conference tables.

June 1, 1967 — The International Amateur Basketball Federation (FIBA) declined to extend BFUSA's international scheduling, basing its decision upon the AAU's claim that it represented 70 percent of the nation's amateur basketball.

August 15, 1967 — The Executive Committee appropriated $15,000 to underwrite the cost of research projects to analyze football injuries.

October 3, 1967 — The NCAA became a member of the United States Collegiate Sports Council, the prime function of which would be to prepare entries for the World University Games.

October 24, 1967 — The NCAA Council appointed a committee to study the feasibility of establishing appropriate machinery for the development and supervision of women's intercollegiate athletics.

January 9, 1968 — Leverett Saltonstall, former Massachusetts governor who served the state as a U.S. Senator for 23 years, was named recipient of the Theodore Roosevelt Award; also honored were 12 outstanding and nationally known businessmen who were former varsity athletes at NCAA member institutions.

January 10, 1968 — The 62nd annual Convention voted freshmen eligible for all NCAA championships except basketball and football; adopted legislation governing the opening of fall football practice; voted to strengthen the 1.600 legislation, the new provisions encouraging all institutions to use national tables; defeated an amendment to abolish the 1.600 legislation; voted to resume certification of noncollegiate track and field meets that had been suspended in deference to the U.S. Senate Commerce Committee's attempts to resolve the track and field dispute.

March 7-9, 1968 — First National College Division Gymnastics Championships held at Springfield College, Springfield, Massachusetts.

April 27, 1968 — The NCAA and USTFF rejected the Sports Arbitration Board's decision regarding the track and field dispute, holding that the board's proposal did not solve basic issues or recognize the school-college educational responsibilities to certify the conditions under which students participate in outside meets.

May 31, 1968 — Report No. 3 of "The Sports and Recreational Programs of the Nation's Universities and Colleges" reflected a significant growth in sports participation, facilities, budget and personnel over that reported in 1962.

June 5-7, 1968 — First National College Division Baseball Championship held at Southwest Missouri State College, Springfield.

June 15, 1968 — The United States Gymnastics Federation was granted international status by the International Gymnastics Federation.

August 19, 1968 — In conjunction with the 100th anniversary of collegiate football (1969), the NCAA and the Chevrolet Motor Division announced that a college football centennial queen would be selected from nominating universities to reign over the anniversary's festivities.

August 19, 1968 — The Council announced the strengthening of procedures to be applied to track and field certification as that program was reinstated November 1, 1969.

September 1, 1968 — In accordance with legislation adopted by the 61st annual Convention requiring members to designate College or University Division in all sports rather than sport-by-sport, 223 members selected University Division and 386 chose College Division.

September 9, 1968 — Sixty-eight NCAA college track and field athletes were selected to participate in the Olympic trials conducted September 9-17 at Lake Tahoe.

January 1, 1969 — Responding to an NCAA survey, 469 athletic directors reported that 76 percent of deans and directors, 75 percent of alumni officers and 72 percent of student newspapers were favorable toward and cooperative with intercollegiate athletics.

January 7, 1969 — Byron O. White, U.S. Supreme Court justice, was named recipient of the Theodore Roosevelt Award. Receiving NCAA honor plaques were 17 luminaries in the performing arts field, all former varsity letter winners at NCAA member institutions.

January 8, 1969 — The 63rd annual Convention voted to sustain freshman eligibility for all NCAA championships except basketball and football; relaxed the junior college transfer rule for those high school students with at least a 1.600 prediction on the national table; clarified 1.600 procedures; separated indoor and outdoor track and field for purposes of eligibility.

March 1, 1969 — The NCAA and the President's Council on Physical Fitness announced the initiation of a jointly sponsored, Federally assisted National Summer Youth Sports Program to provide on-campus sports activities, medical examinations and a lunch program for underprivileged boys and girls.

April 19, 1969 — First National Collegiate Trampoline Championships held at the University of Michigan, Ann Arbor.

August 18, 1969 — The Executive Committee appointed an Investment Committee to examine Association finances and study the feasibility of constructing a headquarters building in the Kansas City area.

September 1, 1969 — The NCAA membership prepared for the 100th anniversary of college football with Rutgers University hosting Princeton University as it did in 1869. Barbara Specht, Texas Tech University, was elected Centennial Queen.

October 1, 1969 — The Council issued a strong reminder about the Association's legislation prohibiting staff members from accepting compensation from professional sports for scouting or evaluating talents of or negotiating contracts for student-athletes.

November 28-29, 1969 — First National Collegiate Water Polo Championship held at California State College, Long Beach.

November 29, 1969 — First College Division (II) Regional Football Championship games (Amos Alonzo Stagg and Knute Rockne Bowls) played at Springfield, Ohio, and Bridgeport, Connecticut.

1970-1974

January 13, 1970 — Frederick L. Hovde, president, Purdue University, was named recipient of the Theodore Roosevelt Award. Receiving NCAA honor plaques were U.S. cabinet members and state governors who were former varsity letter winners at NCAA member institutions.

January 14, 1970 — The 64th annual Convention increased the number of in-season football games from 10 to 11 and further restricted campus visitation by prospective student-athletes.

April 24-25, 1970 — First National Collegiate Volleyball Championship held at the University of California, Los Angeles.

April 26, 1970 — The Council approved the January 11, 1970, action by the Executive Committee to acquire 3.36 acres of land in Mission, Johnson County, Kansas, and proceed with architectural plans for a headquarters building.

April 28, 1970 — The Council received the first draft of the recodified constitution and bylaws; also received a report from its special committee studying the feasibility of divided voting; i.e., College and University Divisions.

June 15, 1970 — The NCAA and the U.S. Department of Defense jointly sponsored the first Vietnam tour by NCAA student-athletes.

June 15, 1970 — In recognition of the formal organization of the International Basketball Board, an interim coalition of AAU and basketball federation interests, there was a resumption of foreign basketball competition by NCAA members.

June 15, 1970 — The Special Committee on Financial Aid released its report on the increasing financial pressures being felt by all members. Among the committee's recommendations were limitations of the number of financial aid grants, awards made on the basis of the student's economic need and a candidate's declaration (letter-of-intent) program.

July 1, 1970 — The Special Committee on Intercollegiate Athletics Costs released an impressive and detailed accounting of intercollegiate athletics costs; the study was conducted and compiled by Mitchell H. Raiborn, University of Missouri, Columbia.

August 1, 1970 — The Council determined that Tier I Canadian ice hockey leagues and teams were professional organizations and their players would be ineligible at NCAA member institutions.

August 18, 1970 — The Executive Committee adopted 1970-71 general operating budgets, as follows: NCAA, $795,500; National Collegiate Sports Services, $285,500; College Athletics Publishing Service, $210,800.

August 20, 1970 — The Council approved the revised recodification of the Association's constitution and bylaws, voting to submit it to the 65th annual Convention.

August 20, 1970 — Concerned that divided voting might create a divided membership, the Council endorsed the concept of "conscience voting"; i.e., institutions having no direct interest in a specific amendment should abstain from voting.

October 30, 1970 — The United States Gymnastics Federation was selected as the United States representative in the International Gymnastics Federation, replacing the AAU.

January 11, 1971 — Prior to its consideration of proposed legislation, the 65th annual Convention adopted the Council's recommendation of "conscience voting."

January 12, 1971 — Dr. Christopher C. Kraft Jr., deputy director of NASA Manned Space Center, was named recipient of the Theodore Roosevelt Award; receiving NCAA honor plaques were 14 winners of the Congressional Medal of Honor, all former varsity letter winners at NCAA member institutions.

January 13, 1971 — To combat rising costs in athletics, the Financial Aid Committee recommended to the 65th annual Convention that all financial aid be based on need and that the number of annual new grants be reduced to 30 in football and six in basketball. The Convention deferred action.

January 13, 1971 — The 65th annual Convention made freshmen eligible for all NCAA championships except University Division basketball and postseason football; defeated an amendment to eliminate the 1.600 rule, and adopted the recodified constitution and bylaws.

March 1, 1971 — The Drug Education Committee launched a national program to combat the use of drugs by all students, particularly athletes.

March 1, 1971 — Intercollegiate athletics in member institutions continued to expand, with the average number of sports sponsored by each member being 9.66. Basketball led the list, with all but one member sponsoring that sport.

May 6, 1971 — Representatives of the NCAA and NAIA met to discuss matters related to a national letter of intent, eligibility and transfer student-athletes.

May 16, 1971 — As directed by the 65th annual Convention, the Financial Aid Committee continued its study and expanded its report to include financial aid based on need, limitations on grants in all sports, candidate's declaration, limiting award of grants to one year and limiting the number of coaches in each institution.

June 5, 1971 — First National Collegiate Lacrosse Championship held at Hofstra University, Hempstead, New York.

October 4, 1971 — Meeting in special session, the Council approved four of five recommendations included in the Financial Aid Committee's report, rejecting only that limiting the size of institutional coaching staffs.

October 27, 1971 — The Council approved a recommendation by the Special Committee on Enforcement authorizing the Committee on Infractions to act on cases without presenting them to the Council, with the Council serving as an appeals agency only; also, membership of the infractions committee would be increased from three to five.

October 27, 1971 — The Council voted to support participation in the World University Games as a normal extension of intercollegiate athletics and as a means of further developing skilled international performers.

October 27, 1971 — The Council heard a report from the Special Committee on Legislative Reorganization, directed the committee to continue its study and planned a meeting at the 66th annual Convention for a thorough review of financial aid and reorganization.

January 1, 1972 — Attendance at 1971 college football games involving 618 members reached a new high of 30,455,442.

January 7, 1972 — Jerome H. "Brud" Holland, U.S. Ambassador to Sweden, was named recipient of the Theodore Roosevelt Award; receiving NCAA honor plaques were nationally prominent journalists who had been varsity letter winners at NCAA member institutions.

January 8, 1972 — The 68th annual Convention rejected a proposal to call a special 1972 Convention to consider financial aid and legislative reorganization; voted to make freshmen eligible for University Division basketball and postseason football competition; continued its study of the NCAA's position and responsibilities in women's athletics.

February 25, 1972 — Ground was broken for construction of the Association's headquarters building in Mission, Kansas.

May 3, 1972 — The NCAA urged the U.S. Senate Subcommittee on Antitrust and Monopoly to subject professional sports to United States antitrust laws.

September 17, 1972 — The Council met in special session and approved a two-division legislative reorganization plan and proposed new legislation governing financial aid; voted to circularize the membership in October with a complete description of the proposed legislation.

October 25, 1972 — The NCAA terminated its long-held membership in the United States Olympic Committee but voted to continue its support of the Olympic movement.

November 15, 1972 — Participation records of the 1972 Olympics indicated that in sports in which there are NCAA championships, 194 out of a total of 260 Olympic team athletes were either enrolled in or had been trained at NCAA member institutions.

January 12, 1973 — General of the Army Omar N. Bradley was named as the recipient of the Theodore Roosevelt Award; receiving NCAA honor plaques were five Silver Anniversary and five Today's Top athletes.

January 13, 1973 — The 67th annual Convention abolished the 1.600 legislation; rejected a proposal to reorganize the Association for legislative purposes but voted to meet in special Convention no later than August 1973 to reconsider the matter; voted to make the Association's Committee on Infractions a judiciary body and increase its membership from three to five.

February 19, 1973 — The Committee for a Better Olympics recommended a completely new structure for the United States Olympic Committee.

March 15, 1973 — Dacia Schileru, Wayne State University diver, became the first female to compete in an NCAA championship, entering the College Division Swimming and Diving Championships.

April 6, 1973 — The NCAA national office moved into the Association's new building in Mission, Kansas, and the headquarters was dedicated April 28.

May 1, 1973 — The Federal District Court, Alexandria, Virginia, dismissed an action brought by two student-athletes (financed by the AAU) against the NCAA, holding that NCAA rules of eligibility were reasonable.

August 1, 1973 — The NCAA and the National Federation of State High School Athletic Associations, along with other amateur sports organizations, joined to oppose Senate Bill 2365, which would have placed certain phases of intercollegiate and high school athletics under jurisdiction of a Federal board.

August 6, 1973 — The membership, meeting in special Convention, overwhelmingly approved reorganization of the Association's legislative and competitive structure, creating three divisions.

October 3, 1973 — The U.S. Senate voted to return Senate Bill 2365 to the Senate Commerce Committee, reflecting the Senate's reluctance to create Federal control over amateur athletics.

November 10, 1973 — First National Collegiate Division III Championships took place in cross country, hosted by Wheaton College, Wheaton, Illinois.

December 1, 1973 — The College Athletics Publishing Service completed its move from Phoenix, Arizona, to the new national office building in Mission, Kansas, and was renamed NCAA Publishing Service.

December 8, 1973 — First National Collegiate Division III Football Championship (Amos Alonzo Stagg Bowl) held in Phenix City, Alabama.

December 15, 1973 — First National Collegiate Division III Football Championship (Camellia Bowl) held in Sacramento, California.

January 1, 1974 — Attendance at 1973 college football games involving 630 members was a record 31,300,000.

January 8, 1974 — Jesse Owens, Ohio State University, one of the century's greatest track and field athletes, was named recipient of the Theodore Roosevelt Award. Receiving NCAA honor plaques were five Silver Anniversary and five Today's Top athletes.

January 9, 1974 — The 68th annual Convention adopted legislation to strengthen the enforcement program and voted substantial changes in the Association's amateur rules; Division I rejected the dollar-equivalency system in favor of individual count in determining the number of permissible grants; also, Division I retained the 2.000 grade-point average as an eligibility standard.

March 1, 1974 — Interpretations by the Department of Health, Education and Welfare of antidiscrimination provisions in Title IX of the Education Amendments of 1972 threatened the financial structure of intercollegiate athletics.

March 1-2, 1974 — First National Collegiate Division III Wrestling Championships held at Wilkes College, Wilkes-Barre, Pennsylvania.

May 5, 1974 — The Council adopted a resolution supporting U.S. Senate Bills 1018 and 3500, which would provide for Federal review procedures of the administration of amateur international athletic competition; also, the Council adopted a resolution calling for the orderly development of women's intercollegiate athletics.

May 25, 1974 — First National Collegiate Division II Lacrosse Championship held at Cortland State College, Cortland, New York.

May 29-31, 1974 — First National Collegiate Division III Outdoor Track Championships held at Eastern Illinois University, Charleston, Illinois.

August 1, 1974 — The U.S. Senate passed Senate Bills 1018 and 3500.

August 1, 1974 — The Amateur Basketball Association of the United States (successor to the Basketball Federation of USA) was named to membership in the International Amateur Basketball Federation (FIBA) as holder of the United States franchise in the sport of basketball, bringing an end to the AAU's control over international basketball in the United States.

August 12, 1974 — Failure by the AAU to take action on a request by the U.S. Wrestling Federation for sanction of good-will tour by high school all-star wrestlers to Finland caused cancellation of the tour.

August 26, 1974 — Report No. 4 of "The Sports and Recreational Programs of the Nation's Universities and Colleges" confirmed, as did previous reports, the widening scope of intercollegiate athletics and related activities.

November 30, 1974 — First National Collegiate Division III Soccer Championship held at Wheaton College, Wheaton, Illinois.

December 1, 1974 — Westminster College, Fulton, Missouri, became the Association's 800th member.

1975-1979

January 7, 1975 — President Gerald R. Ford was named recipient of the Theodore Roosevelt Award; receiving NCAA honor plaques were five Silver Anniversary and five Today's Top athletes.

January 8, 1975 — The 69th annual Convention approved the Association's first dues increase since 1951 with the generated revenue earmarked for an expanded enforcement program; adopted resolutions calling for a comprehensive report and plan on administration of women's intercollegiate athletics; authorized a select meeting to discuss problems of economy in intercollegiate athletics.

March 20-22, 1975 — First National Collegiate Division III Swimming Championships held at Allegheny College, Meadville, Pennsylvania.

April 24-25, 1975 — A Select Meeting on Economy in Intercollegiate Athletics met in Kansas City; recommended several cost-cutting proposals; requested the Council to call a second special Convention to enact legislation prompted by these recommendations.

June 10-13, 1975 — First National Collegiate Division III Golf Championships held at the University of Tennessee, Martin, Tennessee.

July 1, 1975 — National Collegiate Sports Services moved from New York City to the national office in Mission, Kansas, and was renamed NCAA Statistics Service.

August 4, 1975 — Signed an agreement with Descente, Ltd., permitting use of the NCAA name and logo in manufacturing and marketing sportswear and sports accessories in Japan. The agreement marked the beginning of the NCAA marketing program.

August 14-15, 1975 — The second special Convention adopted legislation to restrict recruiting activities, the number and amount of financial aid awards, size of football and basketball coaching staffs and size of practice squads. Unfinished business was to be completed at a third special Convention to be held in conjunction with the 70th annual Convention in January 1976.

January 1, 1976 — Attendance at 1975 college football games involving 634 members was a record 31,700,000.

January 16, 1976 — Rear Adm. Thomas J. Hamilton, U.S. Navy Retired, was named recipient of the Theodore Roosevelt Award; receiving NCAA honor plaques were five Silver Anniversary and five Today's Top athletes.

January 14-17, 1976 — The third special Convention and 70th annual Convention rejected aid based on need after first roll-call vote in history of NCAA Convention; decided not to apply NCAA rules to all-female teams; defeated proposals requiring equal distribution of television revenues to all members sponsoring football.

May 19-23, 1976 — First National Collegiate Division III Tennis Championships held at Millsaps College, Jackson, Mississippi.

June 4-6, 1976 — First National Collegiate Division III Baseball Championship held at Marietta College, Marietta, Ohio.

January 11, 1977 — Tom Bradley, mayor of Los Angeles, was named recipient of the Theodore Roosevelt Award. Receiving NCAA honor plaques were five Silver Anniversary and five Today's Top athletes.

January 10-12, 1977 — The 71st annual Convention rejected Council-sponsored plan to restructure Division I; defeated proposals dealing with aid based on need; approved proposal to remove June 15 recruiting limitation in all sports except football and basketball.

May 1977 — Home Box Office, Inc., purchased the cable television rights for the 1977 College World Series championship game.

August 1977 — Guaranteed payment of 100 percent of transportation expenses incurred by teams and individual medal winners in all NCAA championships, beginning 1977-78 academic year.

August 1977 — Volunteers for Youth program established under auspices of the Association.

September 1977 — Entered first four-year football TV contract. Previous television plans for football were limited to two-year agreements. The agreement with ABC was for the football seasons 1978-1981.

January 11, 1978 — Gerald B. Zornow, former chair of the board of Eastman Kodak, was named recipient of the Theodore Roosevelt Award. Receiving NCAA honor plaques were five Silver Anniversary and five Today's Top athletes.

January 11-13, 1978 — The 72nd annual Convention approved realignment of Division I football with creation of Divisions I-A and I-AA; adopted two regulations designed to support the development of U.S. Olympic team; voted down proposals to alter length of basketball and football seasons.

March 18, 1978 — First Division II Ice Hockey Championship held at Springfield College, Springfield, Massachusetts.

March 1978 — Report No. 5 of "The Sports and Recreational Programs of the Nation's Universities and Colleges" showed that more than four million people were engaged in college sports.

April 14, 1978 — Membership in United States Olympic Committee reestablished.

June 1978 — Division I-AA Football members unanimously approved establishment of a football championship and statistics program.

August 1978 — Executive Committee approved the expansion of the National Collegiate Basketball Championship from 32 to 40 teams.

August 1978 — NCAA and ABC agreed to an out-of-court settlement with Warner Cable Corporation, permitting Warner to cablecast five Ohio State football games into Columbus, Ohio, in both 1978 and 1979 on an experimental basis.

September 27-28, 1978 — NCAA President J. Neils Thompson, Secretary-Treasurer Edgar A. Sherman and Executive Director Walter Byers testified before the House Commerce Subcommittee on Oversight and Investigation.

October 1978 — Internal Revenue Service ruled college sports broadcasts are not taxable.

November 8, 1978 — President Carter signed Amateur Sports Act of 1978.

December 16, 1978 — First Division I-AA Football Championship held at Wichita Falls, Texas.

January 8, 1979 — Otis Chandler was named recipient of the Theodore Roosevelt Award. Receiving NCAA honor plaques were five Silver Anniversary and five Today's Top athletes.

January 8-10, 1979 — The 73rd annual Convention rejected proposal for aid based on need for all sports other than football and basketball; turned down proposal to establish five women's championships in Division III; passed seven proposals affecting enforcement procedures after rejecting a proposal calling for total overhaul of enforcement program.

March 1979 — Reached a two-year agreement with Entertainment and Sports Programming Network, Inc., to cablecast a series of NCAA championships, as well as college and conference regular-season events, in 18 sports. ESPN programming began September 7, 1979.

March 1979 — "The Classic," a history of the NCAA basketball championship written by Ken Rappoport, was published as the Association's first hard-cover book.

August 1979 — Executive Committee approved the expansion of the National Collegiate Basketball Championship field from 40 to 48 teams and eliminated the restriction that permitted the selection of a maximum of two teams from a conference.

October 1979 — Council adopted resolution calling for appointment of Special Committee on NCAA Governance, Organization and Services and charged it to examine and make recommendations regarding the governance structure of the Association, including legislative processes, accommodation of women's interests within the NCAA and development of programs and services for women's intercollegiate athletics and the present and future NCAA district and division structure.

1980-1981

January 7, 1980 — Dr. Denton A. Cooley was named recipient of the Theodore Roosevelt Award. Receiving NCAA honor plaques were five Silver Anniversary and five Today's Top athletes.

January 7-9, 1980 — The 74th annual Convention approved proposal to establish five women's championships in Divisions II and III in the sports of basketball, field hockey, swimming, tennis and volleyball, effective in 1981-82; voted to establish permanent rifle championships; voted to increase number of accredited Convention delegates for each member from three to four.

March 1980 — Use of Spalding Top-Flite 100 ball in NCAA Basketball Championships marked the beginning of the Association's official championship ball program.

April 4-5, 1980 — First pilot National Collegiate Rifle Championships conducted in Johnson City, Tennessee.

April 1980 — Free-lance writer Jack Falla was selected to write the history of the NCAA in conjunction with the Association's 75th anniversary year.

May 1980 — Executive Committee approved change in National Collegiate Skiing Championships, eliminating the ski jumping event, effective following the 1981 championship.

May 25, 1980 — First Division III Lacrosse Championship held at Hobart College, Geneva, New York.

September 29-30, 1980 — Special meeting of selected chief executive officers held in Kansas City to discuss issues of importance in college athletics, including financial aid, recruiting, Title IX and governance of the Association.

October 1980 — Thirty-eight coaches and administrators selected to NCAA Divisions II and III women's sports committees, the first women's committees in the Association.

October 26-28, 1980 — Divisions II and III Women's Basketball Committees convened, marking the first time an NCAA women's committee had met.

November 1980 — NCAA membership set all-time record as 740 institutions held active membership. The old record was 728 members in 1978. Overall membership (active, allied, associate and affiliated) also reached new heights with 883 members. The old record was 862 in 1978.

December 1980 — Division I-A football attendance record was set with 26,515,894 spectators attending college games.

January 12, 1981 — Television and radio personality Art Linkletter received Theodore Roosevelt Award. Five Silver Anniversary and five Today's Top athletes also honored.

January 13, 1981 — The 75th annual Convention adopted governance plan to include women's athletics programs and services within NCAA structure. Delegates also adopted 19 additional women's championships, as follows: National Collegiate Women's Championships in fencing, golf and lacrosse; Division I women's championships in basketball, cross country, field hockey, gymnastics, softball, swimming and diving, tennis, outdoor track and volleyball; additional Division II women's championships in cross country, gymnastics, softball and outdoor track; additional Division III championships in cross country, softball and outdoor track.

On other issues, Convention adopted academic satisfactory-progress requirements, establishing quantitative standards to maintain academic eligibility; tightened rules regarding summer-school courses and nonresident academic credit; created recruiting and evaluation periods for Divisions I and II football and basketball.

February 1981 — New NCAA seal depicting both male and female athletes put into use. Association also adopted a new logo.

March 4, 1981 — CBS Television granted rights to telecast Division I Men's Basketball Championship in 1982, 1983 and 1984.

March 1981 — Figures released for 75th annual Convention showed a record attendance, with total delegate count at 1,314. The old record was 1,109 in 1978.

April 1981 — Changes announced for NCAA publications including discontinuance of football and basketball guides.

April 1981 — "Evaluation of Intercollegiate Athletic Programs: A Suggested Guide for the Process of Self-Study" is completed and made available to member institutions.

April 23-24, 1981 — The Executive Committee voted that transportation expenses would be guaranteed for all men's and women's championships in 1981-82. In other action, the Executive Committee approved the construction of an additional national office building at an anticipated cost of $1.2 million.

April 30, 1981 — Results of a five-year study, conducted for the NCAA by the American College Testing Program (ACT), indicated that male student-athletes at member institutions graduated at a better rate than nonathletes.

May 11, 1981 — The 1982-1983 NCAA Football Television Plan was approved by a margin of 220 to 6. The vote was on a series of football television principles by which the NCAA Television Committee would negotiate with interested parties. The principles provided for two national network packages.

July 30, 1981 — Four-year football television agreement was reached with two national networks for the 1982-1985 seasons. The combined rights fees from ABC and CBS totaled $263.5 million.

APPENDIX B

ALL-TIME ROLL OF MEMBERS

Following is a listing of all those institutions that have held active membership in the Association from 1906 through the 1980-81 academic year. The dates following the institution's name represent the years that the institution held active membership in the NCAA. It should be noted that many institutions have changed their formal names through the years. For sake of clarity, the present name (1981) is used for each institution.

Abilene Christian University, 1951-1974
Adams State College, 1953-1971
Adelbert College, 1968-1972
Adelphi University, 1951-
Adrian College, 1963-
Akron, University of, 1913-1936, 1951-
Alabama, University of, Birmingham, 1979-
Alabama, University of, 1936-
Alabama A&M University, 1951-
Alabama State University, 1956-
Alaska, University of, Anchorage, 1975-
Alaska, University of, Fairbanks, 1959-
Alaska Methodist University, 1970-1976
Albany, State University of New York, 1962-
Albany State College (Georgia), 1968-
Albion College, 1947-
Albright College, 1952-
Albuquerque, University of, 1967-1970
Alcorn State University, 1965-
Alfred University, 1921-
Allegheny College, 1906-
Allen University, 1952-1968
Allentown College of St. Francis de Sales, 1972-
Alma College, 1951-
American International College, 1938-
American University, 1948-
Amherst College, 1906-
Appalachian State University, 1940-1947, 1971-
Aquinas College, 1959-
Arizona, University of, 1936-
Arizona State University, 1946-
Arkansas, University of, Fayetteville, 1909-1916, 1939-
Arkansas, University of, Little Rock, 1975-
Arkansas, University of, Pine Bluff, 1963-
Arkansas State University, 1952-
Armstrong State College, 1971-
Ashland College, 1939-
Assumption College, 1959-
Auburn University, 1910-
Augusta College, 1972-
Augustana College (Illinois), 1952-
Augustana College (South Dakota), 1951-

Aurora College, 1979-
Austin College, 1963-1978
Austin Peay State University, 1957-
Averett College, 1976-
Babson College, 1953-
Bakersfield, California State University, 1972-
Baldwin-Wallace College, 1945-
Ball State University, 1956-
Baltimore, University of, 1935-
Baptist College, 1971-
Barrington College, 1975-1978
Bates College, 1909-
Baylor University, 1922-
Bellarmine College, 1962-
Belmont College, 1956-1960
Belmont Abbey College, 1958-
Beloit College, 1937-
Bemidji State University, 1979-
Benedict College, 1959-1974, 1974-
Bentley College, 1967-
Bernard M. Baruch College, 1972-
Bethany College (West Virginia), 1970-
Bethune-Cookman College, 1952-
Binghamton, State University of New York, 1968-
Biola College, 1966-1971
Biscayne College, 1970-
Bishop College, 1952-
Blackburn College, 1977-
Bloomsburg State College, 1952-
Bluefield State College, 1954-1968
Boise State University, 1969-
Boston College, 1921-
Boston State College, 1966-
Boston University, 1924-
Bowdoin College, 1914-
Bowie State College, 1971-
Bowling Green State University, 1941-
Bradley University, 1926-
Brandeis University, 1954-
Bridgeport, University of, 1955-
Bridgewater College (Virginia), 1958-
Bridgewater State College (Massachusetts), 1960-

Brigham Young University, 1939-
Brockport, State University College, 1958-
Brooklyn College, 1944-
Brown University, 1909-
Bryant College, 1967-
Bucknell University, 1906-1916, 1950-
Buena Vista College, 1958-1968, 1976-
Buffalo, State University College, 1956-
Buffalo, State University of New York, 1929-
Butler University, 1923-
C. W. Post College, 1958-
California, University of, Berkeley, 1929-
California, University of, Davis, 1929-
California, University of, Irvine, 1967-
California, University of, Los Angeles, 1929-
California, University of, Riverside, 1956-
California, University of, San Diego, 1968-
California, University of, Santa Barbara, 1947-
California, University of, Santa Cruz, 1980-
California Institute of Technology, 1945-1947, 1954-
California Lutheran College, 1975-1977
California Polytechnic State University, San Luis Obispo, 1948-
California State College (Pennsylvania), 1968-
California State Polytechnic University, Pomona, 1957-
Calvin College, 1959-
Cameron College, 1974-1977
Campbell University, 1976-
Canisius College, 1936-
Capital University, 1954-
Carleton College, 1951-
Carnegie-Mellon University, 1910-1941, 1972-
Carroll College (Wisconsin), 1948-1973, 1976-
Carthage College, 1965-1971, 1976-
Case Western Reserve University, 1909-
Castleton State College, 1965-
Catholic University, 1915-
Catholic University (Puerto Rico), 1962-1973
Centenary College, 1926-1946, 1952-
Central College (Iowa), 1966-
Central Connecticut State College, 1963-
Central Florida, University of, 1972-
Central Michigan University, 1940-
Central Missouri State University, 1957-
Central State University (Ohio), 1954-
Central State University (Oklahoma), 1937-1939, 1946-1952, 1975-1979
Central Washington University, 1967-1975
Centre College, 1920-1933, 1959-
Chaminade University, 1976-1981
Chapman College, 1951-
Charleston, University of, 1972-
Cheyney State College, 1962-
Chicago, University of, 1907-
Chicago State University, 1961-
Chico, California State University, 1954-
Christopher Newport College, 1974-
Cincinnati, University of, 1919-1933, 1935-
Citadel, The, 1936-1948, 1952-
Claremont Men's-Harvey Mudd-Scripps Colleges, 1959-
Clarion State College, 1967-
Clark College (Georgia), 1952-
Clark University (Massachusetts), 1955-
Clarkson College of Technology, 1928-

Clemson University, 1912-
Cleveland State University, 1948-
Coe College, 1920-
Colby College, 1944-
Colgate University, 1906-
Colorado, University of, 1906-
Colorado College, 1938-
Colorado School of Mines, 1940-
Colorado State University, 1929-
Columbia University, 1909-
Columbus College, 1972-
Columbus University, 1939-1942
Concordia College (Illinois), 1956-1976, 1980-
Concordia College (Minnesota), 1977-
Concordia College (Nebraska), 1975-1978
Connecticut, University of, 1910-
Connecticut College, 1975-
Coppin State College, 1980-
Cornell College, 1920-1927, 1936-
Cornell University, 1920-
Corpus Christi State University, 1971-1974
Cortland, State University College, 1949-
Creighton University, 1923-
Curry College, 1972-
Dartmouth College, 1906-
Davidson College, 1937-
Dayton, University of, 1928-1932, 1951-
Defiance College, 1970-1975
Delaware, University of, 1909-1916, 1923-
Delaware State College, 1958-
Delaware Valley College, 1962-
Delta State University, 1961-
Denison University, 1906-
Denver, University of, 1936-
DePaul University, 1939-
DePauw University, 1920-
Detroit, University of, 1923-
Detroit Institute of Technology, 1952-1954
Dickinson College, 1906-1942, 1954-
Dillard University, 1976-1980
District of Columbia, University of, 1972-
Doane College, 1957-1960, 1962-1979
Dominguez Hills, California State University, 1971-1972, 1980-
Dowling College, 1978-
Drake University, 1912-
Drew University, 1969-
Drexel University, 1935-1946, 1951-
Drury College, 1971-1974
Dubuque, University of, 1940-1942, 1946-1951, 1976-
Duke University, 1925-
Duquesne University, 1929-
Earlham College, 1970-1971
East Carolina University, 1961-
East Stroudsburg State College, 1961-
East Tennessee State University, 1961-
Eastern Connecticut State College, 1967-
Eastern Illinois University, 1954-1955, 1960-
Eastern Kentucky University, 1952-
Eastern Mennonite College, 1975-
Eastern Michigan University, 1927-
Eastern Montana College, 1980-
Eastern Nazarene College, 1974-1979
Eastern New Mexico University, 1962-1970
Eastern Washington University, 1961-1964, 1977-
Eckerd College, 1968-
Edinboro State College, 1972-
Eisenhower College, 1974-1976, 1980-
Elizabeth City State University, 1956-

Elizabethtown College, 1954-
Elmhurst College, 1955-
Elmira College, 1970-
Elon College, 1924-1930
Embry-Riddle Aeronautical University,
   1970-
Emory and Henry College, 1973-
Emory University, 1948-
Emporia State University, 1954-1972
Eureka College, 1978-
Evansville, University of, 1951-
Fairfield University, 1958-
Fairleigh Dickinson University, Madison,
   1963-
Fairleigh Dickinson University, Teaneck,
   1954-
Fayetteville State University, 1953-
Ferris State College, 1975-
Fisk University, 1952-
Fitchburg State College, 1966-
Florida, University of, 1922-
Florida A&M University, 1952-
Florida Institute of Technology, 1979-
Florida International University, 1975-
Florida Southern College, 1957-
Florida State University, 1949-
Fordham University, 1923-
Fort Lewis College, 1965-
Fort Valley State College, 1952-1957, 1959-
Framingham State College, 1971-
Franklin and Marshall College, 1906-
Franklin College, 1978-
Franklin Pierce College, 1972-1980
Fredonia, State University College, 1963-
Fresno, California State University, 1937-
Fresno Pacific College, 1971-1974
Frostburg State College, 1977-
Fullerton, California State University, 1961-
Furman University, 1936-
Gallaudet College, 1957-
Gannon University, 1962-
Geneseo, State University College, 1964-
Geneva College, 1926-1939
George Mason University, 1968-
George Washington University, 1906-1916,
   1939-
Georgetown College (Kentucky), 1978-
Georgetown University, 1926-
Georgia, University of, 1913-
Georgia Institute of Technology, 1917-
Georgia Southern College, 1953-1960, 1968-
Georgia State University, 1964-
Gettysburg College, 1929-
Glassboro State College, 1963-
Gonzaga University, 1938-
Gordon College, 1974-1980
Grambling State University, 1951-
Grand Valley State Colleges, 1975-
Greensboro College, 1974-
Grinnell College, 1910-
Grove City College, 1906-1909, 1958-
Guilford College, 1972-1976
Gustavus Adolphus College, 1951-
Hamilton College, 1916-
Hamline University, 1951-
Hampden-Sydney College, 1957-
Hampton Institute, 1949-
Hardin College, 1949-1950
Hardin-Simmons University, 1946-
Hartford, University of, 1962-
Hartwick College, 1949-

Harvard University, 1909-
Hastings College, 1954-1955
Haverford College, 1906-
Hawaii, University of, 1946-
Hawthorne College, 1972-1980
Hayward, California State University, 1961-
Heidelberg College, 1954-
Herbert H. Lehman College, 1958-
Hillsdale College, 1956-1958, 1974-1978
Hiram College, 1955-
Hobart and William Smith Colleges, 1925-
Hofstra University, 1947-
Holy Cross College, 1938-
Hope College, 1957-
Houston, University of, 1949-
Houston Baptist University, 1969-
Howard University, 1924-
Humboldt State University, 1953-1954,
   1959-
Hunter College, 1968-
Husson College, 1980-
Idaho, University of, 1936-
Idaho, College of, 1953-1965, 1968-1970
Idaho State University, 1949-
Illinois, University of, Champaign, 1914-
Illinois, University of, Chicago Circle, 1968-
Illinois Benedictine College, 1972-
Illinois College, 1978-
Illinois Institute of Technology, 1945-
Illinois State University, 1939-
Illinois Wesleyan University, 1977-
Indiana Central University, 1971-
Indiana State University, Evansville, 1974-
Indiana State University, Terre Haute,
   1936-1939, 1963-
Indiana University, 1909-
Indiana University of Pennsylvania, 1963-
Indiana University-Purdue University, Fort
   Wayne, 1976-
InterAmerican University, 1958-
Iona College, 1952-
Iowa, University of, 1908-
Iowa State University, 1908-
Ithaca College, 1936-
Jackson State University, 1955-
Jacksonville State University, 1971-
Jacksonville University, 1964-
James Madison University, 1969-
Jamestown College, 1974-
Jersey City State College, 1962-
John Carroll University, 1948-
John Jay College of Criminal Justice, 1976-
Johns Hopkins University, 1912-
Johnson C. Smith University, 1955-
Johnson State College, 1966-
Juniata College, 1938-
Kalamazoo College, 1938-
Kansas, University of, 1908-
Kansas State University, 1922-
Kean College, 1974-
Keene State College, 1972-
Kent State University, 1937-
Kentucky, University of, 1936-
Kentucky State University, 1951-
Kentucky Wesleyan College, 1958-
Kenyon College, 1937-
King College (Tennessee), 1936-1946
King's College, 1958-
Knox College, 1921-1942, 1951-
Knoxville College, 1959-
Kutztown State College, 1964-

La Salle College, 1939-
Lafayette College, 1908-
Lake Forest College, 1951-
Lake Superior State College, 1970-
Lamar University, 1957-
Lambuth College, 1970-1971
Lane College, 1959
Lawrence University, 1926-1940, 1948-
Le Moyne College, 1955-
Lebanon Valley College, 1951-
Lehigh University, 1906-
LeMoyne-Owen College, 1952-1956, 1958-
Lewis University, 1980-
Lewis and Clark College, 1952-1963
Lincoln University (Missouri), 1949-
Lincoln University (Pennsylvania), 1951-
Linfield College, 1953-1962
Livingston University, 1973-
Livingstone College, 1961-
Lock Haven State College, 1939-
Long Beach, California State University,
  1955-
Long Island University, 1956-
Longwood College, 1978-
Loras College, 1955-1976
Los Angeles, California State University,
  1952-
Louisiana College, 1960-1969
Louisiana State University, 1923-1927, 1936-
Louisiana Tech University, 1936-1939, 1951-
Louisville, University of, 1947-
Lowell, University of, 1955-
Loyola College (Maryland), 1954-
Loyola Marymount University, 1947-
Loyola University (Illinois), 1940-1946, 1951-
Loyola University (Louisiana), 1927-1941,
  1951-1972
Luther College, 1953-
Lycoming College, 1951-
Lynchburg College, 1958-1971, 1974-
Lyndon State College, 1967-
Macalester College, 1958-
MacMurray College, 1961-
Maine, University of, Farmington, 1966-
Maine, University of, Orono, 1922-
Maine, University of, Presque Isle, 1971-
Maine Maritime Academy, 1972-
Manhattan College, 1910-1915, 1928-
Manhattanville College, 1976-
Mankato State University, 1954-
Mansfield State College, 1972-
Marietta College, 1954-
Marist College, 1968-
Marquette University, 1928-
Marshall University, 1950-
Mary Washington College, 1978-
Maryland, University of, Baltimore County,
  1969-
Maryland, University of, College Park, 1919-
Maryland, University of, Eastern Shore,
  1956-
Maryville College (Missouri), 1978-
Maryville College (Tennessee), 1965-
Massachusetts, University of, Amherst, 1912-
Massachusetts, University of, Boston, 1980-
Massachusetts Institute of Technology, 1920-
Massachusetts Maritime Academy, 1974- *
McMurry College, 1951-1964
McNeese State University, 1965-
Medgar Evers College, 1977-
Memphis State University, 1952-

Mercer University, 1923-1926, 1957-
Mercy College, 1975-
Mercyhurst College, 1980-
Merrimack College, 1954-
Methodist College, 1974-
Miami, University of (Florida), 1936-
Miami University (Ohio), 1906-1910, 1920-
Michigan, University of, 1916-
Michigan State University, 1919-
Michigan Technological University, 1948-
Middle Tennessee State University, 1953-
Middlebury College, 1922-
Midland Lutheran College, 1966-1976
Midwestern University, 1950-1957
Miles College, 1970-
Millersville State College, 1951-
Millikin University, 1951-1958, 1975-
Millsaps College, 1925-1928, 1965-
Minnesota, University of, Duluth, 1956-
Minnesota, University of, Morris, 1972-1974,
  1977-
Minnesota, University of, Twin Cities, 1906-
Mississippi, University of, 1909-1913, 1936-
Mississippi College, 1948-
Mississippi State University, 1923-1931,
  1936-
Mississippi Valley State University, 1970-
Missouri, University of, Columbia, 1906-
Missouri, University of, Kansas City,
  1977-1978
Missouri, University of, Rolla, 1957-
Missouri, University of, St. Louis, 1970-
Missouri Valley College, 1951-1954
Monmouth College (Illinois), 1947-
Monmouth College (New Jersey), 1967-
Montana, University of, 1940-
Montana State University, 1937-
Montclair State College, 1962-
Moorhead State College, 1962-
Moravian College, 1939-
Morehead State University, 1952-
Morehouse College, 1952-
Morgan State University, 1951-
Morningside College, 1958-
Morris Brown College, 1952-
Mount St. Mary's College, 1926-1939, 1954-
Mount Union College, 1910-1933, 1951-
Muhlenberg College, 1938-
Murray State University, 1951-
Muskingum College, 1952-
Nasson College, 1962-1970, 1970-
Nebraska, University of, Lincoln, 1906-
Nebraska, University of, Omaha, 1947-1964,
  1973-
Nebraska Wesleyan University, 1961-
Nevada, University of, Las Vegas, 1965-
Nevada, University of, Reno, 1953-
Newberry College, 1952-1955
New England, University of, 1980-
New England College, 1966-
New Hampshire, University of, 1917-
New Hampshire College, 1974-
New Haven, University of, 1958-1960, 1967-
New Jersey Institute of Technology, 1971-
New Mexico, University of, 1939-
New Mexico State University, 1947-
New Orleans, University of, 1969-
New Paltz, State University College, 1962-
New York, City College of, 1907-
New York, Polytechnic Institute of, 1927-
New York Institute of Technology, 1970-

New York Maritime College, State
  University of, 1953-
New York University, 1906-
Niagara University, 1906-1912, 1924-1930,
  1935-
Nicholls State University, 1965-
Nichols College, 1966-
Norfolk State College, 1958-
North Adams State College, 1967-
North Alabama, University of, 1952-1958,
  1961-1968, 1971-
North Carolina, University of, Chapel Hill,
  1906-
North Carolina, University of, Charlotte,
  1971-
North Carolina, University of, Greensboro,
  1974-
North Carolina, University of, Wilmington,
  1969-
North Carolina A&T State University, 1952-
North Carolina Central University, 1952-
North Carolina State University, 1909-1933,
  1941-
North Carolina Wesleyan College, 1974-
North Central College, 1939-1941, 1954-
North Dakota, University of, 1936-1940,
  1949-
North Dakota State University, 1955-
North Park College, 1961-
North Texas State University, 1949-
Northeast Louisiana University, 1965-
Northeast Missouri State University, 1957-
Northeastern University, 1937-
Northeastern State College (Oklahoma),
  1952-1953
Northern Arizona University, 1949-1954,
  1969-
Northern Colorado, University of, 1940-
Northern Illinois University, 1951-
Northern Iowa, University of, 1936-
Northern Kentucky University, 1974-
Northern Michigan University, 1958-1961,
  1967-
Northern State College (South Dakota),
  1980-
Northridge, California State University,
  1959-
Northwest Missouri State University,
  1938-1946, 1957-
Northwestern State University (Louisiana),
  1965-
Northwestern University, 1908-
Northwood Institute, 1980-
Norwich University, 1908-1914, 1927-
Notre Dame, University of, 1924-
Oakland University, 1967-
Oberlin College, 1906-
Occidental College, 1941-1946, 1951-
Oglethorpe University, 1923-1924,
  1961-1974, 1977-1978
Ohio Northern University, 1936-1937,
  1956-1958, 1961-1966, 1971-
Ohio State University, 1907-
Ohio University, 1916-1920, 1924-
Ohio Wesleyan University, 1906-
Oklahoma, University of, 1916-
Oklahoma City University, 1950-
Oklahoma State University, 1933-
Old Dominion University, 1963-
Olivet College, 1963-
Oneonta, State University College, 1963-

Oral Roberts University, 1971-
Oregon, University of, 1929-
Oregon College of Education, 1955-1976
Oregon State University, 1916-1922, 1925-
Oswego, State University College, 1958-
Otterbein College, 1954-
Pace University, 1961-
Pacific, University of the, 1943-
Pacific Lutheran College, 1955-1970
Pacific University, 1953-1963
Pan American University, 1964-
Parsons College, 1959-1968, 1971-1972
Pembroke State University, 1975-
Pennsylvania, University of, 1906-
Pennsylvania Military College, 1921-1973
Pennsylvania State University, 1908-
Pepperdine University, 1938-
Pfeiffer College, 1975-
Philadelphia College of Textiles and Science,
  1956-
Philander Smith College, 1949-1970
Pittsburgh, University of, 1906-
Pittsburgh, University of, Johnstown, 1975-
Plattsburgh, State University College, 1958-
Plymouth State College, 1966-
Point Park College, 1969-1973
Pomona-Pitzer Colleges, 1924-1927, 1952-
Portland, University of, 1952-
Portland State University, 1958-1963, 1965-
Potsdam, State University College, 1962-
Prairie View A&M University, 1951-
Pratt Institute, 1909-1913, 1955-
Presbyterian College, 1938-1940, 1945-1951
Princeton University, 1913-
Principia College, 1974-
Providence College, 1948-
Purchase, State University College, 1980-
Puerto Rico, University of, Rio Piedras,
  1948-1972
Puerto Rico, University of, 1960-
Puget Sound, University of, 1950-
Purdue University, 1914-
Purdue University, Calumet, 1969-1973
Queens College, 1960-
Quinnipiac College, 1965-
Ramapo College, 1976-
Randolph-Macon College, 1956-
Redlands, University of, 1957-1979
Regis College, 1956-
Rensselaer Polytechnic Institute, 1923-
Rhode Island, University of, 1926-
Rhode Island College, 1967-
Rice University, 1913-
Richmond, University of, 1947-
Ricker College, 1967-1975
Rider College, 1956-
Ripon College, 1954-
Roanoke College, 1957-
Robert Morris College, 1976-
Roberts Wesleyan College, 1980-1981
Rochester, University of, 1906-
Rochester Institute of Technology, 1958-
Rockford College, 1959-1976
Rocky Mountain College, 1975-1978
Roger Williams College, 1974-
Rollins College, 1936-1939, 1947-
Roosevelt University, 1976-
Rose-Hulman Institute of Technology, 1974-
Rust College, 1977-
Rutgers University, Camden, 1956-
Rutgers University, Newark, 1975-

Rutgers University, New Brunswick, 1906-
Sacramento, California State University,
1956-
Sacred Heart University, 1970-
St. Ambrose College, 1948-1965
St. Andrews Presbyterian College, 1974-
St. Anselm's College, 1953-
St. Augustine's College, 1952-
St. Bonaventure University, 1925-1928,
1951-
St. Cloud State University, 1969-
St. Francis College (Maine), 1968-1977
St. Francis College (New York), 1959-
St. Francis College (Pennsylvania), 1950-
St. John Fisher College, 1971-
St. John's College (Maryland), 1928-1933
St. John's University (Minnesota),
1960-1964, 1968-1975, 1976-
St. John's University (New York), 1938-
St. Joseph's College (Indiana), 1963-
St. Joseph's College (Maine), 1974-
St. Joseph's College (Pennsylvania), 1939-
St. Lawrence University, 1929-
St. Leo College, 1969-
St. Louis University, 1934-
St. Mary's College (California), 1952-
St. Mary's College of Maryland, 1977-
St. Michael's College, 1951-
St. Norbert College, 1952-
St. Olaf College, 1954-
St. Paul's College, 1952-
St. Peter's College, 1951-
St. Procopius College, 1962-1972
St. Scholastica, College of, 1979-
St. Stephen's College, 1922-1931
St. Thomas, College of, 1926-1932,
1951-1956, 1964-
Salem State College, 1967-
Salisbury State College, 1974-
Samford University, 1971-
Sam Houston State University, 1951-1953
San Diego, University of, 1961-
San Diego State University, 1947-
San Francisco, University of, 1941-
San Francisco State University, 1952-
San Jose State University, 1936-
Santa Clara, University of, 1938-
Sarah Lawrence College, 1975-1976
Savannah State College, 1952-
Scranton, University of, 1951-
Seattle Pacific University, 1960-
Seattle University, 1950-1980
Seton Hall University, 1906-1912, 1946-
Shaw University (North Carolina), 1952-
Shepherd College, 1966-1976
Shippensburg State College, 1938-1940,
1948-
Siena College, 1947-
Simpson College, 1970-
Slippery Rock State College, 1950-
Sonoma State University, 1965-1974, 1979-
South, University of the (Sewanee), 1913-
South Alabama, University of, 1969-
South Carolina, University of, 1923-1930,
1936-
South Carolina State College, 1955-
South Dakota, University of, 1955-
South Dakota State University, 1951-
South Florida, University of, 1968-
Southampton College, 1965-
Southeast Missouri State University, 1957-

Southeastern Louisiana University, 1965-
Southeastern Massachusetts University,
1974-
Southern California, University of, 1927-
Southern Colorado, University of, 1965-
Southern Connecticut State College, 1961-
Southern Illinois University, Carbondale,
1947-
Southern Illinois University, Edwardsville,
1970-
Southern Maine, University of, 1967-
Southern Methodist University, 1923-
Southern Mississippi, University of, 1952-
Southern Oregon State College, 1970-
Southern Technical Institute, 1974-1978
Southern University, Baton Rouge, 1951-
Southern University, New Orleans, 1973-
Southwest Minnesota State University,
1978-
Southwest Missouri State University, 1957-
Southwest Texas State University,
1953-1956, 1978-
Southwestern College (Tennessee), 1953-
Southwestern Louisiana, University of,
1939-1956, 1965-
Southwestern Oklahoma State University,
1936-1940
Southwestern University (Texas), 1950-1953
Spring Hill College, 1953-1977
Springfield College, 1914-
Stanford University, 1916-
Stanislaus, California State College, 1975-
Staten Island, College of, 1977-
Stetson University, 1922-1935, 1952-
Steubenville, University of, 1960-1974
Stevens Institute of Technology, 1908-
Stillman College, 1963-
Stockton State College, 1976-
Stonehill College, 1964-
Stony Brook, State University College, 1970-
Suffolk University, 1954-
Sul Ross State University, 1951-1955
Susquehanna University, 1924-1946, 1954-
Swarthmore College, 1906-
Syracuse University, 1906-
Tampa, University of, 1971-
Tarkio College, 1939-1946
Tarleton State University, 1976-1977
Temple University, 1919-
Tennessee, University of, Chattanooga, 1953-
Tennessee, University of, Knoxville, 1909-
Tennessee, University of, Martin, 1961-
Tennessee State University, 1951-
Tennessee Technological University, 1951-
Texas, University of, Arlington, 1964-
Texas, University of, Austin, 1907-
Texas, University of, El Paso, 1949-
Texas A&I University, 1980-
Texas A&M University, 1917-
Texas Christian University, 1936-
Texas College, 1952-1958
Texas Southern University, 1952-
Texas Tech University, 1937-
Thiel College, 1954-
Thomas College, 1974-
Thomas More College, 1960-1978
Toledo, University of, 1941-
Tougaloo College, 1970-
Towson State University, 1957-
Transylvania University, 1965-
Trenton State College, 1962-

Trinity College (Connecticut), 1917-
Trinity University (Texas), 1949-
Tri-State University, 1975-
Troy State University, 1971-
Tufts University, 1906-
Tulane University, 1923-
Tulsa, University of, 1936-
Turabo, University of, 1976-1980
Tuskegee Institute, 1940-
U.S. Air Force Academy, 1959-
U.S. Coast Guard Academy, 1930-
U.S. International University, 1966-1969,
    1980-
U.S. Merchant Marine Academy, 1946-
U.S. Military Academy, 1906-
U.S. Naval Academy, 1920-
Union College (New York), 1906-
Union University (Tennessee), 1959-1975
Upper Iowa University, 1959-1973, 1976-
Upsala College, 1950-
Ursinus College, 1911-1919, 1953-
Utah, University of, 1929-
Utah State University, 1938-
Utica College, 1968-
Valdosta State College, 1973-
Valparaiso University, 1926-1930, 1941-
Vanderbilt University, 1906-
Vermont, University of, 1923-
Villanova University, 1927-
Virginia, University of, 1907-
Virginia Commonwealth University, 1971-
Virginia Military Institute, 1923-1932, 1936-
Virginia Polytechnic Institute, 1930-1933,
    1936-
Virginia State College, 1952-
Virginia Union University, 1951-
Virginia Wesleyan College, 1974-
Wabash College, 1943-
Wagner College, 1950-
Wake Forest University, 1930-
Wartburg College, 1949-
Washburn University, 1936-1946
Washington, University of, 1926-
Washington and Jefferson College,
    1906-1933, 1958-
Washington and Lee University, 1912-
Washington College (Maryland), 1938-
Washington State University, 1926-
Washington University (Missouri), 1923-
Wayne State College (Nebraska), 1949-1953
Wayne State University (Michigan), 1937-
Waynesburg College, 1947-1968
Weber State College, 1964-
Wesleyan University, 1906-
West Chester State College, 1933-
West Georgia College, 1973-
West Liberty State College, 1963-1971
West Texas State University, 1923-1928,
    1941-
West Virginia State College, 1952-1961
West Virginia University, 1907-
West Virginia Wesleyan College, 1922-1931,
    1974-1981
Western Carolina University, 1972-
Western Connecticut State College, 1977-
Western Illinois University, 1942-
Western Kentucky University, 1939-
Western Maryland College, 1938-
Western Michigan University, 1929-
Western New England College, 1966-
Western New Mexico University, 1953-1973

Western State College (Colorado), 1948-1979
Western Washington University, 1953-1966
Westfield State College, 1965-
Westmar College, 1967-1974
Westminster College (Missouri), 1974-1979
Westminster College (Pennsylvania),
    1906-1930, 1944-1972
Westminster College (Utah), 1965-1973
Westmont College, 1966-1980
Wheaton College, 1946-
Whitman College, 1949-1951, 1954-1963
Whittier College, 1953-1958, 1974-
Whitworth College, 1951-1967
Wichita State University, 1928-1939, 1945-
Widener University, 1921-
Wilberforce University, 1948-1952,
    1970-1977
Wiley College, 1951-1971
Wilkes College, 1951-
Willamette University, 1953-1961
William and Mary, College of, 1936-
William Jewell College, 1950-1974
William Paterson College, 1970-
William Penn College, 1976-
Williams College, 1906-
Wilmington College, 1951-1971, 1976-1980
Windham College, 1968-1979
Winona State University, 1959-1960,
    1967-1972, 1977-
Winston-Salem State University, 1956-
Wisconsin, University of, Green Bay, 1973-
Wisconsin, University of, LaCrosse, 1975-
Wisconsin, University of, Madison, 1910-
Wisconsin, University of, Milwaukee, 1959-
Wisconsin, University of, Oshkosh, 1974-
Wisconsin, University of, Parkside,
    1974-1976, 1977-
Wisconsin, University of, Platteville, 1980-
Wisconsin, University of, River Falls,
    1976-1978
Wisconsin, University of, Stevens Point,
    1980-
Wisconsin, University of, Stout, 1951-1956,
    1980-
Wisconsin, University of, Superior,
    1939-1941, 1943-
Wisconsin, University of, Whitewater,
    1972-1978, 1980-
Wittenberg University, 1906-1912,
    1924-1932, 1954-
Wofford College, 1953-1954
Wooster, College of, 1906-1909, 1915-1942,
    1945-
Worcester Polytechnic Institute, 1921-
Worcester State College, 1967-
Wright State University, 1972-
Wyoming, University of, 1939-
Xavier University (Louisiana), 1937-1960
Xavier University (Ohio), 1954-
Yale University, 1915-
Yankton College, 1938-1941
Yeshiva University, 1956-
York College (Pennsylvania), 1969-
York College of the City University of New
    York, 1973-
Youngstown State University, 1946-

APPENDIX C

PAST NCAA OFFICERS

YEARS	NAME	INSTITUTION
	PRESIDENT	
1906-1913	Capt. Palmer E. Pierce	U.S. Military Academy
1914-1916	LeBaron R. Briggs	Harvard University
1917-1929	Gen. Palmer E. Pierce	U.S. Military Academy
1930-1932	Charles W. Kennedy	Princeton University
1933-1937	Maj. John L. Griffith	Big Ten Conference
1938-1940	William B. Owens	Stanford University
1941-1944	Phillip O. Badger	New York University
1945-1946	Wilbur C. Smith	Tulane University/University of Wyoming
1947-1949	Karl E. Leib	University of Iowa
1950-1952	Hugh C. Willett	University of Southern California
1953-1954	A. B. Moore	University of Alabama
1955-1956	Clarence P. Houston	Tufts College
1957-1958	Frank N. Gardner	Drake University
1959-1960	Herbert J. Dorricott	Western State College (Colorado)
1961-1962	Henry B. Hardt	Texas Christian University
1963-1964	Robert F. Ray	University of Iowa
1965-1966	Everett D. Barnes	Colgate University
1967-1968	Marcus L. Plant	University of Michigan
1969-1970	Harry M. Cross	University of Washington
1971-1972	Earl M. Ramer	University of Tennessee, Knoxville
1973-1974	Alan J. Chapman	Rice University
1975-1976	John A. Fuzak	Michigan State University
1977-1978	J. Neils Thompson	University of Texas, Austin
1979-1980	William J. Flynn	Boston College
1981-1982	James Frank	Lincoln University (Missouri)
	SECRETARY-TREASURER	
1906-1908	Louis Bevier Jr.	Rutgers University, New Brunswick
1908	W. A. Lambeth	University of Virginia *(Treasurer only)*
1909-1939	Frank W. Nicolson	Wesleyan University
1940-1944	Maj. John L. Griffith	Big Ten Conference
1945-1951	Kenneth L. Wilson	Big Ten Conference
1952-1954	Earl S. Fullbrook	University of Nebraska, Lincoln
1955-1956	Ralph W. Aigler	University of Michigan
1957-1958	Edwin D. Mouzon Jr.	Southern Methodist University
1959-1960	Percy L. Sadler	Lehigh University
1961-1962	Rev. Wilfred H. Crowley	University of Santa Clara
1963-1964	Everett D. Barnes	Colgate University
1965-1966	Francis E. Smiley	Colorado School of Mines
1967-1968	Ernest B. McCoy	Pennsylvania State University
1969-1970	William J. Flynn	Boston College
1971-1972	Samuel E. Barnes	Howard University/D.C. Teachers College
1973-1974	Richard P. Koenig	Valparaiso University
1975-1976	Stanley J. Marshall	South Dakota State University
1977-1978	Edgar A. Sherman	Muskingum College
1979-1980	James Frank	Lincoln University (Missouri)
1981-1982	John L. Toner	University of Connecticut

APPENDIX D

NCAA COUNCIL — ALL-TIME LISTING

NAME	INSTITUTION	YEARS SERVED
Adams, J. C.	Yale University	1926-27
Ahearn, M. F.	Kansas State University	1923
Aigler, Ralph W.	University of Michigan	1923, 1936-37, 1952-54
Arlanson, Harry	Tufts University	1966-68
Armstrong, A. H.	Georgia Institute of Technology	1940-41
Arnold, S. T.	Brown University	1934
Ayer, L. J.	University of Washington	1923
Badger, Phillip O.	New York University	1937-39
Barnes, Everett D.	Colgate University	1959-62
Barnes, Samuel E.	Howard University	1966-70
Barr, J. Shober	Franklin and Marshall College	1953-55
Berg, Sherwood O.	South Dakota State University	1977-79
Berry, Romeyn	Cornell University	1929-36
Betz, Edward S.	University of the Pacific	1975-78
Beyer, S. W.	Iowa State University	1924-31
Bilheimer, C. E.	Gettysburg College	1937-41
Bingham, William J.	Harvard University	1928-35, 1940-42
Blaik, Earl H.	U.S. Military Academy	1949
Blommers, Paul J.	University of Iowa	1955
Bolles, Thomas D.	Harvard University	1955-56
Bonner, Francis W.	Furman University	1981
Booth, Bradford A.	University of California, Los Angeles	1965-68
Bray, Hubert E.	Rice University	1945-47
Breneman, William R.	Indiana University	1951
Breternitz, Louis A.	University of Denver	1948
Brewer, C. L.	University of Missouri, Columbia	1933-34, 1936
Broshous, Lt. Col. C. R.	U.S. Military Academy	1948
Bryant, Walter D. Jr.	University of the South	1963-65
Byrd, H. C.	University of Maryland, College Park	1923-24, 1950
Caldwell, Capt. H. H.	U.S. Naval Academy	1949
Carlson, Harry G.	University of Colorado	1948
Carpenter, H. V.	Washington State University	1926-27
Carver, Frank R.	University of Pittsburgh	1967-71
Casale, Ernest C.	Temple University	1971-77
Chapman, Alan J.	Rice University	1968-72
Chellman, John	Indiana University of Pennsylvania	1978-80
Chrouser, Harvey C.	Wheaton College	1965-67
Clark, Andrew G.	Colorado State University	1946
Clausen, M. R.	University of Arizona	1965-67
Coleman, Cecil N.	University of Illinois, Champaign	1976-78
Cornwell, Oliver K.	University of North Carolina, Chapel Hill	1956-61
Crisler, H. O.	University of Michigan	1958-59
Cross, Harry M.	University of Washington	1971-73
Crowley, Rev. Wilfred H.	University of Santa Clara	1952-55
Davies, Thurston J.	Colorado College	1937, 1939, 1945-48
Davis, Earle	Kansas State University	1949-50
Davis, Howard	Tuskegee Institute	1980-81
Davis, J. William	Texas Tech University	1967-73
Davis, John R.	Oregon State University	1979-81
DeGroot, Dudley	University of Rochester	1942

NAME	INSTITUTION	YEARS SERVED
Dennett, Tyler	Williams College	1935
Diederichs, H.	Cornell University	1936
Dolley, J. C.	University of Texas, Austin	1938-40
Dorricott, Herbert J.	Western State College (Colorado)	1954-58
Dougherty, N. W.	University of Tennessee, Knoxville	1930, 1937-39
Eckel, C. L.	University of Colorado	1938
Eddy, C. L.	Case Western Reserve University	1934-35
Eiler, John R.	East Stroudsburg State College	1975-77
Ellickson, Raymond T.	University of Oregon	1969-70
Emmons, Lloyd C.	Michigan State University	1948-50
Everest, H. P.	University of Washington	1950-51, 1953-56
Ewerhardt, F. H.	Washington University (Missouri)	1938-40
Exum, William	Kentucky State University	1972-74
Fadum, Ralph E.	North Carolina State University	1972-75
Farmer, Malcolm	Yale University	1936-38
Fauver, Edwin	University of Rochester	1926
Fetzer, Robert A.	University of North Carolina, Chapel Hill	1935-37, 1950
Fitterer, J. C.	Colorado School of Mines	1935, 1941
Folsom, F. G.	University of Colorado	1924
Ford, Jeremiah II	University of Pennsylvania	1958-59
Frank, James	Lincoln University (Missouri)	1975-78
Freeborn, Stanley B.	University of California, Berkeley	1947-49
French, Thomas E.	Ohio State University	1924-28
Friley, C. E.	Texas A&M University	1929-32
Fuzak, John A.	Michigan State University	1971-74
Funkhouser, W. D.	University of Kentucky	1938
Gardner, Frank N.	Drake University	1952-56
Gentry, Howard C.	Tennessee State University	1971-73
Geraud, Joseph R.	University of Wyoming	1978-81
Gilmore, Ralph J.	Colorado College	1928, 1945
Ginn, Ralph A.	South Dakota State University	1961-63
Griffith, John L.	Big Ten Conference	1924-32
Groneman, Chris H.	Texas A&M University	1963-66
Hamilton, Thomas J.	University of Pittsburgh	1952-54
Harder, Theodore	University of California, Santa Barbara	1956-60
Hardt, Henry B.	Texas Christian University	1954-58
Harmon, John M.	Boston University	1942-44
Hartvigsen, Milton F.	Brigham Young University	1962-64, 1966-69
Hass, Walter L.	University of Chicago	1962-64, 1972-74
Hawkins, James E.	Fort Valley State College	1974-76
Heitman, Hubert Jr.	University of California, Davis	1975-77
Hendricks, King	Utah State University	1950-55
Henry, D. H.	Clemson University	1931-32
Herrick, Kenneth W.	Texas Christian University	1977-80
Hibbs, Lt. Col. Louis E.	U.S. Military Academy	1941-42
Hixson, Chalmer C.	Wayne State University (Michigan)	1978-81
Hobbs, A. W.	University of North Carolina, Chapel Hill	1942-47
Holcomb, Glenn W.	Oregon State University	1961-67
Holland, Jerome H.	Hampton Institute	1964-66
Holland, Judith R.	University of California, Los Angeles	1981
Houston, Clarence P.	Tufts College	1945-48, 1951, 1954
Hubbard, Wilbur V.	San Jose State University	1958-59
Hume, William II	University of New Mexico	1942
Humphreys, Capt. Charles O.	U.S. Naval Academy	1944-46
Hurlbert, John B.	Stanford University	1952
Ilg, George F.	California State University, Fresno	1971-74
Johnston, Frontis W.	Davidson College	1960-62
Jones, Col. L. McC.	U.S. Military Academy	1943-47
Jordan, Lloyd P.	Amherst College	1948-50
Kane, Robert J.	Cornell University	1948-49
Kennedy, Charles W.	Princeton University	1925, 1929
Ketz, Wilford H.	Union College	1968-71
King, H. H.	Kansas State University	1932-33, 1935-47
Kiphuth, DeLaney	Yale University	1957-58
Knapp, E. J.	University of Texas, El Paso	1959-61
Knight, S. L.	University of Wyoming	1926-27

NAME	INSTITUTION	YEARS SERVED
Koenig, Richard P.	Valparaiso University	1969-72
Kollevoll, Olav B.	Lafayette College	1978-81
Kruczek, Elizabeth A.	Fitchburg State College	1981
Kurtz, Capt. T. R.	U.S. Naval Academy	1924
LaPorte, W. R.	University of Southern California	1924-25, 1929, 1933-34
Larkins, Richard C.	Ohio State University	1956-57
Larson, Emil L.	University of Arizona/ Border Conference	1938-40, 1948-49
Lawrence, Edwin W.	Cheyney State College	1981
Lendall, H. N.	Rutgers University, New Brunswick	1923-24
Lewis, Fred	Vanderbilt University	1951, 1954-55
Lindeburg, Franklin A.	University of California, Riverside	1974-76
Little, Kenneth	University of Wisconsin, Madison	1951
Livingston, W. J.	Denison University	1937
Long, O. F.	Northwestern University	1929-33
Lory, Earl C.	Montana State University	1959-61
Loveless, James C.	DePauw University	1960-63
Macdonald, S. L.	Colorado State University	1934
MacKesey, Paul F.	Brown University	1952-57
Malan, Edward W.	Pomona-Pitzer Colleges	1978-81
Manly, George C.	University of Denver	1923
Marsh, A. W.	Amherst College	1928, 1930-33
Marshall, H. L.	University of Utah	1929-33, 1937
Marshall, Stanley J.	South Dakota State University	1973-74
Martin, J. Frederick	Wesleyan University	1947
Marvel, Fred W.	Brown University	1925
Masters, Alfred R.	Stanford University	1945-50
May, C. C.	University of Washington	1927, 1938-40
McAfee, Arthur J. Jr.	Morehouse College	1978-79
McAlister, D. S.	The Citadel	1954-59
McCarter, William H.	Dartmouth College	1951-53
McCormick, Frank J.	University of Minnesota, Twin Cities	1940
McCoy, Ernest B.	Pennsylvania State University	1960-66
McCoy, James R.	Ohio State University	1967-70
McCurdy, J. H.	Springfield College	1923-24
McDiarmid, E. W.	Texas Christian University	1935-37
McGuirk, Warren P.	University of Massachusetts, Amherst	1958-61
McIntosh, J. S.	Southern Methodist University	1941-44
McIntyre, W. E.	University of Washington	1936
McKenzie, R. Tait	University of Pennsylvania	1923, 1928
McKnight, Nicholas M.	Columbia University	1951
McWhinnie, R. E.	University of Wyoming	1940
McWhorter, H. Boyd	University of Georgia	1968-71
Mendell, C. W.	Yale University	1923-24
Mercer, E. LeRoy	Swarthmore College/ University of Pennsylvania	1926-27, 1934-36, 1940-41, 1950
Metcalf, T. N.	University of Chicago	1937-41
Metzenthin, W. E.	University of Texas, Austin	1936
Meylan, George L.	Columbia University	1923-24, 1926-27
Miles, C. P.	Virginia Polytechnic Institute	1952-53
Mooradian, Andrew T.	University of New Hampshire	1981
Moore, A. B.	University of Alabama	1948-52
Moore, F. W.	Harvard University	1925
Moran, T. F.	Purdue University	1926-27
Morrison, W. R.	Oberlin College	1928
Mouzon, Edwin D. Jr.	Southern Methodist University	1951-56
Murphy, Rev. John H.	University of Notre Dame	1949
Muto, Edwin D.	State University of New York, Buffalo	1981
Myers, Louis A.	University of Arizona	1970-73
Nebel, Arthur W.	University of Missouri, Columbia	1965-70
Neidlinger, L. K.	Dartmouth College	1939-44
Nelson, A. C.	University of Denver	1936
Nettleton, G. H.	Yale University	1929
Nichols, J. H.	Oberlin College	1949, 1952-55
Norrell, Gwendolyn	Michigan State University	1981
Nottelmann, R. H.	University of Washington	1945-46
Olle, Edwin W.	University of Texas, Austin	1962-63
Olmsted, John W.	University of California, Los Angeles	1941-44
Olson, Howard M.	Colorado College	1951-52

NAME	INSTITUTION	YEARS SERVED
Orwig, J. William	Indiana University	1973-75
Owens, William B.	Stanford University	1928-33, 1935
Palmer, S. C.	Swarthmore College	1923, 1937-40
Parsons, Edward S.	Northeastern University	1945-47, 1951
Penick, D. A.	University of Texas, Austin	1923-34
Picard, Fred	Ohio University	1977-80
Plant, Marcus L.	Univesity of Michigan	1963-66
Pont, John	Northwestern University	1979-80
Pritchard, Robert W.	Worcester Polytechnic Institute	1970-73
Pritchett, Norton	University of Virginia	1941-46
Provost, Leo G.	University of Utah	1949
Pyre, J. F. A.	University of Wisconsin, Madison	1925
Ramer, Earl M.	University of Tennessee, Knoxville	1964-70
Ray, Robert F.	University of Iowa	1959-62
Raycroft, Joseph E.	Princeton University	1923-35, 1937
Reed, Dwight T.	Lincoln University (Missouri)	1969-71
Reid, William A.	Colgate University	1943-47
Reynolds, Arthur R.	Colorado State University	1962-68
Richardson, J. P.	Dartmouth College	1925
Rider, George L.	Miami University (Ohio)	1944-47, 1950
Riedel, Robert F.	Geneseo State University College	1979-80
Rockafeller, Harry J.	Rutgers University, New Brunswick	1956-57
Rolfe, Robert A.	Dartmouth College	1959-61
Russell, Donald M.	Wesleyan University	1980-81
Sackett, R. L.	Pennsylvania State University	1930-35
Sadler, Percy L.	Lehigh University	1955-58
St. John, L. W.	Ohio State University	1929-36, 1938-39, 1941-44, 1946-47
Samborski, Adolph W.	Yankee Conference	1966-72
Samson, Charles H.	Texas A&M University	1981
Sanford, S. V.	University of Georgia	1923-34
Sarratt, C. M.	Vanderbilt University	1948
Sawyer, John W.	Wake Forest University	1980-81
Saxer, Edwin L.	University of Toledo	1975-76
Schmidt, Victor O.	Pacific Coast Intercollegiate Athletic Conference	1956-57
Schott, Carl P.	Pennsylvania State University	1950-51
Scott, Alfred W.	University of Georgia	1962-63
Scott, Charley	University of Alabama	1976-79
Scott, Harry A.	Rice University	1942-44
Sebben, Aldo A.	Southwest Missouri State University	1979-81
Shrider, Richard G.	Miami University (Ohio)	1981
Signer, M. I.	Colorado School of Mines	1947
Small, George D.	University of Tulsa	1950-54
Smith, Ross H.	Massachusetts Institute of Technology	1973-77
Smith, Wilbur C.	Tulane University	1933-36
Sneed, Earl	University of Oklahoma	1961-64
Snyder, Rixford K.	Stanford University	1957-60
Sorenson, A. N.	Utah State University	1939
Sours, James K.	Wichita State University	1959-64
Southern, C. E.	Arizona State University	1948-49
Stetson, Willis J.	Swarthmore College	1963-65
Stinson, Wade	University of Kansas	1972
Stovall, Frank L.	University of Houston	1957-58
Strimer, Robert M.	Ohio Wesleyan University	1975-77
Stuhldreher, Harry	University of Wisconsin, Madison	1950
Sullivan, James P.	Boston State College	1978-79
Swank, David	University of Oklahoma	1968-74
Swartz, Delbert	University of Arkansas, Fayetteville	1959-62
Sweat, P. Laverne	Hampton Institute	1981
Taylor, Capt. E. B.	U.S. Naval Academy	1947-48
Thompson, Herbert B.	Fisk University	1977
Thompson, J. Neils	University of Texas, Austin	1973-76
Thompson, Warren O.	University of Colorado	1955-60
Thoms, Frank R. Jr.	Williams College	1962-65
Toner, John L.	University of Connecticut	1977-80
Trevor, Dean S.	Knox College	1964-67
Troxel, O. L.	University of Northern Colorado	1943-44
Troxell, Harry E.	Colorado State University	1974-77
Turner, Marshall S. Jr.	Johns Hopkins University	1967-69

NAME	INSTITUTION	YEARS SERVED
Van Leer, Blake R.	Georgia Institute of Technology	1949
Weller, Kenneth J.	Central College (Iowa)	1980-81
West, R. B.	Utah State University	1925
Whelchel, Capt. John E.	U.S. Naval Academy	1943
Whispell, Raymond J.	Muhlenberg College	1974-78
Wieman, E. E.	University of Denver	1957-58
Willett, Hugh C.	University of Southern California	1934-44, 1953
Williams, D. W.	Texas A&M University	1950-53
Williams, Robley C.	University of California, Berkeley	1970
Williamson, Ivan B.	University of Wisconsin, Madison	1960-61
Williamson, Walter	City College of New York	1928
Winkin, John W.	Colby College/	
	University of Maine, Orono	1974-76
Wood, Harold S.	Beloit College	1956-58

APPENDIX E

NCAA EXECUTIVE COMMITTEE — ALL-TIME LISTING

NAME	INSTITUTION	YEARS SERVED
Abercrombie, R. T.	Johns Hopkins University	1913, 1917-1918
Adams, J. C.	Yale University	1927
Ahearn, M. F.	Kansas State University	1920
Aigler, Ralph W.	University of Michigan	1952
Arbuckle, P. H.	Rice University	1914
Armstrong, Ike J.	University of Utah	1950
Ashburn, I. S.	Texas A&M University	1921-22
Ayer, L. J.	University of Washington	1921-22
Badger, Phillip O.	New York University	1935-40
Barnes, Everett D.	Colgate University	1967-68
Bates, Stan	Western Athletic Conference	1970-77
Bell, William M.	Fayetteville State University	1974-76
Bellis, A. E.	Colorado School of Mines	1921
Berry, Romeyn	Cornell University	1930-37
Bevier, Louis Jr.	Rutgers University, New Brunswick	1909
Beyer, S. W.	Iowa State University	1910, 1921, 1929-31
Bezdek, Hugo	University of Arkansas, Fayetteville	1913
Bible, Dana X.	University of Texas, Austin	1945-46
Bingham, William J.	Harvard University	1928-39
Blommers, Paul J.	University of Iowa	1955
Bohler, F. W.	Washington State University	1919
Bolles, Thomas D.	Harvard University	1957-60
Bosler, C. E.	Dartmouth College	1913
Botsford, E. Herbert	Williams College	1918
Bragg, Thomas	Auburn University	1920
Brewer, C. L.	University of Missouri, Columbia	1916, 1933
Brown, C. S.	Vanderbilt University	1919
Brown, O. E.	Vanderbilt University	1915
Browne, A. D.	Oregon State University	1917-18
Bryant, George	Coe College	1917
Buchanan, H. E.	University of Tennessee, Knoxville	1914, 1916-17
Bushnell, Asa S.	Eastern College Athletic Conference	1943-44, 1947-51
Carpenter, P. R.	Worcester Polytechnic Institute	1922
Carver, Frank.	University of Pittsburgh	1964-66
Casale, Ernest C.	Temple University	1980-81
Castleman, Frank	University of Colorado	1913
Chase, H. G.	Tufts University	1911
Clapp, R. G.	University of Nebraska, Lincoln	1911
Clark, H. W.	Lafayette College	1940-42
Coleman, A. M.	Southeastern Conference	1971
Coleman, Cecil N.	University of Illinois, Champaign	1979
Coleman, Jefferson J.	University of Alabama	1958-62
Conner, Mike S.	Southeastern Conference	1945-46
Coons, C. D.	Denison University	1917
Crenshaw, J. B.	Georgia Institute of Technology	1918
Crowley, Rev. Wilfred H.	University of Santa Clara	1959-60, 1963-64
Davies, Thurston J.	Colorado College	1938-44
Dorricott, Herbert J.	Western State College (Colorado)	1955-56, 1958, 1961-65
Dougherty, N. W.	University of Tennessee, Knoxville	1947-49
Driver, W. L.	Texas A&M University	1917
Dudley, William L.	Vanderbilt University	1906-09
Duke, R. Wayne	Big Eight/Big Ten Conferences	1970-75
Ehler, G. W.	University of Wisconsin, Madison	1911
Erdle, Col. Philip J.	U.S. Air Force Academy	1978

NAME	INSTITUTION	YEARS SERVED
Estes, Linda K.	University of New Mexico	1981
Ewerhardt, F. H.	Washington University (Missouri)	1938-39
Fairman, R. Kenneth	Princeton University	1942
Farr, H. A.	Yale University	1916
Fauver, Edwin	University of Rochester	1926
Fetzer, Robert A.	University of North Carolina, Chapel Hill	1938-41, 1949
Flynn, William J.	Boston College	1967-68, 1971-74
French, Thomas E.	Ohio State University	1919
Fullbrook, Earl	University of Nebraska, Lincoln	1950-51
Furey, Ralph S.	Columbia University	1953-58
Futrall, J. C.	University of Arkansas, Fayetteville	1918
Golden, W. N.	Pennsylvania State University	1910
Goodenough, G. A.	University of Illinois, Champaign	1916, 1921
Grice, J. William	Case Western Reserve University	1977-81
Griffith, John L.	Big Ten Conference	1924-32
Grubbs, Howard	Southwest Athletic Conference	1952-55
Hamilton, Thomas J.	University of Pittsburgh	1952-54
Hardt, Henry B.	Texas Christian University	1963-66
Herty, C. H.	University of North Carolina, Chapel Hill	1916
Hetherington, C. W.	University of Missouri, Columbia	1907-1910
Hill, Jesse T.	University of Southern California	1964-69
Holgate, T. F.	Northwestern University	1915
Houston, Clarence P.	Tufts College	1942-44
Howe, H. C.	University of Oregon	1920
Huff, George	University of Illinois, Champaign	1918
Hullihen, Walter	University of the South	1913
Hunter, J. A.	University of Colorado	1920
Huntington, C. E.	Colgate University	1920
James, Robert C.	Atlantic Coast Conference	1976-81
Johns, Wilbur C.	University of California, Los Angeles	1951-55, 1960-63
Judd, A. F.	University of Pittsburgh	1914
Kane, Robert J.	Cornell University	1950-51
Keene, Roy S.	Oregon State University	1956-59
Kennedy, Charles W.	Princeton University	1929
King, H. H.	Kansas State University	1937
Larkins, Richard C.	Ohio State University	1958-63
Lee, H. B.	Kansas State University	1965-69
Lefevre, Albert	University of Virginia	1914, 1919
Leib, Karl E.	University of Iowa	1941-46
Lendall, H. N.	Rutgers University, New Brunswick	1923-24
Lester, O. C.	University of Colorado	1914
Lewis, E. M.	University of Massachusetts, Amherst	1920
Lonborg, Arthur C.	University of Kansas	1959-64
Long, O. F.	Northwestern University	1929-32
Lowe, Henry T.	University of Missouri, Columbia	1979-81
Macdonald, S. L.	Colorado State University	1915
Manley, W. G.	University of Missouri, Columbia	1913
Manly, George C.	University of Denver	1922
Martin, J. Frederick	Wesleyan University	1946
Marvel, Fred W.	Brown University	1910
Mather, W. T.	University of Texas, Austin	1915
Maxcy, C. L.	Williams College	1917
May, C. C.	University of Washington	1940-41
McCarter, William H.	Dartmouth College	1953
McCoy, Ernest B.	Pennsylvania State University	1969
McCurdy, J. H.	Springfield College	1923-24
McKenzie, R. Tait	University of Pennsylvania	1919
Meanwell, W. E.	University of Missouri, Columbia	1918
Mercer, E. LeRoy	Swarthmore College/ University of Pennsylvania	1926-27, 1934-36, 1945-49
Meylan, George L.	Columbia University	1911, 1921-24
Miller, J. A.	Swarthmore College	1915
Miller, Ogden D.	Yale University	1943-45
Moore, Bernie H.	Southeastern Conference	1950-57
Moore, F. W.	Harvard University	1925
Moran, T. F.	Purdue University	1922
Morehouse, D. W.	Drake University	1914, 1922
Morgan, J. D.	University of California, Los Angeles	1977-79
Motten, Roger H.	Colorado College	1918-19

NAME	INSTITUTION	YEARS SERVED
Mouzon, Edwin D. Jr.	Southern Methodist University	1956, 1962
Murray, E. W.	University of Kansas	1915
Neidlinger, L. K.	Dartmouth College	1940-41
Nelson, Thomas	North Carolina State University	1921-22
Nichols, J. H.	Oberlin College	1950-51
Nicolson, Frank W.	Wesleyan College	1908
Norlin, George	University of Colorado	1911
Ogilby, R. B.	Trinity College (Connecticut)	1921
Owen, B. G.	University of Oklahoma	1916
Owens, William B.	Stanford University	1941-44
Paige, James	University of Minnesota, Twin Cities	1913
Palmer, Erastus	City College of New York	1917
Palmer, S. C.	Swarthmore College	1923
Parmelee, H. C.	Colorado School of Mines	1917
Patterson, A. H.	University of North Carolina, Chapel Hill	1910
Peck, H. A.	Syracuse University	1908
Peters, Reaves E.	Missouri Valley Conference	1949, 1951-53
Peters, Seaver	Dartmouth College	1977-81
Phillips, Henry D.	University of the South	1921
Phillips, Paul C.	Amherst College	1909
Plant, Marcus L.	University of Michigan	1969-73
Pritchett, Norton	University of Virginia	1947-48
Pyre, J. F. A.	University of Wisconsin, Madison	1914, 1920
Ramer, Earl M.	University of Tennessee, Knoxville	1973-78
Ray, Robert F.	University of Iowa	1965-70
Raycroft, Joseph E.	Princeton University	1916, 1923-37
Richardson, J. P.	Dartmouth College	1925
Richey, J. J.	Texas A&M University	1920
Riddick, W. C.	North Carolina State University	1911
Riedel, Robert F.	Geneseo State University College	1981
Robison, Polk F.	Texas Tech University	1970-76
Rockafeller, Harry J.	Rutgers University, New Brunswick	1959-61
Sackett, R. L.	Pennsylvania State University	1932-36
St. John, C. E.	Oberlin College	1907
St. John, L. W.	Ohio State University	1929-40, 1945
Sanford, S. V.	University of Georgia	1922, 1925-28
Satterfield, H. E.	North Carolina State University	1920
Savage, C. W.	Oberlin College	1910
Scott, Charley	University of Alabama	1980-81
Shannon, E. F.	Washington and Lee University	1915
Sherman, Edgar A.	Muskingum College	1974-76
Shirky, Sam B.	University of Missouri, Columbia	1946-48
Shively, Bernie A.	University of Kentucky	1966-67
Sills, K. C. M.	Bowdoin College	1919
Singleton, Joe L.	University of California, Davis	1977-81
Steitz, Edward S.	Springfield College	1974-80
Stewart, E. J.	Oregon State University	1916
Stewart, James H.	Southwest Athletic Conference	1947-50
Small, George D.	University of Tulsa	1954-58
Smiley, Francis E.	Colorado School of Mines	1967-71
Smith, Wilbur C.	Tulane University	1941-44
Stagg, Amos Alonzo	University of Chicago	1908-09
Stout, R. Victor	Boston University	1961-66
Strong, Frank	University of Kansas	1906
Swank, David	University of Oklahoma	1975-76
Turner, Marshall S. Jr.	Johns Hopkins University	1972-73
Weaver, James H.	Atlantic Coast Conference	1968-70
Welch, Rev. Herbert	Ohio Wesleyan University	1906
Whittier, F. N.	Bowdoin College	1915
Wild, H. D.	Williams College	1906-07
Willett, Hugh C.	University of Southern California	1937-39, 1945-49
Williams, C. C.	University of Kansas	1919
Williams, Henry L.	University of Minnesota, Twin Cities	1908-09
Williamson, Walter	City College of New York	1928
Wilson, Kenneth L.	Big Ten Conference	1952, 1954, 1956-57
Wilson, W. L.	Lehigh University	1913
Woll, F. A.	City College of New York	1918
Wren, F. G.	Tufts University	1914
Zimmerman, Mary M.	University of South Dakota	1981

APPENDIX F

GENERAL COMMITTEE CHAIRS — ALL-TIME LISTING

Listed below are the chairs of the various standing committees established by the NCAA constitution and bylaws. Numerous other committees have existed for periods of time for the purpose of dealing with specific assignments; while important, they are not listed. Through the years, the names of various committees have changed although their functions basically have not. For example, the Professional Relations Committee of years past is now called Professional Sports Liaison. Each committee is listed by its present (1981) name.

YEARS	NAME	AFFILIATION
ACADEMIC TESTING AND REQUIREMENTS		
1963-69	James H. Weaver	Atlantic Coast Conference
1970	John A. Fuzak	Michigan State University
1971-72	Alan J. Chapman	Rice University
1973-75	Rixford N. Yard	Tulane University
1976-77	E. John Larsen	University of Southern California
1978-81	H. Boyd McWhorter	Southeastern Conference
ALL-STAR HIGH SCHOOL GAMES		
1962	Henry B. Hardt	Texas Christian University
1963	Robert F. Ray	University of Iowa
1964-66	Arthur C. Lonborg	University of Kansas
1967	Charles A. Taylor	Stanford University
1968	Henry T. Bream	Gettysburg College
1969-70	Cameron S. Deeds	California State University, Los Angeles
1971-73	Gordon H. Chalmers	Indiana State University, Terre Haute
1974-75	Hayden Fry	North Texas State University
1976	Fred L. Miller	Arizona State University
1977-78	Harry H. Fouke	University of Houston
1979-81	Ade L. Sponberg	North Dakota State University
CLASSIFICATION		
1976-79	Louis A. Myers	University of Arizona
1980-81	Capt. John O. Coppedge	U.S. Naval Academy
COLLEGE		
(Formerly Small College)		
1941	H. W. Clark	Lafayette College
1942-45	Clarence P. Houston	Tufts University
1946-50	J. H. Nichols	Oberlin College
1951-52	C. E. Bilheimer	Gettysburg College
1953	Willis J. Stetson	Swarthmore College
1954-55	Marshall S. Turner Jr.	Johns Hopkins University
1956-60	Ralph A. Ginn	South Dakota State University
1961-62	Harold J. Beatty	California State University, Fresno
1963-64	Francis E. Smiley Jr.	Colorado School of Mines
1965	Harry Arlanson	Tufts University
1966	Don Adee	California State University, Chico
1967	Wilford H. Ketz	Union College (New York)
1968	James H. Witham	University of Northern Iowa

YEARS	NAME	AFFILIATION
1969-70	J. Lewis Comer	California State University, Hayward
1971-72	Stanley J. Marshall	South Dakota State University
1973-74	Franklin A. Lindeburg	University of California, Riverside

*COMMITTEE ON COMMITTEES, MEN'S

1940-44	Thomas E. French	Ohio State University
1945	L. W. St. John	Ohio State University
1946-50	Hugh C. Willett	University of Southern California
1951	Earl S. Fullbrook	University of Nebraska, Lincoln
1952	Stanley B. Freeborn	University of California, Berkeley
1953-54	Harry Carlson	University of Colorado
1955	Howard Grubbs	Southwest Athletic Conference
1956-57	E. E. Wieman	University of Denver
1958-59	Richard C. Larkins	Ohio State University
1960	Ivan B. Williamson	University of Wisconsin, Madison
1961	Paul F. MacKesey	Brown University
1962-63	Howard Grubbs	Southwest Athletic Conference
1964	James H. Weaver	Atlantic Coast Conference
1965	Asa S. Bushnell	Eastern College Athletic Conference
1966-67	E. Hoyt Brawner	University of Denver
1968	Richard C. Larkins	Ohio State University
1969-70	J. Neils Thompson	University of Texas, Austin
1971	Robert C. James	Mid-American Conference
1972	Lloyd P. Jordan	Southern Conference
1973	Karl Kurth Jr.	Trinity College (Connecticut)
1974-75	James B. Higgins	Lamar University
1976-77	Eugene F. Corrigan	University of Virginia
1978	Peter R. Elliott	University of Miami (Florida)
1979-80	George S. King Jr.	Purdue University
1981	John Caine	University of Oregon
1982	Fred Jacoby	Mid-American Conference

*Records prior to 1940 are incomplete. In 1981, the Committee on Committees became the men's committee and a new women's committee was appointed.

COMMITTEE ON COMMITTEES, WOMEN'S

1981	Emma J. Best	University of District of Columbia

COMPETITIVE SAFEGUARDS AND MEDICAL ASPECTS OF SPORTS

1959-64	Ernest B. McCoy	Pennsylvania State University
1965-68	Carl S. Blyth	University of North Carolina, Chapel Hill
1969-71	Donald L. Cooper, M.D.	Oklahoma State University
1972	Walter C. Schwank	University of Montana
1973-75	Kenneth S. Clarke	Pennsylvania State University
1976-81	Fred L. Miller	Arizona State University

CONSTITUTION AND BYLAWS

1954-56	Victor O. Schmidt	Pacific Coast Conference
1957-61	Marcus L. Plant	University of Michigan
1962-64	Earl Sneed	University of Oklahoma
1965-67	Harry M. Cross	University of Washington
1968-71	Frank J. Remington	University of Wisconsin, Madison
1972	John E. Kane	University of Arkansas, Fayetteville
1973-77	Marcus L. Plant	University of Michigan
1978-79	Stanley J. Marshall	South Dakota State University
1980-81	Alan J. Chapman	Rice University

CREDENTIALS

1945-46*	Robert A. Fetzer	University of North Carolina, Chapel Hill
	Z. G. Clevenger	Indiana University
1947-48*	Robert A. Fetzer	University of North Carolina, Chapel Hill
	Sam B. Shirky	University of Missouri, Columbia
1949*	Robert A. Fetzer	University of North Carolina, Chapel Hill
	George A. Rider	Miami University (Ohio)
1950*	Robert A. Fetzer	University of North Carolina, Chapel Hill
	Sam B. Shirky	University of Missouri, Columbia
1951*	Robert A. Fetzer	University of North Carolina, Chapel Hill

YEARS	NAME	AFFILIATION
	David Bjork	University of California, Los Angeles
	Dean Kenny	Brown University
1952	Edward Parsons	Northeastern University
1953	Rev. Wilfred H. Crowley	University of Santa Clara
1954	Henry B. Hardt	Texas Christian University
1955	Hugh C. Willett	University of Southern California
1956	Forrest U. Lake	Tulane University
1957	Sam B. Shirky	University of Missouri, Columbia
1958	Verne C. Freeman	Purdue University
1959-62	Marshall S. Turner Jr.	Johns Hopkins University
1963	Alfred W. Scott	University of Georgia
1964-66	James C. Loveless	DePauw University
1967	Eugene L. Shirk	Albright College
1968	Frank L. Stovall	University of Houston
1969-70	Robert T. Bronzan	San Jose State University
1971	R. R. Ritchie	Clemson University
1972	J. Lewis Comer	California State University, Long Beach
1973	Carl E. Abner	University of Louisville
1974	Kenneth N. Vickery	Clemson University
1975	H. Evan Zeiger	Samford University
1976	Vannette W. Johnson	University of Arkansas, Pine Bluff
1977	Ralph H. Coleman	University of Evansville
1978	John W. Sawyer	Wake Forest University
1979	T. H. Anderson	Northern Arizona University
1980-81	Paul V. Amodio	Youngstown State University/ Kent State University
1982	Richard A. Clower	Western Maryland College

Records prior to 1945 are incomplete. *No chair designated.

DRUG EDUCATION

1973-77	Robert W. Pritchard	Worcester Polytechnic Institute
1978-81	Carl S. Blyth	University of North Carolina, Chapel Hill

ELIGIBILITY

1939-44	Thomas E. French	Ohio State University
1945-49	Hugh C. Willett	University of Southern California
1950	E. LeRoy Mercer	University of Pennsylvania
1951-56	Victor O. Schmidt	Pacific Coast Conference
1957-64	Rev. Wilfred H. Crowley	University of Santa Clara
1965-67	Ernest B. McCoy	Pennsylvania State University
1968	Marcus L. Plant	University of Michigan
1969-72	J. William Davis	Texas Tech University
1973	Ernest C. Casale	Temple University
1974	Stanley J. Marshall	South Dakota State University
1975-77	Louis A. Myers	University of Arizona
1978-80	John L. Toner	University of Connecticut
1981	Olav B. Kollevoll	Lafayette College

EXTRA EVENTS
(also see Postseason Football)

1981	Clarence E. Gaines	Winston-Salem State University

GOVERNMENTAL AFFAIRS

1962-65	William R. Reed	Big Ten Conference
1966-74	Robert C. James	Mid-American Conference/ Atlantic Coast Conference
1975	J. William Orwig	Indiana University
1976-78	Ferdinand A. Geiger	University of Pennsylvania
1979-80	James Frank	Lincoln University (Missouri)
1981	John R. Davis	Oregon State University

INFRACTIONS

1956-59	A. D. Kirwan	University of Kentucky
1960-73	George H. Young	University of Wisconsin, Madison
1974-77	Arthur R. Reynolds	University of Northern Colorado
1978-81	Charles Alan Wright	University of Texas, Austin

YEARS	NAME	AFFILIATION

INSURANCE

YEARS	NAME	AFFILIATION
1952-63	Edwin D. Mouzon Jr.	Southern Methodist University
1964-66	Walter L. Hass	University of Chicago
1967-68	Ralph H. Wherry	Pennsylvania State University
1969-70	Walter L. Hass	University of Chicago
1971-75	Rixford N. Yard	Tulane University
1976	M. R. Clausen	University of Arizona
1977	Harold C. Krogh	University of Kansas
1978-81	Kenneth W. Herrick	Texas Christian University

INTERNATIONAL RELATIONS
(formerly Olympic)

1954-61	Willis O. Hunter	University of Southern California
1962-65	Clarence L. Munn	Michigan State University
1966-70	William R. Reed	Big Ten Conference
1971-72	Edward S. Steitz	Springfield College
1973-77	Charles M. Neinas	Big Eight Conference
1978-81	David L. Maggard	University of California, Berkeley

JUNIOR COLLEGE RELATIONS

1974-79	H. Boyd McWhorter	Southeastern Conference
1980-81	Kenneth W. Herrick	Texas Christian University

LONG RANGE PLANNING

1964	James K. Sours	Wichita State University
1965-70	Francis E. Smiley	Colorado School of Mines
1971-73	William H. Baughn	University of Colorado
1974	John A. Fuzak	Michigan State University
1975-81	Alan J. Chapman	Rice University

MEMORIAL RESOLUTIONS

1940*	R. E. Whinnie	University of Wyoming
	H. H. King	Kansas State University
1941	William B. Owens	Stanford University
1942	Thurston Davies	Colorado College
1943-44	Karl E. Leib	University of Iowa
1945	Records incomplete	
1946*	E. LeRoy Mercer	University of Pennsylvania
	Dana X. Bible	University of Texas, Austin
	Mike S. Conner	Southeastern Conference
1947-48	J. Frederick Martin	Wesleyan University
1949*	Brutus Hamilton	University of California, Berkeley
	Asa S. Bushnell	Eastern College Athletic Conference
1950	Records incomplete	
1951	Dean Moore	University of Alabama
1952	King Hendricks	Utah State University
1953	Paul MacKesey	Brown University
1954	King Hendricks	Utah State University
1955	Marshall S. Turner Jr.	Johns Hopkins University
1956	Rev. Edmund P. Joyce	University of Notre Dame
1957	Rev. Wilfred H. Crowley	University of Santa Clara
1958-59	Rev. Charles L. Sanderson	St. Louis University
1960	Rev. Edmund P. Joyce	University of Notre Dame
1961	Rev. Wilfred H. Crowley	University of Santa Clara
1962	Edwin D. Mouzon Jr.	Southern Methodist University
1963	Carl Erickson	Kent State University
1964	Rev. Wilfred H. Crowley	University of Santa Clara
1965	Rev. Edmund P. Joyce	University of Notre Dame
1966	Robert L. Hoggson	Georgetown University
1967	Henry B. Hardt	Texas Christian University
1968-69	Aloysius B. Begley	Providence College
1970	John E. Faber	University of Maryland, College Park
1971-72	John J. Horgan	Seton Hall University
1973	Edwin P. Horner	Baylor University
1974	Charles D. Henry	Grambling University
1975-76	Robert H. Frailey	American University
1977**	Ronald D. Roberts	Lawrence University
	Rev. John Carven	Niagara University

YEARS	NAME	AFFILIATION
1978-80	Jack C. Patterson	Baylor University
1981-82	Rev. Joseph Eagan	University of San Francisco

Records prior to 1940 are incomplete. *No chair designated. **Both served as chair.

NATIONAL YOUTH SPORTS PROGRAM

1970	Richard C. Larkins	Ohio State University
1971-79	William Exum	Kentucky State University
1980-81	Warren K. Giese	University of South Carolina

NOMINATING

1906	E. J. Barlett	Dartmouth College
1907	Louis Bevier Jr.	Rutgers University, New Brunswick
1908	Records incomplete	
1909	Frank W. Nicolson	Wesleyan University
1910	Amos Alonzo Stagg	University of Chicago
1911	Records incomplete	
1912	C. C. Maxey	Williams College
1913	W. G. Manley	University of Missouri, Columbia
1914	J. H. McCurdy	Springfield College
1915	T. F. Moran	Purdue University
1916	C. W. Savage	Oberlin College
1917	H. C. Swan	Trinity College (Connecticut)
1918	L. W. St. John	Ohio State University
1919	E. M. Botsford	Williams College
1920	J. H. McCurdy	Springfield College
1921	Paul C. Phillips	Amherst College
1922	Clarence P. Houston	Tufts University
1923	S. W. Beyer	Iowa State University
1924	R. Tait McKenzie	University of Pennsylvania
1925	S. W. Beyer	Iowa State University
1926-27	J. H. McCurdy	Springfield College
1928-30	T. A. Storey	Stanford University
1931	Thomas E. French	Ohio State University
1932	C. L. Brewer	University of Missouri, Columbia
1933	Records incomplete	
1934	Thomas E. French	Ohio State University
1935	Romeyn Berry	Cornell University
1936	Thomas E. French	Ohio State University
1937-38	Wilbur C. Smith	Tulane University
1939-41	H. W. Clark	Lafayette College
1942-45	Clarence P. Houston	Tufts University
1946	Karl E. Leib	University of Iowa
1947	William J. Bingham	Harvard University
1948	Norton Pritchett	University of Virginia
1949	Robert J. Kane	Cornell University
1950	N. W. Dougherty	University of Tennessee, Knoxville
1951-53	J. H. Nichols	Oberlin College
1954	Rev. Wilfred H. Crowley	University of Santa Clara
1955	Paul MacKesey	Brown University
1956	H. P. Everest	University of Washington
1957	Herbert J. Dorricott	Western State College (Colorado)
1958	Henry B. Hardt	Texas Christian University
1959	Warren O. Thompson	University of Colorado
1960	Rixford K. Snyder	Stanford University
1961	Warren P. McGuirk	University of Massachusetts, Amherst
1962	Glen W. Holcomb	Oregon State University
1963	James K. Sours	Wichita State University
1964	Chris H. Groneman	Texas A&M University
1965	Frank R. Thoms Jr.	Williams College
1966	Ernest B. McCoy	Pennsylvania State University
1967	Earl M. Ramer	University of Tennessee, Knoxville
1968	Bradford A. Booth	University of California, Los Angeles
1969	Adolph W. Samborski	Harvard University
1970	J. William Davis	Texas Tech University
1971	H. Boyd McWhorter	University of Georgia
1972	Alan J. Chapman	Rice University
1973	Louis A. Myers	University of Arizona
1974	John A. Fuzak	Michigan State University

YEARS	NAME	AFFILIATION
1975	Ralph E. Fadum	North Carolina State University
1976	J. Neils Thompson	University of Texas, Austin
1977	Harry E. Troxell	Colorado State University
1978	Edward S. Betz	University of the Pacific
1979	John L. Toner	University of Connecticut
1980	Fred Picard	Ohio University
1981	Joseph R. Geraud	University of Wyoming
1982	John R. Davis	Oregon State University

POSTGRADUATE SCHOLARSHIP

1966	A. D. Kirwan	University of Kentucky
1967-71	Laurence C. Woodruff	University of Kansas
1971-75	Capt. John O. Coppedge	U.S. Naval Academy
1976-80	Joe L. Singleton	University of California, Davis
1981	Fred Jacoby	Mid-American Conference

POSTSEASON FOOTBALL
(formerly Extra Events)

1952-58	Wilbur C. Johns	University of California, Los Angeles
1959-61	Paul W. Brechler	University of Iowa
1962-64	James R. Jack	University of Utah
1965-69	Stan Bates	Washington State University
1970-72	Wade R. Stinson	University of Kansas
1973-76	Robert C. James	Atlantic Coast Conference
1977-79	David H. Strack	University of Arizona
1980	Eugene F. Corrigan	University of Virginia
1981	Milo R. Lude	University of Washington

PROFESSIONAL SPORTS LIAISON

*1962-65	Rev. Joseph A. Glavin	Holy Cross College/Boston College
1962-64	William R. Reed	Big Ten Conference
1965-66	James J. Corbett	Louisiana State University
1967-70	David M. Nelson	University of Delaware
1971-73	Robert M. Whitelaw	Eastern College Athletic Conference
1974-77	R. Wayne Duke	Big Ten Conference
1978	J. D. Morgan	University of California, Los Angeles
1979-81	Wiles Hallock	Pacific-10 Conference

*Professional Baseball Committee combined with Professional Relations Committee (now Professional Sports Liaison Committee) in 1966.

PROMOTION

1971-76	Donald B. Canham	University of Michigan
1977-79	Wiles Hallock	Pacific-10 Conference
1980-81	Joseph L. Kearney	Western Athletic Conference

PUBLIC RELATIONS

1956-57	H. P. Everest	University of Washington
1958-61	C. Robert Paul	University of Pennsylvania
1962-64	Fred W. Stabley	Michigan State University
1965	Baaron B. Pittenger	Harvard University
1966-67	Ernest Goodman	Harvard University
1968-69	Robert Cheyne	University of Arkansas, Fayetteville
1970-71	Bill Young	University of Wyoming
1972-75	Bill Callahan	University of Missouri, Columbia
1976-79	Charles J. Thornton	University of Alabama
1980-81	Don W. Bryant	University of Nebraska, Lincoln

PUBLICATIONS

1915-24	Joseph E. Raycroft	Princeton University
1925-44	No committee	
1945-51	Ralph Furey	Columbia University
1952-53	Robert A. Hall	Yale University
1954-63	James V. Gilloon Jr.	New York University
1964	Walter T. McLaughlin	St. John's University (New York)

RECRUITING

1977-81	Robert C. James	Atlantic Coast Conference

YEARS	NAME	AFFILIATION

RESEARCH
1977-81	Fred Jacoby	Mid-American Conference

STEERING COMMITTEE — DIVISION I
1978-79	Charley Scott	University of Alabama
1980-81	Joseph R. Geraud	University of Wyoming

STEERING COMMITTEE — DIVISION II
1978	James Frank	Lincoln University (Missouri)
1979-80	Chalmer G. Hixson	Wayne State University (Michigan)
1981	Aldo A. Sebben	Southwest Missouri State University

STEERING COMMITTEE — DIVISION III
1978	Raymond J. Whispell	Muhlenberg College
1979-80	Edward W. Malan	Pomona-Pitzer Colleges
1981	Donald M. Russell	Wesleyan University

SUMMER BASEBALL
1924	Roger Lee	Harvard University
1925	John L. Griffith	Big Ten Conference
1926-59	No committee	
1960	Bernie A. Shively	University of Kentucky
1961-68	George L. Shiebler	Eastern College Athletic Conference
1969-73	J. A. Tomlinson	Arkansas State University
1974-79	Clifton M. Speegle	Southwest Athletic Conference
1980-81	John W. Winkin	University of Maine, Orono

TELEVISION, FOOTBALL
1951*	Thomas J. Hamilton	University of Pittsburgh
	Ralph Furey	Columbia University
1952	Robert A. Hall	Yale University
1953	Robert J. Kane	Cornell University
1954	Harvey Cassill	University of Washington
1955	E. L. Romney	Mountain States Conference
1956	Howard Grubbs	Southwest Athletic Conference
1957	Robert J. Kane	Cornell University
1958	Rixford N. Yard	Denison University
1959	Howard Grubbs	Southwest Athletic Conference
1960	Rixford N. Yard	Denison University
1961	James J. Corbett	Louisiana State University
1962	William J. Flynn	Boston College
1963-64	Paul W. Brechler	Western Athletic Conference
1965-66	Herbert J. Dorricott	Western State College (Colorado)
1967-68	William J. Flynn	Boston College
1969-70	Forest Evashevski	University of Iowa
1970	William J. Flynn	Boston College
1971-72	James H. Decker	Syracuse University
1973-76	Seaver Peters	Dartmouth College
1977-78	Capt. John O. Coppedge	U.S. Naval Academy
1979	Cecil N. Coleman	University of Illinois, Champaign
1980-81	Wiles Hallock	Pacific-10 Conference

*No chair designated.

TELEVISION, GENERAL
1981	Seaver Peters	Dartmouth College

THEODORE ROOSEVELT AWARD
1969-81	Committee chaired by current NCAA president	

TOP TEN SELECTION
1974-79	Robert F. Ray	University of Iowa
1980-81	Wilbur Evans	Salado, Texas (formerly Southwest Athletic Conference)

YEARS	NAME	AFFILIATION

VOTING

1952	Rev. Wilfred H. Crowley	University of Santa Clara
1953	A. E. Lumley	Amherst College
1954-56	N. W. Dougherty	University of Tennessee, Knoxville
1957	Henry A. Hardt	Texas Christian University
1958	Verne C. Freeman	Purdue University
1959-62	Alfred W. Scott	University of Georgia
1963	Frank L. Stovall	University of Houston
1964-65	Willis J. Stetson	Swarthmore College
1966	Wallis Beasley	Washington State University
1967-69	William R. Maybry	Southwestern College (Tennessee)
1970	Rixford N. Yard	Tulane University
1971	Frank L. Forbes	Morehouse College
1972	Albert W. Twitchell	Rutgers University, New Brunswick
1973	Thomas J. Frericks	University of Dayton
1974-75	H. Boyd McWhorter	Southeastern Conference
1976-77	Aldo A. Sebben	Southwest Missouri State University
1978-79	Brig. Gen. Philip J. Erdle	U.S. Air Force Academy
1980	Charles D. Henry	Big Ten Conference
1981-82	Frank Windegger	Texas Christian University

WOMEN'S INTERCOLLEGIATE ATHLETICS

1977-79	Edward S. Betz	University of the Pacific

APPENDIX G

SPORTS COMMITTEE CHAIRS — ALL-TIME LISTING
Through the years, the names of various committees have changed although their functions basically have not. For example, the Baseball Rules Committee is now the Men's Baseball Committee. Each committee is listed by its present (1981) name.

YEARS	NAME	AFFILIATION

MEN'S BASEBALL

1927-32	Edgar Fauver	Wesleyan University
1933-36	No committee	
1937-38	Edgar Fauver	Wesleyan University
1939	L. C. Boles	College of Wooster
1940-46	No committee	
1947-49	Frank G. McCormick	University of Minnesota, Twin Cities
1950-53	Everett D. Barnes	Colgate University
1954-60	John K. Kobs	Michigan State University
1961-64	J. Kyle Anderson	University of Chicago
1965-68	L. C. Timm	Iowa State University
1969-74	Charles Brayton	Washington State University
1975-76	Chalmers Port	The Citadel
1977	Kal H. Segrist	Texas Tech University
1978	Donald K. Edwards	University of California, Riverside
1979-81	Dick Bergquist	University of Massachusetts, Amherst

*DIVISION I MEN'S BASKETBALL

1938-46	Harold G. Olsen	Ohio State University
1947-59	Arthur C. Lonborg	University of Kansas
1960-65	Bernie A. Shively	University of Kentucky
1966-69	H. B. Lee	Kansas State University
1970-74	Tom Scott	Davidson College
1975-76	Stanley H. Watts	Brigham Young University
1977-80	R. Wayne Duke	Big Ten Conference
1981	David R. Gavitt	Providence College

*In 1957, a separate College Division Basketball Committee was formed.

*MEN'S BASKETBALL, COLLEGE DIVISION

1957-59	Willis J. Stetson	Swarthmore College
1960-61	Harvey Chrouser	Wheaton College
1962	J. Shober Barr	Franklin and Marshall College
1963-67	Richard P. Koenig	Valparaiso University
1968-70	Walter L. Hass	University of Chicago
1971-73	Wilbur Renken	Albright College

*In 1957, this committee was separated from what was then called the "University Division Basketball Committee." In 1974, this committee (Men's Basketball, College Division) was disbanded and separate committees were formed for Division II and Division III basketball.

DIVISION II MEN'S BASKETBALL

1974	Howard Gentry	Tennessee State University
1975	Andrew Laska	Assumption College
1976	Richard F. Scharf	St. Joseph's College (Indiana)
1977-78	Thomas J. Martin	Roanoke College

YEARS	NAME	AFFILIATION
1979	Thomas J. Niland Jr.	Le Moyne College
1980	Floyd A. Walker	Central Missouri State University
1981	Paul Rundell	San Francisco State University

DIVISION III MEN'S BASKETBALL

1974	Wilbur Renken	Albright College
1975-77	Herbert B. Thompson	Fisk University
1978	Paul M. Maaske	Cornell College
1979-80	Russell B. DeVette	Hope College
1981	Willie Shaw	Lane College

DIVISION I WOMEN'S BASKETBALL

1981	Nora Lynn Finch	North Carolina State University

DIVISION II WOMEN'S BASKETBALL

1981	Mary M. Zimmerman	University of South Dakota

DIVISION III WOMEN'S BASKETBALL

1981	Harriett K. Hamilton	Fisk University

MEN'S BASKETBALL RULES

1906-09	R. B. Hyatt	Yale University
1910*	R. B. Hyatt	Yale University
	Joseph E. Raycroft	University of Chicago
1911-20	Joseph E. Raycroft	University of Chicago/Princeton University
1921-37	L. W. St. John	Ohio State University
1938-39	H. H. Salmon Jr.	New York, New York
1940-45	James W. St. Clair	Southern Methodist University
1946	Harold G. Olsen	Ohio State University
1947-50	George R. Edwards	University of Missouri, Columbia
1951-54	Bruce Drake	University of Oklahoma
1955-59	Paul D. Hinkle	Butler University
1960-65	Harold E. Foster	University of Wisconsin, Madison
1966**	Polk Robison	Texas Tech University
	John Wooden	University of California, Los Angeles
1967-74	Norvall Neve	Missouri Valley Conference
1975	Richard E. Wilson	Amherst College
1976-77	John B. Carpenter	Rider College
1978-79	Jack M. Thurnblad	Carleton College
1980-81	C. M. Newton	Southeastern Conference/Vanderbilt University

*No chair designated. **Both served as chair.

BOXING

1919-31	R. Tait McKenzie	University of Pennsylvania
1932-34	Francis C. Grant	Philadelphia, Pennsylvania
1935-37	Hugo Bezdek	Pennsylvania State University
1938-39	W. H. Cowell	University of New Hampshire
1940-48	I. F. Toomey	University of California, Davis
1949-53	William J. Bleckwenn	University of Wisconsin, Madison
1954-56	I. F. Toomey	University of California, Davis
1957-59	Edmund R. LaFond	Catholic University
1960-63	Anthony R. Curreri	University of Wisconsin, Madison

MEN'S FENCING

1935-38	Hugh V. Alessandroni	Columbia University
1939	Malcolm Farmer	Yale University
1940-42	John Huffman	New York University
1943-46	Frank A. Riebel	Ohio State University
1947-59	Alvar Hermanson	University of Chicago
1960-65	Miguel de Capriles	New York University
1966-69	Walter M. Langford	University of Notre Dame
1970-72	Robert Kaplan	Ohio State University
1973-76	Muriel Bower	California State University, Northridge
1977-79	Charles Simonian	Ohio State University
1980-81	Michael A. DeCicco	University of Notre Dame

WOMEN'S FENCING

1981	Muriel Bower	California State University, Northridge

YEARS	NAME	AFFILIATION

FIELD HOCKEY
1981	Mikki Flowers	Old Dominion University

FOOTBALL RULES
1906-15	Henry L. Williams	University of Minnesota, Twin Cities
1916	E. K. Hall	Dartmouth College
1917-18	Henry L. Williams	University of Minnesota, Twin Cities
1919	E. K. Hall	Dartmouth College
1920	Henry L. Williams	University of Minnesota, Twin Cities
1921-32	E. K. Hall	Dartmouth College
1933-43	Walter R. Okeson	Lehigh University
1944-49	Lt. Col. Wm. J. Bingham	Harvard University
1950-58	H. O. Crisler	University of Michigan
1959-61	R. R. Neyland	University of Tennessee, Knoxville
1962	H. O. Crisler	University of Michigan
1963-67	Ivan B. Williamson	University of Wisconsin, Madison
1968-74	John Waldorf	Big Eight Conference
1975-76	Clifton M. Speegle	Southwest Athletic Conference
1977-79	Harold W. Lahar	Southwest Athletic Conference
1980-81	John R. Adams	Western Athletic Conference

FOOTBALL, COLLEGE DIVISION
1965	Don Adee	California State University, Chico
1966	Ross H. Smith	Massachusetts Institute of Technology
1967-69	Cecil N. Coleman	California State University, Fresno
1970-73	Edgar A. Sherman	Muskingum College

DIVISION I-AA FOOTBALL
1978-80	Lyle H. Smith	Boise State University
1981	Milton D. Hunter	South Carolina State College

DIVISION II FOOTBALL
1974-75	Milton E. Weisbecker	Illinois State University
1976-77	Robert A. Latour	Bucknell University
1978-79	Gordon K. Larson	University of Akron
1980-81	Victor A. Buccola	California Polytechnic State University, San Luis Obispo

DIVISION III FOOTBALL
1974	Edgar A. Sherman	Muskingum College
1975	George A. Hansell	Widener University
1976-78	William C. Stiles	Hobart College
1979-80	J. William Grice	Case Western Reserve University
1981	Ronald Schipper	Central College (Iowa)

MEN'S GOLF
1940-43	Charles Evans Jr.	U.S. Golf Association
1943-46	James Hagan	University of Pittsburgh
1947-58	Ted B. Payseur	Northwestern University
1959	Robert H. Kepler	Ohio State University
1960	Charles E. Finger	Stanford University
1961	Charles P. Erickson	University of North Carolina, Chapel Hill
1962	Labron Harris	Oklahoma State University
1963-65	Robert H. Kepler	Ohio State University
1966	Stan Wood	University of Southern California
1967-68	Dick McGuire	University of New Mexico
1969-71	Vic Kelley	University of California, Los Angeles
1972-74	Bruce Fossom	Michigan State University
1975-76	Herb Wimberly	New Mexico State University
1977-80	Roderick W. Myers	Duke University
1981	William D. Johnson	Dartmouth College

WOMEN'S GOLF
1981	JoAnne Lusk	University of Arizona

MEN'S GYMNASTICS
1928-31	Charles W. Graydon	Dartmouth College
1932-36	Christopher Beling, M.D.	Newark, New Jersey
1937-41	D. L. Hoffer	University of Chicago
1942-47	Maximilian Younger	Temple University

YEARS	NAME	AFFILIATION
1948-52	Erwin F. Beyer	University of Chicago
1953-56	Ralph Piper	University of Minnesota, Twin Cities
1957-59	Lyle Welser	Georgia Institute of Technology
1960	Eugene Wettstone	Pennsylvania State University
1961-64	Harold J. Fred	University of California, Berkeley
1965-69	Eugene Wettstone	Pennsylvania State University
1970-74	Edward R. Gagnier	Iowa State University
1975-78	Roger Counsil	Indiana State University, Terre Haute
1979-81	William Roetzheim	University of Illinois, Chicago Circle

WOMEN'S GYMNASTICS

1981	Jackie Walker	Stanford University

MEN'S ICE HOCKEY

1924-25	Alfred Winsor	Harvard University
1926-46	Albert I. Prettyman	Hamilton College
1947-51	Louis F. Keller	University of Minnesota, Twin Cities
1952	J. Howard Starr	Colgate University
1953-57	Herbert W. Gallagher	Northeastern University
1958-59	Amo Bessone	Michigan State University
1960	Herbert W. Gallagher	Northeastern University
1961-63	Murray Murdoch	Yale University
1964-66	R. Victor Stout	Boston University
1967-69	Herbert W. Gallagher	Northeastern University
1970-74	John McComb	Ohio University
1975-79	J. Burt Smith	Michigan State University/ Western Collegiate Hockey Association
1980-81	Charles E. Holt	University of New Hampshire

MEN'S LACROSSE

1922-26	Ronald T. Abercrombie	Johns Hopkins University
1927-29	Roy Taylor	Cornell University
1930-35	L. J. Korns	Swarthmore College
1936	R. D. Root	Yale University
1937-49	Harry J. Rockafeller	Rutgers University, New Brunswick
1950-53	Morris D. Gilmore	U.S. Naval Academy
1954-60	Ferris Thomsen	Princeton University
1961-62	William C. Stiles	Hobart College
1963-65	W. Kelso Morrill	Johns Hopkins University
1966-69	Avery Blake	University of Pennsylvania
1970-73	R. Bruce Allison	Union College (New York)
1974-77	James F. Adams	University of Pennsylvania/University of Virginia
1978-79	Mortimer LaPointe	Bowdoin College
1980-81	E. Richard Watts	University of Maryland, Baltimore County

WOMEN'S LACROSSE

1981	Margaret Faulkner	Towson State University

MEN'S RIFLE

1980-81	Kenneth G. Germann	Southern Conference

MEN'S SKIING

1953-54	Paul W. Wright	Western State College (Colorado)
1955-56	Thomas Jacobs	University of Colorado
1957	Elvin R. Johnson	Whitman College
1958-64	Willy Schaeffler	University of Denver
1965	Bob Beattie	University of Colorado
1966-67	Robert H. Sheehan	Middlebury College
1968-71	Willy Schaeffler	University of Denver
1972-74	John Bower	Middlebury College
1975-77	William C. Marolt	University of Colorado
1978-81	Lloyd F. LaCasse	University of Vermont

MEN'S SOCCER

1912-16	James A. Babbitt	Haverford College
1917*	James A. Babbitt	Haverford College
	George W. Orton	University of Pennsylvania
1918	George W. Orton	University of Pennsylvania
1919-26	James A. Babbitt	Haverford College
1927	A. W. Marsh	Amherst College

YEARS	NAME	AFFILIATION
1928-30	John B. Thayer	University of Pennsylvania
1931	A. W. Marsh	Amherst College
1932-36	H. W. Clark	Harvard University
1937	Burnham Dell	Princeton University
1938-41	Douglas Stewart	University of Pennsylvania
1942-48	Robert H. Dunn	Swarthmore College
1949-52	William Jeffrey	Pennsylvania State University
1953-59	J. J. Reed	Princeton University
1960	John Y. Squires	University of Connecticut
1961-62	Clifford Stevenson	Brown University
1963-64	Hugh G. McCurdy	Wesleyan University
1965-66	Charles R. Scott	University of Pennsylvania
1967-70	Robert Baptista	Wheaton College
1971-74	Julius Menendez	San Jose State University
1975-76	Robert Guelker	Southern Illinois University, Edwardsville
1977-78	Robert Seddon	University of Pennsylvania
1979-81	Jerad L. Yeagley	Indiana University

* No chair designated.

WOMEN'S SOFTBALL

1981	Mary Higgins	Creighton University

MEN'S SWIMMING

1914	R. Tait McKenzie	University of Pennsylvania
1915*	Paul Withington	Harvard University
	F. W. Luehring	Princeton University
1916-36	F. W. Luehring	Princeton University
1937-45	R. J. H. Kiphuth	Yale University
1946-52	Edward T. Kennedy	Columbia University
1953-54	Howard W. Stepp	Princeton University
1955-56	Robert Royer	Indiana University
1957-58	Alfred Barr	Southern Methodist University
1959-61	Philip E. Moriarity	Yale University
1962-63	Gordon Scott Little	Cornell University
1964-65	Karl B. Michael	Dartmouth College
1966-68	G. Robert Mowerson	University of Minnesota, Twin Cities
1969	Jay S. Markley	University of Oklahoma
1970-71	Don Van Rossen	University of Oregon
1972-75	Charles J. Butt	Bowdoin College
1976-81	Robert F. Busbey	Cleveland State University

*No chair designated.

WOMEN'S SWIMMING

1981	Susan J. Petersen	U.S. Merchant Marine Academy

MEN'S TENNIS

1938-41	C. S. Garland	Baltimore, Maryland
1942	T. N. Metcalf	University of Chicago
1943-46	Paul Bennett	Northwestern University
1947-50	William C. Ackerman	University of California, Los Angeles
1951-58	Paul Bennett	Northwestern University
1959-60	Harvey J. Schmidt	Iowa State University
1961-64	J. D. Morgan	University of California, Los Angeles
1965	William E. Murphy	University of Michigan
1966	Robert Renker	Stanford University
1967	David Snyder	University of Arizona
1968-72	Dale A. Lewis	University of Miami (Florida)
1973	Clarence Mabry	Trinity University (Texas)
1974-75	Rolla L. Anderson	Kalamazoo College
1976-78	Dan Magill	University of Georgia
1979-81	David A. Benjamin	Princeton University

WOMEN'S TENNIS

1981	Carol J. Arrowsmith	University of Maryland, Baltimore County

MEN'S TRACK AND FIELD

1907-09	W. A. Lambeth	University of Virginia
1910*	Fred W. Marvel	Brown University

YEARS	NAME	AFFILIATION
	Amos Alonzo Stagg	University of Chicago
1911*	W. A. Lambeth	University of Virginia
	Fred W. Marvel	Brown University
	Amos Alonzo Stagg	University of Chicago
1912-14	Fred W. Marvel	Brown University
1915-20	Frank Castleman	Ohio State University
1921-29	John L. Griffith	Big Ten Conference
1930-36	T. N. Metcalf	Iowa State University
1937-45	Kenneth L. Wilson	Northwestern University
1946-49	Wilbur Hutsell	Auburn University
1950-58	Brutus Hamilton	University of California, Berkeley
1959	Frederic D. Tootell	University of Rhode Island
1960	Leo T. Johnson	University of Illinois, Champaign
1961-63	William J. Bowerman	University of Oregon
1964-66	Weems O. Baskin Jr.	University of South Carolina
1967	Hugh Hackett	University of New Mexico
1968-70	Bill McClure	Abilene Christian University
1971-76	DeLoss Dodds	Kansas State University
1977-79	John Randolph	U.S. Military Academy/University of Florida
1980	Cleburne Price Jr.	University of Texas, Austin
1981	Albert Buehler	Duke University

*No chair designated.

WOMEN'S TRACK AND FIELD

1981	Mary Alice Hill	San Diego State University

MEN'S VOLLEYBALL

1918-27	George L. Meylan	Columbia University
1928-32	J. H. McCurdy	Springfield College
1933-69	No committee	
1970	Edward S. Steitz	Springfield College
1971-73	Allen Scates	University of California, Los Angeles
1974	Donald S. Shondell	Ball State University
1975-77	Walter G. Versen	University of Illinois, Chicago Circle
1978	Albert E. Negratti	University of California, Santa Barbara
1979-80	Donald S. Shondell	Ball State University
1981	Richard H. Perry	University of Southern California

DIVISION I WOMEN'S VOLLEYBALL

1981	Libba Birmingham	Mississippi State University

DIVISION II WOMEN'S VOLLEYBALL

1981	Susan Gibbons	Le Moyne College

DIVISION III WOMEN'S VOLLEYBALL

1981	Carol Pipkorn	MacMurray College

WATER POLO

1970-74	James W. Schultz	California State University, Long Beach
1975-76	John Williams	University of Southern California
1977-79	Ken Lindgren	California State University, Long Beach
1980-81	Jerry W. Hinsdale	University of California, Davis

MEN'S WRESTLING

1919-20	Dana M. Evans	Indiana University
1921-23	Charles W. Mayser	Iowa State University
1924-27	H. R. Reiter	Lehigh University
1928-45	R. G. Clapp	University of Nebraska, Lincoln
1946-51	B. R. Patterson	Kansas State University/ University of Nebraska, Lincoln
1952	E. F. Caraway	Lehigh University
1953-55	Henry A. Stone	University of California, Berkeley
1956	Arthur Griffith	Oklahoma State University
1957-58	Raymond Sparks	Springfield College
1959	Charles W. Parker	Davidson College
1960	Fritz G. Knorr	Kansas State University
1961	Richard L. Voliva	Rutgers University, New Brunswick
1962	John W. Hancock	Colorado State University
1963-64	Harold J. Nichols	Iowa State University

YEAR	NAME	AFFILIATION
1965-67	Wallace J. Johnson	University of Minnesota, Twin Cities
1968-70	Marvin Hess	University of Utah
1971-76	LeRoy A. Alitz	U.S. Military Academy
1977	Charles A. Patten	University of Northern Iowa
1978-81	John K. Johnston	Princeton University

APPENDIX H

ALL-TIME NCAA
TEAM CHAMPIONS

Following is a listing of all teams that have ever reached the ultimate of NCAA competition — a National Collegiate Championship.

BASEBALL

DIVISION I

Year	Champion	Year	Champion	Year	Champion
1947	California	1959	Oklahoma State	1971	Southern Cal
1948	Southern Cal	1960	Minnesota	1972	Southern Cal
1949	Texas	1961	Southern Cal	1973	Southern Cal
1950	Texas	1962	Michigan	1974	Southern Cal
1951	Oklahoma	1963	Southern Cal	1975	Texas
1952	Holy Cross	1964	Minnesota	1976	Arizona
1953	Michigan	1965	Arizona State	1977	Arizona State
1954	Missouri	1966	Ohio State	1978	Southern Cal
1955	Wake Forest	1967	Arizona State	1979	Fullerton State
1956	Minnesota	1968	Southern Cal	1980	Arizona
1957	California	1969	Arizona State	1981	Arizona State
1958	Southern Cal	1970	Southern Cal		

DIVISION II

Year	Champion	Year	Champion	Year	Champion
1968	Chapman	1973	Cal-Irvine	1978	Florida Southern
1969	Illinois State	1974	Cal-Irvine	1979	Valdosta State
1970	Northridge State	1975	Florida Southern	1980	Cal Poly-Pomona
1971	Florida Southern	1976	Cal Poly-Pomona	1981	Florida Southern
1972	Florida Southern	1977	Cal-Riverside		

DIVISION III

Year	Champion	Year	Champion	Year	Champion
1976	Stanislaus State	1978	Glassboro State	1980	Ithaca
1977	Stanislaus State	1979	Glassboro State	1981	Marietta

BASKETBALL

DIVISION I

Year	Champion	Year	Champion	Year	Champion
1939	Oregon	1950	CCNY	1961	Cincinnati
1940	Indiana	1951	Kentucky	1962	Cincinnati
1941	Wisconsin	1952	Kansas	1963	Loyola (Ill.)
1942	Stanford	1953	Indiana	1964	UCLA
1943	Wyoming	1954	La Salle	1965	UCLA
1944	Utah	1955	San Francisco	1966	Texas-El Paso
1945	Oklahoma State	1956	San Francisco	1967	UCLA
1946	Oklahoma State	1957	North Carolina	1968	UCLA
1947	Holy Cross	1958	Kentucky	1969	UCLA
1948	Kentucky	1959	California	1970	UCLA
1949	Kentucky	1960	Ohio State	1971	UCLA

Year	Champion	Year	Champion	Year	Champion
1972	UCLA	1976	Indiana	1980	Louisville
1973	UCLA	1977	Marquette	1981	Indiana
1974	N. C. State	1978	Kentucky		
1975	UCLA	1979	Michigan State		

DIVISION II

Year	Champion	Year	Champion	Year	Champion
1957	Wheaton	1966	Ky. Wesleyan	1975	Old Dominion
1958	South Dakota	1967	Winston-Salem	1976	Puget Sound
1959	Evansville	1968	Ky. Wesleyan	1977	Tenn.-Chatt.
1960	Evansville	1969	Ky. Wesleyan	1978	Cheyney State
1961	Wittenberg	1970	Phila. Textile	1979	North Alabama
1962	Mt. St. Mary's	1971	Evansville	1980	Virginia Union
1963	South Dakota St.	1972	Roanoke	1981	Florida Southern
1964	Evansville	1973	Ky. Wesleyan		
1965	Evansville	1974	Morgan State		

DIVISION III

Year	Champion	Year	Champion	Year	Champion
1975	LeMoyne-Owen	1978	North Park	1981	Potsdam State
1976	Scranton	1979	North Park		
1977	Wittenberg	1980	North Park		

CROSS COUNTRY

DIVISION I

Year	Champion	Year	Champion	Year	Champion
1938	Indiana	1952	Michigan State	1967	Villanova
1939	Michigan State	1953	Kansas	1968	Villanova
1940	Indiana	1954	Oklahoma State	1969	Texas-El Paso
1941	Rhode Island	1955	Michigan State	1970	Villanova
1942	Indiana & Penn State (tie)	1956	Michigan State	1971	Oregon
		1957	Notre Dame	1972	Tennessee
1943	No meet held	1958	Michigan State	1973	Oregon
1944	Drake	1959	Michigan State	1974	Oregon
1945	Drake	1960	Houston	1975	Texas-El Paso
1946	Drake	1961	Oregon State	1976	Texas-El Paso
1947	Penn State	1962	San Jose State	1977	Oregon
1948	Michigan State	1963	San Jose State	1978	Texas-El Paso
1949	Michigan State	1964	Western Mich.	1979	Texas-El Paso
1950	Penn State	1965	Western Mich.	1980	Texas-El Paso
1951	Syracuse	1966	Villanova		

DIVISION II

Year	Champion	Year	Champion	Year	Champion
1958	Northern Ill.	1966	San Diego State	1974	SW Missouri St.
1959	South Dakota St.	1967	San Diego State	1975	Cal-Irvine
1960	Central Ohio	1968	Eastern Illinois	1976	Cal-Irvine
1961	Southern Ill.	1969	Eastern Illinois	1977	Eastern Illinois
1962	Central Ohio	1970	Eastern Mich.	1978	Cal Poly-SLO
1963	Emporia State	1971	Fullerton State	1979	Cal Poly-SLO
1964	Kentucky State	1972	North Dakota St.	1980	Humboldt State
1965	San Diego State	1973	South Dakota St.		

DIVISION III

Year	Champion	Year	Champion	Year	Champion
1973	Ashland	1976	North Central	1979	North Central
1974	Mount Union	1977	Occidental	1980	Carleton
1975	North Central	1978	North Central		

FENCING

Year	Champion	Year	Champion	Year	Champion
1941	Northwestern	1944	No meet held	1947	New York U.
1942	Ohio State	1945	No meet held	1948	CCNY
1943	No meet held	1946	No meet held	1949	Army & Rutgers (tie)

Year	Champion	Year	Champion	Year	Champion
1950	Navy	1961	New York U.	1972	Detroit
1951	Columbia	1962	Navy	1973	New York U.
1952	Columbia	1963	Columbia	1974	New York U.
1953	Pennsylvania	1964	Princeton	1975	Wayne St. (Mich.)
1954	Columbia & New York U. (tie)	1965	Columbia	1976	New York U.
		1966	New York U.	1977	Notre Dame
1955	Columbia	1967	New York U.	1978	Notre Dame
1956	Illinois	1968	Columbia	1979	Wayne St. (Mich.)
1957	New York U.	1969	Pennsylvania	1980	Wayne St. (Mich.)
1958	Illinois	1970	New York U.	1981	Pennsylvania
1959	Navy	1971	New York U. &		
1960	New York U.		Columbia (tie)		

FOOTBALL

DIVISION I-AA

Year	Champion	Year	Champion	Year	Champion
1978	Florida A&M	1979	Eastern Ky.	1980	Boise State

DIVISION II

Year	Champion	Year	Champion	Year	Champion
1973	Louisiana Tech	1976	Montana State	1979	Delaware
1974	Central Mich.	1977	Lehigh	1980	Cal Poly-SLO
1975	Northern Mich.	1978	Eastern Illinois		

DIVISION III

Year	Champion	Year	Champion	Year	Champion
1973	Wittenberg	1976	St. John's (Minn.)	1979	Ithaca
1974	Central (Iowa)	1977	Widener	1980	Dayton
1975	Wittenberg	1978	Baldwin-Wallace		

GOLF

(1897-1938 Results)

Year	Champion	Year	Champion	Year	Champion
1897	Yale	1910	Yale	1925	Yale
1898	Harvard (spring)	1911	Yale	1926	Yale
	Yale (fall)	1912	Yale	1927	Princeton
1899	Harvard	1913	Yale	1928	Princeton
1900	No meet held	1914	Princeton	1929	Princeton
1901	Harvard	1915	Yale	1930	Princeton
1902	Yale (spring)	1916	Princeton	1931	Yale
	Harvard (fall)	1917	No meet held	1932	Yale
1903	Harvard	1918	No meet held	1933	Yale
1904	Harvard	1919	Princeton	1934	Michigan
1905	Yale	1920	Princeton	1935	Michigan
1906	Yale	1921	Dartmouth	1936	Yale
1907	Yale	1922	Princeton	1937	Princeton
1908	Yale	1923	Princeton	1938	Stanford
1909	Yale	1924	Yale		

DIVISION I

(1939-1981 Results)

Year	Champion	Year	Champion	Year	Champion
1939	Stanford	1947	Louisiana State	1958	Houston
1940	Princeton &	1948	San Jose State	1959	Houston
	Louisiana State	1949	North Texas St.	1960	Houston
	(tie)	1950	North Texas St.	1961	Purdue
1941	Stanford	1951	North Texas St.	1962	Houston
1942	Louisiana State	1952	North Texas St.	1963	Oklahoma State
	& Stanford (tie)	1953	Stanford	1964	Houston
1943	Yale	1954	Southern Meth.	1965	Houston
1944	Notre Dame	1955	Louisiana State	1966	Houston
1945	Ohio State	1956	Houston	1967	Houston
1946	Stanford	1957	Houston	1968	Florida

Year	Champion	Year	Champion	Year	Champion
1969	Houston	1974	Wake Forest	1979	Ohio State
1970	Houston	1975	Wake Forest	1980	Oklahoma State
1971	Texas	1976	Oklahoma State	1981	Brigham Young
1972	Texas	1977	Houston		
1973	Florida	1978	Oklahoma State		

DIVISION II

Year	Champion	Year	Champion	Year	Champion
1963	SW Missouri St.	1970	Rollins	1977	Troy State
1964	Southern Ill.	1971	New Orleans	1978	Columbus
1965	Middle Tenn.	1972	New Orleans	1979	Cal-Davis
1966	Chico State	1973	Northridge State	1980	Columbus
1967	Lamar	1974	Northridge State	1981	Florida Southern
1968	Lamar	1975	Cal-Irvine		
1969	Northridge State	1976	Troy State		

DIVISION III

Year	Champion	Year	Champion	Year	Champion
1975	Wooster	1978	Stanislaus State	1981	Stanislaus State
1976	Stanislaus State	1979	Stanislaus State		
1977	Stanislaus State	1980	Stanislaus State		

GYMNASTICS

DIVISION I

Year	Champion	Year	Champion	Year	Champion
1938	Chicago	1955	Illinois	1970	Michigan
1939	Illinois	1956	Illinois		Michigan (trampoline)
1940	Illinois	1957	Penn State	1971	Iowa State
1941	Illinois	1958	Michigan State &	1972	Southern Ill.
1942	Illinois		Illinois (tie)	1973	Iowa State
1943	No meet held	1959	Penn State	1974	Iowa State
1944	No meet held	1960	Penn State	1975	California
1945	No meet held	1961	Penn State	1976	Penn State
1946	No meet held	1962	Southern Cal	1977	Indiana State &
1947	No meet held	1963	Michigan		Oklahoma (tie)
1948	Penn State	1964	Southern Ill.	1978	Oklahoma
1949	Temple	1965	Penn State	1979	Nebraska
1950	Illinois	1966	Southern Ill.	1980	Nebraska
1951	Florida State	1967	Southern Ill.	1981	Nebraska
1952	Florida State	1968	California		
1953	Penn State	1969	Iowa		
1954	Penn State		Michigan (trampoline)		

DIVISION II

Year	Champion	Year	Champion	Year	Champion
1968	Northridge State	1973	Southern Conn.	1978	Ill.-Chi. Circle
1969	Northridge State	1974	Fullerton State	1979	Ill.-Chi. Circle
1970	NW Louisiana	1975	Southern Conn.	1980	Wis.-Oshkosh
1971	Fullerton State	1976	Southern Conn.	1981	Wis.-Oshkosh
1972	Fullerton State	1977	Springfield		

ICE HOCKEY

DIVISION I

Year	Champion	Year	Champion	Year	Champion
1948	Michigan	1957	Colorado Col.	1966	Michigan State
1949	Boston College	1958	Denver	1967	Cornell
1950	Colorado Col.	1959	North Dakota	1968	Denver
1951	Michigan	1960	Denver	1969	Denver
1952	Michigan	1961	Denver	1970	Cornell
1953	Michigan	1962	Michigan Tech	1971	Boston U.
1954	Rensselaer	1963	North Dakota	1972	Boston U.
1955	Michigan	1964	Michigan	1973	Wisconsin
1956	Michigan	1965	Michigan Tech	1974	Minnesota

Year	Champion	Year	Champion	Year	Champion
1975	Michigan Tech	1978	Boston U.	1981	Wisconsin
1976	Minnesota	1979	Minnesota		
1977	Wisconsin	1980	North Dakota		

DIVISION II

Year	Champion	Year	Champion	Year	Champion
1978	Merrimack	1980	Mankato State	1981	Lowell
1979	Lowell				

LACROSSE

DIVISION I

Year	Champion	Year	Champion	Year	Champion
1971	Cornell	1975	Maryland	1979	Johns Hopkins
1972	Virginia	1976	Cornell	1980	Johns Hopkins
1973	Maryland	1977	Cornell	1981	North Carolina
1974	Johns Hopkins	1978	Johns Hopkins		

DIVISION II

Year	Champion	Year	Champion	Year	Champion
1974	Towson State	1977	Hobart	1980	Md.-Balt. County
1975	Cortland State	1978	Roanoke	1981	Adelphi
1976	Hobart	1979	Adelphi		

DIVISION III

Year	Champion	Year	Champion
1980	Hobart	1981	Hobart

RIFLE

Year	Champion	Year	Champion
1980	Tennessee Tech	1981	Tennessee Tech

SKIING

Year	Champion	Year	Champion	Year	Champion
1954	Denver	1964	Denver	1974	Colorado
1955	Denver	1965	Denver	1975	Colorado
1956	Denver	1966	Denver	1976	Colorado &
1957	Denver	1967	Denver		Dartmouth (tie)
1958	Dartmouth	1968	Wyoming	1977	Colorado
1959	Colorado	1969	Denver	1978	Colorado
1960	Colorado	1970	Denver	1979	Colorado
1961	Denver	1971	Denver	1980	Vermont
1962	Denver	1972	Colorado	1981	Utah
1963	Denver	1973	Colorado		

SOCCER

DIVISION I

Year	Champion	Year	Champion	Year	Champion
1959	St. Louis	1967	Michigan State &	1973	St. Louis
1960	St. Louis		St. Louis*	1974	Howard
1961	West Chester St.	1968	Maryland &	1975	San Francisco
1962	St. Louis		Michigan State**	1976	San Francisco
1963	St. Louis	1969	St. Louis	1977	Hartwick
1964	Navy	1970	St. Louis	1978	San Francisco***
1965	St. Louis	1971	Howard***	1979	SIU-Edwardsville
1966	San Francisco	1972	St. Louis	1980	San Francisco

*Game called due to inclement weather.
**Two overtimes, 2-2 tie.
***Championship subsequently vacated as a result of participation of an ineligible student-athlete in the event.

DIVISION II

Year	Champion	Year	Champion	Year	Champion
1972	SIU-Edwardsville	1975	Baltimore	1978	Seattle Pacific
1973	Mo.-St. Louis	1976	Loyola (Md.)	1979	Alabama A&M
1974	Adelphi	1977	Alabama A&M	1980	Lock Haven State

DIVISION III

Year	Champion	Year	Champion	Year	Champion
1974	Brockport State	1977	Lock Haven State	1980	Babson
1975	Babson	1978	Lock Haven State		
1976	Brandeis	1979	Babson		

SWIMMING

DIVISION I

Year	Champion	Year	Champion	Year	Champion
1937	Michigan	1952	Ohio State	1967	Stanford
1938	Michigan	1953	Yale	1968	Indiana
1939	Michigan	1954	Ohio State	1969	Indiana
1940	Michigan	1955	Ohio State	1970	Indiana
1941	Michigan	1956	Ohio State	1971	Indiana
1942	Yale	1957	Michigan	1972	Indiana
1943	Ohio State	1958	Michigan	1973	Indiana
1944	Yale	1959	Michigan	1974	Southern Cal
1945	Ohio State	1960	Southern Cal	1975	Southern Cal
1946	Ohio State	1961	Michigan	1976	Southern Cal
1947	Ohio State	1962	Ohio State	1977	Southern Cal
1948	Michigan	1963	Southern Cal	1978	Tennessee
1949	Ohio State	1964	Southern Cal	1979	California
1950	Ohio State	1965	Southern Cal	1980	California
1951	Yale	1966	Southern Cal	1981	Texas

DIVISION II

Year	Champion	Year	Champion	Year	Champion
1964	Bucknell	1970	Cal-Irvine	1976	Chico State
1965	San Diego State	1971	Cal-Irvine	1977	Northridge State
1966	San Diego State	1972	Eastern Mich.	1978	Northridge State
1967	Cal-Santa Barb.	1973	Chico State	1979	Northridge State
1968	Long Beach State	1974	Chico State	1980	Oakland
1969	Cal-Irvine	1975	Northridge State	1981	Northridge State

DIVISION III

Year	Champion	Year	Champion	Year	Champion
1975	Chico State	1978	Johns Hopkins	1981	Kenyon
1976	St. Lawrence	1979	Johns Hopkins		
1977	Johns Hopkins	1980	Kenyon		

TENNIS

DIVISION I

Year	Champion	Year	Champion	Year	Champion
1946	Southern Cal	1959	Notre Dame &	1971	UCLA
1947	William & Mary		Tulane (tie)	1972	Trinity (Tex.)
1948	William & Mary	1960	UCLA	1973	Stanford
1949	San Francisco	1961	UCLA	1974	Stanford
1950	UCLA	1962	Southern Cal	1975	UCLA
1951	Southern Cal	1963	Southern Cal	1976	Southern Cal &
1952	UCLA	1964	Southern Cal		UCLA (tie)
1953	UCLA	1965	UCLA	1977	Stanford
1954	UCLA	1966	Southern Cal	1978	Stanford
1955	Southern Cal	1967	Southern Cal	1979	UCLA
1956	UCLA	1968	Southern Cal	1980	Stanford
1957	Michigan	1969	Southern Cal	1981	Stanford
1958	Southern Cal	1970	UCLA		

DIVISION II

Year	Champion	Year	Champion	Year	Champion
1963	Los Angeles St.	1970	Cal-Irvine	1976	Hampton Inst.
1964	Los Angeles St. &	1971	Cal-Irvine	1977	Cal-Irvine
	Southern Ill. (tie)	1972	Cal-Irvine &	1978	SIU-Edwardsville
1965	Los Angeles St.		Rollins (tie)	1979	SIU-Edwardsville
1966	Rollins	1973	Cal-Irvine	1980	SIU-Edwardsville
1967	Long Beach St.	1974	San Diego	1981	SIU-Edwardsville
1968	Fresno State	1975	Cal-Irvine & San		
1969	Northridge State		Diego (tie)		

DIVISION III

Year	Champion	Year	Champion	Year	Champion
1976	Kalamazoo	1979	Redlands	1981	Swarthmore &
1977	Swarthmore	1980	Gust. Adolphus		Claremont-Mudd-
1978	Kalamazoo				Scripps (tie)

INDOOR TRACK

Year	Champion	Year	Champion	Year	Champion
1965	Missouri	1971	Villanova	1977	Washington St.
1966	Kansas	1972	Southern Cal	1978	Texas-El Paso
1967	Southern Cal	1973	Manhattan	1979	Villanova
1968	Villanova	1974	Texas-El Paso	1980	Texas-El Paso
1969	Kansas	1975	Texas-El Paso	1981	Texas-El Paso
1970	Kansas	1976	Texas-El Paso		

OUTDOOR TRACK

DIVISION I

Year	Champion	Year	Champion	Year	Champion
1921	Illinois	1943	Southern Cal	1965	Oregon &
1922	California	1944	Illinois		Southern Cal (tie)
1923	Michigan	1945	Navy	1966	UCLA
1924	No meet held	1946	Illinois	1967	Southern Cal
1925	Stanford*	1947	Illinois	1968	Southern Cal
1926	Southern Cal*	1948	Minnesota	1969	San Jose State
1927	Illinois*	1949	Southern Cal	1970	Brigham Young,
1928	Stanford	1950	Southern Cal		Kansas & Oregon
1929	Ohio State	1951	Southern Cal		(tie)
1930	Southern Cal	1952	Southern Cal	1971	UCLA
1931	Southern Cal	1953	Southern Cal	1972	UCLA
1932	Indiana	1954	Southern Cal	1973	UCLA
1933	Louisiana State	1955	Southern Cal	1974	Tennessee
1934	Stanford	1956	UCLA	1975	Texas-El Paso
1935	Southern Cal	1957	Villanova	1976	Southern Cal
1936	Southern Cal	1958	Southern Cal	1977	Arizona State
1937	Southern Cal	1959	Kansas	1978	Southern Cal**
1938	Southern Cal	1960	Kansas	1979	Texas-El Paso
1939	Southern Cal	1961	Southern Cal	1980	Texas-El Paso
1940	Southern Cal	1962	Oregon	1981	Texas-El Paso
1941	Southern Cal	1963	Southern Cal		
1942	Southern Cal	1964	Oregon		

*Unofficial championship.
**Championship subsequently vacated as a result of participation of an ineligible student-athlete in the event.

DIVISION II

Year	Champion	Year	Champion	Year	Champion
1963	Md.-East. Shore	1970	Cal Poly-SLO	1975	Northridge State
1964	Fresno State	1971	Kentucky State	1976	Cal-Irvine
1965	San Diego State	1972	Eastern Mich.	1977	Hayward State
1966	San Diego State	1973	Norfolk State	1978	Los Angeles St.
1967	Long Beach St.	1974	Eastern Illinois &	1979	Cal Poly-SLO
1968	Cal Poly-SLO		Norfolk State	1980	Cal Poly-SLO
1969	Cal Poly-SLO		(tie)	1981	Cal Poly-SLO

DIVISION III

Year	Champion	Year	Champion	Year	Champion
1974	Ashland	1977	Southern-N.O.	1980	Glassboro State
1975	Southern-N.O.	1978	Occidental	1981	Glassboro State
1976	Southern-N.O.	1979	Slippery Rock		

VOLLEYBALL

Year	Champion	Year	Champion	Year	Champion
1970	UCLA	1974	UCLA	1978	Pepperdine
1971	UCLA	1975	UCLA	1979	UCLA
1972	UCLA	1976	UCLA	1980	Southern Cal
1973	San Diego State	1977	Southern Cal	1981	UCLA

WATER POLO

Year	Champion	Year	Champion	Year	Champion
1969	UCLA	1973	California	1977	California
1970	Cal-Irvine	1974	California	1978	Stanford
1971	UCLA	1975	California	1979	Cal-Santa Barb.
1972	UCLA	1976	Stanford	1980	Stanford

WRESTLING

DIVISION I

Year	Champion	Year	Champion	Year	Champion
1928	Oklahoma State*	1946	Oklahoma State	1965	Iowa State
1929	Oklahoma State	1947	Cornell College	1966	Oklahoma State
1930	Oklahoma State	1948	Oklahoma State	1967	Michigan State
1931	Oklahoma State*	1949	Oklahoma State	1968	Oklahoma State
1932	Indiana*	1950	Northern Iowa	1969	Iowa State
1933	Oklahoma State	1951	Oklahoma	1970	Iowa State
	& Iowa State*	1952	Oklahoma	1971	Oklahoma State
1934	Oklahoma State	1953	Penn State	1972	Iowa State
1935	Oklahoma State	1954	Oklahoma State	1973	Iowa State
1936	Oklahoma	1955	Oklahoma State	1974	Oklahoma
1937	Oklahoma State	1956	Oklahoma State	1975	Iowa
1938	Oklahoma State	1957	Oklahoma	1976	Iowa
1939	Oklahoma State	1958	Oklahoma State	1977	Iowa State
1940	Oklahoma State	1959	Oklahoma State	1978	Iowa
1941	Oklahoma State	1960	Oklahoma	1979	Iowa
1942	Oklahoma State	1961	Oklahoma State	1980	Iowa
1943	No meet held	1962	Oklahoma State	1981	Iowa
1944	No meet held	1963	Oklahoma		
1945	No meet held	1964	Oklahoma State		

*Unofficial champions.

DIVISION II

Year	Champion	Year	Champion	Year	Champion
1963	Western St. (Colo.)	1970	Cal Poly-SLO	1977	Bakersfield St.
1964	Western St. (Colo.)	1971	Cal Poly-SLO	1978	Northern Iowa
1965	Mankato State	1972	Cal Poly-SLO	1979	Bakersfield St.
1966	Cal Poly-SLO	1973	Cal Poly-SLO	1980	Bakersfield St.
1967	Portland State	1974	Cal Poly-SLO	1981	Bakersfield St.
1968	Cal Poly-SLO	1975	Northern Iowa		
1969	Cal Poly-SLO	1976	Bakersfield St.		

DIVISION III

Year	Champion	Year	Champion	Year	Champion
1974	Wilkes	1977	Brockport State	1980	Brockport State
1975	John Carroll	1978	Buffalo	1981	Trenton State
1976	Montclair State	1979	Trenton State		

APPENDIX I

THEODORE ROOSEVELT AWARD HONOREES

The "Teddy" Award is the highest honor the National Collegiate Athletic Association may confer on an individual. It is presented annually to a distinguished citizen of national reputation and outstanding accomplishment who, having earned a varsity athletic award in college, has by his continuing interest and concern for physical fitness and competitive sport and by the example of his own life exemplified most clearly and forcefully the ideals and purposes to which college athletic programs and amateur sports competition are dedicated.

1967 **Dwight D. Eisenhower**
General of the Army,
President of the United States
U.S. Military Academy, 1915

1968 **Leverett Saltonstall**
U.S. Senator,
Governor of Massachusetts
Harvard University, 1914

1969 **Byron R. White**
Justice, U.S. Supreme Court
University of Colorado, 1938

1970 **Frederick L. Hovde**
President, Purdue University
University of Minnesota,
Twin Cities, 1929

1971 **Christopher C. Kraft Jr.**
National Aeronautics and
Space Administration
Virginia Polytechnic Institute, 1944

1972 **Jerome H. Holland**
U.S. Ambassador to Sweden
Cornell University, 1939

1973 **Omar N. Bradley**
General of the Army
U.S. Military Academy, 1915

1974 **Jesse Owens**
Jesse Owens, Inc.,
Public Relations
Ohio State University, 1937

1975 **Gerald R. Ford**
President of the United States
University of Michigan, 1935

1976 **Thomas J. Hamilton**
Rear Admiral, U.S. Navy
U.S. Naval Academy, 1927

1977 **Tom Bradley**
Mayor of Los Angeles
University of California,
Los Angeles, 1941

1978 **Gerald B. Zornow**
Eastman Kodak Company
University of Rochester, 1937

1979 **Otis Chandler**
Publisher, Los Angeles Times
Stanford University, 1950

1980 **Denton A. Cooley**
Heart Surgeon
Texas Heart Institute
University of Texas, Austin, 1941

1981 **Arthur G. Linkletter**
Entertainer and Author
San Diego State University, 1934

APPENDIX J

NCAA ADMINISTRATIVE STAFF — ALL-TIME LISTING

Following is a listing of all those individuals who have served in an administrative position for the NCAA. Many individuals have held several administrative positions with the Association; the position listed is the last position held.

NAME	POSITION	YEARS
Alejos, Maxine R.	Circulation Manager (Publishing)	1972-
Barning, Frank	Compilations (Statistics)	1972-73
Bergstrom, Arthur J.	Controller	1956-76
Berkey, Ruth M.	Director of Women's Championships	1980-
Berst, S. David	Director of Enforcement	1972-
Boda, Steve	Associate Director of Statistics	1968-
Bork, Patricia E.	Assistant Director of Championships	1978-
Bortstein, Larry	Associate Editor	1964-66
Bowyer, Michael F.	Administrative Assistant (Statistics)	1978-
Boyer, Jennifer A.	Production Coordinator	1979-
Brown, Warren S.	Assistant Executive Director (Enforcement)	1966-77
Bump, Janice I.	Administrative Assistant (Enforcement)	1970-
Burks, Lester J.	Executive Assistant	1972-73
Bushnell, Asa S.	Consultant (Television Committee)	1954-73
Byers, Walter	Executive Director	1947-
Cawood, David E.	Director of Public Relations	1974-
Chesley, Castleman D.	Liaison Officer (Television Committee)	1955-57
Clark, Jack N.	Director of Productions and Marketing	1974-76
Clark, Joe Brent	Enforcement Representative	1975-77
Clark, Jonathan	Assistant Director of Publishing	1970-76
Cleary, Michael J.	Events Director	1964-66
Combs, Thomas C.	Events Manager	1971-74
Cooke, Homer F. Jr.	Director of Publishing	1959-74
Cryder, C. Dennis	Director of Productions	1977-
Daniel, Dave R.	NCAA News Editor	1972-75
Delany, James E.	Enforcement Representative	1975-79
Didion, David A.	Enforcement Representative	1978-
Dodd, Melvin D.	Enforcement Representative	1977-81
Doherty, Walter G.	General Editor	1959-60
Duffy, Eugene R.	Director of Events	1966-72
Duke, R. Wayne	Assistant to Executive Director	1952-63
Dunlop, Douglas W.	Enforcement Representative	1974-76
Eaton, Paul	Compilations-Research (Statistics)	1969-70
Erles, Christian W.	Compilations (Statistics)	1959-76
Farrell, James T.	Compilations (Statistics)	1961
Fieber, Marjorie K.	Business Manager	1952-
Flanagan, Sheila M.	Publications Editor	1974-77
Foley, Jon A.	Promotion Director	1968-70
Gabrielli, Albert P.	General Editor	1962-64
Giannini, Richard	Director of Productions/Film Service	1976-77
Gilleran, Michael M.	Enforcement Representative	1976-
Glazier, Michael S.	Enforcement Representative	1979-
Gleason, Timothy W.	Administrative Assistant (Statistics)	1980-
Gutierrez, Abe R.	Associate Editor	1967-70
Guss, Steven J.	General Editor	1971-72
Hallock, Wiles	Director of Public Relations	1963-67

NAME	POSITION	YEARS
Hansen, Thomas C.	Assistant Executive Director (Communications)	1967-
Hill, Thomas L. "Danny"	Associate Director (Publishing)	1959-63
Holmes, James D.	Associate Editor	1960-62
Howlett, Grayle W.	Director of Marketing	1970-75
Howard, Bruce L.	Publications Editor	1979-
Hunt, William B.	Assistant Executive Director (Enforcement)	1972-
Hunter, Richard D.	Assistant Director of Championships	1978-
Hutchings, Linda N.	Administrative Assistant (Gen. Adm.)	1971-79
Jacobs, C. Eugene	Assistant Director of Publishing	1973-77
Jensen, Nels N.	NCAA News Editor	1972
Jernstedt, Thomas W.	Assistant Executive Director (Championships)	1972-
Kelley, Victor M.	Liaison Officer (Television Committee)	1962-63
Klein, Gerald R.	Compilations (Statistics)	1970-75
Klein, Lawrence M.	Director of Service Bureau (Statistics)	1964-72
Lee, Gary M.	NCAA News Editor	1977
Link, Richard J.	Compilations (Statistics)	1967-68
MacIntyre, Richard	Administrative Assistant (Publishing)	1962-66
Mauldin, Gregory L.	Administrative Assistant (Statistics)	1975-78
McFillen, Ralph W.	Assistant Director of Championships	1972-
McMenamin, J. Hale	Assistant Director of Enforcement	1975-
Mead, Douglas	Publications Editor	1978
Meggas, Dale M.	Research Assistant	1977-81
Mesh, Michael C.	Enforcement Representative	1977-79
Miles, Jerry A.	Director of Men's Championships	1971-
Minnix, Robert J.	Enforcement Representative	1975-
Montana, Marie	Assistant Director of Publishing	1959-74
Morgan, Stephen R.	Executive Assistant (Enforcement)	1977-
Nance, Lynn	Enforcement Representative	1973-74
Neinas, Charles M.	Assistant to Executive Director	1961-71
Olnick, Jerome	Associate Editor	1965-66
Onofrio, Louis A.	Enforcement Representative	1979-
Paul, Geraldine	Circulation Manager (Publishing)	1966-73
Pickle, David	Assistant Director of Publishing	1977-
Pierce, Edward E.	Associate Editor	1961-62
Poppe, Dennis L.	Assistant Director of Championships	1974-
Price, G. David	Publications Editor	1964-66
Renfro, Wallace I.	Director of Publishing	1972-
Rogers, Roberta A.	Administrative Assistant (Communications)	1977-
Schlanaer, Herbert J.	Associate Editor	1967
Schmad, Timothy D.	Publications Editor	1979-
Schwartz, Ronald	Director of Television News Service	1968-
Seifert, David P.	Executive Assistant (General Administration)	1977-
Seifert, S. Lavonne	Assistant Director of Publishing	1977-
Shaffer, James W.	Assistant Director of Productions	1976-
Shaw, Karen	Administrative Assistant (Statistics)	1976-79
Shawver, Thomas W.	Enforcement Representative	1976
Sheldon, James A.	Publications Editor	1981-
Sirianni, Stephen J.	Associate Editor	1964-68
Skinner, Bruce E.	NCAA News Editor	1970-71
Smith, Cynthia L.	Assistant Director of Championships	1981-
Smith, R. Dale	Enforcement Representative	1979-
Soldenwagner, John G.	Associate Editor	1961-66
Solomon, George M.	Associate Editor	1963-64
Spry, Louis J.	Controller	1966-
Starr, Kenneth R.	Research-Compilations (Statistics)	1968
Stratten, Ronald J.	Assistant Director of Enforcement	1975-
Thornton, Charles J.	Assistant to Executive Director	1963-64
Tow, Ted C.	Assistant Executive Director (Publishing)	1972-
Van Valkenburg, James M.	Director of Statistics	1968-
Vaughan, Fannie B.	Administrative Assistant (Gen. Adm.)	1963-
Wall, Patricia W.	Assistant Director of Championships	1981-
Waters, John T.	Director of Promotions	1959-
Whereatt, E. G. "Ted"	Assistant to Executive Director	1954-55
Whitacre, Shirley M.	Administrative Assistant (Communications)	1964-
Wilkinson, James H.	Assistant Executive Director (Gen. Adm.)	1969-
Winn, Jules L.	Administrative Assistant (Statistics)	1973-79
Wright, James F.	Administrative Assistant (Statistics)	1975-
Yeager, Thomas E.	Enforcement Representative	1976-
Zipperlen, Skipper	Administrative Assistant (Gen. Adm.)	1974-

INDEX

NOTE: The following index is for text pages only and does not include photo section and appendices.